CQ's Vital Issues Series

Capital Punishment

Ann Chih Lin, editor

Raphael Goldman, author

CQ PRESS

A Division of Congressional Quarterly Inc.

WASHINGTON, D.C.

CQ Press
A Division of Congressional Quarterly Inc.
1255 22nd St. N.W., Suite 400
Washington, DC 20037

(202) 822-1475; (800) 638-1710

www.cqpress.com

Printed in the United States of America
05 04 03 02 01   5 4 3 2 1

Grateful acknowledgment is made to the following for granting permission to reprint material: Amnesty International; Death Penalty Information Center; *Northwestern School of Law Journal of Criminal Law and Criminology*, "Criminal Law: The Proportionality Review of Capital Cases by State High Courts After *Gregg:* Only the 'Appearance of Justice'?" by Leigh B. Bienen; CQ Press, *The CQ Researcher* (January 8, 1999): "Death Penalty Update," by Mary H. Cooper; *Constitutional Law for a Changing America: Rights, Liberties, and Justice*, 4th ed., by Lee Epstein and Thomas G. Walker (CQ Press, 2000); and *International Encyclopedia of Human Rights: Freedoms, Abuses, and Remedies*, by Robert L. Maddex (CQ Press, 2000).

Cover design: Debra Naylor

(∞) The paper used in this publication meets the minimum requirements of the American National Standard for Information Sciences—Permanence of Paper for Printed Library Materials, ANSI Z39.48-1992.

Library of Congress Cataloging-in-Publication Data

Goldman, Raphael.
    Capital punishment / by Raphael Goldman; Ann Chih Lin, editor.
        p. cm. — (CQs vital issues series)
    Includes bibliographical references and index.
    ISBN 1-56802-657-9 (pbk.) — ISBN 1-56802-658-7
        1. Capital punishment—United States. 2. Capital punishment. I. Lin, Ann Chih. II. Title. III. Series.

    HV8699.U5 G66 2002
    364.66'0973—dc21   2001052439

8/02

Contents

Preface   v

Introduction   vii

1. Issues, Viewpoints, and Trends / *The CQ Researcher* Death Penalty Update   1

The Issues   1
Background   15
Current Situation   20
Outlook   28
Notes   31
Bibliography   32

2. Politics and Policy   42

The United States Supreme Court and the Constitutionality of Capital
  Punishment   42
The Jurisdictions: Capital Punishment Laws   53
Application of Capital Punishment Policy   74
Arguments about Capital Punishment   90
Notes   101

3. Agencies, Organizations, and Individuals   114

Important Abolitionist Organizations and Individuals   114
Important Retentionist Groups and Individuals   132
Important Governmental Actors   142
Notes   153

4. International Implications   158

The International Trend   158

The U.S. Trend   166

International Criticism of U.S. Death Penalty Policies   169

Collaboration between International and National Abolitionists   179

The United States' Response to International Criticism   181

Notes   186

Appendix

Further Research and Chronology   195

Bibliography of Print Sources   195

Bibliography of Internet Sources   206

Chronology   208

Facts, Policies, and Commentary   212

U.S. Jurisdictions that Lack the Death Penalty   212

An Example of Aggravating Factors: Alabama's Murder Statute   215

Limiting Proportionality Review   216

Capital Punishment Policies in Nations Worldwide   217

Notable Quotes on Capital Punishment   221

Encyclopedia Articles   223

Capital Punishment   223

International Bill of Human Rights   224

Universal Declaration of Human Rights   226

Primary Documents   229

Fact Sheet: The International Bill of Human Rights   229

UN Report on the Use of the Death Penalty in the United States   242

Selected Supreme Court Cases   250

Index   277

Preface

CQ Press is pleased to present CQ's Vital Issues Series, a new reference collection that provides unparalleled, unbiased analyses of controversial topics debated at local, state, and federal levels. The series covers all sides of issues equally, delving into the topics that dominate the media, shape election-year politics, and confront the American public. Each book includes an issue from *The CQ Researcher* that introduces the subject; in-depth explanations of relevant politics, policy, and political actors; analyses of major for-profit and nonprofit business interests; and discussion of international reaction to how the United States handles the issue. In addition, each volume features extensive appendixes to aid in further research. Titles in the series include *Capital Punishment, Welfare Reform,* and *Immigration.* We believe CQ's Vital Issues Series is an exceptional research tool, and we would like your feedback. Please send your comments to aforman@cqpress.com.

Introduction

As I write this introduction barely three weeks after the tragedies of September 11, 2001, the political landscape of a year ago seems as different, and distant, as the moon's. In autumn 2000 domestic political issues were in the ascendancy. Only one presidential debate dealt with foreign policy in any detail, and "security" meant programs for the elderly rather than protection from terrorist attacks. The economy was showing signs of a slowdown, but times were still easy in America. When we sat transfixed by the news, it was the collapse of ballot boxes that caught our attention. Some comics wondered, as weeks went by without a decision from the November election, if we would be better off without a new president.

Today I write in a country where issues other than criminal investigation and economic downturn have all but vanished from the political agenda. Our grief over the deaths of thousands, admiration for heroic rescue workers, and anger at the perpetrators have pushed aside, for the moment, much partisan rhetoric and debate. Was it really only this spring when a "bill of rights" referred to patients and their HMOs? Were competing versions of education legislation, just months ago, the subjects of congressional compromise and recriminations?

Yet in some ways our national tragedy has confirmed the continuing relevance of the public policy issues with which we inaugurate CQ Press's new Vital Issues Series. Capital punishment, welfare reform, and immigration: all are issues at the core of our national sense of justice, our definition of who is part of our country, and our understanding of rights and responsibilities. As we try to understand the crimes that led to such a massive loss of life, will our evaluations of the death penalty change? As we see Muslims and Arab immigrants targeted indiscriminately, will we think about immigration policy differently? As we struggle through layoffs and economic retrenchment, hard times that hurt everyone but affect the poor the most, will our view of the legacy of welfare reform change?

These questions deserve careful thought and thorough knowledge. The volumes in CQ's Vital Issues Series seek to provide the answers. They gather together a clear summary of the various dimensions of each of these important issues; a comprehensive look at the politics and policy developments of the past decade; a discussion of the various business, nonprofit, and political actors who influence the debate; and a view of the international context of U.S. policy. For those new to the subject, a Vital Issues book provides the necessary background in a readable and accessible format. For readers already acquainted with the debates, a Vital Issues volume is a useful reference for facts on various aspects of the issues, for an analysis of how those aspects fit together, and for further sources of information.

Each book in the series follows a format designed to make research and understanding as easy as possible. The first chapter of each book, "Issues, Viewpoints, and Trends," is a lively, succinct, and balanced account of the current policy debate. Reprinted from *The CQ Researcher,* this section is a primer for the novice. The second chapter, "Politics and Policy," presents a thorough look at policymaking and implementation: What have been the major developments of the past decade? How have debates at the level of policy formulation been translated into policy on the ground? This section pays particular attention to variations at the state and local levels: a Vital Issues book gives readers the story not only from Washington, D.C., but also from around the country, with an account of innovations and a summary, where appropriate, of each state's experience.

The third chapter, "Agencies, Organizations, and Individuals," explains the specific role that business, nonprofit, and political actors play in shaping—and continuing to shape—policy developments. Sketches of important organizations and their contributions are included, along with contact information and Web addresses. The final chapter, "International Implications," draws attention to the international context of our policy debates. Americans tend to forget that policies affect and are affected by events and policies in other countries and ignore the experience of other nations in struggling with similar problems. One of the distinctive contributions of CQ's Vital Issues Series is that it summarizes this international context, reporting accurately—but simply—the major worldwide trends, comparisons, and reactions that Americans need to know to make good policy at home.

As debates over capital punishment, immigration, and welfare reform recur—and they loom just over the horizon—we may find ourselves, more self-consciously than before, speaking both as interested individuals with differing points of view and as citizens with a responsibility to our common life. We hope that CQ's Vital Issues Series will provide readers with the information and perspective necessary to have these conversations. Whether you are a student, a journalist, an activist, or a concerned citizen, this series is for you. Let us know if we have been successful.

Ann Chih Lin
University of Michigan

1   Issues, Viewpoints, and Trends

The CQ Researcher Death Penalty Update

A series of shocking murders in the past few years has focused public attention once again on the death penalty. The deaths caused by the Oklahoma City bombers, the "Unabomber," and others have lent support to advocates of capital punishment. They continue to argue that capital punishment not only deters crime but also helps the families of murder victims find "closure." But opponents call for reform, if not abolition, of the death penalty. They point to disturbing evidence that nonwhite offenders are more likely to be executed for their crimes than white offenders and that poor inmates often do not receive adequate legal counsel. As proof they cite the cases of ninety-four people released from death row since 1973 after courts reversed their convictions.

The Issues

It had been more than three years since Rolando Cruz was cleared of the charges that landed him on death row, but there was still bitterness in his voice. "I did twelve years, three months, and three days," he told a conference on capital punishment. "They did kill me. I am who I am now because this is who they made."[1]

Cruz and another man, Alejandro Hernandez, were sentenced to death for the 1983 abduction, rape, and murder of ten-year-old Jeanine Nicarico of Naperville, Illinois. It was the kind of high-profile crime that prompts communities to demand quick action by law enforcement officers. DuPage County authorities complied by charging Cruz and Hernandez with Jeanine's murder.

This article was written by Mary H. Cooper for *The CQ Researcher* (January 8, 1999): 3–23.

Both men were tried, convicted, and sentenced to death in 1985. Their convictions were based largely on the testimony of jailhouse informants and a deputy sheriff who said Cruz's description of a dream included details about the murder that only the killer would have known.

In 1995, after more than ten years on death row, Cruz and Hernandez were released from prison after DNA testing proved that another man had raped Jeanine. At the time of the murder, Brian Dugan, a repeat sex offender and confessed murderer, had told authorities that he alone had committed the crime—a fact that the Cruz and Hernandez juries were not told. Three prosecutors and four law enforcement officers have since been charged with obstruction of justice for concealing evidence that would have exonerated the men a decade earlier.[2]

The Cruz and Hernandez cases may be dramatic, but they are hardly unique. More than seven hundred people have been executed in the United States since the Supreme Court reinstated the death penalty in 1976. Over that same period, ninety-four condemned inmates have been released since 1973 after evidence showed they had been wrongfully convicted. That equates to roughly one exoneration for every seven executions.

"If you had to go to a hospital for a life-and-death operation and found that hospital misdiagnosed [one out of every seven] cases, you'd run," said lawyer Barry Scheck, a member of O.J. Simpson's defense team. "It's an intolerable level of error, regardless of your views on the death penalty."[3]

Scheck spoke at a November 1998 national conference on wrongful conviction and the death penalty at Northwestern University Law School. "We don't have a position on the ultimate morality of the death penalty," says conference participant Richard C. Dieter, executive director of the Death Penalty Information Center in Washington, D.C. "It's how the death penalty is applied in the United States that we are critical of. We say that there's a lot of unfairness and that mistakes are made, and that at least we should attempt to change and correct those things."

Indeed, no one is predicting the death penalty will be abolished anytime soon in the United States. Capital punishment is on the books in thirty-eight states, plus the federal government and the military. There are now 3,726 prisoners around the country awaiting execution.

A large majority of Americans still support capital punishment, and that support seems unlikely to wane in the wake of several horrific crimes in the past few years. Few protested the death sentence meted out to an unrepentant Timothy J.

McVeigh for his role in the 1995 bombing of the Alfred P. Murrah Federal Building in Oklahoma City, which killed 168 people. And many Americans were angered when Susan Smith was sentenced in South Carolina to life in prison rather than death after drowning her two young children in 1994 and charging a mysterious black man with the crime. Similarly, many thought "Unabomber" Theodore Kaczynski deserved the death penalty for mailing letter bombs that left three people dead and twenty-two others injured.

Death penalty advocates say leniency in some of these cases shows that the system works by sparing mentally ill or mentally retarded criminals. But many legal experts point to flaws in the death penalty's application that open the criminal justice system to charges of pervasive unfairness. Recent studies have documented longstanding allegations of racial discrimination in capital cases. Statistics show that prisoners of all races are more likely to be executed if the victim was white than some other race. Although about half the homicide victims are people of color, more than 80 percent of the prisoners on death row were convicted of killing whites.[4] A 1999 study also suggests that blacks are the most likely to receive the death penalty, regardless of the victim's race.[5]

"These studies are trying to determine whether race discrimination accounts for the race disparities in sentencing," says Dieter, author of the latest such study. "The odds of getting the death penalty are much higher if you're black than if you're white."

Defenders of capital punishment counter that any racial discrimination that may exist in its application argues for expanding the use of capital punishment, not abolishing it. "If it is true that people who kill black victims are less likely to get sentenced to death, that doesn't show the death penalty is discriminatorily imposed," says Kent S. Scheidegger, legal director at the Criminal Justice Legal Foundation in Sacramento, California. "It shows the death penalty is discriminatorily withheld. And the answer to that is more death sentences, not fewer, for the same kinds of crime in black-victim cases."

Another area of concern has been the death penalty's application to mentally retarded or mentally ill prisoners. The U.S. Supreme Court ruled in 1986 that the Eighth Amendment prohibits the execution of insane prisoners, but the definition of insanity varies widely among jurisdictions. Although evidence of mental illness led courts to spare Kaczynski and Smith, many less notorious killers have been executed despite evidence that they were unable to discern the seriousness of their crimes. In fact, thirty-five mentally retarded people have been executed since 1976; only fourteen states prohibit the death penalty for the mentally retarded.[6]

Much of the current criticism of capital punishment concerns recently implemented restrictions on habeas corpus, a procedure for challenging a state conviction or sentence in federal court on constitutional grounds after normal appeals have been exhausted. The Constitution enshrines this right in Article 1, Section 9, and forbids the suspension of habeas corpus except in cases involving rebellion or invasion that threaten the public safety.

The mounting crime rates of the late 1980s prompted Congress to pass the 1996 Anti-Terrorism and Effective Death Penalty Act. Among other things, the sweeping measure not only set a one-year deadline for submitting a habeas corpus petition after state appeals are exhausted but also limited prisoners to one appeal in most cases. Supporters of the measure wanted to deter prisoners from launching repeated and groundless petitions to stall their executions.

Critics say the 1996 law fails to recognize the importance of the appeals process, compounding the unfairness of capital punishment. Most defendants in capital cases cannot afford experienced defense attorneys, and many do not receive adequate counsel, critics say, either at trial or during the appeals process.

In 1997, the American Bar Association (ABA) called for a moratorium on executions, citing "a haphazard maze of unfair practices with no internal consistency." But public support for the death penalty continues to run high, making the prospects doubtful for substantive reform in the near future.

As the debate over the fairness of the death penalty continues, these are some of the questions being asked:

Should recent restrictions on the right to appeal be rolled back?

One of the main complaints of death penalty advocates has been the growing delay between sentencing and execution. From 1977 to 1996, the average stay on death row increased from 51 months to 125 months, as prisoners appealed their sentences at the state level and, if those failed, at the federal level, all the way to the Supreme Court.[7] Critics claimed that most of the appeals were without merit and intended only to stall for time, and they called on Congress and the courts to do something.

Over the last decade the Supreme Court and Congress have responded, restricting men and women on death row from seeking habeas corpus review of their convictions. Chief Justice William Rehnquist has led the high court's efforts to streamline the handling of death row appeals. In 1991, for example, the Supreme Court ruled that an appeal filed three days late is not entitled to federal court review. In 1998, it made it harder for appeals court judges to delay executions, ruling that a federal court had committed a "grave abuse of discretion" when it halted the execution of convicted rapist and murderer Thomas Thompson in California.

Congress also ratcheted up the effort to curtail death row appeals. The 1996 Anti-Terrorism and Effective Death Penalty Act set a limit of one year for state prisoners to petition to the federal level after exhausting their appeals in state courts. But in states that meet the law's standards for providing adequate counsel to defendants, the limit is only six months. The law also made it difficult to file more than one habeas petition by requiring federal judges to defer to state court rulings on constitutional and other issues unless the state rulings were deemed "unreasonable."

"If a second or successive habeas petition raises the same claim that has been raised and decided adversely to the petitioner, then it must be dismissed," says Ira Robbins, a law professor at the American University's Washington College of Law and an expert on capital appeals. "There is no discretion there."

Even if a new claim is presented in a second or successive appeal, under the 1996 law the petition cannot be filed without authorization by a federal appeals court. Such courts have only limited discretion in authorizing the filing because they must examine a combination of reasons why the new claim was not presented earlier, including possible changes in the law, as well as evidence of innocence. "The court of appeals must look at that combination, which is a very hard test to satisfy," Robbins says. "So there has been a striking limitation on the ability to file second or successive petitions in the district court because of this gatekeeping provision that has to be ruled on by the court of appeals."

The other main restriction to death row appeals, the one-year statute of limitations on habeas petitions, marks a clear departure from previous law. "There was no statute of limitations prior to April 24, 1996, when the law was passed," Robbins says.

Critics say the new combination of restrictions could make it harder for innocent prisoners to make their case in time to avoid execution. "The restrictions impinge right at the point where these kinds of cases might run into trouble," Dieter says. "Some of the evidence of DNA doesn't show up until a number of years later. Not everybody needs twenty years to make their case, but there needs to be an exception for credible claims of innocence that allows that door to be open. These re-

Capital Punishment in the United States

Since the Supreme Court declared the death penalty constitutional in 1976, twenty-nine of the thirty-eight states with death penalty statutes have held executions.* Texas, Virginia, and Florida conducted more than half of the 713 executions since 1976. Eighty-five people were executed nationwide in 2000.

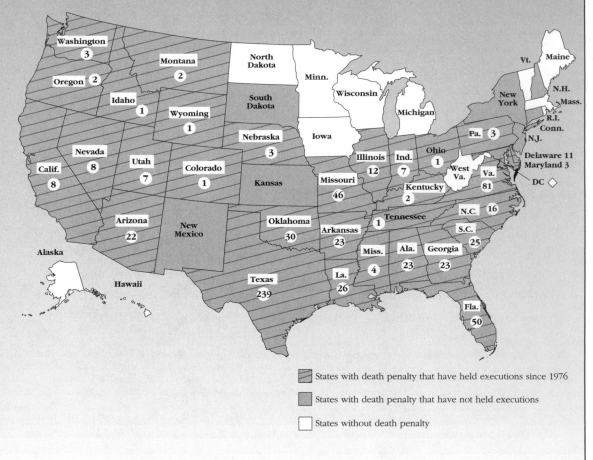

Washington 3
Oregon 2
Idaho 1
Montana 2
North Dakota
Minn.
Wisconsin
Michigan
Vt. Maine
N.H.
New York
Mass.
R.I.
Conn.
N.J.
Nevada 8
Utah 7
Wyoming 1
South Dakota
Iowa
Pa. 3
Calif. 8
Colorado 1
Nebraska 3
Illinois 12
Ind. 7
Ohio 1
West Va.
Va. 81
Delaware 11
Maryland 3
DC ◇
Kansas
Missouri 46
Kentucky 2
Arizona 22
New Mexico
Oklahoma 30
Arkansas 23
Tennessee 1
N.C. 16
S.C. 25
Alaska
Miss. 4
Ala. 23
Georgia 23
Hawaii
Texas 239
La. 26
Fla. 50

States with death penalty that have held executions since 1976

States with death penalty that have not held executions

States without death penalty

* Numbers on the map indicate the number of executions held in each state since 1976.

Source: Death Penalty Information Center.

strictions make it more likely not only that innocent people will be sentenced to death but that some will be executed."

In Dieter's view the federal restrictions on death row appeals are especially onerous in light of obstacles that already block appeals at the state level. In most states, a death row appeal goes from the trial court straight to the state supreme court. "These cases are reviewed at the state level, and that's where the mistakes should be found," Dieter says. "But what you find on the state level are comparable or even worse restrictions on appeals. The standard to get a review in some states is almost insurmountable. A lot of states have passed measures to limit the state part of the appeal, and when you tack on the federal limitations, you have a very difficult situation for anybody who has evidence of their innocence to get anywhere."

But other legal experts say the appeals process needs more, not fewer, restrictions. "Successive petitions," Scheidegger says, "are almost always without merit." He cites the 1997 *Lindh v. Murphy* case, in which the Supreme Court held that the 1996 law's provisions could not apply to petitions that were pending before the law was passed. "This was a quite wrong decision, in my opinion, that has postponed most of the law's benefits by eliminating a very large class," he says.

With 591 prisoners on death row and only eight executions since 1976, California has the biggest backlog of death penalty cases in the country. "As far as the existing backlog goes," Scheidegger says, "the new law is doing us no good at all."

Critics say the anti-terrorism act has failed to streamline the appeals process in large part because it gave federal judges the authority to decide whether states qualify for the six-month deadline by providing competent legal counsel to indigent prisoners. In 1998, Andrew Peyton Thomas, a former assistant attorney general for Arizona, wrote:

> Congress gave this critical responsibility to the very federal judges whom the act was meant to control. Not surprisingly, they have been in no hurry to declare the states in compliance. To date, not a single state has been permitted to opt in to the [anti-terrorism act's] system of expedited capital appeals. Two years after passage of the [law], death penalty appeals in the federal courts remain as protracted as ever.[8]

Critics of the anti-terrorism act cite studies suggesting that innocent people have already been executed in the United States and predict that the law makes such mistakes more likely to occur. A landmark 1987 study concluded that twenty-three innocent prisoners were executed from 1900 to 1987.[9] But some supporters of streamlining the appeals process for death row inmates question the findings and even suggest that executing the occasional innocent may be an acceptable price to pay.

"There is no proof that an innocent has been executed since 1900," affirms Justice for All, a Houston-based victims'-rights group. "In the context that hundreds of thousands of innocents have been murdered or seriously injured, since 1900, by criminals improperly released by the U.S. criminal justice system (or not incarcerated at all!), the relevant question is: Is the risk of executing the innocent, however slight, worth the justifications for the death penalty—those being retribution, rehabilitation, incapacitation, required punishment, deterrence, escalating punishments, religious mandates, cost savings, the moral imperative, just punishment and the saving of innocent lives?" [10]

Should behavior in prison be considered in decisions to carry out executions?

In 1983, Karla Faye Tucker and a male companion broke into a Houston apartment to steal some motorcycle parts. But they encountered two occupants and brutally killed them with a pickax. Both were convicted and sentenced to death. Tucker's codefendant died in prison of natural causes, but as Tucker's date with the executioner neared, Pope John Paul II and other religious leaders urged then-governor George W. Bush to spare her life.

"She is not the same person who committed those heinous ax murders," said televangelist Pat Robertson on *The 700 Club*. "She is totally transformed, and I think to execute her is more of an act of vengeance than it is appropriate justice." [11]

To Tucker's supporters, she had earned clemency throughout her fourteen years of incarceration. Soon after arriving on death row, she became a born-again Christian. Prison guards attested to her exemplary behavior over the years, including her efforts to help other prisoners learn from her experience. By all accounts, Tucker appeared to have been completely rehabilitated.

Governors in Texas, which leads the country in executions—239 since 1976—have offered clemency to about a fifth of the prisoners scheduled for execution. Despite the appeals and the protesters outside the Huntsville prison complex calling for mercy, Bush allowed the thirty-eight-year-old Tucker to be executed by lethal injection on February 3, 1998. But the controversy over what role postconviction behavior should play in carrying out the death penalty continues.

Males typically commit capital crimes. Of the total U.S. death row population of 3,726, only 53 are women. Before Tucker, only one woman had been executed in the United States since 1976 and only one in Texas since the Civil War. (Since her execution five more women have been put to death.)

Tucker's conversion to an evangelical form of Christianity also made her attractive to conservative religious leaders like Robertson, who normally support the death penalty.

"We believe that to not have the death penalty on the books would lower the value of life itself by suggesting that there is no crime worthy of the penalty of death," says Richard Cizik, acting director of the National Association of Evangelicals. "But that position does not suggest that the death penalty is appropriate in any particular case. We weren't arguing for Karla Faye Tucker's release. We were arguing for commutation of her death sentence on the grounds she would do much greater good to society alive in prison than she could dead."

Death penalty critics say Tucker's execution forces society to examine what it is trying to accomplish with capital punishment. "Are we trying to prevent future crime, or are we trying to punish because someone is so horrible?" Dieter asks. "If we look at the reasons for the death penalty and then try to see if it still makes sense, then I think it is worth looking at whether a person has changed in prison."

This is especially true in Tucker's case, Dieter says, because the key standard Texas jurors must use in deciding whether to apply the death sentence is whether the convicted person poses a future danger to society. "From that perspective, Tucker—like some other prisoners—was not much of a danger to anyone in prison," Dieter says. "She wasn't knifing guards or fellow inmates. She seems to have been a lovable person. If a prisoner's future danger is one of the criteria for the death penalty—and Texas isn't the only state where that applies—then we should reevaluate it if we have the chance. Rehabilitation should make a difference in clemency proceedings."

But by its very nature, clemency is outside the judicial process. After all appeals have been exhausted through the courts, the final decision on execution rests solely with the governor of the state. This is as it should be, in Scheidegger's view. "Post-conviction behavior is something a governor may choose to consider," he says. "The clemency proceedings have, by and large, gone the way they should. There hasn't been the kind of abuse of the process that would get us concerned."

Conference Highlights Incredible Journey from Death Row to Freedom

Conferences on legal issues rarely attract public attention, given their dry discussions of arcane legal matters. But a November 1998 meeting in Chicago drew worldwide press coverage. Among the lawyers and professors attending the conference on wrongful convictions and the death penalty were more than thirty former death row inmates. They were among ninety-four people who have been sentenced to death in the United States since 1973 and later released from prison after being declared innocent or after charges against them were dropped due to overwhelming evidence of innocence. The wrongfully convicted include:

JAMES RICHARDSON

The migrant farmworker was convicted in 1968 of poisoning seven of his children with pesticide. Prosecutors claimed he had bought life insurance policies for the children the day before they died and presented testimony of two jailhouse informants who said they had heard Richardson incriminate himself. Lawyers who later took on the case discovered that Richardson had not bought life insurance and that a babysitter who was with the children the night they died had been convicted of poisoning her husband. She later confessed to killing the children. Richardson was released in 1989 after a review of his case by then–Dade County state attorney Janet Reno. Richardson spent twenty-one years on death row, the longest for a wrongfully convicted person.

SABRINA BUTLER

She was sentenced to death in 1990 in Mississippi for murdering her nine-month-old baby. One of two women on the list of wrongfully convicted people, Butler said she performed CPR on her child when she found him not breathing and then took him to the hospital. The Mississippi Supreme Court overturned the conviction in 1992, and in 1995 Butler was acquitted on evidence that the baby had died of kidney disease or sudden infant death syndrome.

DENNIS WILLIAMS AND VERNEAL JIMERSON

They were convicted along with two others for the 1978 murder of a young Illinois couple and spent eighteen years on death row before three journalism students gathered new evidence showing that all four men had been wrongly convicted. The students interviewed suspects seen leaving the crime scene by a witness whose testimony police had ignored after charging the four with the crime. Two of the suspects confessed. DNA tests indicated that none of the four were involved in the crime. After charges were dropped, the Cook County state's attorney apologized to the four men, calling the case a "glaring example" of the justice system's fallibility.

JONATHAN TREADWAY

Convicted in 1974 of sodomizing and killing a six-year-old boy in Arizona and sentenced to death, Treadway was granted a retrial by the state Supreme Court based on the incompetence of his trial counsel. He was acquitted of all charges after five pathologists testified that there was no evidence of sodomy and that the child had probably died of natural causes.

JOSEPH GREEN BROWN

Sentenced to death in 1974 for murder, rape, and robbery, Brown spent thirteen years on Florida's death row before the Eleventh U.S. Circuit Court of Appeals ruled that prosecutors had knowingly allowed false testimony to be introduced at trial. The key evidence used against him was testimony of Ronald Floyd, whom Brown had turned in to police for an unrelated crime. Floyd later admitted that he had lied at trial and that he had testified in return for not being prosecuted himself for the same murder. After state courts rejected Brown's appeals, Brown filed a habeas corpus petition, and a federal court overturned his conviction. He came within thirteen hours of execution.

Opponents of capital punishment took heart from the conference and the media coverage it attracted. "Certainly the American people are not in favor of executing innocent people," says Richard C. Dieter, executive director of the Death Penalty Information Center, who attended the Chicago conference. "People don't always realize that there are people on death row who don't have lawyers. They see the federal cases, which are well represented and take weeks. They don't see the quick trial in Alabama, where they pay attorneys $2,000 maximum to take a death penalty case. If more people realized this, they would accept a greater requirement of fairness, and many would be more open to applying a sentence of life without parole."

Other legal experts are less sanguine about the conference's impact. "People who want to abolish the death penalty get energized by these kinds of conferences," says Victor Streib, dean of Ohio Northern University Law School and an opponent of capital punishment for juvenile offenders. "They think something like this will end support for the death penalty. I think people are concerned about wrongfully convicted people, but if you keep your finger on the public pulse with the polls, you'll find that support for the death penalty remains strong."

For their part, supporters of capital punishment are skeptical about the innocence of former death row inmates. "Of the seventy-five exonerated prisoners that they highlighted at the conference, even the conference organizers said they could not prove innocence," says Diane Clements, president of Justice for All, a Houston victims' rights group. "Along with everybody else in the United States, Justice for All does not want to see innocents wrongly convicted. But were these people really innocent?"

Other death penalty advocates say postconviction behavior should not be taken into account because it does not accurately predict a person's behavior upon release. "Death row is a very cloistered, structured environment," says Diane Clements, president of Justice for All. "I don't believe that behavior on death row is a barometer as to how we would measure someone's behavior outside death row. That is why in Texas we sentence people to death, not only because of the crime they have committed, but also whether the individual is a future threat."

Ultimately, supporters of Bush's decision to deny Tucker clemency say the crime is more important than any subsequent change of heart. "Capital punishment is the redemption of a contract society owes to all human beings," writes William F. Buckley Jr. "To protect them and to guard posthumously their dignity, by taking the life of those who took their lives." [12]

Should minors be subject to capital punishment?

Shareef Cousin was just sixteen when he was arrested, tried, and convicted of fatally shooting Michael Gerardi in the face during a holdup outside a restaurant in New Orleans's French Quarter. In 1996, Cousin became the youngest death row inmate in the country when he began awaiting execution by lethal injection. He was seventeen. Cousin continued to proclaim his innocence, and last spring the Louisiana Supreme Court granted him a new trial. Justices determined that prosecutors had failed to disclose that Gerardi's date, an eyewitness to the crime, had initially told authorities she was not wearing her glasses at the time and could see only patterns and shapes. At the trial, however, she positively identified Cousin as the murderer.

Dwayne Wright was not so lucky. Like Cousin, Wright was black, and he grew up in a poor, crime-ridden neighborhood of Washington, D.C. His father was imprisoned when Dwayne was four; his mother was mentally ill and often unemployed. When Dwayne was ten, his older brother was murdered. As a teenager, Dwayne was hospitalized for major depression and psychosis and was held in juvenile detention facilities. He was evaluated as borderline retarded. A month after his seventeenth birthday, Dwayne went on a two-day crime spree that culminated in the robbery, attempted rape, and shooting death of a thirty-three-year-old woman in Virginia. He confessed after his arrest and was tried and sentenced to death in 1991. [13]

In his appeal, Wright contended that his defense attorney had failed to discover that an expert witness for the prosecution, a psychologist, had once concluded in a study that mental illness and environment are not responsible for a criminal's behavior. The appeal was rejected, however, and Gov. James Gilmore III, R-Va., a former prosecutor and a death penalty advocate, declined to stop the execution by lethal injection. On October 14, 1998, Wright, then twenty-six, became the twelfth person to be executed in the United States since 1976 for a crime committed as a minor.

Few other countries in the world have executed juvenile offenders in recent years. Iran, Nigeria, Pakistan, Saudi Arabia, and Yemen are the only other countries since 1990 known to have executed people for crimes they committed as minors. The United States has sentenced to death 200 juvenile offenders since 1973.[14]

"We are literally the only country in the world that does this now," says Victor Streib, dean of Ohio Northern University's law school and an expert on condemned teens. "It was very rare in other countries until recently, and then because of some international treaties other countries have stopped it altogether."

The United States signed the International Covenant on Civil and Political Rights in 1992 but reserved the right to ignore the treaty's stipulation that "sentence of death shall not be imposed for crimes committed by persons below 18 years of age."

Supporters of harsher treatment of juvenile offenders point to the recent spate of schoolyard killings by teenagers and even preteens as evidence that a crackdown is needed to protect society from its youngest predators. In March 1998, a thirteen-year-old and his eleven-year-old schoolmate were arrested for killing four students and a teacher at a Jonesboro, Arkansas, school.

In several states, no child is too young to be charged as an adult for certain violent crimes.[15] Federal law allows defendants as young as thirteen to be tried as adults. In 1998 U.S. Sen. Orrin G. Hatch, R-Utah, sponsored legislation that would require all states to lower the threshold to fourteen for violent crimes. "Kids all over America are laughing at the juvenile courts," said Sen. Jeff Sessions, R-Ala., one of the bill's twenty-five cosponsors, all Republicans. "We're having more kids commit murder, armed robbery, the most serious offenses." [16]

Schoolyard shootings also have generated support for lowering the minimum age when a defendant can receive the death penalty. Of the thirty-nine jurisdictions (thirty-eight states and the federal government) with capital punishment, sixteen set the minimum age at the time of the crime at eighteen; five set it at seventeen; and the other eighteen set it at sixteen.[17]

In Mississippi, where a high school student killed two classmates in October 1997, lawmakers considered a bill that would allow prosecutors to seek the death penalty for juveniles when slayings occur on school grounds.[18] Other lawmakers went further, proposing death for younger offenders no matter where the killings occur.

"These children are not like they were when you and I were growing up," said Texas state representative Jim Pitts. In the wake of the Jonesboro shootings, Pitts proposed lowering the age at which juveniles are eligible for the death penalty in Texas from seventeen to eleven. "They're not what I call the Beaver Cleavers of the world," he said. "These kids are different. And, yes, I do feel that an eleven-year-old should be . . . accountable for what [he or she] commit[s]."[19] While Texans overwhelmingly support death for adults, only 25 percent of the respondents to a recent poll supported lowering the age of eligibility to eleven.[20]

A rise in juvenile crime in the mid-1980s sparked a nationwide crackdown. But critics of the death penalty for juveniles point to statistics showing a fall in violent crime among teenagers since 1993 and suggest that the juvenile justice system does not need to be made tougher. "A tremendous amount of publicity has been given to a few, terribly horrific crimes, but the fact is that youth crime has gone down," says Brian Henninger, program coordinator for the National Coalition to Abolish the Death Penalty. "Instead of looking at this fact, as well as what has been working to get the youth crime rate down and doing more of that, we're looking at our gut instinct, at how we can punish more and make clear that these crimes can't happen again."

Some legal experts and child advocates say that any benefits the death penalty may have for adult offenders in deterring crime are utterly lost on juveniles. "Mostly, we know that kids don't think before they act," Streib says. "So threatening them with any kind of consequences doesn't seem to work. If you stopped a kid in a parking lot as he went into a store with a gun and warned him what would happen to him, it wouldn't work," Streib says.

"They're often high, they're excited, and hormones are flying around," he continued. "So someone who says we need to increase the punishment for these crimes as a way to somehow prevent these kids from doing this, I say that's somebody who doesn't understand kids. It will not work."

Background

Early Reforms

The death penalty arrived in America with the English, whose laws ruled the Colonies for a century and a half. Public hanging was mandatory for a number of crimes, and the first colonist executed, George Kendall, died in 1608 at Jamestown.[21]

After the Revolution, English common law remained the basis of the U.S. justice system. Neither the Bill of Rights nor the Eighth Amendment to the Constitution prohibiting "cruel and unusual punishment" were construed to prohibit executions. But modifications to English legal precedents soon distanced the U.S. criminal justice system from the English model.

Bowing to Quakers and other opponents of the death penalty, Pennsylvania in 1793 introduced the distinction between first-degree and second-degree murder. Capital punishment was reserved for offenses that were deemed more brutal because they involved premeditation. Most other jurisdictions also adopted this distinction.

The United States also ended the spectacle of public executions that were the rule in England. Rioting was not uncommon at hangings, especially when the condemned, rather than dying instantly of a broken neck, slowly strangled or was decapitated. Philadelphia physician Benjamin Rush, a vocal opponent of the death penalty, criticized the circuslike atmosphere at hangings. In 1835, New York began conducting hangings in enclosed yards before official witnesses only. The other states eventually followed New York's example, though Kentucky and Missouri continued public hangings until the late 1930s.

English law mandated the death sentence for capital offenses. But American jurisdictions, bowing to populist sentiment, allowed trial juries to make binding sentence recommendations of either death or life in prison. Introduced in 1841 in Alabama and Tennessee, jury sentencing discretion spread to other jurisdictions in the nineteenth century and has applied to virtually all capital cases as a result of Supreme Court rulings in the 1970s.

American criminal law also reduced the number of offenses punishable by death under the English system. However, a variety of capital offenses other than homicide, including kidnapping, treason, rape, and armed robbery, remained on the books in many jurisdictions until recently. In 1977, for example, the Supreme Court abolished the death penalty for rape. Homicide is the only crime punishable by death that the Supreme Court has upheld as constitutional. But the 1994 Federal Death Penalty Act authorizes the death penalty for some federal crimes that do not involve homicide, such as espionage and treason.

Abolition Movement

The movement to abolish the death penalty made its greatest headway early in the twentieth century. Nine states repealed capital punishment, joining Michigan, Rhode Island, and Wisconsin, which had abolished the death penalty in the mid-1800s.

By the late 1920s, the abolition movement had lost its momentum. Partly as a result of public anxiety over "crime waves" during Prohibition and the Great Depression, the number of executions rose sharply in the 1930s and 1940s.

This period saw two important changes in capital punishment. The first was the widespread adoption of the electric chair as an alternative to hanging. Developed in the late 1880s as a more humane method of execution, electrocution itself came under attack as cruel and barbaric and was replaced in some jurisdictions by the gas chamber and later by lethal injection. Today, all but four states provide lethal injection as at least an alternative for execution.

The other major change during the 1930s and 1940s was the involvement of federal appeals courts in reviewing state court death sentences. Until then, death sentences had almost always been carried out without review of any kind, state or federal. A few landmark cases, such as the Scottsboro Boys rape case (*Powell v. Alabama*, 1932), set precedents for federal review of appeals based on charges that state courts had violated the federal Bill of Rights.*

Delaware's repeal of capital punishment in 1958 revived the abolition movement. The movement peaked in 1966, the only time that Americans opposed to the death penalty outnumbered advocates, though by a narrow margin of 47 percent to 42 percent. Also in the mid-1960s, three states abolished the death penalty, bringing the number of states without capital punishment to twelve, plus the District of Columbia. (See map, p. 6.)

---

*The rape convictions and death sentences of the defendants in the Scottsboro case were overturned because the state failed to provide adequate defense counsel.

The growing sentiment against capital punishment was accompanied by a steady decrease in executions from a peak of 199 in 1935 to just 1 in 1966. Between 1968 and 1976, while the constitutionality of the death penalty was tested in the courts, no executions were held in the United States. The courts continued to sentence prisoners to death, however, and the decline in executions was accompanied by the growth of the death row population from just over 500 in 1970 to more than 3,000 by 1995.

Two landmark cases decided the fate of capital punishment in the United States. In June 1972 the Supreme Court ruled in *Furman v. Georgia* that the death penalty as administered by thirty-five states at the time was unconstitutional. Because the ruling essentially nullified the sentences of the more than 600 prisoners on death row, state courts were required to resentence them. The court later made several important changes to capital punishment—prohibiting mandatory death penalties, limiting death sentences to some form of criminal homicide, and requiring each death sentence to undergo review by a state appeals court.

Although the Supreme Court placed restrictions on certain aspects of the death penalty in *Furman,* the decision marked the end of the most recent drive to eliminate capital punishment in the United States. Within months of the ruling, state legislatures had overhauled their capital punishment laws to comply with the new guidelines. In the mid-1970s, the court ruled in *Gregg v. Georgia* (1976) and other cases that the death penalty as applied under revised state laws did not violate the Eighth Amendment's prohibition of "cruel and unusual punishment." Executions resumed in 1977.

Support for Executions

The resumption of executions coincided with a surge in violent crime that began in the late 1960s and continued, for two decades. Popular support for the death penalty rose rapidly during this period, surpassing 70 percent of Americans by the early 1990s. At the same time, victims' rights advocates fought for, and obtained, the right of families of homicide victims to participate in the sentencing process.[22]

In campaigns for public office, including Ronald Reagan's successful bid for the California governorship in 1966 and George Bush's presidential campaign of 1988, candidates won votes by presenting themselves as tough on crime and supportive of capital punishment. Accordingly, governors and presidents alike have refrained

Chronology

1970s *Executions are suspended in the United States pending court review of capital punishment's constitutionality.*

1972   The U.S. Supreme Court holds in *Furman v. Georgia* that the death penalty, as administered by thirty-five states, is unconstitutional. The Court later prohibits mandatory death penalties, limits death sentences to some form of criminal homicide, and requires that each death sentence undergo review by a state appeals court.

1976   The Supreme Court reinstates the death penalty in *Gregg v. Georgia,* holding that it does not violate the Eighth Amendment's prohibition of "cruel and unusual punishment" as applied under revised state laws. Executions resume the next year.

1980s *The incidence of violent crimes punishable by death rises rapidly.*

1986   The Supreme Court rules that the Eighth Amendment prohibits the execution of insane people.

1987   The Supreme Court rules in *McCleskey v. Kemp* that defendants may not use evidence of racial disparities in death sentences as evidence of racial discrimination in their own sentences.

1990s *Horrific crimes bolster public support for the death penalty amid concerns about the fairness with which it is applied.*

1992   The United States signs the International Covenant on Civil and Political Rights but reserves the right to ignore the treaty's ban on executing individuals for crimes committed when they were under age eighteen.

1994   Susan Smith is sentenced to life in prison in South Carolina for drowning her two young children. Congress authorizes the death penalty for numerous federal crimes. Justice Harry Blackmun reverses his earlier support for the death penalty.

1995   Timothy J. McVeigh and Terry Nichols are convicted of blowing up the Alfred P. Murrah Federal Building in Oklahoma City, killing 168 people. McVeigh is later sentenced to death; Nichols receives a life sentence.

APRIL 24, 1996 Congress passes the Anti-Terrorism and Effective Death Penalty Act restricting convicted criminals' rights to file habeas corpus appeals of their sentences. The measure sets a one-year deadline for submitting such petitions after state appeals are exhausted and limits prisoners to one such hearing in most cases.

1997 Citing due-process questions raised by the 1996 law and other concerns, the American Bar Association calls for a moratorium on executions in the United States. The Supreme Court holds that the Anti-Terrorism Act does not apply to petitions pending before the law was passed, excluding a number of backlogged cases in California and other states.

FEBRUARY 1998 Then-governor George W. Bush, R-Texas, refuses to grant clemency to Karla Faye Tucker, a condemned murderer who became a born-again Christian on death row.

APRIL 1998 The Supreme Court rules that a federal appeals court committed a "grave abuse of discretion" by halting the execution of a convicted rapist and murderer in California; the Court makes it harder for appeals court judges to delay executions. It also rules that an appeals court may change a death sentence handed down by a state court only if presented with "clear and convincing evidence" of the defendant's innocence. Kentucky passes the Racial Justice Act, becoming the first state to allow defendants to challenge a death sentence on grounds of racial disparity in sentencing.

MAY 4, 1998 "Unabomber" Theodore Kaczynski is sentenced to life in prison for mailing letter bombs that killed three people and injured twenty-two others.

NOVEMBER 13–15, 1998 Northwestern University Law School holds a conference on wrongful convictions, featuring more than thirty former death row inmates whose sentences were overturned.

from granting clemency. The average number of clemency awards each year fell from eighteen in the 1960s to one a year in the decade ending in 1994.

Meanwhile, evidence of unfairness in the administration of capital punishment prompted a renewal of the death penalty debate. Beginning in the 1980s, a number of studies concluded that racial discrimination was common in meting out death sentences.[23] The first was a study by Iowa researcher David C. Baldus showing that killers of white victims in Georgia were more likely to receive the death penalty than killers of black victims. Based on Baldus's study, the Supreme Court ruled in *McCleskey v. Kemp* (1987) that defendants could not use evidence of racial disparities in death sentences as evidence of racial discrimination in their own sentences. Subsequent studies have found such evidence stemming from the overall number of black inmates on death row and the overwhelming prevalence of white prosecutors in capital cases.[24]

The vast majority of death sentences have been handed out by state courts. But Congress responded in 1994 to public anger over terrorism and drug-related killings by passing a massive crime bill that authorized the death penalty for several dozen federal crimes, including drug trafficking by "drug kingpins," treason, espionage, or causing a death by mailing explosives. Since the law took effect the death penalty has been sought in about 159 federal cases, up from just 7 in 1994, the year before the law took effect.[25]

Current Situation

Questions of Fairness

While Congress and the Supreme Court have acted to speed executions in recent years, concerns about the death penalty's fairness have led several prominent jurists who had not opposed the death penalty to reverse course. "From this day forward, I no longer shall tinker with the machinery of death," declared then–Supreme Court justice Harry Blackmun in 1994. "For more than 20 years I have endeavored—indeed, I have struggled—along with a majority of this Court, to develop procedural and substantive rules that would lend more than the mere appearance of fairness to the death penalty endeavor. Rather than continue to coddle the Court's delusion that the desired level of fairness has been achieved and the need for regulation eviscerated, I feel morally and intellectually obligated to concede that the death penalty experiment has failed." [26]

Despite Global Trend, U.S. Executions Continue

On November 12, 1998, while attempting to pass through Italian customs on a false passport, Abdullah Ocalan was arrested and detained in Rome. Ocalan, leader of the Kurdish Workers' Party, had led a bloody campaign for Kurdish self-rule in southeastern Turkey for fourteen years. He asked for political asylum in Italy. But the Turkish government holds Ocalan responsible for the deaths of 30,000 citizens and demanded his extradition to face charges of terrorism and treason. Ocalan also was wanted on terrorism charges in Germany.

If convicted in a Turkish court of law, Ocalan would almost certainly receive a death sentence. But Italy, which does not have the death penalty, is barred by its constitution from extraditing foreigners to countries with capital punishment. Outraged over Italy's refusal to hand over its most wanted criminal, the Turkish government threatened economic retaliation. The incident became a major diplomatic crisis between the two NATO members that escalated in late December 1998, when Italian Premier Massimo D'Alema announced that Ocalan had been released following Germany's cancellation of its warrant.

The controversy swirling around Ocalan's treatment in Europe stands in stark contrast to the death penalty debate in the United States. As Kurdish and Turkish protesters clashed outside the Rome building where Ocalan was held, the American criminal justice system quietly executed its 500th prisoner since 1976, when the Supreme Court upheld the constitutionality of capital punishment.

Of course, the United States is hardly alone in executing its most vicious criminals. Since 1996, when China launched its "Strike Hard" anti-crime campaign, more than 6,000 people have been sentenced to die in China, of whom more than 4,000 were executed in 1997.[1] A number of Caribbean countries, including Jamaica and Trinidad and Tobago, have taken steps to increase capital punishment in an attempt to curb rising violent crime rates linked to the region's thriving drug traffic.[2]

But more than half the countries in the world have abandoned capital punishment, either by statute or in practice. Today, the United States is one of eighty-eight countries that have the death penalty; sixty-three have abolished capital punishment, while another twenty—including Turkey—are considered to be de facto abolitionists because they have not executed anyone for at least twenty-five years or since gaining independence. Of the ninety countries with the death penalty, thirteen reserve it for "extraordinary crimes," such as treason and espionage.[3] Among the countries with capital punishment, only a handful

---

1. "China's Crimes and Punishments" *Harper's*, November 1997.

2. Larry Rohter, "In the Caribbean, Support Growing for the Death Penalty," *New York Times*, October 4, 1998.

3. Data from Amnesty International USA.

apply it frequently: Only China, Iran, and Saudi Arabia are known to have executed more prisoners than the United States in 1997.[4]

But over the past several decades, as the pace of executions picked up in the United States, there has been a global trend to abandon capital punishment. The Universal Declaration of Human Rights adopted in 1948 by the United Nations does not specifically ban capital punishment, but many critics say the document does so implicitly. "The Declaration proclaims each person's right to protection from deprivation of life, and it categorically states that no one shall be subjected to cruel or degrading punishment," states Amnesty International USA. "The death penalty—the premeditated and cold-blooded killing of prisoners in state custody—violates both of these rights." [5]

Other international agreements address specific issues related to capital punishment. The 1992 International Covenant on Civil and Political Rights forbids the execution of offenders younger than eighteen. Upon ratifying that agreement, the United States reserved the right to carry out such executions. In May 1989, the United Nations Economic and Social Council recommended "eliminating the death penalty for persons suffering from mental retardation or extremely limited mental competence." In 1997, the U.N. Commission on Human Rights passed a resolution calling for all states with capital punishment to consider suspending executions with a view to abolishing the death penalty.

In April 1998, the commission released a report condemning the application of capital punishment in the United States. Specifically, the report says that some of the states carry out executions in an arbitrary and discriminatory manner that does not spare juveniles, the mentally retarded, or the mentally ill.

Congressional conservatives, including longtime critics of the United Nations and U.S. support of the institution, quickly responded to the report. "With all the abuses in places like Burma, China, Cuba, and Iraq, to be wasting time and money to investigate the freest country in the world shows what a strange and distant planet the United Nations inhabits," said Marc Thiessen, a spokesman for Senate Foreign Relations Committee Chairman Jesse Helms, R-N.C. "I hope the U.N. will send this report to every single U.S. citizen so they can see how their money is being spent by an institution so badly in need of top-to-bottom reform." [6]

---

4. Amnesty International USA, "United States of America: 'A Macabre Assembly Line of Death,'" Death Penalty Developments in 1997, April 1998.

5. Amnesty International USA, "A Violation of Human Rights," U.S. Death Penalty Fact Sheet #10, September 1998. For background, see Kenneth Jost, "Human Rights," *CQ Researcher*, November 13, 1998, 977–999.

6. Quoted in John M. Goshko, "U.N. Panel Calls On U.S. To Halt Death Penalty," *Washington Post*, April 4, 1998.

The victims' rights movement has broadened the debate over the death penalty beyond concern about fair treatment of defendants and capital punishment's effectiveness in deterring future crimes. It is only right, many victims' advocates say, that murderers pay for their crime with their lives. Until an inmate is executed, they say, victims' families are unable to reach "closure," to reconcile themselves to the crime that has torn apart their lives. "We believe that the death penalty is appropriate because it is a deterrent," says Clements of Justice for All. "We also believe it is the ultimate punishment for the ultimate crime. We must respect life."

The author of *Dead Man Walking*, Sister Helen Prejean, came to understand the need for retribution through her work as a spiritual consultant to prisoners on death row in Louisiana. As Prejean recounted in her book, later made into a popular movie, the family of a young man who had been brutally murdered desperately wanted his murderer, Robert Willie, to be executed. Moreover, they had been angered by Prejean, who had ministered to Willie but had ignored the victim's family.

The victim's girlfriend, who had been kidnapped and raped by the same man, was more ambivalent about the execution's role in enabling her to get on with her life. "Robert Willie's death . . . definitely reduced the fear I had to live with, [and] while I wasn't at all sure that was justification enough to execute a man, I couldn't help the fact that I simply felt better knowing Robert Willie was dead," wrote Debbie Morris. "But I do know this: Justice didn't do a thing to heal me. Forgiveness did."[27]

Death penalty opponents decry the focus on retribution, no matter what the crime. "To say that unless we get the death penalty for this person we are depreciating the value of the lost victim is simply a basic sickness," says juvenile crime expert Streib. "If somebody, God forbid, were to kill my child, I would not measure the value of my child's life on this Earth by whatever happened to the guy who killed her. But society to some degree has bought into the notion that you can put a price on the victim's pain by the punishment given the offender. That puzzles me because it has absolutely nothing to do with crime control. It has to do with satisfying the victim's family by killing yet somebody else by feeding that appetite we have for violent revenge."

Streib acknowledges that his views are not widely shared. "Between 75 and 80 percent of Americans support the death penalty," he says, "and that hasn't changed very much in the last ten to fifteen years."

There are some signs that recent studies tracking racial disparities in sentencing are beginning to influence the administration of capital punishment, however. In April 1998, Kentucky became the first state to allow defendants to challenge a death sentence on grounds of racial disparity in sentencing. "Under Kentucky's Racial Justice Act," says Dieter of the Death Penalty Information Center, "a defendant in whose case the death penalty is being sought no longer must prove purposeful racial discrimination, but may challenge the decision by simply introducing evidence of a pattern of racial bias or disparity in death sentencing against whatever minority group he or she belongs to."

But most statutory changes in recent years have made it easier, not harder, for prosecutors to seek the death sentence. In 1996, for example, a number of states added to the list of aggravating circumstances* in death penalty cases, including murder of a witness (South Carolina); murder of a firefighter, paramedic, or emergency rescue worker engaged in official duties when the defendant had reason to know the victim's occupation (Tennessee); and mutilation or torture of a murder victim while still alive (Indiana).[28] After the slashing death of a nine-year-old boy in Oceanside, California, legislators called for a change in the law to allow the death penalty in the murder of a child under fourteen.[29]

The pace of executions also has quickened. In 1997, seventeen states executed seventy-four prisoners—twenty-nine more than in 1996 and the highest number since the 1950s. Texas led the way, with thirty-seven executions. In 1998, there were sixty-eight executions. Thirty-eight-year-old Andrew Smith, convicted of the 1983 stabbing deaths of two elderly relatives, died by lethal injection on December 18, 1998, in South Carolina. He was the last person to be executed in 1998, and the 500th since capital punishment was reinstated in 1976. Executions in 1999 jumped to ninety-eight and fell only slightly to eighty-five in 2000.

Anti-Terrorism Law

Passage of the Anti-Terrorism and Effective Death Penalty Act in 1996 was greeted enthusiastically by conservatives, who had long opposed the repeated filing of habeas corpus petitions to delay executions. At issue was what conservatives called

---

*Aggravating and mitigating circumstances in capital cases are facts that can be weighed during the sentencing phase in deciding whether to sentence a defendant to death or a lesser sentence, such as life in prison without parole.

prisoners' meritless claims that their constitutional rights had been violated during the trial or appeals phase.

Capital punishment advocates were soon disappointed, however, as attorneys for death row prisoners took advantage of a rarely used avenue to pursue their cases, asking federal appellate courts to review death sentences based on procedural flaws at trial or on new evidence.

In April 1998 the Supreme Court shut the door on this type of petition by ruling that an appeals court can only change a state court's death sentence if presented with "clear and convincing evidence" of the defendant's innocence. That decision paved the way for the execution in California of Thomas Thompson, a convicted rapist and murderer scheduled to die the previous August.

"The Thompson execution could not go forward until the Supreme Court jumped in to enforce the law," says Scheidegger of the Criminal Justice Legal Foundation. With the Supreme Court ruling, he says "The law has already had the effect of cutting off repeated petitions in all but the most rare cases." Thompson was executed on July 14, 1998.

Some conservatives say the 1996 law does not go far enough, however, in restricting the authority of federal appellate courts to defy state court decisions by prolonging the appeals process. A frequent target of such criticism is the Ninth U.S. Circuit Court of Appeals in San Francisco, which ruled on the Thompson case.

"The [anti-terrorism law] seemed a reasonable, studied response to the seemingly interminable delays in executions of first-degree murderers across the land," writes Thomas, the former assistant attorney general for Arizona. "But it already seems clear that [it] is an abject failure, a metaphor for the very problem it was meant to help remedy: an out-of-control federal judiciary, impervious to the claims of the rest of the political system, or even of simple justice."

Thomas wants Congress to repeal the law's requirement that states provide competent counsel to indigent defendants in capital cases.

"The states should be trusted once again to hire qualified counsel for capital appeals without supervision by the same federal judges the [anti-terrorism law] is meant to curb," he writes. "[H]ardened murderers on death row have been able to avoid execution for more than a decade on average, in large part because their advocates are quite competent indeed—seated on the bench, with gavels in hand." [30]

But other legal experts say the law exacerbates longstanding flaws in the death penalty's administration. The ABA has long criticized the death penalty for people

Should the death penalty be abolished?

YES

Amnesty International USA,
Program to Abolish the Death Penalty
From Fact Sheets, September 1998.

Extensive evidence shows that death sentencing continues to be arbitrary in the United States. The death penalty is applied neither fairly nor consistently. Several thousand defendants are convicted of murder each year, and less than 1 percent of them receive death sentences.

Gravity of crime and culpability are not always factors in determining the sentence. Race, social and economic status, level of education, location of crime, and pure chance play significant roles in the legal processes which send some defendants to prisons, others to death. Offenders who commit similar crimes under similar circumstances have received widely differing sentences.

In almost all jurisdictions throughout the United States, the prosecutor is an elected official. It is the prosecutor who decides whether to seek the death penalty. Some prosecutors rarely seek the death penalty; some seek it whenever possible. Some prosecutors call for capital punishment only if a case is widely publicized, a focus of community pressure, or an issue among defense attorneys or local police. Some prosecutors demonstrate racial bias in their decisions to seek the death penalty. Prosecutors settle many cases through plea bargaining. More culpable defendants at high risk of receiving a death sentence often plea bargain in return for a reduced sentence. Their less culpable accomplices, however, may receive the death penalty.

In addition, prosecutors seek the death penalty far more frequently when the victim of the homicide is white than when the victim is black. . . .

In most states prosecutors may reject potential jurors who oppose the death penalty. Potential black jurors are often removed by peremptory challenge—that is, without any stated reason—in cases involving black defendants. Since reinstatement of the death penalty in 1976, only five white persons have been executed for killing a black person.

Jury interpretations of aggravating or mitigating circumstances also cause discrepancies in death sentencing. In Texas a defendant's life or death may depend on a jury's prediction of his or her future conduct. In Alabama, Delaware, Florida, and Indiana, trial judges may override the jury's sentencing recommendation. . . .

Even with the costly safeguards required by the United States judicial systems, gross miscarriages of justice occur. Innocent people have been executed in the past and statistics show that several innocent people are convicted of capital crimes in the United States each year.

Should the death penalty be abolished?

NO

David Gelernter
A professor of computer science at Yale University
who was letter-bombed and nearly killed in June 1993
From "What Do Murderers Deserve?"
Commentary, **April 1998.**

Why execute murderers? To deter? To avenge? Supporters of the death penalty often give the first answer, opponents the second. But neither can be the whole truth. If our main goal were deterring crime, we would insist on public executions. . . . If our main goal were vengeance, we would allow the grieving parties to decide the murderer's fate. . . . In fact, we execute murderers in order to make a communal proclamation: that murder is intolerable. A deliberate murderer embodies evil so terrible that it defiles the community. . . .

When a murder takes place, the community is obliged, whether it feels like it or not, to clear its throat and step up to the microphone. Every murder demands a communal response. Among possible responses, the death penalty is uniquely powerful because it is permanent and can never be retracted or overturned. . . .

Of course, we could make the same point less emphatically if we wanted to—for example, by locking up murderers for life (as we sometimes do). The question then becomes: Is the death penalty overdoing it? Should we make a less forceful proclamation instead?

The answer might be yes if we were a community in which murder was a shocking anomaly and thus, in effect, a solved problem. But we are not. Our big cities are full of murderers at large. . . .

Granted (some people say), the death penalty is a communal proclamation; it is nevertheless an incoherent one. If our goal is to affirm that human life is more precious than anything else, how can we make such a declaration by destroying life? . . . [But] the point of capital punishment is not to pronounce on life in general but on the crime of murder. . . .

A newer objection grows out of the seemingly random way in which we apply capital punishment. . . . We can grant that, on the whole, we are doing a disgracefully bad job of administering the death penalty. After all, we are divided and confused on the issue. The community at large is strongly in favor of capital punishment; the cultural elite is strongly against it. Our attempts to speak with assurance as a community come out sounding in consequence like a man who is fighting off a choke-hold as he talks. But a community as cavalier about murder as we are has no right to back down. That we are botching things does not entitle us to give up.

who committed crimes as juveniles or who are mentally impaired. In August 1997, in response to concerns about the anti-terrorism law, the ABA finally called for a moratorium on executions altogether.

"The anti-terrorism statute was really the impetus for getting this done now," says Kenneth Goldsmith, staff counsel for the ABA's criminal justice section. Because the ABA represents practitioners of all branches of the law, including criminal prosecutors, Goldsmith says, there had not been enough support to pass a moratorium resolution until the new law raised due-process concerns. "The anti-terrorism statute created an atmosphere which otherwise would not have been conducive to the ABA's taking on the death penalty," he says.

Anti–death penalty advocates see another danger in the law. "In states like Missouri, this law has actually been applied retroactively, which is disturbing in its own right," says Henninger of the National Coalition to Abolish the Death Penalty. "Missouri doesn't by a long shot meet the requirements that are necessary to fall under the act, yet they're processing appeals faster than any other state in the country right now."

Henninger says the Eighth U.S. Circuit Court of Appeals, which presides over Missouri, has not looked at the fact that three Missouri inmates have been executed since passage of the anti-terrorism law without recourse to the federal appeals process.

"That is very disturbing, and if we see other circuits follow suit, we could have a real problem on our hands," he says.

Outlook

Piecemeal Reforms?

The courts have yet to grapple with a key issue raised by the 1996 Anti-Terrorism and Effective Death Penalty Act.

"When you enact a statute of limitations to cut off habeas cases—or you enact such a strict gatekeeping provision as for second or successive habeas petitions and you say they can't be filed if they are same-claims successive petitions—does that violate the [Constitution's] suspension clause?" asks Robbins of the Washington College of Law. "A good argument could be made that it does, but a good argument could also be made that it doesn't."

At the time the clause was written, Robbins points out, habeas corpus relief was available only to federal prisoners. State prisoners, the vast majority of death row inmates, were not allowed to file habeas claims until passage of the Habeas Corpus Act in 1867.

"So you could argue that what Congress gave in 1867 Congress can take away, and say that habeas for state prisoners is not a constitutional matter," Robbins says. "You could also argue that it is a constitutional matter because habeas corpus has become the primary vehicle for testing constitutional criminal procedures for state prisoners for more than 130 years now. There is a nice argument on both sides. Ultimately, as with all nice questions, the answer is whether you can get five votes at the Supreme Court level, and that would be an uphill battle."

Meanwhile, death penalty opponents are pushing for piecemeal reforms in an effort to lessen the 1996 law's impact.

"We're not going for abolition or even a moratorium on executions," Henninger says. Instead, his group wants to prevent a lowering of the minimum age for death sentences and eliminate them for the mentally retarded. "We are just trying to scale back the law in ways that legislatures can see it more as a fairness issue rather than deciding whether the death penalty in and of itself is right or wrong."

At the same time, death penalty supporters are backing proposals to extend capital sentencing to yet more crimes. Murder alone is not enough to bring down a death sentence in many states. In Texas, for example, capital punishment is reserved for cases in which murder is accompanied by another felony crime such as burglary or rape.

Clements of Justice for All advocates mandatory application of the death sentence to murderers of senior citizens, a provision recently adopted by the Washington state legislature. She also would like to see killers in domestic violence cases subject to the death penalty.

"Most often these horrible crimes involve a woman with a protective order against an assaultive, stalking ex-boyfriend or husband," she says. "They've done everything they can to protect themselves—they've moved, changed jobs, gone to the courts, gone to the police, and nobody can do anything for them. All they can do is hope and pray that whoever the protective order is against has enough respect for the fact that there is a protective order not to assault, stalk, or murder them, but very, very often they do."

For More Information

American Bar Association, 740 15th St. N.W., Washington, D.C. 20005; (202) 662-1500; www.abanet.org. The leading organization of lawyers has called for a moratorium on executions, citing inconsistencies and unfairness in its application.

Criminal Justice Legal Foundation, P.O. Box 1199, Sacramento, California 95812; (916) 446-0345; www.cjlf.org. The public interest law organization seeks to "enhance public safety and victims' rights" and provides the media with a "balancing perspective to the well-publicized advocates of criminals' rights."

Death Penalty Information Center, 1320 18th St. N.W., Fifth Floor, Washington, D.C. 20036; (202) 293-6970; www.deathpenaltyinfo.com. This nonprofit organization provides information on issues concerning capital punishment.

Justice for All, P.O. Box 55159, Houston, Texas 77255; (713) 935-9300. This victims' rights organization supports the death penalty and aids victims of violent crime and their families.

National Association of Evangelicals, 1001 Connecticut Ave. N.W., Suite 522, Washington, D.C. 20036; (202) 789-1011; www.nae.net. The leading membership group of conservative Christian churches and individuals recently raised questions about capital punishment, citing inequities in its application.

National Coalition to Abolish the Death Penalty, 1436 U St. N.W., Suite 104, Washington, D.C. 20009; (202) 387-3890; www.ncadp.org. This advocacy group opposes the death penalty and calls it an instrument of racial oppression against minority groups.

Notes

1. Quoted in *Chicago Sun-Times*, November 15, 1998, 15.

2. Amnesty International USA, "Fatal Flaws: Innocence and the Death Penalty," November 12, 1998.

3. Quoted in Vince Beiser, "Lucky to Be Alive," *Maclean's*, November 30, 1998, 49.

4. U.S. General Accounting Office, "Death Penalty Sentencing," February 1990.

5. Richard C. Dieter, "The Death Penalty in Black & White," Death Penalty Information Center, 1998.

6. Death Penalty Information Center, www.deathpenaltyinfo.org. Accessed spring 2001.

7. Tracy L. Snell, "Capital Punishment 1996," U.S. Department of Justice, Bureau of Justice Statistics, February 6, 1998.

8. Andrew Peyton Thomas, "Penalty Box: A Much-Needed Reform Seemed Poised to Hasten Executions Until Federal Judges Got Their Hands on It," *National Review*, May 4, 1998, 40.

9. H. A. Bedau and Michael L. Radelet, "Miscarriages of Justice in Potentially Capital Cases," *Stanford Law Review*, November 1987.

10. Justice for All, "Death Penalty and Sentencing Information in the United States," October 1, 1997.

11. Quoted in "Conservatives Rethink the Death Penalty," *Christianity Today*, April 6, 1998, 19.

12. William F. Buckley Jr., "Miss Tucker's Plea," *National Review*, March 9, 1998, 71.

13. Amnesty International USA, *On the Wrong Side of History: Children and the Death Penalty in the USA*, October 1998.

14. Victor L. Streib, "The Juvenile Death Penalty Today: Death Sentences and Executions for Juvenile Crimes, January 1, 1973–December 31, 2000," February 2001. Accessed at http://www.law.onu.edu/faculty/streib/juvdeath.htm.

15. See Patrick Griffin, Patricia Torbet, and Linda Szymanski, "Trying Juveniles as Adults in Criminal Court: An Analysis of State Transfer Provisions," U.S. Department of Justice, December 1998.

16. Quoted by Arlene Levinson, "States Steadily Lower Age When Child Becomes Adult in Eyes of Law," Associated Press, March 27, 1998.

17. Death Penalty Information Center, www.deathpenaltyinfo.org. Accessed fall 2001.

18. Arlene Levinson, "States Steadily Lower Age when Child Becomes Adult in Eyes of Law," Associated Press, March 27, 1998.

19. Speaking April 20, 1998, on NBC's *Today* show.

20. John W. Gonzalez, "Many in Poll Want Stiffer Laws on Juvenile Criminals; Support Growing to Punish Parents," *Houston Chronicle,* June 21, 1998.

21. Information in this section is based on Hugo Adam Bedau, *The Death Penalty in America: Current Controversies* (1997), 3–24. See also Richard L. Worsnop, "Death Penalty Debate," *CQ Researcher,* March 10, 1995, 193–216.

22. For background, see Charles S. Clark, "Crime Victims' Rights," *CQ Researcher,* July 22, 1994, 625–648.

23. The results of the study were published later in David C. Baldus, Charles Pulanski, and George Woodworth, *Equal Justice and the Death Penalty* (1990).

24. Dieter, *op. cit.*

25. Roberto Suro, "How a Federal Case Becomes a Capital Case," *Washington Post,* January 11, 1998; "The Federal Death Penalty System: A Statistical Study (1988–2000)," U.S. Department of Justice, September 12, 2000.

26. From a dissenting opinion by Blackmun in *Callins v. Collins* (1994).

27. Debbie Morris, *Forgiving the Dead Man Walking* (1998), 232, 251.

28. Snell, *op. cit.*

29. Tony Perry, "Boy's Slaying Sparks Call for Expansion of Death Penalty Law," *Los Angeles Times,* December 3, 1998.

30. Thomas, *op. cit.*

Bibliography

Books

Bedau, Hugo Adam, ed. *The Death Penalty in America: Current Controversies*. Oxford University Press, 1997.

A noted legal scholar presents forty essays by legal experts that examine various elements of the debate over capital punishment in the United States.

Jackson, Rev. Jesse. *Legal Lynching: Racism, Injustice, and the Death Penalty*. Marlowe, 1996.

Jackson presents the findings of numerous studies of racial disparity in sentencing and concludes that black Americans, as well as the poor and residents of southern states, are discriminated against in capital cases.

Morris, Debbie. *Forgiving the Dead Man Walking*. Zondervan Publishing, 1998.

The author survived kidnapping, rape, and her boyfriend's shooting at the hands of Robert Willie, one of the inmates portrayed in the book and film entitled *Dead Man Walking*. After suffering severe emotional distress, Morris forgave her assailant and remained ambivalent about the death penalty.

Prejean, Helen. *Dead Man Walking: An Eyewitness Account of the Death Penalty in the United States*. Random House, 1993.

Sister Prejean's account of serving as spiritual adviser to death row inmates in Louisiana was portrayed in a popular film of the same title. The experience galvanized her opposition to capital punishment while forcing her to sympathize with the frustration and anger of victims' families who supported capital punishment.

Weinglass, Leonard. *Race for Justice*. Common Courage Press, 1995.

The author served as chief defense counsel for Mumia Abu-Jamal, a black activist condemned to death for murdering a Philadelphia police officer. He describes numerous discrepancies in the case that prompted an international appeal for Jamal's release.

Articles

Buckley, William F. Jr. "Miss Tucker's Plea." *National Review*, March 9, 1998, 71.

A conservative supporter of capital punishment justifies the February 1998 execution of Karla Faye Tucker as a possible deterrent to future crime and the fulfilling of society's need for retribution.

Farley, Christopher John, and James Willwerth. "Dead Teen Walking." *Time*, January 19, 1998, 50–57.

This account of the trial and conviction of Shareef Cousin helped draw attention to the case involving a juvenile condemned to death for murder under questionable evidence. Cousin was subsequently granted a retrial.

"The Lesson of Karla Faye Tucker: Evangelical Instincts Against Her Execution Were Right, but Not Because She Was a Christian." *Christianity Today*, April 6, 1998, 15–16.

With this editorial, the leading magazine of conservative Christians broke with tradition by calling for the abolition of the death penalty. "The death penalty as it is practiced in this country is unfair and discriminatory," the editorial states. "It has not made the United States a safer country or a more equitable one."

McCormick, John. "The Wrongly Condemned." *Newsweek,* **November 9, 1998, 64–66.**

A recent conference in Chicago highlighted the cases of seventy-five former death row prisoners who were released after evidence of innocence or of procedural flaws at trial prompted courts to overturn their death sentences.

Schlosser, Eric. "The Prison-Industrial Complex." *Atlantic Monthly,* **December 1998, 51–77.**

To house the nearly two million Americans who are currently behind bars, a vast industry has emerged involving architectural firms, Wall Street banks, and an array of contractors providing goods and services to prisons.

Reports and Studies

Amnesty International. *The United States of America: Rights for All.* **Amnesty International Publications, 1998.**

This report on the status of human rights in the United States includes a chapter on the death penalty, which Amnesty opposes as "cruel, inhuman, and degrading" punishment.

Dieter, Richard C. *Innocence and the Death Penalty: The Increasing Danger of Executing the Innocent.* **Death Penalty Information Center, July 1997.**

Of the sixty-nine prisoners sentenced to death and later released on evidence of their innocence described in this report, the average time spent on death row was about seven years. With recent steps to shorten the appeals process, the author predicts that more innocent prisoners will be executed.

Streib, Victor L. *Another Kind of Innocence: The Death Penalty for Children.* **November 14, 1998.**

This paper, presented at the Chicago conference on wrongful convictions by an expert on juvenile crime, examines the application of capital punishment to prisoners who committed their crimes before age eighteen.

THE NEXT STEP: ADDITIONAL INFORMATION

Death Row Mistakes

Bailey, Eric. "With Inmate's Execution Looming, Some Doubt Guilt, Death Row; His Attorneys Cite New Evidence and Gain Support; As Governor Weighs Pleas, Victim's Family Remains Convinced He Killed Woman." *Los Angeles Times*, **July 28, 1997, A3.**

His death sentence seems to fit the crime—the rape and brutal murder of a Newport Beach woman not yet twenty-one years old. But one nagging uncertainty remains as Thomas Thompson nears his fate. Unlike the four men who preceded him to California's death chamber, Thompson claims he is innocent. His legal appeals virtually exhausted, Thompson's fate now rests with Gov. Pete Wilson, who is pondering pleas that the death sentence be nudged down to life in prison without the possibility of parole.

Endres, Krista. "The Frustrations of Fighting for a Life." *Human Rights* **(spring 1997): 9.**

The author, a lawyer, shares her frustration over the conviction of Willie Enoch for murder in 1983 in Peoria, Illinois. She believes Enoch was mistakenly convicted and should not be facing the death penalty.

Herbert, Bob. "Wrongful Death Penalty." *New York Times*, **July 14, 1997, A15.**

"Perhaps the bleakest fact of all," said Supreme Court Justice William J. Brennan in 1994, "is that the death penalty is imposed not only in a freakish and discriminatory manner but also in some cases upon defendants who are actually innocent." Justice Brennan's observation is cited in the introduction to a frightening new report released by the Death Penalty Information Center in Washington, D.C. According to the report, there have been sixty-nine cases since 1973 in which people have been released from death row because they were improperly convicted or evidence of their innocence was uncovered after they were sentenced to die.

Leo, Richard A., and Richard J. Ofshe. "The Consequences of False Confessions: Deprivations of Liberty and Miscarriages of Justice in the Age of Psychological Interrogation." *Journal of Criminal Law and Criminology* **(winter 1998): 429–496.**

The authors present documentation that police in the United States continue to elicit false confessions even though the era of third-degree interrogation has passed. Sixty cases of false confessions are summarized.

Ross, Michael B. "The Execution of Innocence." *Peace Review* **(September 1998): 481–483.**

The U.S. judicial system is grounded in the belief that a person is innocent until proven guilty, but no justice system is foolproof. The author examines the conviction and execution of innocents in the United States.

Shapiro, Joseph P. "The Wrong Men on Death Row." *U.S. News & World Report,* **November 9, 1998, 22–26.**

A growing number of bad convictions have turned the public spotlight on the death penalty and its fairness. Several false convictions are examined.

"Too Many Close Calls on Death Row." *Chicago Tribune,* **July 19, 1997, 22.**

The article contends that something has gone terribly wrong in enforcement of the death penalty in Illinois. Since capital punishment was reinstated in the state in 1977, Illinois has achieved the dubious distinction of having the highest number of defendants known to have been wrongfully sentenced to die. A study by the Death Penalty Information Center in Washington, D.C., found twenty-one such cases nationwide in the last four years, of which seven were in Illinois, more than in any other state.

Weinstein, Henry. "Death Penalty Foes Focus Effort on the Innocent." *Los Angeles Times,* **November 16, 1998, A1.**

Prominent opponents of capital punishment have launched a nationwide effort to recruit law schools to train students to work on cases that might lead to freedom for wrongly convicted people—particularly inmates facing capital punishment. The campaign seeks to take advantage of new DNA technologies that can identify innocent people who have been wrongly convicted.

Zuckoff, Mitchell. "Death Row Survivors Tell How Justice Errs; Conference Puts Death Penalty on Trial." *Boston Globe,* **November 15, 1998, A1.**

Watching them assemble yesterday in the first large-scale meeting of wrongfully convicted death row inmates, it was easy to imagine the walk each was supposed to take alone, from a prison cell down a hall to a waiting death chamber. The gathering at Northwestern University Law School had particular resonance for Massachusetts, where Republican governor Argeo Paul Cellucci has made restoring the death penalty among his top priorities.

Deterrence

Bailey, William C. "Deterrence, Brutalization, and the Death Penalty: Another Examination of Oklahoma's Return to Capital Punishment." *Criminology* (November 1998): 711–733.

A replication and extension of an analysis that appeared in *Criminology* confirms that Oklahoma's return to capital punishment in 1990 after a twenty-five-year moratorium was followed by a significant increase in killings involving strangers.

Levy, David A. "Violent Criminals Must Stay in Prison." *USA Today: The Magazine of the American Scene*, May 1994, 48–49.

Communities in the United States are living in fear of violent crimes. The author discusses the need for convicted felons to stay in prison longer.

Van Den Haag, Ernest, and Oliver Starr Jr. "How to Cut Crime." *National Review*, May 30, 1994, 30–35.

The main reason crime has skyrocketed since the 1960s is that the risk of punishment has plummeted. The authors say Attorney General Janet Reno is so busy looking for root causes of crime that she has no time to look for solutions, and that Richard Davis, who murdered Polly Klaas, is a career criminal who made the system work for him.

Minors

"Should Juveniles Be Eligible for the Death Penalty?" *Cosmopolitan*, August 1998, 60.

People share their views on the death penalty for juveniles who commit murder. Of those surveyed, 41 percent of men and 35 percent of women believe that juveniles as young as eleven should face the death penalty.

Lhotka, William C. "Teen Charged in Killing May Be Facing Death Penalty." *St. Louis Post-Dispatch*, August 25, 1998, B4.

If teenager DeShun S. Washington is convicted of first-degree murder, he will be the youngest defendant in St. Louis County to face the death penalty since Missouri's capital punishment law was reinstated twenty years ago. He is accused of murdering Michele Holt in North St. Louis County.

Munz, Michele. "Officials Want to Try Boy, Fifteen, as Adult in Girl's Beheading, Hearing Is Set for July 13 in St. Charles County; Teen-Ager Could Face Death Penalty." *St. Louis Post-Dispatch*, **June 10, 1998, B1.**

St. Charles County youth services officials say they will ask that a fifteen-year-old accused in the rape, murder, and beheading of a teen-age girl be certified to stand trial as an adult. If the boy is convicted as an adult of first-degree murder and the other charges, he could face the death penalty, prosecutors say. A judge would consider the rape and the boy's age in the sentencing.

Walt, Kathy. "Lawmaker Seeks to Lower Age on Death Penalty to Eleven." *Houston Chronicle*, **April 7, 1998, A13.**

As abolitionists denounced Texas's "diabolical appetite" for executions, a state lawmaker said he will push to change Texas law to allow children as young as eleven to be sentenced to death. The proposal by state representative Jim Pitts, R-Waxahachie, is part of a five-point plan he announced to increase the penalties that could be leveled against violent juvenile offenders.

Popular Opinion

Matier, Phillip, and Andrew Ross. "74 Percent Support for Death Penalty an About-Face From the '50s." *San Francisco Chronicle*, **July 15, 1998, A13.**

All of this year's major candidates for California governor and attorney general—Republicans and Democrats alike—favored the death penalty.

Ryan, John Paul, and John Michael Eden. "Teaching About the Death Penalty." *Social Education* **(February 1998): 88–91.**

The authors discuss the death penalty beliefs of a panel gathered by the American Bar Association's Division for Public Education. The panel says that open discussion of capital punishment will help to increase students' awareness of political, legal, ethical, and philosophical issues.

Shepard, Scott. "More Blacks Support Death Penalty; Increased Crime May Be Part of Reason." *Atlanta Journal Constitution*, **April 18, 1998, A1.**

African Americans no longer oppose capital punishment with the same vigor as in past decades, even though the death penalty still falls disproportionately on black people. African Americans have had a gradual but profound change of heart on the issue, largely the result of improving economic status as well as outrage over violent crime in their own communities, according to death penalty experts, sociologists, and political scientists.

Walt, Kathy. "Death Penalty's Support Plunges to a Thirty-Year Low; Karla Faye Tucker's Execution Tied to Texans' Attitude Change." *Houston Chronicle*, **March 15, 1998, A1.**

A new Scripps-Howard Texas poll found 68 percent of Texans favor capital punishment, down a whopping 18 percentage points from a 1994 survey. "The whole Karla Faye Tucker deal focused people on this issue. That's got to have something to do with it," Texas poll director Ty Meighan said of the new survey findings. Tim Flanagan, dean of the criminal justice college at Sam Houston State University, said the Texas poll findings are consistent with other state and national polls, which have shown declining support for capital punishment in recent years.

Racial Issues

"Study Cites Link Between Death Penalty and Race." *Jet*, **June 22, 1998, 46.**

The Washington, D.C.–based Death Penalty Information Center recently prepared a study indicating that nearly all of the prosecutors who pursue capital cases are white. Blacks are four times more likely to get the death sentence than whites.

Bienen, Leigh B. "Can the Death Penalty Be Administered Fairly? No." *Spectrum: The Journal of State Government* **(winter 1998): 29.**

The author argues that it is impossible to administer the death penalty fairly. The reason for abolishing it is very simple: It is not just.

Fields, Gary, and Charisse Jones. "Studies Find Death Penalty Links to Race; Nearly All Lead Prosecutors in Capital Cases are White." *USA Today*, **June 4, 1998, A3.**

"The Death Penalty in Black and White: Who Lives, Who Dies, Who Decides," includes two studies. One conducted by a professor and researchers at St. Mary University Law School in Texas found that 1,794 of the 1,838 lead prosecutors in the thirty-eight states that have the death penalty are white, twenty-two are black, and twenty-two are Hispanic.

Page, Clarence. "Race Clouds Death Penalty Fairness." *Chicago Tribune*, **June 7, 1998, 23.**

A study by University of Iowa Law School researchers David Baldus and George Woodworth analyzed 667 murders that occurred in Philadelphia from 1983 to 1993. Of the 520 cases involving black defendants, 95 were sentenced to die, while 19 of the 147 non-black defendants received the death penalty. Baldus conducted a similar study in the mid-1980s that showed the killers of whites were far more likely to receive the death penalty than the killers of blacks. The study became part of a death penalty challenge that reached the Supreme Court. In 1987, the Court accepted the statistics but rejected the argument that even when the statistics clearly showed Georgia's death penalty enforcement to be unfair to blacks, statistics were not enough to prove that race was an issue in individual cases.

Price, David Andrew. "Death Penalty is a Black and White Issue." *USA Today*, **November 19, 1998, A15.**

Does the death penalty in America discriminate against African American defendants? Today, one opinion poll after another shows that about 70 percent of Americans support the death penalty for the most heinous offenses. Against that consensus, the charge of racism is the most cutting and effective argument used by the penalty's opponents—from the Rev. Jesse Jackson to Sister Helen Prejean in her book *Dead Man Walking*. But there is precious little support for the mythology that prosecutors are more zealous about seeking the death penalty against African Americans, or that biased juries are sending African Americans to death row more often. Another inconvenient fact for those playing the race card: White death row prisoners are more likely than African Americans to have their death sentences carried out: 7.2 percent of white prisoners were executed, compared with 5.9 percent of African Americans.

Rovella, David E. "Race Pervades Death Penalty." *National Law Journal* **(June 8, 1998): A20.**

A recently released two-year study discussed the role race plays in death sentences; black defendants were found to be four times more likely than whites to receive the death penalty. The report may breathe new life into the Racial Justice Act, a bill that would allow defendants to argue racial disparity as a defense against execution.

Reforms

Mehren, Elizabeth. "Grisly Murder Fuels Death Penalty Debate." *Los Angeles Times*, **November 17, 1998, A5.**

Death penalty opponents here realized a narrow victory last year when a push to reinstitute capital punishment lost by a single vote with state lawmakers. With the 1998 conviction of one of two defendants in the especially horrific murder of a ten-year-old child, that margin may grow shakier still. In a fractious campaign against Democrat and death penalty supporter Scott Harshbarger, Republican governor Argeo Paul Cellucci pledged to return capital punishment to Massachusetts, one of only twelve states without the death penalty.

Mooney, Brian C. "On the Death Penalty, Two Sides Weigh Each Move." *Boston Globe*, November 11, 1998, B2.

The Massachusetts House will probably vote on whether to reinstate the death penalty in the state in January. In the incoming House, which includes twenty new members, the death penalty died on an 80–80 vote in 1997. Currently, members are split 79–79, with two undecideds. The Massachusetts Senate, meanwhile, maintains a pro–death penalty majority.

Savage, David G. "State's Legal Morass Numbs Death Penalty." *Los Angeles Times*, May 31, 1998, A1.

It often takes four or five years for a federal judge in California to rule on a habeas corpus appeal filed by a state death row inmate, and then, after that appeal has failed, several more years for the U.S. Ninth Circuit Court of Appeals to review the case. And this process begins only after several years of unsuccessful appeals in the California state courts.

Whitehead, John T. " 'Good Ol' Boys' and the Chair: Death Penalty Attitudes of Policy Makers in Tennessee." *Crime & Delinquency* (April 1998): 245–256.

The author summarizes a survey of Tennessee chief prosecutors, chief public defenders, and state legislators concerning their attitudes toward capital punishment. When given the option of life imprisonment without parole, support for the death penalty decreased.

2   Politics and Policy

Capital punishment in the United States has a long history; it has been used almost continuously since the nation gained its independence, with the exception of a few years in the 1970s. Yet the details of its use are constantly in flux. The frequency with which the government imposes the death penalty, and the crimes it punishes, for instance, have varied considerably over the years. The manner in which the punishment is used at any time is a function of many political forces, including the action of all of the branches of government at every level of government. This chapter examines how these forces have impacted the use of the death penalty in the United States and describes their result: the death penalty as it is applied today.

The United States Supreme Court and the Constitutionality of Capital Punishment

Since the earliest days of the republic, capital punishment has been a part of the United States' legal landscape. The United States Constitution, in fact, explicitly addresses the use of the death penalty in the Fifth Amendment:

> No person shall be held to answer for a *capital,* or other wise infamous crime, unless on a presentment or indictment of a Grand Jury, except in cases arising in the land or naval forces, or in the militia, when in actual service in time of War or public danger . . . nor be deprived of life . . . without due process of law.[1]

The Fourteenth Amendment, adopted in 1868, has a similar provision, designed to prevent the government from depriving people of "*life,* liberty, or property, without due process of law."[2] Thus, the Constitution seems to state that, if a person is accorded "due process of law," it is permissible to deprive that person of his or her life.

Indeed, the death penalty was a common form of punishment in the first century of United States' history.[3] Although states began to reform the methods by which they implemented capital punishment in the late eighteenth century,[4] the first state did not even partially abolish the practice until 1846.[5] Over the ensuing years, other states also discarded capital punishment, but by 1972 thirty-nine states still had death penalty statutes on their books.[6]

Despite this long history, and the seeming constitutional endorsement of capital punishment, in 1972 the U.S. Supreme Court struck down a Georgia death penalty law as unconstitutional. In *Furman v. Georgia* (1972), in a close 5–4 decision, the Court held that the Georgia statute and laws like it in other states, which gave the jury in capital cases (cases in which a prosecutor seeks the death penalty) complete discretion in deciding whether to impose the death penalty, violated the Eighth Amendment's protections against cruel and unusual punishment.[7]

The case concerned a black man, William Furman, accused of killing a white father of five. Furman was convicted and sentenced to death under Georgia's murder statute. The NAACP Legal Defense and Educational Fund (LDF) handled Furman's subsequent appeal, arguing that Georgia's law gave the jury too much discretion in deciding whether to sentence a defendant to death. According to the LDF, the system allowed jurors' prejudices to impact sentencing decisions and resulted in an unfair disparity: black defendants convicted of killing whites were far more likely to receive the death penalty than were white defendants convicted of killing other whites.

The Supreme Court agreed. Yet, even among the five justices that voted to strike down the law, two of the justices—William J. Brennan and Thurgood Marshall—accepted the argument that society had finally progressed to the point where capital punishment was *invariably* cruel and unusual and could never be constitutionally imposed. The other three—William O. Douglas, Potter Stewart, and Byron R. White—did not agree that the death penalty was always unconstitutional. Instead, they argued that the manner in which Georgia and other states applied capital punishment was cruel and unusual, because it afforded jurors too much discretion. Under those laws, the decision whether to impose the sentence was too vulnerable to jurors' prejudices, and therefore the system was "arbitrary and capricious." The justices who voted against striking down the law—Warren E. Burger, Harry A. Blackmun, Lewis F. Powell Jr., and William H. Rehnquist—felt both that the death penalty could constitutionally be used and that Georgia's system of doing so was acceptable.

Furman had a wide impact because all death penalty statutes in the United States were similar to the Georgia law that had now been ruled unconstitutional. Yet legislators realized that, though the Supreme Court had invalidated a death penalty law, only two justices had written that the death penalty could never be used. A majority of the Court—seven justices—had held that capital punishment could be constitutional if it was applied in a noncapricious manner. So, many states revised their death penalty statutes in attempts to meet the demands of *Furman*. In 1973 Congress, too, passed a new law (P.L. 93-366) imposing the death penalty for anyone guilty of conducting an aircraft hijacking that resulted in a death.[8] (See Table 2-1.)

The first real test of these efforts came four years later, when the Supreme Court decided *Gregg v. Georgia* (1976).[9] Georgia had passed a new death penalty statute that mandated a "bifurcated trial" in capital cases. Under this system the trial to determine guilt or innocence would proceed as normal. If the defendant was found guilty of a capital offense, the prosecution could choose to seek the death penalty in a special sentencing stage. In this second stage, the prosecution would tell the jury about the aggravating facts of the crime—facts that make the crime more heinous and would allow a jury to impose the death penalty. The defense would present mitigating facts about the defendant, which make the crime seem less awful and would be likely to lead a juror to vote against imposing the death penalty. These facts were not set in law and could be anything, including the defendant's age, criminal record, family history, chances for rehabilitation, and so on. The prosecution, on the other hand, had to prove that one of ten specific aggravating factors applied, such as the fact that the murder was committed to achieve monetary gain. If no such factor existed, the death penalty could not be imposed. After hearing the presentations by the prosecution and defense, the jury was to decide whether one of the aggravating factors was present, and if so, whether to impose the death penalty in light of the mitigating factors presented by the defense. It was hoped that this system would limit the jury's discretion and the chance that members' prejudices would affect the sentence—and thus that the new law would pass constitutional muster.

In *Gregg*, the defendant, Troy Gregg, was tried for murdering two men that had given Gregg and a hitchhiking friend a ride. He was convicted and sentenced to death under the new bifurcated death penalty procedure. Gregg challenged his sentence as a constitutional violation, and his appeal went all the way to

Table 2-1 Jurisdictions Imposing Capital Punishment

Jurisdiction	Jurisdictions with Capital Punishment in 1972	Jurisdictions Passing Law after 1972	Year Post-Furman Capital Statute Adopted
Alabama	*	*	1976
Alaska			
Arizona	*	*	1973
Arkansas	*	*	1973
California	*	*	1974
Colorado	*	*	1975
Connecticut	*	*	1973
Delaware	*	*	1974
District of Columbia			
Florida	*	*	1972
Georgia	*	*	1973
Hawaii			
Idaho	*	*	1973
Illinois	*	*	1974
Indiana	*	*	1973
Iowa			
Kansas		*	1994
Kentucky	*	*	1975
Louisiana	*	*	1973
Maine			
Maryland	*	*	1975
Massachusetts	*	*	1979 (since repealed)
Michigan			
Minnesota			
Mississippi	*	*	1974
Missouri	*	*	1975
Montana	*	*	1974
Nebraska	*	*	1973

Table 2-1 *continued*

Jurisdiction	Jurisdictions with Capital Punishment in 1972	Jurisdictions Passing Law after 1972	Year Post-Furman Capital Statute Adopted
Nevada	*	*	1973
New Hampshire	*	*	1991
New Jersey	*	*	1982
New Mexico	*	*	1979
New York	*	*	1995
North Carolina	*	*	1977
North Dakota			
Ohio	*	*	1974
Oklahoma	*	*	1973
Oregon	*	*	1978
Pennsylvania	*	*	1974
Rhode Island	*	*	1973 (since repealed)
South Carolina	*	*	1974
South Dakota	*	*	1979
Tennessee	*	*	1974
Texas	*	*	1974
Utah	*	*	1973
Vermont			
Virginia	*	*	1975
Washington	*	*	1975
West Virginia			
Wisconsin			
Wyoming	*	*	1977
Federal system	*	*	1974
U.S. military	*	*	1984

Sources: Death Penalty Information Center, www.deathpenaltyinfo.org; and Christopher Z. Mooney and Mei-Hsein Lee, "Morality Policy Reinvention: State Death Penalties," *Annals of the American Academy of Political and Social Science* 566 (1999): 88.

the Supreme Court. In a 7–2 decision, the Court denied his appeal and upheld the new Georgia law. In doing so, it explicitly rejected the notion that the death penalty invariably violates the Eighth Amendment. The Court noted that the Constitution, in the Fifth and Fourteenth Amendments, discusses the use of capital punishment.

The Court also rejected the argument that Justices Brennan and Marshall had made in *Furman.* In that case, the two justices had argued that, despite the seeming constitutional endorsement of capital punishment, the Eighth Amendment's prohibition on cruel and unusual punishment "must draw its meaning from the evolving standards of decency that mark the progress of a maturing society."[10] Brennan and Marshall argued that by the contemporary standards of morality in the United States, the death penalty had indeed become cruel and unusual. The majority in *Gregg* rebuffed this contention, noting several indications that most Americans still supported use of the death penalty. These included the facts that, since *Furman* was decided in 1972, Congress and thirty-five state legislatures had already passed new statutes imposing capital punishment for certain crimes; that the voters of California had adopted an amendment to their state constitution authorizing capital punishment; and that many juries were still willing to impose the sentence.

The majority further held that the bifurcated trial system proscribed by the new Georgia law was adequate to rein in the discretion of the jury and to avoid the risk of "wholly capricious" sentences. Thus, the Court had finally and firmly declared the death penalty constitutional and had endorsed a method by which criminal justice systems could avoid running afoul of the Eighth Amendment. *Gregg* delineated the fundamental constraints on government's use of capital punishment. In fact, in the next two years, the Court made some elements of the Georgia law requirements for any death penalty statute. In *Roberts v. Louisiana* (1977)[11] the Court held that a defendant in a capital case must be allowed to present mitigating factors to the jury; and in another pair of cases the Court ruled that there can be no statutory limitations on the sorts of mitigating factors that defendants may use in their defense.[12]

The Court's job was not finished, however. In the years since *Gregg,* it has issued many opinions refining its death penalty jurisprudence. The Court has limited the use of capital punishment in two important ways. First, it has clarified the notion of "proportionality"—the idea that the death penalty must properly fit the magnitude of the crime it punishes or else the sentence is cruel and unusual. In short, the

Court has stated that a capital sentence may not be imposed unless the defendant is culpable for the death of another person. In *Coker v. Georgia* (1977)[13] the Court ruled that states may not impose the death penalty to punish the crime of rape of an adult woman. In another series of cases, *Enmund v. Florida* (1982),[14] *Cabana v. Bullock* (1986),[15] and *Tison v. Arizona* (1987),[16] the Court concluded that the Eighth Amendment prohibits the imposition of the death penalty for mere participation in a robbery in which an accomplice takes a life, but it does not necessarily prohibit the death penalty when the defendant simply lacked an outright *intent* to kill. An individual who knowingly engages in a crime that is likely to cause the death of another person may be executed. The second major way the Court limited the use of the death penalty was by ruling that the government may not execute an insane person.[17] The Court noted that, since only one jurisdiction in the United States at the time imposed the penalty upon insane murderers, modern "standards of decency" clearly prohibited the practice.

The Court has also made several rulings since 1976 that specifically endorse more expansive uses for capital punishment. In *Penry v. Lynaugh* (1989) the Court ruled that, under the Eighth Amendment, mentally retarded people may be sentenced to death.[18] In *Stanford v. Kentucky* (1989) the Court concluded that the Eighth Amendment does not prohibit the government from executing juveniles who committed crimes at ages sixteen or seventeen.[19] The Court has also endorsed a procedural rule that makes the sentence of death more likely: in *Payne v. Tennessee* (1991) the Court ruled that the Eighth Amendment does not bar juries from hearing "victim impact evidence" during the sentencing phase of a capital trial.[20] This is evidence "relating to the personal characteristics of the victim and the emotional impact of the crimes on the victim's family."[21] The Court held that a state may legitimately decide that such evidence is relevant to the jury's decision.[22]

Finally, in *McCleskey v. Kemp* (1987) the Court directly addressed, and rejected, a petitioner's argument based on recent academic research that showed that defendants of any race who killed white victims were much more likely to receive the death penalty than were defendants of any race who killed nonwhites.[23] The defendant, Warren McCleskey, backed by the LDF, contended that this disparity represented unconstitutional discrimination in the application of the sentence of death. The Court disagreed, ruling that, despite this general statistical evidence, a death sentence issued under such a system does not contravene the tenets of the Constitution if the defendant can prove no discrimination in his or her particular case.

McCleskey did not deny committing the murder with which he was charged, and the imposition of a capital sentence for such a crime is not in itself disproportionate under the Constitution. The Court ruled that capital defendants may not present evidence about systemic discrimination during their trial.

The Supreme Court jurisprudence described above provides the parameters within which state and federal capital punishment statutes must fit. Under the Supreme Court's interpretation of the Constitution, any state may choose to implement capital punishment, as long as the application of the sentence conforms to the strictures laid out in *Furman, Gregg,* and the other Supreme Court cases. Many states have elected to do so. By 1982, all but one of the states that had a death penalty statute prior to *Furman* had readopted the practice.[24] By fall 2001, thirty-eight states and the federal system had death penalty laws on the books.[25]

The Post-Conviction Judicial Process: Capital Appeals

Supreme Court justice Stewart once wrote, "There is no question that death as a punishment is unique in its severity and irrevocability."[26] It is the ultimate punishment a society can impose. Because of its special nature, the courts strive to ensure that every safeguard is afforded to capital defendants. The justice system, if it is to take a life, wants to be certain that it is doing so justly. This concern has led the Supreme Court to adopt singular requirements for the appeals process that follows a death sentence.

As the Court made clear in *Furman* and subsequent cases, the imposition of the death penalty by the government must not be arbitrary. States that use capital punishment must take steps to ensure that the sentence is applied fairly and without discrimination. Some commentators have even described the constraints as "super due process" requirements, since they go beyond the normal constraints imposed by the due process clause of the Fifth and Fourteenth Amendments.[27]

Capital justice systems must have some degree of reliability—that is, they must avoid mistakenly executing innocent persons, and they must perform in a somewhat predictable and even manner.[28] The Court requires that "the sentencing authority [be] given adequate information and guidance."[29] Part of this requirement is the obligation to provide "meaningful appellate review" of death sentences.[30] By providing a system for adjudicating appeals, jurisdictions are more likely to catch instances in which the jury acted in an unfair manner, whether on its own initiative or because of some other circumstance. For instance, death sentences are some-

Table 2-2 Major U.S. Supreme Court Decisions since *Gregg v. Georgia*

Case	*Summary of Court's Holding*
Roberts v. Louisiana (1977)	Defendant must be allowed to present mitigating evidence during sentencing phase of capital trial.
Coker v. Georgia (1977)	Capital punishment may not be imposed for rape of adult woman.
Locket v. Ohio (1978) and *Eddings v. Oklahoma* (1982)	There can be no statutory limitations on the types of mitigating evidence defendant can present during sentencing phase of capital trial.
Enmund v. Florida (1982)	Eighth Amendment prohibits the imposition of the death penalty for mere participation in a robbery in which an accomplice takes a life.
Pulley v. Harris (1984)	Automatic review and proportionality review are not constitutional requirements.
Cabana v. Bullock (1986) and *Tison v. Arizona* (1987)	Eighth Amendment does not prohibit the death penalty when the defendant lacked an outright intent to kill. A person who knowingly engages in a crime that is likely to cause the death of another may be executed.
Murray v. Carrier (1986)	State prisoners must first exhaust all state court remedies before filing federal habeas corpus writs.
Ford v. Wainwright (1986)	Government may not execute an insane person.
McCleskey v. Kemp (1987)	A death sentence imposed by a system containing racial disparities does not contravene the tenets of the Constitution if the defendant can prove no discrimination in his particular case.
Penry v. Lynaugh (1989)	Government may execute a mentally retarded person.
Stanford v. Kentucky (1989)	Government may execute persons for crimes committed at age sixteen or older.
Payne v. Tennessee (1991)	Eighth Amendment does not prohibit juries from hearing victim impact evidence during sentencing phase of trial.

times overturned when, upon appeal, it is discovered that the jury was not allowed to hear about some important mitigating fact that might have led to leniency.

The Court, in effect, requires that jurisdictions provide some mechanism by which errors, oversights, or other problems can be caught. One way to do so is to require that *all* capital sentences be reviewed by a state supreme court or other appellate court—a system called "automatic review." Under such a system, every time a person is sentenced to death in the jurisdiction in question an appellate court must conduct a review of the sentence to determine whether or not it was fair.

Courts in many jurisdictions also use "proportionality review." Under this system, the reviewing court examines the facts of the case under review to make sure that when a death sentence is imposed, it is "proportional" to the punishments handed down in similar cases in that jurisdiction. If the court finds that other juries in the jurisdiction have not imposed the death penalty for similar crimes, it strikes down the sentence. Some jurisdictions provide automatic proportionality review. For example, the Georgia law at issue in *Gregg*, which won approval by the Supreme Court, provided for automatic proportionality review. Since *Gregg*, many states have also adopted automatic proportionality review.

Automatic review and proportionality review are not, however, constitutional requirements in and of themselves.[31] Rather, the Supreme Court has left it to the relevant legislatures to craft statutes that ensure "meaningful appellate review." Ten states do not provide proportionality review.[32] There, the legislatures have provided for appeals that do not address the notion of proportionality. Moreover, though a majority of states provide automatic capital appeals, some do not. Instead, in those states, capital convicts must bring appeals on their own initiative, hiring a lawyer and petitioning for their appeal to be heard by a higher court. Congress, in the Federal Death Penalty Act of 1995 (FDPA), provided for neither type of review.[33] Under the FDPA, appellate review of a capital sentence takes place only upon a petition from the defendant. The act allows for review of "all substantive and procedural issues raised on the appeal," but it does not call for the appellate court to check the proportionality of the sentence against other cases with similar facts.

Persons sentenced to death have options for appeal outside of the court system in which they were sentenced, too. The Constitution guarantees that all prisoners have the right to file a writ of habeas corpus to the federal courts.[34] This is a petition that alleges the prisoner's constitutional rights were violated during his or her trial and that therefore he or she is being wrongfully held. Until recently, the repeated filing of writs of habeas corpus was commonplace among convicts on death row. After all, the prisoner in such a situation has nothing to lose and only time to gain by bringing many appeals.

Defense lawyers and many civil rights advocates argue that, despite the time they took, these multiple appeals had value in that they helped avoid putting an innocent person to death. A June 2000 Columbia University study notes that, of the 5,760 people who spent time on death row between 1973 and 1995, 237 had their sentences overturned as a result of federal habeas corpus appeals. More strikingly, capital habeas appeals were successful 40 percent of the times they were heard by federal courts.[35]

Others, though, including many conservative congressmen and even former president George H. W. Bush, have felt that, since they brought essentially meritless appeals, the many writs were taking too much time and energy from the federal courts and needlessly delaying the execution of condemned criminals.[36] In recent years, these concerns have begun to take effect: the ability of capital convicts to file multiple habeas corpus writs has been substantially reduced over the past decade.

The Supreme Court itself has actively participated in this process. It ruled in *Murray v. Carrier* (1986) that state prisoners must first exhaust all state court remedies before filing federal habeas writs.[37] The Court also ruled that "successive federal habeas review should be granted only in rare cases"[38] and only if the petitioner can "establish 'cause and prejudice' sufficient to excuse his failure to present his evidence in support of his first federal petition."[39] These provisions may only be circumvented if "the failure to hear the claims would constitute a 'miscarriage of justice,'" and the petitioner can show by clear and convincing evidence that, without some constitutional error, no juror would have sentenced him or her to death.[40]

Also damaging to the capital convict's habeas options is an act of Congress: the 1996 Anti-Terrorism and Effective Death Penalty Act, intended to reduce the time between sentencing and execution of capital criminals, sets a one-year statute of limitations on habeas writs. Under the law, a convict has just one year to submit his or her petition.[41] Previously, there had been no statute of limitations on filing habeas writs.[42] This new law was upheld by the Supreme Court in 2000.

A final important issue relating to capital appeals is assistance of counsel. The constitution guarantees a lawyer to help defend any person accused of a crime during his or her trial. If the defendant cannot afford a lawyer, the state or jurisdiction trying the case must provide one.[43] This right, of course, extends to persons accused of capital crimes.

The Supreme Court has held that the right to assistance of counsel also extends to the initial appeal afforded by the jurisdiction in which the appellant was convicted.[44] However, the right to counsel extends no further. The government need not provide lawyers to help capital convicts prepare second and subsequent appeals to state courts or habeas corpus petitions to federal courts. Indigent convicts who wish to file these later appeals must rely on death penalty resource centers and other sources of nonprofit legal aid. In 1988 Congress established resource centers to help ensure the availability of qualified counsel for those wishing to file federal writs, but this funding was cut in 1996.[45]

The constitutional requirements and legislation detailed above constitute the main procedural boundaries within which governments—and capital convicts—must operate. States must provide an opportunity for meaningful review of capital sentences, though the methods for doing so are not constitutionally mandated. The federal judiciary must hear habeas petitions, though the conditions under which the writs may be filed have become more restricted than in the past. Finally, the jurisdiction that tries a capital case must provide a lawyer for the defendant to prepare the defense at trial (if he or she cannot afford one) and to prepare the first state-level appeal.

The Jurisdictions: Capital Punishment Laws

Given the Supreme Court's decisions about the death penalty, the jurisdictions within the United States—the federal government, states, and military—have many choices about the death penalty. As long as they keep within the boundaries the Court has set, these jurisdictions may choose among a range of options: whether or not to have the death penalty, which crimes constitute capital offenses within the jurisdiction, whether juveniles or retarded defendants are subject to execution, who will defend indigent capital defendants, how the postconviction appellate process within the jurisdiction works, and how the death penalty is actually expedited. This section will examine the choices that the states and federal government have made on this issue—the laws by which capital punishment is actually applied in the United States.

How the Jurisdictions Make Capital Punishment Policy

Before looking at the jurisdictions' actual policies, it is important to examine the ways in which the policies are made. There are four basic decision-making methods that can impact the behavior of jurisdictions in this area: legislation, court rulings, constitutional amendments, and referenda.

Legislation is probably the most common method by which death penalty policy is made. Under this system, Congress or a state legislature simply passes a law concerning the death penalty. For instance, after *Furman* and *Gregg,* many state legislatures passed laws that changed the death penalty procedure within their states to conform with the constitutional requirements expounded in those cases. Congress, too, passes laws that govern capital punishment in the federal criminal system and the military. For instance, in 1988 Congress passed a new drug kingpin statute that provides for the death penalty for cases of murder in the course of a drug-trafficking crime.[46]

The laws of the various jurisdictions are also determined in part by court rulings. In the case of the federal jurisdictions (the federal criminal justice system and the military), the governing courts are federal. Those jurisdictions are limited only by the strictures laid out by the Supreme Court. States, however, each have their own court systems and constitutions. State supreme courts can limit or prohibit the death penalty based on interpretation of their state constitutions. In fact, in Massachusetts and California the state high court has at one point ruled the death penalty unconstitutional under the state's constitution.[47] Each of these state court rulings was later overcome, however, by an amendment to the respective state's constitution. Unlike Massachusetts and California, where the state constitutions do not explicitly deal with the death penalty, one state constitution does address capital punishment: Michigan's expressly forbids it.

The final important method through which states make death penalty policy is direct citizen referenda. Under a referendum system, the citizens of a state directly vote on a policy proposal that, if passed, becomes law without any action by the state legislative or executive branches. Many states have such procedures, and they can be used to enact death penalty policy as long as the policy satisfies the state and federal constitutions. In fact, referenda may sometimes be used to change a state's constitution itself. In California, the state supreme court's decision striking down the use of capital punishment was rendered moot by a statewide referendum to amend the California constitution. The citizens added a clause to the constitution that allowed for the death penalty.

These methods—legislation, court decision, constitutional amendment or interpretation, and referendum—are the mechanisms by which the various jurisdictions make their death penalty choices. Using these tools, the jurisdictions have generated a surprising diversity of death penalty policy.

To Execute or Not

The most fundamental decision a jurisdiction must make is whether or not to use the death penalty as a method of punishment at all. At present, thirty-eight states, the federal justice system, and the military all have some form of the death penalty. Twelve states and the District of Columbia do not. (See Table 2-3.) Native American tribes on reservations, which in some senses have separate legal systems from the rest of the United States, may opt to use the federal death penalty system or not. Almost all tribes have decided not to use it.[48]

In English law before the Unites States' secession, and in early American law, the death penalty was universal. In fact, capital punishment was a part of the "common law" on which the American legal system was founded. Therefore, the jurisdictions that do not use capital punishment had to affirmatively abolish the practice within their borders. The thirteen jurisdictions that have abandoned the death penalty have done so in a variety of ways. Michigan became the first government in the English-speaking world to ban the punishment in 1846, when it adopted a constitutional amendment that proscribed death penalty statutes.[49] Most jurisdictions that lack the death penalty have simply abolished the practice through legislative efforts. In two cases, old death penalty laws were struck down by courts or in some other way and never reinstated by the state legislature. A final method for abandonment is for a state supreme court to strike down the death penalty as unconstitutional under the state constitution. This has occurred twice, in California and Massachusetts (in each case, however, the rulings were overturned by constitutional amendments).

Other than thirteen jurisdictions, all states and the federal government have the death penalty. Among the death penalty states, there is tremendous variation in the actual application of the punishment. These differences are discussed next.

Table 2-3 Jurisdictions with and without Capital Punishment

With Capital Punishment		Without Capital Punishment
Alabama	Oklahoma	Alaska
Arizona	Oregon	Hawaii
Arkansas	Pennsylvania	Iowa
California	South Carolina	Maine
Colorado	South Dakota	Massachusetts
Connecticut	Tennessee	Michigan
Delaware	Texas	Minnesota
Florida	Utah	North Dakota
Georgia	Virginia	Rhode Island
Idaho	Washington	Vermont
Illinois	Wyoming	West Virginia
Indiana	Federal system	Wisconsin
Kansas	U.S. military	District of Columbia
Kentucky		
Louisiana		
Maryland		
Mississippi		
Missouri		
Montana		
Nebraska		
Nevada		
New Hampshire		
New Jersey		
New Mexico		
New York		
North Carolina		
Ohio		

Source: www.deathpenaltyinfo.org.

Variations among the Jurisdictions with Capital Punishment

Laws vary considerably among jurisdictions that impose capital punishment. Each jurisdiction's statutes are slightly different from the others'. The various policies can, however, be classified along several important lines: the crimes for which the death penalty is available, the types of defendants who are eligible to receive the death penalty, the procedures for conducting capital trials, the postconviction appellate and clemency processes, and the methods of execution.

Types of Crime Punished. In all jurisdictions with the death penalty, the sentence may be imposed for some type of first-degree or aggravated murder. In many jurisdictions, first-degree murder or its equivalent is the only crime that may be punished with execution. (See Table 2-4.)[50]

Even among those states, though, some differences exist. Since the Supreme Court in *Gregg* approved the use of statutorily defined aggravating factors—which must be found true if the death penalty is to be imposed—many jurisdictions with capital punishment have codified them. The aggravating factors codified in each jurisdiction are different. Thus, for instance, Alabama's capital murder statute delineates eighteen aggravating circumstances; other states have nine aggravating factors, others ten, still others fourteen, and so on.

Table 2-4 States that Apply Capital Punishment Only in Cases of First-Degree Murder

Alabama	Nevada	South Carolina
Arizona	New Hampshire	Tennessee
Delaware	New Mexico	Texas
Illinois	North Carolina	Utah
Indiana	Ohio	Virginia
Kansas	Oklahoma	Washington
Missouri	Oregon	Wyoming
Nebraska	Pennsylvania	

Source: www.deathpenaltyinfo.org.

Some jurisdictions impose the death penalty for offenses other than first-degree murder. Frequently, these other crimes are types of homicide. Some jurisdictions impose the death penalty for felony murder, which occurs when a person recklessly, but not intentionally, causes a death while he or she is engaged in another felony. As noted earlier, the Supreme Court in *Cabana* and *Tison* upheld the use of the sentence in such cases. Florida and Maryland allow the death penalty for any felony murder.

Other jurisdictions apply the death penalty to felony murder only in cases of certain felonies. Federal law, for instance, provides for the death penalty if a death is caused during the commission of a civil rights offense.[51] Several states impose the death penalty for kidnapping resulting in death, though sometimes only certain types of kidnapping count, like the kidnapping of a minor. California allows the death penalty in cases of perjury that lead to an execution.

Some crimes punished with execution do not involve the taking of life at all. Treason is a fairly common capital offense, and its penalty of death has common-law roots stemming from early English law. The federal government, California, Colorado, Georgia, and Louisiana allow for executions in cases of treason. The United States Code (the federal criminal code) adds espionage to the list of death penalty crimes, as well.

A couple of jurisdictions also impose the sentence for certain drug-related offenses. The United States Code allows for executions for the crime of trafficking in large quantities of drugs, and Florida has a similar law. A few allow the death penalty for certain types of aggravated rape. Although the Supreme Court has said that the death penalty is disproportionate as a punishment for the rape of an adult woman, a few jurisdictions apply the sentence to other types of rape, like the rape of a child under twelve.

The United States Military Code makes certain crimes capital if they are committed in times of war. These include the crimes of desertion, assaulting or disobeying a superior officer, improper use of a countersign, spying, and misbehavior of a sentinel. Other crimes, like misbehavior before the enemy, could only occur in a time of war, and are punishable by death. In all military cases, the death penalty, when imposed by a court-martial, must be approved by the president.

Types of Defendants Who Are Eligible for the Death Penalty. Another important policy area on which the jurisdictions differ is the people who may be executed. Although the Supreme Court allows retarded individuals and persons who committed capital crimes as juveniles to receive the death penalty, not all states impose the sentence on those groups. Twenty-five states allow the execution of the mentally retarded, and twenty-four allow the sentence for crimes committed by sixteen- or seventeen-year-olds. (See Table 2-5.)[52]

Table 2-5 Capital Punishment for Juvenile and Mentally Retarded Criminals in U.S. Jurisdictions

Death Penalty Jurisdiction	Allows Execution of Retarded Defendants?	Allows Execution of Juvenile Criminals?
Alabama	Yes	Yes
Arizona	Yes	Yes
Arkansas	No	Yes
California	Yes	No
Colorado	No	No
Connecticut	Yes	No
Delaware	Yes	Yes
Florida	Yes	Yes
Georgia	No	Yes
Idaho	Yes	Yes
Illinois	Yes	No
Indiana	No	Yes
Kansas	No	No
Kentucky	No	Yes
Louisiana	Yes	Yes
Maryland	No	No
Mississippi	Yes	Yes
Missouri	Yes	Yes
Montana	Yes	Yes
Nebraska	No	No
Nevada	Yes	Yes
New Hampshire	Yes	Yes
New Jersey	Yes	No

Table 2-5 *continued*

Death Penalty Jurisdiction	Allows Execution of Retarded Defendants?	Allows Execution of Juvenile Criminals?
New Mexico	No	No
New York	No*	No
North Carolina	Yes	Yes
Ohio	Yes	No
Oklahoma	Yes	Yes
Oregon	Yes	No
Pennsylvania	Yes	Yes
South Carolina	Yes	Yes
South Dakota	Yes	Yes
Tennessee	No	No
Texas	Yes	Yes
Utah	Yes	Yes
Virginia	Yes	Yes
Washington	No	No
Wyoming	Yes	Yes
Federal system	No	No
U.S. military	NA	No

*Except in cases of murder by a prisoner.

Source: www.deathpenaltyinfo.org.

Despite the fact that more than half of the death penalty–allowing states permit the executions of these special classes of defendants, the policies remain controversial. They even have affected presidential races. During the 1992 contest, then-candidate Bill Clinton was the governor of Arkansas. At the time, the state allowed the execution of mentally retarded individuals. Just before the crucial New Hampshire primary, Clinton made a special trip home to Arkansas to authorize the execution of a retarded black man, Ricky Ray Rector. In some commentators' estimations, the gesture was an attempt to show that he was "tough on crime."[53] Yet it was a controversial move: according to reports, when Rector was given his last meal, "he was so simple he asked to save the pecan pie for later."[54] Clinton's move angered many voters, especially African Americans.

In another case, after the Supreme Court stayed the Texas execution of John Paul Penry in order to determine if Penry's jury had been properly informed about his disability, that state became a center of attention on the issue. A bill outlawing the execution of the mentally retarded passed the Texas legislature in 2001, but Gov. Rick Perry, a Republican, vetoed the bill on June 17.[55]

On June 4, 2001, the Supreme Court overturned Penry's sentence, holding that the jury had not been adequately instructed about how to account for mental retardation as a mitigating factor.[56] In 2001 Arizona, Connecticut, Florida, Missouri, and North Carolina banned the execution of mentally retarded murderers. This brings to eighteen the total number of states that use the death penalty but do not put the mentally retarded to death. Moreover, the Supreme Court agreed to hear *McCarver v. North Carolina* in order to reconsider whether executing the mentally retarded offends the nation's "evolving standards of decency" and thus violates the Eighth Amendment's ban on cruel and unusual punishment.

The execution of defendants who committed crimes as juveniles is controversial, too. In fact, of the states that permit such executions, only seven have actually done so since 1978. In 2000 just four such executions occurred in the United States: two in Texas and two in Virginia. Moreover, in 1995 President Clinton signed the United Nations' Convention on the Rights of the Child, which prohibits execution for crimes committed as a juvenile. The Senate, however, did not ratify the accord.[57]

Defense Lawyers. Another important difference among the jurisdictions is the methods by which they provide defense counsel to indigent capital defendants. The Constitution guarantees that criminal defendants have lawyers to represent them during trial. If the defendant cannot afford a lawyer, the state or jurisdiction trying the case must provide one.[58] It does not speak, however, to the methods by which the counsel should be chosen; nor does it require legal representation for the appeals process.

According to the Justice Department, there are three main methods by which jurisdictions fulfill their duty to provide trial counsel to defendants who cannot afford their own lawyers: public defender offices, assigned counsel systems, and contract attorneys.[59] Public defender programs are public or nonprofit organizations with full-time staff lawyers who defend indigent criminal defendants. Assigned counsel systems are those in which the courts appoint private attorneys to defend individuals as the need arises. Under contract attorney systems, the government reaches an agreement with private attorneys or bar associations to provide services to indigent defendants for a specified amount of money.

The decision about how to provide legal representation to indigent defendants may be made by state legislatures, or it may even be left to a county-by-county determination. Some areas just use public defenders, others assign counsel or contract defenders, and still others use a combination of the three.

A large proportion of people charged with crimes must use the services described above. In 1992, about 80 percent of defendants charged with felonies in large urban areas relied on assigned counsel or public defenders for legal representation.[60] In 1996, about 75 percent of inmates in state prisons had received publicly funded legal counsel for the offense for which they were serving time.[61]

Many capital defendants, too, must make use of those services. The differences in legal aid services available to defendants charged with capital crimes has at times sparked controversy, because some observers feel that the representation afforded by certain systems is inadequate. Texas, which has only appointed counsel systems, is a case in point. The American Civil Liberties Union (ACLU) of Texas recently joined a lawsuit seeking better legal aid for capital defendants in Harris County.[62] The lawsuit charges that Texas's assigned counsel system, because of cronyism and local politics, often provides ineffective counsel to capital defendants. In a similar case, also in Texas, convicted murderer Calvin J. Burdine asked a federal court to overturn his conviction because his assigned counsel slept through large portions of his 1984 trial in Houston.[63] His lawyer, Joe Frank Cannon, has represented nine other clients who were sentenced to death.

Systems that assign all indigent capital defendants to a public defender's office have come under criticism, too. Public defenders are often overburdened, and since the workload of even one capital case can be enormous, the public defender's office may simply be overwhelmed if it must handle too many capital cases. In 1995, five states were sued because their public defender organizations were so overburdened that the plaintiffs felt they had been inadequately defended.[64] The Louisiana Supreme Court found the state's system of representation through the public defender's office to be unconstitutional because of the burden put on the office.

A report for the American Bar Association (ABA), written in the first half of the

1990s, found that the state of indigent criminal defense was in crisis in many juris-dictions.[65] The differences in this area play a crucial role in shaping capital systems. Since many defendants accused of capital crimes must make use of indigent de-fense networks, the quality of the networks may have a significant effect on the number and the accuracy of capital sentences.

Who Decides the Sentence? Another difference among death penalty jurisdictions concerns who decides if the sentence shall be imposed in a given case. In the ma-jority of death penalty jurisdictions, the trial jury has sole sentencing authority; in the others, a judge makes the decision.

Jury sentencing is a departure from normal criminal practice. For most crimes, the jury determines guilt or innocence, but the judge handles sentencing. Although jury sentencing is unusual, it has long been the practice in capital cases. In fact, in all state death penalty statutes preceding *Furman* the jury had complete discretion in deciding whether to impose the punishment. As discussed earlier, since *Furman* the jurisdictions have been required to avoid the arbitrary application of the sen-tence. Some have attempted to accomplish this aim through a return to sentencing by judges or at least oversight of sentencing by judges. Others have followed the type of jury sentencing system approved by the Supreme Court in *Gregg*.

In thirty-one of the forty death penalty jurisdictions, the jury has sole authority to determine if a convicted person will be put to death. In the nine others, a judge or group of judges has the final say. In some of these states, such as Delaware, Florida, and Indiana, the jury recommends a sentence, but the judge may override it. In California and Nebraska, the sentence is determined by a panel of judges.[66] (See Table 2-6.)

Jurisdictions' Postconviction Processes: Appeals and Clemency. Other differences among the jurisdictions concern the methods by which they handle the postcon-viction appeals process for capital convicts. As discussed earlier, all jurisdictions must provide some kind of "meaningful appellate review." The exact types of pro-visions are not set in stone, however.

Most jurisdictions that use capital punishment provide an automatic review process by the court of last resort.[67] A few jurisdictions, including the federal government, do not. Often, the automatic review concerns issues of "proportional-ity"—the court examines the facts of the crime at bench to make sure it roughly corresponds to the seriousness of other crimes punished with death in that juris-diction.

Table 2-6 Final Capital Sentencing Authority in U.S. Jurisdictions

Jurisdiction	Final Capital Sentencing Authority	
	Judge	Jury
Alabama	*	
Arizona		*
Arkansas		*
California	* (Panel of three)	
Colorado	*	
Connecticut		*
Delaware	*	
Florida	*	
Georgia		*
Idaho	*	
Illinois		*
Indiana	*	
Kansas		*
Kentucky		*
Louisiana		*
Maryland		*
Mississippi		*
Missouri		*
Montana	*	
Nebraska	* (Panel)	
Nevada		*
New Hampshire		*
New Jersey		*
New Mexico		*
New York		*
North Carolina		*
Ohio		*
Oklahoma		*

Table 2-6 *continued*

Jurisdiction	Final Capital Sentencing Authority	
	Judge	Jury
Oregon		*
Pennsylvania		*
South Carolina		*
South Dakota		*
Tennessee		*
Texas		*
Utah		*
Virginia		*
Washington		*
Wyoming		*
Federal system		*
U.S. military		*

Source: www.deathpenaltyinfo.org.

Proportionality review is an area of major divergence among the jurisdictions. (See Table 2-7.) In the years directly following *Furman,* as the jurisdictions attempted to craft death penalty statutes that would withstand the demands of the Supreme Court, most adopted proportionality review.[68] In some cases, the legislatures enacted laws specifically requiring an appellate court to conduct the review. In others, the state supreme court made proportionality review mandatory.[69] In still others, the state supreme court began conducting this type of review on its own initiative, though it was required to do so neither by statute nor by constitutional ruling.

However, in the mid-1980s, the Supreme Court began to make clear that it was more willing than previously thought to allow states a certain level of discretion in implementing capital punishment. For example, in *Pulley v. Harris* (1984) the Supreme Court rejected a constitutional challenge to California's capital sentenc-

Table 2-7 Proportionality Review in the Jurisdictions

Jurisdiction	None	Discretionary	Required
Alabama			*
Arizona	*		
Arkansas			*
California		*	
Colorado	*		
Connecticut			*
Delaware			*
Florida		*	
Georgia			*
Idaho			*
Illinois		*	
Indiana	*		
Kansas	*		
Kentucky			*
Louisiana			*
Maryland	*		
Mississippi			*
Missouri			*
Montana			*
Nebraska			*
Nevada	*		
New Hampshire			*
New Jersey			*
New Mexico			*
New York			*
North Carolina			*
Ohio			*
Oklahoma	*		
Oregon	*		

Table 2-7 *continued*

Jurisdiction	None	Discretionary	Required
Pennsylvania			*
South Carolina			*
South Dakota			*
Tennessee			*
Texas	*		
Utah		*	
Virginia			*
Washington			*
Wyoming	*		
Federal system			
U.S. military			

Source: Leigh B. Bienen, "Criminal Law: The Proportionality Review of Capital Cases by State High Courts After *Gregg:* Only the 'Appearance of Justice'?" *Northwestern School of Law Journal of Criminal Law and Criminology* 87 (fall 1996): 130.

ing system, which lacked proportionality review.)[70] The Court held, in effect, that jurisdictions were not constitutionally required to conduct the review.[71]

Since the early 1990s, the general trend among the jurisdictions has been to back away from strictly enforced proportionality review.[72] Seven state legislatures repealed their proportionality review requirements (though Tennessee reinstated the practice in 1992). In other states, high courts charged with conducting the review have simply let it "wither on the vine."[73]

One method of doing so has been to narrowly define the set of cases against which each death penalty sentence is compared. The courts can compare the sentence only against other cases in which the death penalty has actually been imposed, rather than against all cases in which it might have been imposed. As Professor Leigh B. Bienen of the Northwestern School of Law has noted, "Except in states where the death row populations are very large, this limitation essentially reduces proportionality review to a perfunctory exercise," since the goal of proportionality review is "to make sure that the death sentence under review belongs with the class of other death sentences," and not with the class of cases in which the sentence was not imposed.[74] If a jurisdiction limits the comparison pool in this way, a judge might look at a death sentence up for review and note that the crime committed is fairly similar to other cases in which executions have been ordered, but he or she might miss the fact that there are many more cases quite similar to the one in question in which a death sentence was not imposed. In jurisdictions that limit the comparison pool in this manner, only one death sentence since *Gregg* has been overturned on the basis of a proportionality review.[75]

Other courts limit the pool of comparison to all cases that resulted in a conviction for capital murder. This set is broader, because it includes cases in which the sentencing authority declined to administer the death penalty. It is still narrow enough to limit the effectiveness of proportionality review, however, since it excludes cases in which the prosecutor opted not to pursue the death penalty, though the facts might have supported such an endeavor.

At present, according to critics like Bienen, few jurisdictions have effective proportionality review procedures. Capital convicts there must rely on other postconviction options. If an automatic or proportionality review does not turn up any problem, or if the jurisdiction does not have those types of review, the defendant may still appeal his or her conviction through normal appellate methods. Most death penalty jurisdictions do not provide any special dispensation for these appeals, but some states allow capital appeals to be heard directly by the highest court, skipping intermediate courts of appeals.[76]

The last resort of a capital convict is an appeal for clemency. All jurisdictions provide some procedure by which a government authority can commute a sentence of death. The exact procedures, however, differ by jurisdiction.

In the majority of states (twenty-three of the thirty-eight death penalty states), the governor has sole and complete authority to grant clemency. In some of these states, the governor must solicit the recommendation of a parole board, but the board's advice is nonbinding. In nine other jurisdictions, the governor has the final authority, but he or she cannot act without the recommendation of a board of pardons or parole board. If the board recommends clemency, the governor decides whether or not to grant it. If the board recommends against clemency, the governor may not act. In three states—Connecticut, Georgia, and Idaho—the governor has no power to grant clemency whatsoever; a board of pardons has the full authority. In Nebraska, Nevada, and Utah, the governor is one member of a board that has final authority over the clemency decision. California has a unique system under which the governor has complete authority to grant clemency, unless the appellant has been convicted of a felony twice. In that case, the governor cannot grant clemency without a favorable recommendation by at least four of the state supreme court justices. (See Table 2-8.)

In most cases, when a death sentence is commuted it automatically becomes a life sentence, often without the possibility of parole. In some jurisdictions, though, the authority granting clemency may decide on the alternative punishment. In many states, the governor or some other authority may also grant reprieves, which

Table 2-8 Clemency Authority in the Jurisdictions

Capital Punishment Jurisdiction	Governor Alone	Governor upon Recommendation of Board	Governor Is Part of Board	Board Alone
Alabama	*			
Arizona		*		
Arkansas	*			
California	*			
Colorado	*			
Connecticut				*
Delaware		*		
Florida		*		
Georgia				*
Idaho				*
Illinois	*			
Indiana		*		
Kansas	*			
Kentucky	*			
Louisiana		*		
Maryland	*			

Table 2-8 *continued*

Capital Punishment Jurisdiction	Governor Alone	Governor upon Recommendation of Board	Governor Is Part of Board	Board Alone
Mississippi	*			
Missouri	*			
Montana		*		
Nebraska			*	
Nevada			*	
New Hampshire	*			
New Jersey	*			
New Mexico	*			
New York	*			
North Carolina	*			
Ohio	*			
Oklahoma		*		
Oregon	*			
Pennsylvania		*		
South Carolina	*			
South Dakota	*			
Tennessee	*			
Texas		*		
Utah			*	
Virginia	*			
Washington	*			
Wyoming	*			
Federal system	* (president)			

Source: www.deathpenaltyinfo.org.

are temporary stays of execution; or he or she may pardon a convict completely.

In the federal system, the president has the sole power to grant clemency, reprieves, or pardons. Under guidelines issued in 2000, federal capital convicts must be warned of their upcoming execution 120 days before its date. The guidelines allow a 30-day period after that warning for convicts to file a clemency petition.

Although every jurisdiction has some type of clemency process, in recent years the authorities in charge of granting clemency have been increasingly reluctant to use the power.

Methods of Execution. The final major point of divergence among jurisdictions' capital punishment policies is in the process by which executions are undertaken. In the United States, there are five different methods used to carry out death sentences: lethal injection, electrocution, hanging, firing squad, and lethal gas. (See Table 2-9.) Lethal injection is by far the most common method; it is employed by thirty-six states, the military, and the federal government. Of the 693 executions conducted in the United States between 1976 and January 29, 2000, a total of 528 (over 76 percent) were carried out using lethal injection.

Many death penalty jurisdictions use more than one method. In some of these jurisdictions, persons sentenced to death may choose their preferred method of dying. In others, because of statutory changes, one method is used for individuals sentenced before a certain date, and another for those sentenced after that date. For instance, in Georgia, convicts who were sentenced before May 1, 2000, must suffer death by electrocution. Those sentenced after that date have to be given a lethal injection.

Of the states that employ methods other than lethal injection, only two do not authorize lethal injection in any cases: Alabama and Nebraska permit only electrocution to execute capital convicts. All other jurisdictions that use electrocution—and those that authorize hanging, firing squad, or lethal gas—employ lethal injection in at least some instances.

In general, criminals sentenced to death in the federal system receive lethal injections. For offenses prosecuted under the Violent Crime Control and Law Enforcement Act of 1994, however, the method used is that of the state in which the conviction takes place. If the state has no death penalty, the prisoner is transferred to another state for execution. Capital sentences pronounced by military courts are carried out via lethal injection.

Table 2-9 Methods of Execution Authorized (In at Least Some Cases)

Death-Penalty Jurisdiction	Lethal Injection	Electrocution	Hanging	Firing Squad	Lethal Gas
Alabama		*			
Arizona	*				*
Arkansas	*	*			
California	*				*
Colorado	*				
Connecticut	*				
Delaware	*		*		
Florida	*	*			
Georgia	*	*			
Idaho	*			*	
Illinois	*				
Indiana	*				
Kansas	*				
Kentucky	*	*			
Louisiana	*				
Maryland	*				*
Mississippi	*				
Missouri	*				*
Montana	*				
Nebraska		*			
Nevada	*				
New Hampshire	*		*		
New Jersey	*				
New Mexico	*				
New York	*				
North Carolina	*				
Ohio	*	*			
Oklahoma	*	*		*	

Table 2-9 *continued*

Death-Penalty Jurisdiction	Lethal Injection	Electrocution	Hanging	Firing Squad	Lethal Gas
Oregon	*				
Pennsylvania	*				
South Carolina	*	*			
South Dakota	*				
Tennessee	*	*			
Texas	*				
Utah	*			*	
Virginia	*	*			
Washington	*		*		
Wyoming	*				*
Federal System	*	*	*	*	*
U.S. Military	*				

Source: www.deathpenaltyinfo.org/methods.html.

Electrocution, the second most commonly used method of execution (149 enforced since 1976), has recently been challenged as unconstitutional in several different cases. In *Fierro v. Gomez* (1996)[77] the Ninth Circuit Court of Appeals held that execution by electrocution is unconstitutional. The court noted that the U.S. Supreme Court, in *Louisiana ex rel. Francis v. Resweber* (1947),[78] had ruled that the "infliction of unnecessary pain in the execution of the death sentence" constitutes cruel and unusual punishment and therefore violates the Eighth Amendment. The *Fierro* court concluded that electrocution does inflict extreme pain and is therefore unconstitutional. On the other hand, the Fourth and Fifth Circuit Courts had previously held that electrocution was *not* cruel and unusual.[79]

Fierro was appealed to the Supreme Court. But while the Court considered the case, California changed its statute to allow convicts to choose between electrocution and lethal injection. The Supreme Court remanded the case to the Ninth Circuit for consideration in light of this development. When the defendant, David

Fierro, chose lethal injection, the case was rendered moot, and neither the Ninth Circuit nor the Supreme Court rendered a final decision on the constitutionality of execution by electrocution.

The electrocution statutes of Florida and Georgia have also been challenged in recent cases. The *New York Times* gave the following grisly account of the electrocution of "Tiny" Davis in Florida: "When the executioner pulled the switch, Davis'[s] face contorted horribly, he made loud moaning sounds, and then a bright-red spew of blood burst from his nose onto his white shirtfront."[80] The paper also noted that in two earlier executions, the heads of the convicts had caught fire.[81] Nevertheless, the Florida Supreme Court has upheld the method as constitutional, most recently in 1999, but that decision was appealed to the U.S. Supreme Court.[82] Since Florida changed its statute to allow for a choice of lethal injection instead of electrocution, however, the Court did not take the appeal.[83] The issue had been rendered moot, and by fall 2001 the Court still had not ruled on the constitutionality of electrocution.

Other, less common execution methods could theoretically be subject to a similar constitutional challenge. All states that might use lethal gas, hanging, or firing squad, however, also allow lethal injection. This fact makes it unlikely that any will suffer a serious constitutional challenge in the near future; since no one will be forced to undergo those methods of execution, Eighth Amendment issues are not raised. In any event, between *Gregg* and January 29, 2001, only sixteen executions by any of those methods were imposed.

It is evident that, among death penalty jurisdictions, capital punishment policy varies widely, even within the parameters set by the Supreme Court. The jurisdictions use execution to punish different crimes and different types of people. They differ in their systems for providing indigent defense, for making sentencing decisions, and for providing review of the sentences. They even differ on the method authorized for carrying out the sentence. The ways in which the jurisdictions' death penalty laws are actually enforced and carried out are examined next.

Application of Capital Punishment Policy

Earlier, after examining the constitutional framework within which capital punishment policy must fit, we discussed the policies that United States jurisdictions have promulgated within that framework. Both subjects are important to understanding capital punishment in America, but neither goes deep enough to give one an in-depth understanding of how the death penalty is used in this country. One can know that forty jurisdictions use capital punishment, and the various ways they authorize using it, without knowing the frequency with which people are actually sentenced and put to death, whether capital convicts manage to have their convictions overturned with any regularity, and so on. This section examines those issues: how the death penalty policies are actually applied.

Overall Trend: More Executions

The most striking recent trend in the application of capital punishment has been the increasing number of executions over the past fourteen years—especially since the early 1990s. In 1976, the year the Supreme Court ruled the death penalty constitutional in *Gregg,* no one was executed in the United States. The following year, Utah executed the nation's first post-*Gregg* capital convict. Gary Mark Gilmore, after a protracted legal battle spearheaded by the ACLU (over the objections of Gilmore himself, who preferred to "die like a man" rather than face a life in prison), was shot to death by a firing squad.[84]

Over the following six years, no more than two people were put to death in America. Between 1984 and 1991, the number of executions did not exceed twenty-five in any year. After 1991, however, the numbers began to increase steadily: ninety-eight people were executed in 1999. (See Figure 2-1.) In total, 731 executions were performed in the United States between January 1, 1976, and August 31, 2001, over 78 percent of which occurred in 1992 or thereafter.

The size of the national death row population has also grown steadily since 1976. (See Figure 2-2.) In that year there were 420 convicts awaiting execution. Ten years later, the number had increased nearly fourfold, to 1,591. At the end of 2000, there were 3,703 death row inmates.

This growth seems to be due to the fact that convicted criminals are sentenced to death much faster than they are actually put to death, rather than an increase in the number of death sentences imposed each year.[85] The average time between sentencing and execution for convicts who are eventually put to death is about ninety-one months.[86] In no year have more than ninety-eight people been executed, but in every year since 1982, more than 250 have been sentenced to death.[87]

Number of executions

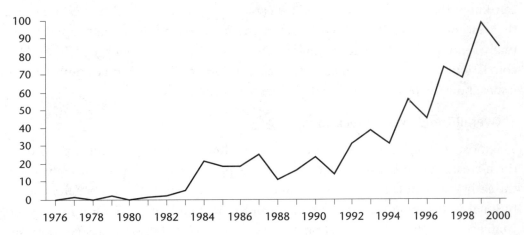

Source: www.deathpenaltyinfo.org.

Figure 2-1 Number of Executions in the United States

Number of prisoners

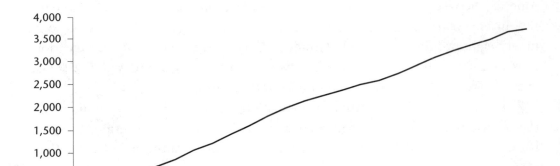

Source: www.deathpenaltyinfo.org.

Figure 2-2 U.S. Death Row Population by Year

Characteristics of Persons Sentenced to Death

Death row inmates, as a group, are disproportionately minority, male, and poorly educated. Of the 3,703 death row inmates at the end of 2000, 43 percent were black and about 9 percent were Latino.[88] Of the eighty-five people executed in 2000, 51 percent were white, 40 percent were black, 7 percent were Latino, and 2 percent were Native American.[89]

Capital convicts tend to be male. As of October, 2000, there were just fifty-three women on death row in the United States—about 1.5 percent of the total death row population.[90] Since 1976 a total of seven women have been executed; the most recent, Marilyn Plantz, was killed by lethal injection in Oklahoma on May 1, 2001.[91] Interestingly, women are much more likely than men to fall out of the capital sentencing process the further it progresses.[92] Women account for 13 percent of all murder arrests in America, yet they have comprised less than 2 percent of the people sentenced to death at trial. They account for only 1.4 percent of death row inmates and just 0.6 percent of the executions in America since 1976. And of the 132 women condemned to death between 1973 and 2000, the sentences of 76 were reversed or commuted to life imprisonment.

This reluctance to execute women likely stems from the social controversy that surrounds such acts. Although the law does not formally consider a person's gender, the execution of a woman often generates a political firestorm. A good example occurred in 1998, when Karla Faye Tucker was executed in Texas. An axe-murderer who had become a born-again Christian while in jail, Tucker and her case attracted an unusual amount of attention. Death penalty opponents—celebrities like Bianca Jagger, televangelist Pat Robertson, and even Pope John Paul II—called for clemency.[93] After her execution, many predicted that the United States was entering a new phase wherein women capital offenders would be executed at the same rate as men. However, the very intensity of the media attention surrounding her case belied that idea: the execution of a woman is still considered especially controversial.

Despite the fact that many jurisdictions authorize capital punishment for juvenile crimes, such sentences are fairly rare. Just 74 of the 3,703 death row inmates in February 2000 had been convicted of crimes they committed as juveniles.[94] Similarly, while there are various crimes for which a person may be sentenced to death, in recent years murder has been the only crime punished with execution in America.[95]

Another telling characteristic about capital convicts is their education level. Over half do not have a high-school degree.[96] They also tend to be single. More than half of all death row inmates in 1998 had never married, and nearly a quarter were divorced, separated, or widowed.[97] Defendants convicted of capital crimes, not surprisingly, have often committed numerous other offenses. In 1998 about two-thirds had past criminal convictions, including 8 percent who had past homicide convictions.[98] Fully 40 percent of the death row population had been arrested for their capital offense while on an active criminal justice status like parole or probation.[99] About one in every seven inmates had received multiple death sentences.[100]

A final important characteristic of people sentenced to death concerns the racial characteristics of the *victims* in death penalty cases: criminals who kill whites are much more likely to receive the death penalty than those who kill victims of other races. Of the victims in cases that resulted in execution in 2000, 76 percent were white.[101] This continues an overall trend: despite the fact that blacks and whites are murder victims in approximately equal numbers, 83 percent of victims whose cases resulted in an execution since 1976 have been white.[102] This trend applies to capital defendants of all races. That is, any person, regardless of his or her race, is much more likely to be sentenced to death in a case involving a white victim than a victim of any other race.[103]

Differences among Jurisdictions in Numbers of Executions and Capital Sentences

As discussed earlier, the many death penalty jurisdictions in the United States have widely differing laws about how the punishment may be used. Those jurisdictions differ in another manner, too: their application of their death penalty laws varies quite a bit. Some jurisdictions have many death row inmates and conduct numerous executions, while others have not executed anyone. In part, these variations are due to the differences in the laws: a state that punishes many types of homicides is likely to sentence more people to death than a jurisdiction that only imposes capital punishment for first-degree murder. Another cause of the variation among the jurisdictions is differences in population. A large state like California is likely to have more crime, more murders, and thus more death penalties than a smaller state like New Hampshire. Yet statutory dissimilarity and differences in size do not account for all of the variations in the application of capital punishment. To put it simply, certain jurisdictions are more active in seeking and carrying out the death penalty than others.

A first important fact to note about the application of the death penalty is that states in the South perform a vast majority of all the executions in the nation. In 2000, 89 percent of all executions in the United States took place in southern states.[104] Of the eighty-five executions that took place in 2000, forty were in Texas, eleven were in Oklahoma, and eight were in Virginia. The distribution in 2000 was not an aberration: since *Gregg* was decided, the South has far and away led the country in executions. Eight of the ten states with the most executions since 1976 are in the South,[105] with Texas leading all jurisdictions by a wide margin.[106] (See Table 2-10.)

Interestingly, this skew toward the South in numbers of executions does not match the number of people *sentenced* to death. Many jurisdictions in other areas of the country have large death row populations but have not executed as high a number of those convicts as the southern states. For instance, California, Illinois, Ohio, and Pennsylvania—all with large death row populations—together executed only one person in 2000 and twenty-four individuals between 1976 and 2000. At 454 convicts, Texas had the second-largest death row population in June 2001 and has had the largest total number of people put to death since 1976.[107]

Clearly, certain states are more prepared to put their sentenced offenders to death than others. In general, southern states are the most willing, though that is not universally true. Texas and Virginia are among the states with the highest proportions of sentenced offenders executed. Yet, though Florida has had a relatively high number of executions (fifty-one between 1976 and August 31, 2001), this is due mostly to its large death row population; the state actually puts a fairly low percentage of its death row inmates to death.[108] Delaware and Utah, neither of which is in the South, are among the jurisdictions that have executed the highest percentages of their death row inmates. The total number of executions in those two states has been low because of small death row populations.[109]

Notably, eight death penalty jurisdictions, including the military, have not put anyone to death since 1976.[110] The federal government, which had not executed anyone since 1963, put two inmates to death during the first half of 2001. Timothy McVeigh, the man who in 1995 killed 168 people when he bombed the Alfred P.

Table 2-10 Numbers of Executions and Death Row Inmates in U.S. Jurisdictions

Jurisdiction	Number of Executions in 2000	Number of Executions since 1976	Death Row Population
Alabama	4	23	188
Arizona	3	22	122
Arkansas	2	23	40
California	1	8	591
Colorado	0	1	7
Connecticut	0	0	7
Delaware	1	11	17
Florida	6	50	387
Georgia	0	23	135
Idaho	0	1	21
Illinois	0	12	176
Indiana	0	7	44
Kansas	0	0	4
Kentucky	0	2	42
Louisiana	1	26	94
Maryland	0	3	16
Mississippi	0	4	66
Missouri	5	46	81
Montana	0	2	6
Nebraska	0	3	11
Nevada	0	8	92
New Hampshire	0	0	0
New Jersey	0	0	17
New Mexico	0	0	5
New York	0	0	6
North Carolina	1	16	236
Ohio	0	1	202
Oklahoma	11	30	138

Table 2-10 *continued*

Jurisdiction	Number of Executions in 2000	Number of Executions Since 1976	Death Row Population
Oregon	0	2	28
Pennsylvania	0	3	243
South Carolina	1	25	70
South Dakota	0	0	3
Tennessee	1	1	103
Texas	40	239	448
Utah	0	7	11
Virginia	8	81	29
Washington	0	3	15
Wyoming	0	1	2
Federal system	0	0	25
U.S. military	0	0	7

Source: www.deathpenaltyinfo.org.

Murrah Federal Building in Oklahoma City, was put to death on June 11.[111] Just eight days later, Juan Raul Garza, whose case received substantial media attention because of claims of racial bias and because the Clinton administration had twice delayed his execution to further study problems of racial bias in the capital justice system, was also executed.[112]

The Capital Appellate System

A 2000 study conducted by Columbia University professor James Liebman and his colleagues reveals that a significant number of capital sentences and even many capital convictions are overturned at some point during the appeals process.[113] Between 1973 and 1995, 68 percent of all capital sentences reviewed in the United States were found to contain "prejudicial error."[114] This means that an appellate court found an error in the trial-court proceedings that was serious enough to command a reversal of the death sentence.

In about 90 percent of the cases in which a death penalty sentence was overturned, a state court found the error and ordered the reversal.[115] In the other 10 percent, the reversals were the result of a federal habeas petition or some other type of federal appeal. Liebman is careful to point out that, despite the fact that only 10 percent of reversals took place at the federal level, 40 percent of all capital appeals that made it into a federal court were successful and the sentences reversed.[116] The reversal rate in the initial state appeals courts was even higher, at about 47 percent.[117]

It is important to note that a reversal of a death sentence is not the same thing as a rejection of the defendant's conviction. In most cases, when a death sentence is overturned, the conviction underlying the sentence stands—the defendant is still considered guilty of murder and must serve a jail term instead of being put to death. For instance, appellate courts sometimes find that, during the sentencing phase of a trial, the prosecutor presented evidence that he or she should not have presented to the jury. In a Nevada case, *Dawson v. State* (1987), the state supreme court overturned a death sentence because the prosecutor had improperly emphasized the black defendant's relationship with a white woman during the sentencing phase of the trial.[118] The court held that such behavior by the prosecutor could have inflamed racial prejudice in the jury, thereby rendering their decision to impose the death sentence unfair and illegitimate. The court overturned the death sentence and ordered a new sentencing hearing. In such a case, the appellate courts do not overturn the jury's conviction of the defendant but find only a *sentencing* error—the conviction stands, but the death sentence is thrown out. According to some scholars who have reexamined Liebman's data, only about 27 percent of capital *convictions* were set aside upon appeal between 1973 and 1995.[119]

Even when a conviction is set aside, though, the defendant is usually retried. Of the overturned guilty verdicts that Liebman and his colleagues sampled, 75 percent were reaffirmed by a new jury and resulted in a jail sentence.[120] In another 18 percent, the defendant's guilt was reaffirmed and he or she was sentenced to death again.[121] In the remaining 7 percent, the defendant was acquitted of the charges.[122] According to the scholars who critiqued Liebman's study, combined data show that about 95 percent of convictions for capital murder are eventually upheld by an appeals court or reaffirmed by a new jury.[123]

Liebman's study shows that error rates between 1973 and 1995 were fairly high across most states that had had enough capital sentences to make reasonable statistical inferences, though they varied quite widely. In the great majority of death penalty states, more than 50 percent of capital sentences were overturned at some point during the state or federal appeals process.[124] In three states—Kentucky, Maryland, and Tennessee—the error rate was 100 percent.[125] Only two states had overall error rates less than 50 percent: Virginia's was 18 percent and Missouri's was 32 percent.[126] Two other states' error rates could not be computed because of the small number of cases and lack of appeals that had progressed through the entire review process.[127]

Another important statistic concerns the proportion of death sentences that are overturned in the state review process in the various states (as opposed to being thrown out by a federal court). According to the Columbia study, state courts exhibited quite different levels of error detection between 1973 and 1995. Wyoming state courts overturned 78 percent of that state's death sentences, while Virginia courts overturned just 13 percent.[128] Other states fell between those two. Interestingly, many southern states were among the top state courts in error detection: Louisiana, Kentucky, Florida, Alabama, North Carolina, South Carolina, and Mississippi state courts overturned more than 50 percent of all death sentences imposed by juries.[129]

A high level of error detection can be a product of several factors. State courts probably could not find a high number of errors unless a large number of errors were actually made during trials in the state, of course. But the percentage is also a function of how vigorously the courts review capital sentences. Liebman points out that many state court judges are elected and are under considerable political pressure to appear "tough on crime," so they face a disincentive to overturn death sentences.[130] He hypothesizes that the level of political pressure may play a role in explaining the variation among state court systems' error detection rates. Other scholars, too, have noted that, in the states with the most intense political pressure surrounding capital punishment, state courts are the least likely to overturn death sentences.[131]

There has been growing concern and much debate in recent years about the error rates described above and their meaning for capital punishment in America. Some commentators (including Liebman) find the error rates to be unacceptably high; others disagree. This growing concern, along with the development of new

DNA-testing technologies, has led to some important changes in the methods by which capital appeals are undertaken.

DNA testing has become an extremely useful tool. It is a process by which crime investigators and chemists can test certain pieces of physical human evidence, like hair or small particles of skin, found at crime scenes to determine whether it came from a certain suspect or defendant. Many regard DNA testing as a vital new piece of the criminal justice system, since it is sometimes very effective at establishing a defendant's guilt or innocence.

DNA testing has also become an important tool for the already convicted to attempt to prove their innocence on appeal. This has been especially true of persons convicted of capital crimes and sentenced to death; a 2000 book, *Actual Innocence*, claims that sixty-seven death row inmates were released between 1992 and 1999 because of newly tested DNA evidence.[132] Traditionally, however, capital convicts' access to DNA testing has been incomplete. Often, they must rely on cooperation from the prosecutor and judge in their case to be allowed to test evidence.

The concern about error rates has led several members of Congress to introduce legislation to aid prisoners' access to DNA testing. In 2000, Sen. Patrick Leahy, D-Vt., and Reps. Bill Delahunt, D-Mass., and Ray LaHood, R-Ill., introduced bills providing a federal mandate to ease access.[133] The bills are opposed by some prominent death penalty supporters, but the chairs of the Senate and House Judiciary Committees support a thorough hearing.[134]

Role of the Chief Executive

The chief executive in each death penalty jurisdiction (in the states, the governor, in the federal system, the president) plays a vital role in the application of capital punishment, because he or she plays such an important role in the policymaking of that jurisdiction. Chief executives help make policy in two ways: they carry out the laws of their jurisdiction, and they craft and implement the legislative agenda.

Chief executives are charged with carrying out the laws of their jurisdictions. This is not a merely mechanical function; they may affect the application of the death penalty by the manner in which they execute the laws. Gov. George Pataki, R-N.Y., for instance, is avidly pro–death penalty and has sought zealously to uphold New York's 1995 capital punishment statute, even over the objections of several local prosecutors. Other governors may be less aggressive about death penalty laws.

Perhaps the most dramatic way that chief executives can affect the application of the death penalty is by granting clemency. Most governors and the president have final power to grant clemency to a capital convict. The president or the governor in many states could commute *all* death sentences if he or she wished (though this has never happened). Actually, in recent years neither the governors nor the president have answered very many clemency appeals at all.[135]

According to death penalty experts, governors and clemency boards have granted many fewer clemency appeals since 1976 than was the previous custom. By some estimations, about 25 percent of all death sentences were commuted before *Furman* was handed down in 1972.[136] Others put the proportion at about 20 percent.[137] Scholars cite examples like Gov. Pat Brown of California, who commuted twenty-three of the fifty-nine death sentences imposed in his state between 1959 and 1966, as reflecting the old type of approach to capital clemency.

Between 1976 and the end of 2000, on the other hand, only forty-three death sentences were commuted in all of the United States.[138] This works out to a rate of about 7.5 percent. Moreover, the number of clemency grants was inflated by the actions of just two governors, Richard Celeste of Ohio and Tony Anaya of New Mexico, who, as they left office, commuted the sentences of all thirteen prisoners on their states' death rows.[139] In Oklahoma and Arizona, which have each executed more than twenty people since 1976, no capital convict has been granted clemency.

In fact, some modern governors do all they can to speed up the rate at which capital offenders are executed. Former Florida governor Bob Martinez, a prime example, signed 139 death warrants in the four years he served in the post.[140] And Gov. Tom Ridge, R-Pa., kept his campaign promise to speed up the rate of executions by signing forty-one death warrants in his first year in office.[141]

It is likely that many governors' distaste for clemency grants, and the desire of others to speed up the execution process, stems from the perceived political popularity of capital punishment. By many measures, a large majority of American voters favor the death penalty. Until recently, governors who feared being labeled "soft on crime" felt pressure to allow executions to go forward. This trend may be changing, however. The recent flap about high error rates in capital proceedings has begun to exert a countervailing pressure: voters are beginning to feel concerned about the way capital punishment is applied in the United States. This has led governors, even pro–death penalty governors, to act more carefully in signing death warrants. Even former Texas governor George W. Bush, who vowed that no innocent person was ever sentenced to death under his watch and who never granted a clemency appeal, was moved by political pressure in June 2000 to grant a thirty-day stay of execution to allow for further DNA testing.[142]

This countervailing pressure on chief executives has also manifested itself in the executives' other capital policymaking role: the designing of legislative agendas. Chief executives each have their own agenda—they introduce legislation and veto bills passed by legislatures. These agendas often include stances on the death penalty. For instance, in 2000, when state legislators in New Hampshire passed a bill abolishing the death penalty in the state, pro–capital punishment governor Jeanne Shaheen vetoed the measure, preserving the sentence in her state.[143]

Although many governors have, over the years, supported capital punishment in their legislative agendas, recent skepticism about capital punishment was brought into high relief when Gov. George Ryan, R-Ill., made news by putting a temporary halt to the use of the punishment in his state. Although Ryan is a supporter of the death penalty in principle—and had long supported its use in practice—on January 31, 2000, he called for a moratorium on further executions.[144] Citing "grave concerns about [Illinois's] shameful record of convicting innocent people and putting them on death row," the governor noted that, since the punishment had been reinstated in Illinois in 1977, thirteen of the twenty-five people who were sentenced to death were later exonerated and set free.[145] He appointed a commission to study the administration of the death penalty in Illinois and to recommend improvements,[146] and he promised not to reinstate the death penalty until he could "be sure with moral certainty that no innocent man or woman is facing lethal injection." [147]

No other state executive has declared a similar moratorium, but Ryan's move clearly had a nationwide impact. Five other states began a process of reviewing their death penalty systems,[148] and several state legislatures and even local city councils at least considered moratoriums of their own.[149] Perhaps more significantly, the move injected the anti–death penalty movement with a new vigor and at least temporarily shifted its rhetoric away from outright abolitionism to a focus on functional inadequacies in the capital punishment system.[150] Scholars noted that Illinois's error rate was not unlike those of other states; in fact, its overall error rate (including sentencing and conviction errors) was slightly *less* than the national average.[151] This allowed commentators to argue that other states should follow Illinois's lead in putting a halt to the death penalty until the system could be fixed.

The concerns about error rates have given governors in other states opportunities to display their death penalty agendas, too. In almost all cases, governors have used the opportunities to shore up their pro–capital punishment credentials. For instance, when the Nebraska legislature passed a bill in 1999 imposing a moratorium on all executions, the governor vetoed it.[152]

The administration of capital punishment in America may be affected by presidential policymaking, too. Most presidential candidates have a stance on the issue; in the 2000 election campaign, both candidates from the major parties were proponents of the death penalty. Since the federal criminal system rarely condemns convicts to death, however, these policy postures were largely symbolic.

Still, presidential agendas are not irrelevant to the way in which the death penalty is actually administered. After Governor Ryan declared a moratorium on executions in his state, President Clinton asked the governors of the other death penalty states to carefully assess their systems as well. While this request carried little formal weight, it at least represented a powerful affirmation of Ryan's position. In the eyes of many observers, new president George W. Bush is much less likely to be sympathetic. During his tenure as governor of Texas, more prisoners were executed than in any other state.[153] Moreover, he generally refused to consider the many criticisms of his state's capital punishment system.

Prosecutorial Discretion

The people who, in many senses, have the most direct impact on the application of the death penalty in America are local prosecutors and district attorneys in states that authorize capital punishment. Prosecutors have almost sole discretion in deciding whether or not to press for the death penalty in a given case. When a person suspected of murder is brought to the attention of a prosecutor, that official must decide whether or not to charge the accused with a capital crime like first-degree murder, accept a plea bargain, or press for the death penalty if a capital crime is charged.

The frequency with which prosecutors press for capital sentences has a significant effect on the number of death penalties and executions in each area. Sometimes, discrepancies occur among jurisdictions in such close proximity that they become almost painfully obvious. Baltimore, Maryland, for instance, averaged 320 murders per year in the 1990s, but through 1999 only one of the murderers from that city had been sentenced to death. Neighboring Baltimore County, however, which suffered just twenty-nine murders a year in the 1990s, had four convicts sentenced to death row.[154] Hamilton County, Ohio, had fifty people on death row in

1999, while nearby Franklin County, with a larger population and twice the number of murders, had just eleven death row inmates.[155]

The striking case of Raymond Patterson particularly shows the importance of the behavior of local prosecutors. In 1984, Patterson was arrested for beating and killing an elderly man in a parking lot in South Carolina. It turned out that the line dividing Lexington County and Richland County ran right through that parking lot. Lexington County, at the time, had sent twelve convicts to death row, while Richland County had sent only one. The police determined that Patterson had committed his crime a few feet inside the Lexington County side of the line; he was charged in that county, convicted, and sentenced to death.[156]

Often, prosecutors make their careers by maintaining long records of capital convictions. But there are rare instances in which prosecutors will not seek the death penalty even though state law authorizes them to do so. A famous case occurred in the mid-1990s in New York City. When the state of New York passed new legislation authorizing the death penalty in 1995, Bronx district attorney Robert T. Johnson vowed to refuse to seek the sentence.[157] He said he was morally opposed to taking another person's life, except in self-defense, and that he did not feel confident that the death penalty system adequately guaranteed that an innocent person would not be executed. Johnson's constituents in the Bronx generally felt the same way about executions, and he did not feel at risk in upcoming elections. Johnson did not ever press for the death penalty in any case, and finally Governor Pataki, who had worked for passage of the new capital punishment legislation, stepped in and removed Johnson's authority in the case of a man who had killed a Bronx police officer.[158]

A 2001 case involved a San Francisco district attorney who opposed the death penalty and would not seek it. The prosecutor, Terence Hallinan, refused to seek the sentence even in the case of a convicted killer who wished to be put to death.[159] As in the case of Robert Johnson, the governor of California stepped in and overrode his decision. But both cases of gubernatorial action were special—in New York, the case involved a defendant accused of killing a police officer; in San Francisco, it involved a man who had already been sentenced to death, wanted to die, and merely needed a prosecutor to go to court to get an execution date set. In general, governors do not take the time to meddle in the affairs of local prosecutors. Therefore, in jurisdictions where officials do not wish to seek the death penalty, there are few or no death sentences imposed.

Capital Punishment as a Symbol in American Politics

The death penalty is not merely an instrument for crime deterrence and punishment in the United States. It is also a powerful symbol used by politicians to appeal to the electorate. Some have even argued that its symbolic usefulness is precisely what has allowed capital punishment to continue in the United States while most other countries have abandoned it.[160]

The American public has shown strong support for the death penalty in the past few decades. Very recently, public concern about errors and unfairness in the nation's administration of capital punishment has grown, but the majority of Americans still favor its use. Although support had been waning since its high of around 80 percent in 1994, in May 2001 a *USA Today*/CNN/Gallup poll found that 59 percent of Americans still support capital punishment in general. Moreover, even though 38 percent of the respondents expressed opposition to the death penalty, 16 percent said that they opposed the death penalty in principle but would support putting Timothy McVeigh, the notorious Oklahoma City bomber, to death.[161] Public support for the policy has influenced the behavior of elected legislators, of course, and was a partial reason for the quick reenactment of capital punishment statutes after *Furman* in 1972.

Yet, even leaving aside this direct influence, the death penalty has long served as a useful symbolic tool for legislators. Politicians can, and often do, use their own rhetorical position on the issue to garner electoral support, even when there is no explicit reason for a discussion of capital punishment. In 1988, for instance, Congress used the death penalty as a symbolic method of earning election-year support by passing the drug kingpin death penalty law. Many courts and commentators have pointed out that Congress apparently acted with considerable haste in passing the statute.[162] Congress neglected to include in the statute any provisions dealing with the time, place, or manner in which executions under the law were supposed to take place. Moreover, the law makes one element of the underlying offense—a fact that is necessary for conviction—an aggravating circumstance, as well. As one commentator put it, "That election-year Congress's interest in the death penalty was purely and transparently symbolic."[163]

Local and state politicians, too, are affected by the death penalty's symbolic usefulness. Many fear being labeled "soft on crime," and one simple way of appearing tough is to support capital punishment.[164] A recent study of criminologists found that all of those surveyed agreed with the statement, "Politicians support the death penalty as a symbolic way to show they are tough on crime."[165] The 1994 gubernatorial election cycle is a good example: candidates in at least five states that year exploited the issue to good effect.[166] Illinois governor Jim Edgar, for instance, emphasized his own support for the sentence and derided his opponent's anti–capital punishment stance.[167]

It is important to note that the death penalty is not a symbolic issue only to legislators and executives; it is used by members of the judicial branch who must seek election, too. In states where judges are elected (thirty-two of the thirty-eight death penalty states), capital punishment often becomes an important electoral issue.[168] In Tennessee, for instance, conservatives used state supreme court justice Penny White's record on the death penalty to oust her from her seat. White, a liberal, had voted on just one death penalty case, in which she joined the majority of judges on the panel in overturning a death sentence.[169] Mississippi supreme court justice James Robertson was unseated by an opponent who attacked him for holding that executions were not permitted for the crime of rape—a ruling required by the U.S. Supreme Court's jurisprudence.[170]

Elected prosecutors—some of whom have sole authority in deciding whether to seek the sentence in any given case—also feel the pressure exerted by the symbolic power of the death penalty. Many prosecutors use statistics about their capital punishment records as campaign propaganda. Bob Macy, district attorney of Oklahoma City, is a prime example: his campaign literature lists the number of murderers he has sent to death row.

Arguments about Capital Punishment

A complete treatment of the use of capital punishment in the United States entails examination of the intellectual arguments made by its proponents and opponents. Detailed here are arguments about the death penalty's deterrence effect, debates about the morality of executing criminals, concerns about racism raised by the death penalty, and arguments that have been especially prevalent in recent years about errors in the application of the death penalty and the manner in which those errors should affect policy choices. Each section considers the arguments made by people on both sides of the issue, the evidence supporting their contentions, and the way the debate has affected the policy arena.

Deterrence

One of the fundamental justifications underlying the use of punishment in the criminal law is deterrence. The threat of punishment for crimes is intended, at least in part, to deter would-be criminals from committing a crime. The threat of a traffic ticket and a fine dissuades people from speeding, for instance. For more serious crimes like theft or assault, the threat of a jail term is the deterrent.

Capital punishment, too, is often justified in part by an appeal to its supposed deterrent effect.[171] Proponents claim that the threat of death is the ultimate fear, and that this fear can be harnessed to dissuade people from committing the most heinous crimes. The Supreme Court in *Gregg* listed deterrence as one of the "two principal social purposes" that the punishment might serve.[172] Legislators also often appeal to deterrence rationales when arguing to maintain or pass death penalty statutes.[173] In signing New York's new statute in 1995, for instance, Governor Pataki stated:

> The citizens of New York State have spoken loudly and clearly in their call for justice for those who commit the most serious of crimes by depriving other citizens of their very lives. The citizens of New York State are convinced the death penalty will deter these vicious crimes and I, as their Governor, agree. The legislation I approve today will be the most effective of its kind in the nation. It is balanced to safeguard defendants' rights while ensuring that our state has a fully credible and enforceable death penalty statute. This law significantly buttresses the twin pillars of an effective criminal justice system—deterrence and true justice for those convicted of violent crimes.[174]

Opponents of the death penalty counter these deterrence arguments in several different ways. Some abolitionists have maintained that, far from deterring crime, the death penalty actually *encourages* violent crimes. These critics, like Professor John Kaplan of Stanford Law School, contend that the "state violence" represented by an execution sends the message that killing is an "appropriate method of settling a dispute."[175] Others claim that the availability of the death penalty allows some people to commit state-sponsored suicide, pointing to cases like that of Daniel M. Colwell, who claimed that he killed specifically in order to be executed, since he could not kill himself.[176]

By far the most common retort to the deterrence justification for capital punishment, though, is that the availability of the punishment simply does not deter violent crime more effectively than the threat of long-term imprisonment. Debate about the question has raged for many decades, and there has been no lack of empirical research to support the two sides. One extremely influential study was conducted by the economist Isaac Ehrlich in the 1970s. His data and analysis seemed to show that capital punishment did have a deterrent effect. Ehrlich claimed that each execution between 1933 and 1969 had prevented about eight other homicides from occurring.[177] This study received quite a bit of attention upon its publication. In fact, Solicitor General (and eventual Supreme Court nominee) Robert Bork used the study to support the death penalty after *Furman* temporarily made it illegal.[178]

Many other scholars, however, strongly criticized Ehrlich's study, claiming that it contained significant flaws.[179] For example, Brian Frost, a scholar of criminal law, conducted a reanalysis of Ehrlich's findings that suggested several defects in the statistical models used by the economist.[180] Frost concluded that "on balance the death penalty does not have a perceptible influence on the homicide rate."[181] In fact, most recent research on the deterrence effect of the death penalty has found that it has "virtually the same effect as long-term imprisonment on homicide rates."[182] One recent survey showed that "there is a wide consensus among America's top criminologists that scholarly research has demonstrated that the death penalty does, and can do, little to reduce rates of criminal violence."[183]

Still, death penalty proponents continue to cite Ehrlich's research. Moreover, his student, Stephen Layson, released a study in 1985 that seems to show an even greater deterrence effect than did Ehrlich's.[184] According to Layson, each execution deters eighteen would-be murderers from going through with their crimes.[185] That research, like Ehrlich's, has been criticized as being flawed, but it is often cited by death penalty supporters.[186]

Interestingly, the Supreme Court has acknowledged that some studies show "the death penalty may not function as a significantly greater deterrent than lesser penalties," though it felt the results were inconclusive.[187] The Court was inclined to the view that the death penalty must have a deterrent effect in at least some cases.[188] However, the Court has decided to defer to the judgment of legislatures in this area. In *Gregg*, the Court said:

> The value of capital punishment as a deterrent of crime is a complex factual issue the resolution of which properly rests with the legislatures, which can evalu-

ate the results of statistical studies in terms of their own local conditions and with a flexibility of approach that is not available to the courts.[189]

The Court noted that many legislatures have proclaimed that capital punishment is an effective deterrent and left the issue at that.[190]

In any event, despite scholarly work that casts serious doubt on the death penalty's deterrent effect, deterrence continues to be an important justification for the use of capital punishment in the political world. As noted earlier, legislators and politicians often appeal to the notion of deterrence in supporting death penalty legislation or in carrying out executions. Even the Supreme Court has indirectly relied on the idea that the death penalty deters murders. Perhaps most importantly, voters tend to list deterrence as an important reason for supporting the death penalty. In the mid-1980s, a Gallup poll showed that over 60 percent of respondents believed that the punishment has a deterrent effect.[191] More recent polls confirm that this feeling continues.[192] Moreover, the public seems to think of the deterrent effect as an important justification for the death penalty. When respondents in the 1986 Gallup poll were asked about their feelings "if new evidence proved that the death penalty does not act as a deterrent to murder," their support for capital punishment dropped from 70 percent to 51 percent.[193]

Morality of Capital Punishment

The second type of argument used to evaluate the death penalty concerns the morality of executing convicts. Unlike the deterrence debate, which revolves around a dispute about the practical value of capital punishment, this difference of opinion is purely intellectual in nature: people who feel that capital punishment is immoral will hold that opinion regardless of the efficacy of the death penalty at achieving societal goals. Conversely, some proponents of capital punishment support it on ethical grounds and would not change their minds even if they knew that the punishment did not help reduce crime in any way. Opponents of capital punishment argue that it is immoral, even for the state, to take a life, so capital punishment is unethical. Proponents argue that some murderers deserve to be put to death.

Many opponents of the death penalty who argue from a morality-based position are affiliated with a religious movement of one kind or another. The essential theme of their arguments was well summarized by Rep. Lee Hamilton of Indiana, who stated, "The death penalty demeans our society and violates a basic tenet of most Americans' religious heritage: Thou shalt not kill." Many people of faith believe that killing is a sin, and that it is therefore sinful for the state to condemn a person to death—even someone who has committed a grievous crime.

Of course, it is not only religious groups that argue against capital punishment from moral grounds. Amnesty International, a human rights advocacy group, seeks to abolish the death penalty because it is incompatible with the humanitarian standards agreed on by the international community. The American Ethical Union opposes the death penalty, stating, "The willful taking of human life is cruel and inhuman punishment and violates [the Union's] belief in the intrinsic worth of every human being."[194]

Moral arguments against the death penalty are occasionally used by politicians, as well. Rep. John Lewis, D-Ga., for instance, listed morality as his reason for opposing a 1994 crime bill that would expand the use of the death penalty.[195] Former governor Mario Cuomo repeatedly vetoed death penalty legislation passed by the New York state house because he found capital punishment to be morally repugnant. In fact, in each of his twelve years in office, the governor vetoed a bill aimed at establishing the death penalty in New York. Some politicians with a religious affiliation, like the Reverend Jesse Jackson, oppose the death penalty on moral grounds, too.

Although many religious and nonreligious organizations and leaders oppose capital punishment on ethical grounds, the moral debate has another side. One of the fundamental justifications underlying the punishment of criminals is retribution. Under a retributive theory, society can and should punish criminals because they committed a wrongful act and deserve to be punished. This is considered true regardless of the later consequences of the punishment; that is, even if imprisoning a thief now does not deter other people from stealing tomorrow, a retributive theory of punishment would mandate that the thief be imprisoned because he or she deserves punishment.

The retribution rationale extends to capital punishment, too. To many people's minds, criminals who commit heinous crimes deserve to be put to death, whether or not the execution deters later crime. A British judge put it this way:

> Punishment is the way in which society expresses its denunciation of wrong doing: and, in order to maintain respect for law, it is essential that the punishment inflicted for grave crimes should adequately reflect the revulsion felt by the great

majority of citizens for them. It is a mistake to consider the objects of punishment as being deterrent or reformative or preventive and nothing else. . . . The truth is that some crimes are so outrageous that society insists on adequate punishment, because the wrong-doer deserves it, irrespective of whether it is a deterrent or not.[196]

The Supreme Court in *Gregg* listed retribution as a valid "social purpose" for the death penalty. "In part," wrote Justice Stewart for the majority, "capital punishment is an expression of society's moral outrage at particularly offensive conduct. This function may be unappealing to many, but it is essential in an ordered society that asks its citizens to rely on legal processes rather than self-help to vindicate their wrongs."[197]

Polls and studies of American citizens have found that many supporters of the death penalty do so for reasons of retribution. A 1985 Gallup poll, for instance, found that 48 percent of proponents base their support on ideas of "retribution," "revenge," or "desert."[198] One professor found that "a factor variously called retribution, revenge, or a desire to see criminals receive their just deserts seems to have become the dominant motive for supporters of the death penalty."[199]

Prosecutors often use retributive arguments when trying to convince jurors to impose the death penalty on a defendant. For instance, in a sensational 1999 trial, two Texas white supremacists were tried for chaining James Byrd, a black man, to a truck and driving along a three-mile stretch of road until he was decapitated.[200] During the penalty stage of the capital trial, the prosecutor in the case said he was not worried that the all-white jury would not return a death penalty sentence. He said, "I don't like the death penalty, but that's what [the defendant] deserves. The just punishment for his case and these facts and circumstances is death."[201]

There is a religious justification for retribution, too: a Bible passage in Exodus, "And if any mischief follow, then thou shalt give life for life, eye for eye, tooth for tooth,"[202] is often quoted as support for retributive punishment.[203] In fact, in a 1991 Gallup poll, the most-used justification for supporting capital punishment was the notion of the propriety of taking "a life for a life."[204] Even prosecutors have sometimes used this religious justification for seeking the death penalty.[205]

Opponents of capital punishment attack retributive justifications as inadequate and misguided.[206] Supreme Court justices Marshall and Brennan, who each opposed the death penalty on the Court, wrote, in the course of their own opinions in various death penalty decisions, that retribution is an erroneous rationalization for capital punishment. In *Furman*, Marshall wrote that "retaliation, vengeance, and retribution have been roundly condemned as intolerable aspirations for a government in a free society."[207] Brennan attacked the idea of retribution as an appeal to the value of "naked vengeance."[208]

Others argue that, even if retribution is a theoretically valid purpose, the American capital punishment system applies the sentence in too chaotic a manner to allow for principled punishment.[209] Professor David Gottlieb of the University of Kansas, for example, claims that the capital punishment system "violates notions of just punishment because it is haphazardly administered against a small, almost randomly selected sample of eligible persons."[210] Professor Jack Greenberg of Columbia University Law School contends that the racial disparities in the system undercut "the moral force of any retribution argument."[211]

At present, retribution remains a strong underlying rationalization for the use of capital punishment. Courts rely on it as a justification: perhaps increasingly so, since scholarly evidence seems to be mounting that the other constitutional justification—deterrence—is not well served by the death penalty. It is also a primary value underlying the public's support for the death penalty, and thus serves to further strengthen support for capital punishment among politicians.

Racism and Capital Punishment

Another important area of debate surrounding the death penalty concerns allegations of racism and disproportionate racial impact in the application of capital punishment in America. Opponents of the death penalty who make claims about racism are making instrumental arguments; they do not argue that the death penalty is intrinsically unethical, but rather that, in the United States, it is imposed unfairly. They argue that the sentence is applied in a racially biased manner and has unfair impacts on minority populations in America.

Opponents note several facts about the manner in which race impacts the death penalty. Blacks have constituted 36 percent of all people executed in the United States since 1976, while whites account for 55 percent, Hispanics 7 percent, and other races 2 percent.[212] The numbers are slightly different for death row inmates: 46 percent are white, 43 percent black, 9 percent Hispanic, and 2 percent another race.[213] When compared with census data about the U.S. population, it is clear that the proportions of minorities sentenced to death and executed are larger than their representation in the general population. Whites made up about 82 percent of the U.S. population in November 2000, blacks about 13 percent, and Hispanics about 12 percent.[214]

Of course, the disproportionate numbers of blacks and Hispanics on death row in the United States does not necessarily indicate a racist application of the law. It is likely that the proportions are heavily influenced by the fact that the black and Hispanic populations include large numbers of impoverished people, who are more likely to commit crimes for a variety of reasons. There are some statistics, though, that do point toward racial disparities in the application of capital punishment. For instance, although about 50 percent of the murder victims are white, 83 percent of executions are imposed on criminals who murdered a white person.[215] Moreover, statistical studies appear to show that race plays a role in death penalty sentencing. In 1990, the U.S. General Accounting Office (GAO), at the behest of Congress, reviewed twenty-eight empirical studies about capital sentencing. The GAO stated, "Our synthesis of the 28 studies shows a pattern of evidence indicating racial disparities in the charging, sentencing, and imposition of the death penalty after the *Furman* decision." In the reviewed studies, "race of victim influence was found at all stages of the criminal justice system process."[216]

The racism argument has also been fueled by another recent study conducted by the federal government. In 2000 the Justice Department released the results of a statistical analysis of the federal death penalty. The report noted that, between 1995 and 2000, 80 percent of all the cases submitted by federal prosecutors for death penalty review involved minority defendants. Of these, almost half were black. Even after review by the attorney general, 72 percent of cases in which federal prosecutors pushed for capital punishment involved minorities.[217]

Over that same five-year period, U.S. attorneys were almost twice as likely to push for the death penalty for a black defendant when the victim in the case was not black than when the victim was black. The study also showed that federal prosecutors were much more likely to enter into plea agreements (lessening the severity of the sentence in return for a guilty plea) with white defendants than with minorities. Finally, the study showed that, as of July 2000, 79 percent of federal death row inmates were members of a racial minority.[218] Then–attorney general Janet Reno was so disturbed by these findings that she ordered all federal prosecutors to explain the disparity.

Death penalty proponents respond to these arguments in two major ways. First, they dispute the statistical analyses that purport to show racism. An authority commonly cited by death penalty proponents is the 1991 study of California conducted by Stephen Klein and John Rolph.[219] The researchers found, contrary to a large number of other studies, that the race of a victim was *not* a statistically significant factor in the imposition of the death penalty during the sentencing phase of capital trials.[220] Although a slightly higher percentage of people who murdered white victims were put to death during the study period, the statistical difference disappeared when Klein and Rolph controlled for factors such as severity of the crime and number of victims. Defenders of the death penalty also note that whites convicted of murder are more likely to be sentenced to death than blacks,[221] and that whites sentenced to death are, on average, executed more quickly than blacks.[222]

The second argument used to respond to the racism issue asks, essentially: Even if the death penalty is being applied in a racist manner, why does that mean we should abolish it? Rather, proponents contend, the system should be fixed. Some claim that the system should not be altered to render fewer death sentences for murderers of whites, but to render *more* capital sentences for killers of blacks. Moreover, some proponents argue that capital punishment should be used even if it is used in an unequal manner. Ernest van den Haag, a law professor and proponent of capital punishment, put it this way:

> If and when discrimination occurs it should be corrected. Not, however, by letting the guilty blacks escape the death penalty because guilty whites do, but by making sure that the guilty white offenders suffer it as the guilty blacks do. . . .
> However, even if . . . this cannot be done, I do not see any good reason to let any guilty murderer escape his penalty. It does happen in the administration of criminal justice that one person gets away with murder and another is executed. Yet the fact that one gets away with it is no reason to let another one escape.[223]

Race-based arguments have seen considerable action over the years among lawmakers, jurists, and advocacy organizations. Many civil rights organizations oppose the death penalty because of racial disparities. The NAACP Legal Defense and Educational Fund, for instance, publishes a periodical, *Death Row USA*, that keeps track of death row statistics, especially those having to do with race and the death penalty.

In 2001 Maryland considered legislation that would impose a moratorium on executions because of concerns about racism in the application of the death penalty.[224] The bill would suspend executions until 2003, when a University of Maryland study about race and the death penalty in Maryland is scheduled to be completed. Although other states have or are considering moratoriums, Michael Stark of the Campaign to End the Death Penalty says the effort in Maryland is different because of its focus on racism as a justification.[225] Some other states' campaigns, including the Illinois effort that culminated in an actual moratorium, have focused primarily on error rates. An important reason for the focus on racism in Maryland is that the state's record is seen as particularly bad: nine of the state's thirteen death row inmates are black, the highest such proportion in the nation. Moreover, though about 75 percent of all murder victims in Maryland are black, 75 percent of the convicted murderers on death row killed whites.[226]

In November 2000, a similar argument was made by death penalty opponents in Indiana. A spokesperson for the Church Women United of Indiana told the state's Criminal Law Study Commission that her group had found evidence of racial bias in death penalty cases, and she urged a moratorium.[227] North Carolina's inquiry into a moratorium, too, looked at racism.[228] Several groups in Texas have also used allegations of racism in their advocacy of a moratorium or a death penalty ban. In fact, an October 2000 report by the Texas Defender Service, a nonprofit organization that represents indigent death row inmates, found racism in two important elements of Texas's capital punishment process: the decision about when to ask for the death penalty and the racial composition of death penalty juries.[229]

Some anti–death penalty organizations have attempted to use arguments about racism to impact death penalty policy on the federal level, too. At the end of President Clinton's second term, a group of activists wrote the president, asking him to impose a moratorium on federal executions. Referring to the 2000 Justice Department study, the group's letter stated, "Unless you take action, executions will begin at a time when your own attorney general has expressed concern about racial and other disparities in the federal death penalty process."[230] The group also urged Clinton to intervene in the execution of federal prisoner Juan Raul Garza, a Hispanic man convicted of killing three people as part of his involvement in an illegal drug ring. They wrote that Garza's case "reflects precisely the concerns over racial, ethnic and geographic disparities in capital cases that the Justice Department itself has raised."[231]

A case that has taken on symbolic national importance on the issue of racism in the application of the death penalty is that of Mumia Abu-Jamal, a former radio journalist who was convicted of the 1981 shooting death of a Philadelphia police officer. Abu-Jamal's supporters, including Rep. Maxine Waters, D-Calif., allege that his case is a prime example of the manner in which race can distort the fairness of capital trials. They contend that his conviction rested on numerous civil rights violations. Recently, Abu-Jamal's supporters have attempted to goad the Justice Department into investigating the facts surrounding the case.[232] At the end of 2000, however, they began to express concern that their time was limited, given the impending change of presidential administration. They felt that President Clinton made a much more sympathetic audience than would the new president Bush.

As explained earlier, in *McCleskey v. Kemp* the Supreme Court rebuffed a challenge to the death penalty that was based on the racism argument. Critics of the Supreme Court have tried to circumvent the decision through legislation.[233] As part of its crime legislation, the House of Representatives in 1994 passed a measure requiring states to show that their death penalty system is racially neutral. That provision, however, was deleted by the House-Senate conference committee that drafted the final congressional legislation.[234]

Error Rates

The final important argument concerning the use of the death penalty has become the most widely discussed capital issue in the past few years. As more and more data have been collected about the error rates in death sentencing, death penalty opponents have begun to argue, with increasing success, that use of the sentence ought to be abolished simply because it is not being applied in a reliable manner. They contend that the risk of putting the innocent or undeserving to death is too high and that therefore the nation should stop using the death penalty. Again, this is an instrumental argument: people using the line of reasoning claim that the punishment should be scrapped because of a problem with its application; they are not focusing on the issue of whether putting a criminal to death is theoretically morally justified.

The most successful application of such an argument occurred in Illinois. In January 2000, Governor Ryan, known as a supporter of the death penalty, called a moratorium on executions. He stated, "I have grave concerns about our state's shameful record of convicting innocent people and putting them on death row."[235] Since 1977, appellate courts had exonerated thirteen of the twenty-five persons Illinois juries had sentenced to death row.[236] Although no other state has yet followed

Illinois's lead, five are actively looking into a moratorium, and moratorium movements are plentiful across the nation. Moreover, national politicians like Rep. Henry Hyde, R-Ill., formerly a staunch death penalty supporter, now support a reevaluation.[237] Congress has even considered several bills aimed at ensuring quality counsel for capital defendants.[238]

Death penalty opponents answer these charges in two major ways. First, they dispute the conclusions of the death penalty studies. Pro–capital punishment commentators note that many overturned death sentences are reimposed by a second jury, so that the overall number of sentences that are overturned for good is lower than it would seem.[239] There have also been questions about the methodology of the studies.

The second type of counter-argument grants that there are a fairly high number of reversals in death penalty cases but claims that this is merely proof of a working system. The appellate process is catching the errors, proponents contend, so injustice is not occurring.

Notes

1. United States Constitution, Amendment V (emphasis added).

2. United States Constitution, Amendment XIV (emphasis added).

3. Christopher Z. Mooney and Mei-Hsien Lee, "Morality Policy Reinvention: State Death Penalties," *Annals of the American Academy of Political and Social Science* 566 (1999): 84.

4. Ibid., 85.

5. Michigan was the first state to partially abolish capital punishment. In 1846, it abandoned the use of the death penalty for all crimes except treason and has never again actually imposed the sentence. William J. Bowers, *Legal Homicide: Death as Punishment in America, 1864–1982* (Boston: Northeastern University Press, 1984), 9.

6. Ibid., 526–531.

7. 408 U.S. 238 (1972).

8. Data for this chart comes from the Death Penalty Information Center's Web page, at www.deathpenaltyinfo.org, and Mooney and Lee, "Morality Policy Reinvention," 88.

9. 428 U.S. 153 (1976).

10. *Furman v. Georgia*, 408 U.S. at 327 (J. Marshall, concurring).

11. *Roberts v. Louisiana*, 431 U.S. 633 (1977).

12. The cases were *Lockett v. Ohio*, 438 U.S. 586 (1978), and *Eddings v. Oklahoma*, 455 U.S. 104 (1982).

13. *Coker v. Georgia*, 433 U.S. 584 (1977).

14. *Enmund v. Florida*, 458 U.S. 782 (1982).

15. *Cabana v. Bullock*, 474 U.S. 376 (1986).

16. *Tison v. Arizona*, 481 U.S. 137 (1987).

17. *Ford v. Wainwright*, 477 U.S. 399 (1986).

18. *Penry v. Lynaugh*, 492 U.S. 302 (1989).

19. *Stanford v. Kentucky*, 492 U.S. 361 (1989).

20. *Payne v. Tennessee*, 501 U.S. 808 (1991).

21. Ibid., 817.

22. Ibid.

23. *McCleskey v. Kemp*, 481 U.S. 279 (1987).

24. Mooney and Lee, "Morality Policy Reinvention," 88.

25. Tracy L. Snell, "Capital Punishment 1999," *Bureau of Justice Statistics Bulletin*, U.S. Department of Justice, Office of Justice Programs (December 2000).

26. *Gregg*, 428 U.S., 187.

27. See Radin, "Cruel Punishment and Respect for Persons: Super Due Process for Death," *Southern California Law Review* 53 (1980): 1143.

28. George Wesley Sherrell Jr., "Note: Successive Chances for Life: *Kuhlmann v. Wilson*, Federal Habeas Corpus, and the Capital Petitioner," *New York University Law Review* 64 (1989): 478.

29. *Furman v. Georgia*, 428 U.S., 188.

30. *Gregg v. Georgia*, 428 U.S., 195, 198, 204–206.

31. *Pulley v. Harris*, 465 U.S., 37.

32. Leigh B. Bienen, "Criminal Law: The Proportionality Review of Capital Cases by State High Courts after *Gregg*: Only the 'Appearance of Justice'?" *Northwestern School of Law Journal of Criminal Law and Criminology*, 87 (fall 1996): 130 at 155–59.

33. 18 U.S.C. 3595.

34. United States Constitution, Article I, § 9, cl. 2

35. James S. Liebman, Jeffrey Fagan, and Valerie West, "A Broken System: Error Rates in Capital Cases, 1973–1995," Columbia University School of Law, June 12, 2000.

36. Neil A. Lewis, "Four Key Issues in Dispute on Package to Fight Crime," *New York Times*, November 27, 1991, B8.

37. 477 U.S. 478 (1986).

38. *Kuhlmann v. Wilson*, 477 U.S. 436, 454 (1986).

39. *Schlup v. Delo,* 513 U.S. 298, 314 (1995).

40. *Sawyer v. Whitley,* 505 U.S. 333, 339 (1992).

41. 28 U.S.C. § 2255. The time limit begins to count at the latest of:

(1) the date on which the judgment of conviction becomes final;

(2) the date on which the impediment to making a motion created by governmental action in violation of the Constitution or laws of the United States is removed, if the movant was prevented from making a motion by such governmental action;

(3) the date on which the right asserted was initially recognized by the Supreme Court, if that right has been newly recognized by the Supreme Court and made retroactively applicable to cases on collateral review; or

(4) the date on which the facts supporting the claim or claims presented could have been discovered through the exercise of due diligence.

42. See *Heflin v. United States,*358 U.S. 415, 420 (1959) (Stewart, J., concurring).

43. *Gideon v. Wainwright,* 372 U.S. 335 (1963).

44. *Douglas v. California,* 372 U.S. 353 (1963).

45. P. Davenport, "Death Row Inmates Losing Key Source of Legal Help," *Dallas Morning News,* February 19, 1996.

46. 18 U.S.C. 930.

47. See *People v. Anderson,* 6 Cal. 3d 628 (1972) for the California court's decision, and *District Attorney v. Watson,* 381 Mass. 648 (1980) for the Massachusetts court's decision.

48. "Federal Death Penalty," Death Penalty Information Center, updated November 27, 2000. Available online at www.deathpenaltyinfo.org/feddp.html.

49. See www.deathpenaltyinfo.org/nodp.html.

50. Information in chart from www.deathpenaltyinfo.org.

51. 18 U.S.C. 241, 242, 245, 247.

52. The information in this table comes from www.deathpenaltyinfo.org.

53. "Why Won't They Give the New President a Chance? The Friday Column," *Daily Telegraph* (London), December 15, 2000, 31.

54. Ibid.

55. "Ideas & Trends; Death and the White House," *New York Times,* December 17, 2000, 4:3.

56. *Penry v. Johnson,* 121 S. Ct. 1910; www.deathpenaltyinfo.com.

57. "Meting Death to Juvenile Criminals," *Washington Post,* December 8, 2000, A54.

58. *Gideon v. Wainwright,* 372 U.S. 335 (1963).

59. Bureau of Justice Statistics, http://www.ojp.usdoj.gov/bjs/id.htm.

60. Ibid.

61. Ibid.

62. "ACLU Joins Lawsuit Against County with High Execution Rate," *Chicago Tribune*, October 1, 2000, 12C.

63. "National Perspective; The Law; Attorney's Dozing at Center of Texas Murder Case Challenge; Defendant Facing the Death Penalty Contends His Lawyer in 1984 Trial Was No More Aware 'Than a Potted Plant,' " *Los Angeles Times*, January 23, 2001, A5.

64. E. Gleik, "Rich Justice, Poor Justice," *Time*, June 19, 1995, 40. The states were Connecticut, Illinois, Indiana, Minnesota, and Mississippi.

65. R. Klein and R. Spangenburg, "The Indigent Defense Crisis," prepared for the American Bar Association Section of Criminal Justice Ad Hoc Committee on the Indigent Defense Crisis (1993), 7.

66. The information in this table comes from the individual state information pages found on the Web site of the Death Penalty Information Center, www.deathpenaltyinfo.org.

67. Joan M. Fisher, "Expedited Review of Capital Post-Conviction Claims: Idaho's Flawed Process," *Journal of Appellate Practice and Process* 2 (winter 2000), 85.

68. Leigh B. Bienen, "Criminal Law: The Proportionality Review of Capital Cases by State High Courts After Gregg: Only the 'Appearance of Justice'?" *Northwestern School of Law Journal of Criminal Law and Criminology* 87 (fall 1996): 130.

69. For example, the Arkansas Supreme Court's ruling in *Sheridan v. State*, 852 S.W.2d 772, 780 (Ark. 1993).

70. *Pulley v. Harris*, 465 U.S. 37 (1984).

71. The information in Table 7-1 is extracted from *Bienen* 1996, appendix A.

72. Ibid., 158–177.

73. Ibid., 159.

74. Ibid., 173–174.

75. Ibid., 174, citing Steven M. Sprenger, "Note: A Critical Evaluation of State Supreme Court Proportionality Review in Death Sentence Cases," *Iowa Law Review* 73 (1988): 719. The case was *Coleman v. State*, 378 So.2d 640 (Miss. 1979).

76. Fisher, "Expedited Review of Capital Post-Conviction Claims."

77. *Fierro v. Gomez*, 77 F.3d 301 (1996).

78. *Francis. v. Resweber*, 329 U.S. 459 (1947).

79. *Gray v. Lucas*, 710 F.2d 1048 (5th Cir. 1983); *Hunt v. Nuth*, 57 F.3d 1327 (4th Cir. 1995).

80. Peter Vilbig, "Innocent on Death Row; Cases of Innocent People Sentenced to Die," *New York Times Upfront* no. 2, vol. 133 (September 18, 2000), 10.

81. Ibid.

82. *Provenzano v. Moore,* 744 So. 2d 413 (Fla. 1999).

83. *Provenzano v. Moore,* 120 S. Ct. 1222, cert. denied 2000 U.S. LEXIS 1439.

84. Herbert H. Haines, *Against Capital Punishment: The Anti-Death Penalty Movement in America, 1972–1994,* (Oxford: Oxford University Press, 1996), 57–58.

85. Between 1984, when 283 defendants were sentenced to death, and 1999, when 272 received the sentence, the number of sentences fluctuated but has not shown a general upward or downward trend.

86. Tracy L. Snell, "Capital Punishment 1999," United States Department of Justice, Office of Justice Programs (December 2000), 12.

87. Ibid., 13.

88. "Death Row USA," NAACP Legal Defense and Educational Fund (January 2001).

89. Richard Dieter, "The Death Penalty in 2000: Year End Report," Death Penalty Information Center, December 2000. Since 1976, about 56 percent of all people executed have been white, and 35 percent have been black. "Death Penalty Profile," National Coalition to Abolish the Death Penalty (January 2001).

90. NAACP Legal Defense and Educational Fund, "Death Row U.S.A.: Winter 2000," Death Row U.S.A. Reporter.

91. Death Penalty Information Center's Web page, www.deathpenaltyinfo.org/women-stats.html.

92. Victor L. Streib, "Death Penalty for Female Offenders: January 1, 1973–June 30, 2000," available only on the World Wide Web at www.law.onu.edu/faculty/streib/femdeath.htm or www.law.onu.edu/faculty/streib/femdeath.pdf.

93. Sam Howe Verhovek, "AK-47's, Battery Acid; Dead Women Waiting: Who's Who on Death Row," *New York Times,* February 8, 1998, sec.4, pp. 1, 3.

94. Death Penalty Information Center's Web page, www.deathpenaltyinfo.org/juvchar.html. About three-quarters of these convicts committed the capital crime when they were seventeen years old.

95. Ibid., 9. See also Tracy L. Snell, "Capital Punishment 1998," United States Department of Justice, Office of Justice Programs, December 1999, 9; Tracy L. Snell, "Capital Punishment 1997," United States Department of Justice, Office of Justice Programs, December, 1998, 9; Tracy L. Snell, "Capital Punishment 1996," United States Department of Justice, Office of Justice Programs, December 1997, 8; Tracy L. Snell, "Capital Punishment 1995," United States Department of Justice, Office of Justice Programs, February 1997, 8; Tracy L. Snell and James J. Stephan, "Capital Punishment 1994," United States Department of Justice, Office of Justice Programs, February 1996, 8; James J. Stephan and Peter Brien, "Capital Punishment 1993," United States Department of Justice, Office of Justice Programs, December 1994.

96. The statistics in this paragraph come from Tracy L. Snell, "Capital Punishment 1999," United States Department of Justice, Office of Justice Programs, December 2000, 8.

97. Ibid.

98. Ibid.

99. Ibid., 9.

100. Ibid.

101. Richard Dieter, "The Death Penalty in 2000: Year End Report," Death Penalty Information Center, December 2000.

102. Ibid.

103. NAACP Legal Defense and Educational Fund, "Death Row U.S.A.: Winter 2000," *Death Row U.S.A. Reporter,* 9.

104. Death Penalty Information Center, "The Death Penalty in 2000: Year End Report," December 2000, available online at www.deathpenaltyinfo.org/yrendrpt00 html.

105. "Death Row U.S.A.: Winter 2000," *Death Row U.S.A. Reporter,* NAACP Legal Defense and Educational Fund, 1466.

106. "Death Penalty Profile," National Coalition to Abolish the Death Penalty, January 1, 2001, available at www.ncadp.org/stats.html.

107. Leigh B. Bienin, "The Proportionality Review of Capital Cases by State High Courts After Gregg: Only 'The Appearance of Justice'?" *Northwestern School of Law Journal of Criminal Law and Criminology* 87 (fall 1996): 170.

108. Ibid.

109. Ibid.

110. All except New Hampshire have sentenced criminals to death, so they have at least small death row populations. New Hampshire has not sentenced anyone to death, so it has no death row population. The federal government has a death row population of twenty-five people, but it has not conducted an execution since Victor Feguer was put to death in 1963.

111. Rick Bragg, "The McVeigh Execution: The Overview," *New York Times,* June 12, 2001, A1.

112. Richard Willing, "Even for Death Penalty Foes, McVeigh Is the Exception: Worst Mass Murder in U.S. History Tills Debate Over Capital Punishment," *USA Today,* May 4, 2001, 1A.

113. James S. Liebman, Jeffrey Fagan, and Valerie West, "A Broken System: Error Rates in Capital Cases, 1973–1995," June 12, 2000.

114. Ibid., i.

115. Ibid., ii.

116. Ibid., i.

117. Ibid.

118. *Dawson v. State,* 103 Nev 76 (1987).

119. Barry Latzer and James N. G. Cauthen, "Capital Appeals Revisited," *Judicature* 84, no. 2 (September–October 2000).

120. Ibid.

121. Ibid.

122. Ibid.

123. Ibid.

124. Liebman, et al., "A Broken System," 74.

125. Ibid. Each state has, however, successfully executed one or more persons since 1995.

126. Ibid.

127. Ibid.

128. Ibid., 57.

129. Ibid.

130. Ibid., 47.

131. See Bienen, "Criminal Law," 170: "The high courts of Texas, Florida, and California spend a substantial amount of time on capital appeals, and have a highly developed capital jurisprudence. However, goaded by political pressures, and staffed by judges who know they may be voted out of office if they reverse death sentences, these courts have almost become factories for affirmances." (Footnotes omitted.)

132. Jim Dwyer, Barry Scheck, and Peter Neufeld, *Actual Innocence: Five Days to Execution and Other Dispatches from the Wrongly Convicted* (New York: Doubleday), 2000.

133. Elizabeth A. Palmer, "The Death Penalty: Shifting Perspectives," *CQ Weekly,* June 3, 2000, 1324.

134. Ibid.

135. In the post-*Gregg* era, the use of clemency has mainly been a province of state executives, because the federal system carries out so few executions, and until recently, none had come up for review. Norman L. Greene, "Sparing Cain: Executive Clemency in Capital Cases," *Capital University Law Review* 28 (2000): 571.

136. Henry Weinstein, "Issue of Clemency Is Davis's Most Difficult as Governor," *Los Angeles Times,* February 6, 1991, A1.

137. M. Vandiver, "The Quality of Mercy: Race and Clemency in Florida Death Penalty Cases, 1924–1966," *University of Richmond Law Review* 27 (1993): 315.

138. "Death Penalty Profile," National Coalition to Abolish the Death Penalty, at www. nacdp.org/stats.html. Texas and Virginia each have systems where sentences are "commuted" when an appeals court delivers a favorable sentence to a capital convict—this oc-

curred forty-one times between 1976 and 2000, but these instances are generally not figured into the total numbers of commutations.

139. Greene, "Sparing Cain," 571.

140. M. Hansen, "Politics and the Death Penalty," *Palm Beach Review*, February 25, 1991, 10B.

141. "Pennsylvania Death Penalty Legislative Alert," Pennsylvania Coalition to Abolish the Death Penalty, July 1, 1996.

142. Elizabeth A. Palmer, "The Death Penalty: Shifting Perspectives," *CQ Weekly*, June 3, 2000, 1324.

143. Rachel Collins, "N.H. to Begin Hearings on Death Penalty Today Dozens to Testify About Bill Revisited By N.H. Legislators," *Boston Globe*, January 30, 2001, B8.

144. "Governor Ryan Declares Moratorium on Executions, Will Appoint Commission to Review Capital Punishment System," press release, January 31, 2000, available at www.state.il.us/gov/press/00/jan/morat.htm.

145. Ibid.

146. Illinois Governor's Executive Order Number 4 (2000), "Creating the Governor's Commission on Capital Punishment."

147. Governor Ryan press release, 2000.

148. "Fixing the Death Penalty," *Chicago Tribune*, December 29, 2000, 22.

149. Benjamin Soskis, "Alive and Kicking," *New Republic* (April 17–24, 2000): 26.

150. Benjamin Wallace, "States Follow Illinois Lead on Death Penalty," *Boston Globe*, February 9, 2000, A3.

151. Liebman et al., "A Broken System," ii.

152. Dirk Johnson, "Illinois, Citing Faulty Verdicts, Bars Executions," *New York Times*, February 1, 2000, 1.

153. Sean Higgins, "Death Penalty Is Still Popular in U.S., Despite Growing Campaign to End It," *Investor's Business Daily*, December 29, 2000, A22.

154. Richard Willing and Gary Fields, "Geography of the Death Penalty," *USA Today*, December 20, 1999, 1A.

155. Ibid.

156. Ibid.

157. Adam Nossiter, "Balking Prosecutors: A Door Opens to Death Row Challenges," *New York Times*, March 11, 1995, sec. 1, p. 27.

158. Melissa Block, "New York Governor Removes Bronx D.A. over Death Penalty," *Morning Edition* (National Public Radio), March 22, 1996, transcript #1830-5.

159. Howard Mintz, "Killer Wants Death but San Francisco DA Says 'No,'" *San Jose Mercury News*, January 9, 2001.

160. See, e.g., Craig Haney, "Riding the Punishment Wave: On the Origins of Our Devolving Standards of Decency," *Hastings Women's Law Journal* 9 (winter 1998): 48–49.

161. Gallup poll release, February 24, 2000.

162. See, e.g., *United States v. Pitera*, 795 F. Supp. 546, 569-70 (E.D.N.Y. 1992); and *United States v. Cooper*, 754 F. Supp. 617, 627 (N.D. Ill. 1990); see, e.g., George Kannar, "Federalizing Death," *Buffalo Law Review* 44 (spring 1996): 325; and Sandra D. Jordan, "Death for Drug Related Killings: Revival of the Federal Death Penalty," *Chicago—Kent Law Review* 67 (1991): 92.

163. Kannar, "Federalizing Death," 326.

164. Jason Berry, "Is Justice Forgiving?" *Dallas Morning News,* August 15, 1993, 1J.

165. Michael L. Radelet and Ronald L. Akers, "Policy and Perspective: Deterrence and the Death Penalty: The Views of the Experts," *Northwestern School of Law Journal of Criminal Law and Criminology* 87 (fall 1996): 7.

166. Bob Minzesheimer, "Executioner's Song Heard in Gubernatorial Races," *USA Today,* October 27, 1994, 9A.

167. Gary Marx, "Fear Takes Spotlight in Governor's Race," *Chicago Tribune,* October 19, 1994, A1.

168. S. Bright, "Judges and the Politics of Death: Deciding Between the Bill of Rights and the Next Election in Capital Cases," *Boston University Law Review* 75 (1995): 779.

169. J. Woods, "Public Outrage Nails a Judge," *Nashville Banner,* July 15, 1996, A1.

170. Ibid., 763–764.

171. Phoebe C. Ellsworth and Lee Ross, "Public Opinion and Capital Punishment: A Close Examination of the Views of Abolitionists and Retentionists," *Crime & Delinquency* 29 (1983): 145. ("Belief in the deterrent efficacy of the death penalty has generally been the rationale most frequently offered by Retentionists.")

172. *Gregg v. Georgia,* 428 U.S., 183.

173. Dan M. Kahan, "The Secret Ambition of Deterrence," *Harvard Law Review* 113 (December 1999): 436. The article argues that deterrence is only a symbolic issue that people really care less about than it would seem.

174. William C. Donnino, *Practice Commentary*, N.Y. Penal Law 125.27 (McKinney 1998). Quoting memorandum of New York governor George Pataki on the death penalty.

175. John Kaplan, "The Problem of Capital Punishment," *University of Illinois Law Review* (1983): 561.

176. Trisha Renaud, "Killer Asks Jurors, 'Why Take the Risk?' of Letting Him Live," *Fulton County Daily Report,* October 7, 1998.

177. Isaac Ehrlich, "The Deterrent Effect of Capital Punishment: A Question of Life and Death," *American Economic Review* 65 (1975): 397.

178. Hugo Bedeau, ed., *The Death Penalty in America*, 3d ed., 1982, 95.

179. See, e.g., Lawrence L. Klein et al., "The Deterrent Effect of Capital Punishment: An Assessment of the Estimates," in *Deterrence and Incapacitation: Estimating the Effects of Criminal Sanctions on Crime Rates*, Alfred Blumstein et al., eds., 1978.

180. Brian Frost, "Capital Punishment and Deterrence: Conflicting Evidence?" *Journal of Criminal Law and Criminology* 74 (1983): 927.

181. Ibid., 938.

182. Michael L. Radelet and Ronald L. Akers, "Policy and Perspective: Deterrence and the Death Penalty: The Views of the Experts," *Northwestern School of Law Journal of Criminal Law and Criminology* 87 (fall 1996): 3. Citing Raymond Paternoster, *Capital Punishment in America*, 1991, 217–245.

183. Radelet and Akers, "Policy and Perspective," 10.

184. Stephen K. Layson, "Homicide and Deterrence: A Reexamination of the United States Time-Series Evidence," *S. Econ. Journal* 52 (1985): 80.

185. Ibid.

186. James Alan Fox and Michael L. Radelet, "Persistent Flaws in Econometric Studies of the Deterrent Effect of the Death Penalty," *Loyola Los Angeles Law Review* 23 (1989): 29.

187. *Gregg*, 428 U.S. at p. 185–188.

188. Ibid., 185–186.

189. Ibid.

190. Ibid., 186.

191. "Seven in 10 Favor Death Penalty for Murder," *Gallup Report*, January–February 1986, 10.

192. Alec Gallup and Frank Newport, "Death Penalty Support Remains Strong," *Gallup Poll Monthly*, June 1991, 40.

193. "Seven in 10 Favor Death Penalty for Murder," 1986.

194. American Ethical Union, Resolution on Capital Punishment, adopted September 17, 1976.

195. John Lewis press release, "Crime Bill," *Congressional Press Releases*, August 17, 1994.

196. Lord Justice Denning, *Royal Commission on Capital Punishment, Minutes of Evidence*, December 1, 1949, 207.

197. *Gregg v. Georgia*, 428 U.S., 183.

198. Gallup Organization, *Gallup Report: The Death Penalty*, 1985, 3. Moreover, 51 percent of respondents said they would continue to support the death penalty even if it was conclusively proved that the punishment had no deterrent effect.

199. James O. Finckenauer, "Public Support for the Death Penalty: Retribution As Just Deserts or Retribution as Revenge?" *Justice Quarterly* 5 (1988): 90.

200. Patty Reinert and Richard Stewart, "Doctor Details 'Devastating Pain' of Dragging: Prosecutors Finish Case with Gruesome Testimony," *Houston Chronicle*, September 17, 1999, A33.

201. Paul Duggan, "Second Conviction in Dragging Death: Former Leader of White Supremacist Prison Group Faces Death Penalty in Texas," *Washington Post*, September 21, 1999, A2.

202. Exodus 21:24.

203. See Doug Janicik, "Allowing Victims' Families to View Executions: The Eighth Amendment and Society's Justifications for Punishment," *Ohio State Law Journal* 61 (2000): 967–969.

204. Gallup Poll, Gallup Organization, June 16, 1991, available in LEXIS, News Library, Rpoll File (question 2).

205. Elizabeth A. Brooks, "Thou Shalt Not Quote the Bible: Determining the Propriety of Attorney Use of Religious Philosophy and Themes in Oral Arguments," *Georgia Law Review* 30 (summer 1999).

206. See Earl F. Martin, "Tessie Hutchinson and the American System of Capital Punishment," *Maryland Law Review* 59 (2000): 585–588.

207. *Furman v. Georgia*, 408 U.S. at p. 343 (Marshall, J., concurring).

208. Ibid. at 304 (Brennan, J., concurring).

209. See Martin, "Tessie Hutchinson and the American System of Capital Punishment," 587–588.

210. "The Death Penalty in the Legislature: Some Thoughts about Money, Myth, and Morality," *University of Kansas Law Review* 37 (1989): 457.

211. "Against the American System of Capital Punishment," *Harvard Law Review* 99 (1986): 1687.

212. Death Penalty Information Center, www.deathpenaltyinfo.org/dpicrace.html.

213. "Death Row USA," NAACP Legal Defense and Educational Fund, January 2001.

214. Population Estimates Program, Population Division, U.S. Census Bureau, "Resident Population Estimates of the United States by Sex, Race, and Hispanic Origin," April 1, 1990–July 1, 1999, with Short-Term Projection to November 1, 2000.

215. Death Penalty Information Center, www.deathpenaltyinfo.org/dpicrace.html.

216. U.S. General Accounting Office, "Death Penalty Sentencing," 1990, 5–6.

217. U.S. Department of Justice, "The Federal Death Penalty System: A Statistical Survey

(1988–2000)," September 12, 2000. Available online at www.usdoj.gov/dag/pubdoc/dpsurvey.html.

218. Ibid.

219. Stephen J. Klein and John E. Rolph, "Relationship of Offender and Victim Race to Death Penalty Sentences in California," *Jurimetrics* 32 (1991): 33.

220. The study did not address the sentences that resulted from all crimes that were charged as capital crimes, but only those that actually progressed to the sentencing phase of trial. The researchers stated: "Our research dealt with the issue of possible racial bias in sentencing. . . . We did not examine possible bias at earlier stages such as police investigation and arrest practices, prosecutor charging decisions, case preparation, jury verdicts regarding guilt or innocence, and prosecutor requests for the death penalty." Ibid., 44.

221. See Dudley Sharpe, "Pro & Con: The Death Penalty in Black and White," *Justice for All*, available at www.prodeathpenalty.com/racism.htm; Dudley Sharpe, "Death Penalty and Sentencing Information in the United States," *Justice for All*, available at www.prodeath-penalty,com/DP.html#C; National Center for Policy Analysis, "Myth of Racism in Death Penalty," available at www.ncpa.org/pi/crime/pd111998d.html.

222. Dudley Sharpe, "Pro & Con."

223. Ernest van den Haag, "Refuting Reiman and Nathanson," in *Punishment and the Death Penalty*, eds. Robert M. Baird and Stuart E. Rosenbaum (Amherst, N.Y.: Prometheus Books, 1995), 207–214.

224. Sarah Koenig, "Racial Aspect Complicates Execution Issue; General Assembly Debates Moratorium, End to Death Penalty; Bills Compete for Support," *Baltimore Sun*, February 3, 2001, A1.

225. Ibid.

226. Ibid.

227. "Officials Hear Call for Moratorium on Death Penalty," *South Bend Tribune*, D4.

228. Paul O'Connor, "Racial Bias in Death Penalty Cases Gets a Closer Look," *Asheville Citizen-Times*, September 24, 2000, A10.

229. Steve Mills, "Texas Criticized on Death Penalty; Study by Defenders Group Says System Is Deeply Flawed, Biased," *Chicago Tribune*, October 16, 2000, 3.

230. Jennifer Hoyt, "Death Penalty Opponents Ask Clinton for Moratorium," *Houston Chronicle*, November 22, 2000, A9.

231. Ibid.

232. Craig Linder, "Calling for New Abu-Jamal Trial, Activists Meet With Justice Department," *States News Service*, December 11, 2000.

233. Sanford H. Kadish and Stephen J. Schulhofer, *Criminal Law and Its Processes*, 6th ed., 1995, 544.

234. *New York Times*, July 29, 1994, A1.

235. "Governor Ryan Declares Moratorium on Executions, Will Appoint Commission to Review Capital Punishment System," Governor Ryan press release, January 31, 2000, available at www.state.il.us/gov/press/00/jan/morat.htm.

236. Ibid.

237. Elizabeth A. Palmer, "The Death Penalty: Shifting Perspectives," *CQ Weekly*, June 3, 2000, 1324.

238. Elizabeth A. Palmer, "Congress Considers Taking a Role in Improving Quality of Counsel," *CQ Weekly*, June 3, 2000, 1324.

239. Barry Latzer and James N. G. Cauthen, "Capital Appeals Revisited," *Judicature* 84, no. 2 (September–October 2000).

3   Agencies, Organizations, and Individuals

Like most contentious public policy issues in the United States, capital punishment has strong supporters and opponents. These people's activities determine in part how, when, where, and why the death penalty is used in the United States. Some of these defenders and attackers are people who occupy positions of great institutional power, like the president and the justices of the U.S. Supreme Court. Others, such as the many interest groups dedicated to abolishing or bolstering the sentence, have no formal power but have effectively organized themselves in such a way that they exert formidable pressure on policymakers. Still others have worked to provide strong intellectual frameworks and arguments for both sides of the debate.

This part of the book discusses these various organizations and individuals who have a significant impact on U.S. death penalty policy. It examines nonprofit organizations, politicians, businesses, religious organizations, and others.

Important Abolitionist Organizations and Individuals

The anti–death penalty movement is comprised of many different organizations and individuals. Sometimes, these elements become linked by formal bonds of cooperation; some organizations even make it part of their mission to bind the organizations together to create a more effective movement. Often, however, the elements work together in more informal ways: each of several organizations or individuals decide to work on some common cause—appealing for clemency for a capital convict, for instance—and to bolster each other's efforts through the weight of numbers.

The abolitionists take many different angles on the issue. Some, like Amnesty International, oppose capital punishment because of human rights concerns. Others, like the National Association for the Advancement of Colored People (NAACP), are primarily concerned with issues of racial disparities in capital sentences. Still others, like many religious groups, take a purely moral approach to the death penalty.

Abolitionist, more than retentionist, organizations tend to maintain statistics about capital punishment. The Death Penalty Information Center, the NAACP's publication *Death Row USA,* and Amnesty International are all prime sources from which many political actors gather death penalty data. It is possible that abolitionists play this role more than retentionists because the anti–death penalty arguments often deal with the minutia of its application: error rates, discrepancies, and the large numbers of executions in certain states or counties. Death penalty supporters, on the other hand, tend to be more concerned with general issues of just deserts and victims' rights; their statistics often focus on numbers of murders and characteristics of murderers and their crimes.

Following are discussions of the most important players on the abolitionist scene. These include important nonprofit groups, religious groups, and influential individuals in the anti–death penalty movement.

Abolitionist Nonprofit Groups

ABOLITIONIST ACTION COMMITTEE. The Abolitionist Action Committee (AAC), "an ad-hoc group of individuals committed to highly visible and effective public education for alternatives to the death penalty through nonviolent direct action," is an affiliate of the Citizens United for Alternatives to the Death Penalty (CUADP). The AAC sponsors various actions to bring public attention to its abolitionist message. For instance, each year the group organizes a four-day vigil and fast in front of the Supreme Court to commemorate and protest the 1976 reinstatement of the death penalty and to urge a moratorium on executions.

Abolitionist Action Committee
c/o Citizens United for Alternatives to the Death Penalty
PMB 297
177 U.S. Hwy. #1
Tequesta, FL 33469
Phone: (800) 973-6548
Fax: (561) 743-4483

E-mail: aac@abolition.org
Web: www.abolition.org

AMERICAN BAR ASSOCIATION. The American Bar Association (ABA), the professional association for lawyers in the United States, provides accreditation for law schools and attorneys and seeks to "improve the legal system for the public." In 1986 the ABA injected itself into the death penalty debate by issuing a report on the capital justice system in America and calling for sixteen changes in the way the death penalty is applied.[1] When, in 1998, the ABA determined that these recommendations had not been followed and that "the crisis in capital cases has only worsened," it issued a resolution calling for a moratorium on executions until the problems it perceived could be fixed.[2]

The ABA takes no official position on the death penalty in theory (though it opposes the execution of retarded defendants on principle). It feels, however, that capital defendants in the United States are not currently guaranteed adequate legal representation and that racial discrimination causes the death penalty to be unfairly applied.[3] The 1998 resolution has been a very important development in the anti–death penalty movement, since the ABA has a membership of 400,000 lawyers and exerts quite a bit of influence in the legal world. Moreover, it is regarded as being fairly conservative about making political pronouncements. The ABA's resolution therefore lends an extra element of respectability to the moratorium movement and is often cited by death penalty opponents.

American Bar Association
740 15th St., NW
Washington, DC 20005-1019
Phone: (202) 662-1000
Fax: (202) 662-1032
E-mail: service@abanet.org
Web: www.abanet.org

American Bar Association Service Center
541 N. Fairbanks Ct.
Chicago, IL 60611
Phone: (312) 988-5522
E-mail: service@abanet.org
Web: www.abanet.org

AMERICAN CIVIL LIBERTIES UNION. The American Civil Liberties Union (ACLU) describes itself as "our nation's guardian of liberty, working daily in courts, legislatures and communities to defend the individual rights and liberties guaranteed to all people in this country by the Constitution and laws of the United States."[4] The

ACLU has been in the forefront of the anti–death penalty movement in the United States since 1965, when its board, after much debate, decided to include an anti–death penalty position in the organization's mandate. It was a primary planner and funder (along with the NAACP) of the legal challenges that led to the Supreme Court's decision in *Furman v. Georgia* (1972) that the death penalty as applied in the states was unconstitutional.[5] During the late 1960s and the 1970s, the ACLU also engaged in extensive lobbying and community education about the death penalty, working toward abolition.[6]

Since *Gregg v. Georgia* (1976) reinstated the death penalty, the ACLU has continued to push for abolition and limitation of the punishment and for greater due process protections for capital defendants. The organization operates an active anti–death penalty campaign, calling for a moratorium on all executions and appealing for clemency for capital convicts (though, according to some commentators, the ACLU has put less energy into its abolitionism than some other organizations have).[7] The main rhetorical focus of the campaign in recent years has been on issues of errors in capital sentencing and on perceived disparities in the application of the death penalty to minorities and the poor.

American Civil Liberties Union
125 Broad St.
New York, NY 10004-2400
Phone: (212) 549-2500
E-mail: aclu@aclu.org
Web: www.aclu.org

ACLU Capital Punishment Project
122 Maryland Ave., NE
Washington, DC 20002
Phone: (202) 675-2319
E-mail: DRust-Tierney@dcaclu.org
Web: www.aclu.org

AMNESTY INTERNATIONAL. Amnesty International was originally founded in 1961 as a human rights organization dedicated to the release of political prisoners around the world. Slowly, the organization expanded its repertoire, tackling more and more international human rights issues. It now describes itself as a "worldwide campaigning movement that works to promote all the human rights enshrined in the *Universal Declaration of Human Rights* and other international standards."[8]

Beginning in the 1970s, Amnesty brought a particular perspective to the death penalty debate: the notion that capital punishment is incompatible with international human rights standards.[9] Its opposition to the death penalty grew originally from its work on prisoners of conscience, as it opposed the death penalty for political prisoners. As the organization grew and gained prominence, it quickly moved to a position seeking worldwide abolition of the punishment. Amnesty believes that the fundamental human rights standards it promotes include a prohibition against the death penalty. It regards executions—particularly of mentally retarded persons, foreign nationals, and defendants who committed their crimes as juveniles—as violations of international law. Amnesty has also expressed deep concern about what it views as racism within the capital justice system in America and with errors in capital sentencing. In short, Amnesty believes that even "one execution is too many because, no matter how it is carried out, the death penalty is cruel, inhuman and degrading. It's an assault on human dignity and a violation of human rights."[10]

Amnesty's earliest public action against the death penalty in general came in 1971, when it asked the United Nations and the Council of Europe to work toward abolition and directed its own branch organizations in nations that retained the death penalty to work toward the same end.[11] Amnesty is now arguably the most important international abolitionist organization in the world. One important role it plays is maintaining a comprehensive database on death penalty practices worldwide. Much of this information can be accessed online at www.amnesty.org/rmp/dplibrary.nsf. Amnesty is perhaps the most authoritative source for such data—its information is routinely cited in academic works, by other nonprofit organizations, and even by the United Nations and national governments.

In addition to the international headquarters' focus on the death penalty worldwide, Amnesty International USA (AIUSA) has been a leader in the abolition movement in the United States. The organization supports abolitionist legislation, appeals for executive commutations, and stays of execution for death row inmates, and it cooperates with other U.S. organizations to press for a nationwide moratorium on executions.

Amnesty International
(international secretariat)
1 Easton St.
London, WC1X 0DW
England
E-mail: amnestyis@amnesty.org
Web: www.amnesty.org

Amnesty International USA
(national office)
322 Eighth Ave.
New York, NY 10001
Phone: (212) 807-8400
Fax: (212) 627-1451
E-mail: admin-us@aiusa.org
Web: www.amnestyusa.org

Amnesty International USA
Program to Abolish the Death Penalty
600 Pennsylvania Ave., SE
Fifth Floor
Washington, DC 20003
Phone: (202) 544-0200
Fax: (202) 546-7142
E-mail: www.amnestyusa.org/abolish/

BENETTON. In 1999 and 2000 the Italian clothing manufacturer Benetton, following the lead of photographer Oliviero Toscani, mounted a controversial advertising campaign that featured sympathetic photographs of U.S. death row inmates.[12] The photographs lacked any accompanying text about their crimes or victims, outraging victims' rights groups.[13] Although the company ended the campaign in March 2000 and severed its ties with Toscani, the advertisements may have been effective at drumming up anti–death penalty sentiments.[14] One of the twenty-six inmates featured in the advertisements, Bobbie Lee Harris, received a stay of execution from the North Carolina Supreme Court.[15] The campaign also caused one major client, Sears, Roebuck & Co., to stop selling Benetton products.[16]

Benetton Group Spa
Villa Minelli
31050 Ponzano, Treviso
Italy
Phone: 39-0422-519111
Fax: 39-0422-969501
Web: www.benetton.com

CITIZENS UNITED FOR ALTERNATIVES TO THE DEATH PENALTY. Citizens United for Alternatives to the Death Penalty (CUADP) "works to end the death penalty in the United States through aggressive campaigns of public education, and the promotion of tactical grassroots activism." CUADP attempts to use the mass media to convince the American public that the death penalty is "bad public policy." It also tries to foster effective grassroots organizing in support of abolition.

In 2001 CUADP sponsored an eighty-mile march from the federal courthouse in

Indianapolis to the federal prison in Terre Haute, Indiana, to protest the impending execution of David Paul Hammer (stopped when Hammer decided to resume his appeals). CUADP also runs a campaign to encourage voters to support anti–death penalty politicians. In the 2000 presidential election, the organization was a vocal critic of George W. Bush, whom it dubbed a "serial killer" because of the many executions imposed during his tenure as governor of Texas—more than any other in the state's history.

Citizens United for Alternatives to the Death Penalty
PMB 297
177 U.S. Hwy. #1
Tequesta, FL 33469
Phone: (800) 973-6548
E-mail: cuadp@cuadp.org
Web: www.cuadp.org

DEATH PENALTY INFORMATION CENTER. The Death Penalty Information Center (DPIC) describes itself as "a nonprofit organization serving the media and the public with analysis and information on issues concerning capital punishment. The Center was founded in 1990 and prepares in-depth reports, issues press releases, conducts briefings for journalists, and serves as a resource to those working on this issue." Despite this neutral-sounding depiction, the DPIC is decidedly abolitionist.

The DPIC does not pursue a strategy of proactive advocacy. Rather, it makes its mark on the political scene by disseminating information. The organization maintains a large database of information about capital punishment in America, and its Web site, www.deathpenaltyinfo.org, is an especially useful resource for readers seeking statistics. It also issues many reports about problems it perceives with the death penalty. Each year the DPIC publishes a year-end report describing important events relating to capital punishment, and it has published reports on international condemnation of U.S. policy, racial disparities in the application of the death penalty, capital error rates, and many other topics. These writings make the DPIC an important player in the death penalty debate because it is so frequently cited by anti–death penalty organizations and politicians.

Death Penalty Information Center
1320 18th St., NW
Fifth Floor
Washington, DC 20036
Phone: (202) 293-6970
Fax: (202) 822-4787
E-mail: dpic@essential.org
Web: www.deathpenaltyinfo.org

EQUAL JUSTICE USA. Equal Justice USA, a project of the Quixote Center, was launched in 1990 to work toward abolition of the death penalty. Its most important contribution to the anti–death penalty movement is its Moratorium Now campaign, an effort to encourage legislatures, organizations, and others to pass resolutions supporting a moratorium on executions. It has also conducted grassroots campaigns on behalf of convicted killer and death row inmate Mumia Abu-Jamal, whose case has become a rallying point for many who believe that the capital justice system suffers from problems with racial justice.

Equal Justice USA claims to have recruited more than 1,600 organizations to pass moratorium resolutions, including forty city councils. The organization maintains a list of these groups that can be found at www.quixote.org/ej/. In 2001 Equal Justice USA convinced the New York State Bar Association, the city of Cary, North Carolina, and others to support the effort. It was also instrumental in inducing the Maryland House of Representatives to pass a moratorium bill. Equal Justice USA provides organizing advice and expertise for grassroots groups seeking moratoriums in their own states, including sample moratorium resolutions.

Equal Justice USA
P.O. Box 5206
Hyattsville, MD 20782
Phone: (301) 699-0042
Fax: (301) 864-2182
E-mail: ejusa@quixote.org
Web: www.quixote.org/ej/

HANDS OFF CAIN. Originally founded in Italy, Hands off Cain is an international organization of citizens and parliamentarians dedicated to achieving a worldwide moratorium on executions. In the 1990s Hands off Cain played an important role in the abolition movement in Europe by pushing the European Union and United Nations to adopt abolitionist positions. Hands off Cain was a driving force behind Italy's 1994 proposal that the United Nations (UN) support a ban on capital punishment. Although the proposal did not win the support of the UN that year, similar resolutions against the death penalty have been adopted every year since 1997.

Hands off Cain has also organized several regional and international conferences on death penalty abolition, including the first pan-Arab conference on the death penalty. It continues to push for abolition in all nations. Hands off Cain states that its main focus is to mobilize public and parliamentarian opinion to convince the European Union to adopt an anti–death penalty resolution that did not reach a vote in 1999.[17]

Hands off Cain
(Rome office)
Via di Torre Argentina 76-00186 Rome
Italy
Phone: 39-06-689-791
Fax: 39-06-689-79211
E-mail: hands.off.cain@agora.it

Hands off Cain
(Brussels–European parliament office)
60, Rue Wiertz
2H 356 -1047
Bruxelles, Belgium
Phone: 32-2-284-3377
Fax: 32-2-284-6566

Hands off Cain (New York office)
866 U.N. Plaza #408
New York, NY 10017
Phone: (212) 813-1334
Fax: (212) 980-1072
Web: www.handsoffcain.org

HUMAN RIGHTS WATCH. Human Rights Watch (HRW), another international organization with a vital role in the death penalty debate, is well known and well respected as a human rights "watchdog" group. It opposes the use of capital punishment by any nation "because of its inherent cruelty," and it regards the death penalty as a violation of international human rights standards.

HRW has a presence in domestic U.S. politics because, in cases in which it finds an execution to be "particularly egregious," it often takes steps to raise media and public awareness about the issues surrounding the case. In 2001 HRW began to pay special attention to the execution of the mentally retarded in some states. The group wrote a protest letter to the governors of those states, requesting changes,[18] published an extensive report about the execution of the mentally retarded in the United States,[19] and issued press releases to highlight the issue.[20]

Human Rights Watch	Human Rights Watch
(New York office)	(District of Columbia office)
350 Fifth Ave.	1630 Connecticut Ave., NW
34th Floor	Suite 500
New York, NY 10118-3299	Washington, DC 20009
Phone: (212) 290-4700	Phone: (202) 612-4321
Fax: (212) 736-1300	Fax: (202) 612-4333
E-mail: hrwnyc@hrw.org	E-mail: hrwdc@hrw.org
Web: www.hrw.org	Web: www.hrw.org

MORATORIUM 2000. Moratorium 2000 is an international "campaign to obtain an immediate moratorium on the death penalty."[21] Its primary mode of action is a global petition drive: according to the group's Web site, by the end of 2000, Moratorium 2000 had collected 3.2 million signatures supporting a halt to the death penalty. Secretary General Kofi Annan of the United Nations accepted the petition, saying, "I am deeply moved, as well as pleased, to accept this petition for a universal moratorium on executions, signed by over three million people in over 130 countries around the world. On behalf of the United Nations, I accept your petition, and I congratulate all those who have worked so hard to collect so many signatures. I wish it were in my power to grant their wish, and by so doing to save the lives of thousands of men and women."[22]

The group also helped generate public pressure on President Bill Clinton in his last months in office to commute the death sentence of David Ronald Chandler. Convicted in 1991 of running a marijuana-trafficking ring and of the murder of an associate who became an informer for government agents, Chandler was in line to be the first federally executed man since 1963. In his final hours in office, the president granted him executive clemency.

Moratorium 2000's honorary chairperson is Sister Helen Prejean, author of the book *Dead Man Walking: An Eyewitness Account of the Death Penalty in the United States* and a famous anti–death penalty advocate.

Moratorium 2000
P.O. Box 13727
New Orleans, LA 70185-3727
Phone: (504) 864-1071
Fax: (504) 864-1654
E-mail: info@moratorium2000.org
Web: www.moratorium2000.org

NAACP LEGAL DEFENSE AND EDUCATIONAL FUND. The NAACP Legal Defense and Educational Fund (LDF) is a spin-off of the National Association for the Advancement of Colored People, "the nation's largest and strongest civil rights organization." The LDF has long been a leader in the anti–death penalty movement. Its opposition to the death penalty grew from its work in defending black capital defendants in the South who had no other sources for competent criminal defense lawyers. Over time the LDF lawyers grew to believe that the death penalty was inequitably applied, and the organization decided to oppose its use on those grounds.[26]

The LDF has been a primary moving force behind the race-based constitutional challenges to the death penalty. It handled William Furman's appeal that led to the Supreme Court's groundbreaking decision in *Furman v. Georgia*. The LDF continued to be legally active after *Gregg* reinstated capital punishment, bringing the constitutional challenge based on racial disparities in *McCleskey v. Kemp* (1987).

The LDF continues to call for a moratorium on executions, focusing its attention mainly on issues of racism in the application of capital punishment. Among other things, the LDF publishes *Death Row USA*, a quarterly journal containing statistics on the race and gender of death row inmates and persons who have been executed and on the races of their victims, nationally and in the states. Because of its long history of service to communities of color and its strong national reputation as a champion of civil rights, the LDF is an important player in the anti–death penalty movement.

NAACP Legal Defense and Educational Fund (national headquarters)
99 Hudson St.
16th Floor
New York, NY 10013-2897
Phone: (800) 221-7822
Fax: (212) 219-1595

NATIONAL ASSOCIATION OF CRIMINAL DEFENSE LAWYERS. The National Association of Criminal Defense Lawyers (NACDL) is a trade organization that represents the interests of criminal defense attorneys. It describes itself as "the preeminent organization in the United States advancing the mission of the nation's criminal defense lawyers to ensure justice and due process for persons accused of crime or other misconduct." Not surprisingly, the NACDL opposes the death penalty. It is an important lobbying group on Capitol Hill, supporting legislation that would protect criminal defendants, including those accused of capital crimes.

In 2001 the NACDL was involved in lobbying on behalf of the Innocence Protection Act, a bill the organization believes would reduce the risk of execution of an innocent person. The bill's most important features would expand defendants' access to DNA testing and provide funding to help states improve the quality of their capital defense systems.

National Association of Criminal Defense Lawyers
1025 Connecticut Ave., NW
Suite 901
Washington, DC 20036
Phone: (202) 872-8600
Fax: (202) 872-8690
E-mail: assist@nacdl.com
Web: www.criminaljustice.org and www.nacdl.org

NATIONAL COALITION TO ABOLISH THE DEATH PENALTY. Another group involved in the anti–death penalty movement in America for decades is the National Coalition to Abolish the Death Penalty (NCADP). The NCADP describes itself as "a coalition of organizations and individuals committed to the abolition of capital punishment, [that] provides information, advocates for public policy and mobilizes and supports people and institutions that share our unconditional rejection of the state's use of homicide as an instrument of social policy."[23] The organization was formed in 1976, after the Supreme Court reinstated the death penalty. It was originally intended to serve as a voice for the nation's abolitionists and to coordinate anti–death penalty activities around the country. It now consists of a large network of organizations with abolitionist positions, including Amnesty International USA, the NAACP, and many state-level groups.

The NCADP has at times advocated civil disobedience and similar radical protest gestures to draw attention its cause, though it now pursues an "incremental" strategy intended gradually to limit the applications of the death penalty until it can be phased out completely.[24] In the early 1990s the NDACP operated a campaign called STOP IT! designed to expose what it felt was the cynical manner in which political candidates were using the issue.[25] In 1994 it launched the Mess With Texas campaign to bolster the weak opposition to the death penalty in the state that conducts by far the most executions in the United States.

The NCADP fills an important role in the abolitionist movement as a link between various anti–death penalty organizations. It publishes *Lifelines,* a bi-monthly newsletter; *National Execution Alert,* a profile of death row inmates with imminent execution dates; and the *Abolitionist Directories,* a comprehensive listing of abolitionist groups and individuals in the United States. The list is now on-line at www. ncadp.org/abdir-index.html.

National Coalition to Abolish the Death Penalty
1436 U St., NW
Suite 104
Washington DC, 20009
Phone: (888) 286-2237
Fax: (202) 387-5590
E-mail: info@ncadp.org
Web: www.ncadp.org

SOUTHERN COALITION ON JAILS AND PRISONS. The Southern Coalition on Jails and Prisons (SCJP) "works throughout the South to assist prisoners and their families, reform the criminal justice system, establish alternatives to incarceration, and abolish the death penalty." The organization, through direct-action tactics, has played an important role in garnering visibility for the abolition movement.[27] In 1976, after the Supreme Court reinstated the death penalty, the SCJP coordinated vigils in several states to protest upcoming executions[28] and organized dramatic protests in the streets.[29] This role was especially vital to the movement in the early years after *Gregg* because of the organizational weakness of such institutions as the National Coalition to Abolish the Death Penalty and the ACLU's Capital Punishment Project.

Southern Coalition on Jails and Prisons
Reverend Joseph B. Ingle, director
P.O. Box 30065
Nashville, TN 37202.
Phone: (615) 242-5131

VARIOUS STATE AND LOCAL ABOLITIONIST ORGANIZATIONS. Every death penalty state has at least a few organizations dedicated to abolishing capital punishment or to achieving a moratorium on executions in that state in particular. While no single state or local organization has a nationwide impact on death penalty policy, these groups can be extremely important in local and state politics and in the aggregate serve as an effective nationwide network.

This group of organizations is very diverse. It includes state organizations specifically created to oppose capital punishment, like Alaskans Against the Death Penalty or the Washington Coalition to Abolish the Death Penalty. It also includes local affiliates of national organizations, like local ACLU and Amnesty International chapters. Finally, some of the groups were formed for other reasons but have adopted an abolitionist stance; for example, many state public defender associations fall into this category.

A fairly comprehensive list of state and local anti–death penalty organizations is *The Abolitionist Directories,* published by the National Coalition to Abolish the Death Penalty. It can be found on-line at www.ncadp.org.

Abolitionist Religious Organizations

AMERICAN FRIENDS SERVICE COMMITTEE. The American Friends Service Committee (AFSC) is "a Quaker organization that includes people of various faiths who are committed to social justice, peace, and humanitarian service. Its work is based on the Religious Society of Friends (Quaker) belief in the worth of every person, and faith in the power of love to overcome violence and injustice. [30] Believing that capital punishment is immoral, the organization has played a central role in the anti–death penalty movement for several decades. In fact, it was the AFSC that donated the first office space to the National Coalition to Abolish the Death Penalty in 1983.[31]

The AFSC has been instrumental in organizing religious groups to oppose the death penalty. In 1990 the group joined several others in launching the Lighting the Torch of Conscience campaign, designed to publicize major religious organizations' opposition to capital punishment and to spur local religious involvement in the issue.[32] The AFSC now runs the Religious Organizing Against the Death Penalty Project, which was "created to galvanize and empower the religious community in the United States to work against capital punishment."[33]

American Friends Service Committee
1501 Cherry St.
Philadelphia, PA 19102
Phone: (215) 241-7000
Fax: (215) 241-7275
E-mail: afscinfo@afsc.org
Web: www.afsc.org

Religious Organizing Against the Death Penalty Project
c/o Criminal Justice Program
American Friends Service Committee
1501 Cherry St.
Philadelphia, PA 19102
Phone: (215) 241-7130
Fax (215) 241-7119
E-mail: information@deathpenaltyreligious.org
Web: www.deathpenaltyreligious.org

CATHOLIC CHURCH.   The Catholic Church, led by Pope John Paul II, has called for a moratorium on the death penalty.[34] The church's new Catechism, published by the Vatican in 1997, indicates the skeptical view with which the church approaches capital punishment.[35] While the teaching does allow for the death penalty "if this is the only possible way of effectively protecting human lives against the unjust aggressor," it pronounces the church's belief that such cases are "practically nonexistent" in today's world, and that governments should limit themselves to nonlethal punishments. Such sentences, according to official church doctrine, are "more in keeping with the concrete conditions of the common good and more in conformity with the dignity of the human person."[36]

The Catholic Church has put direct pressure on various government actors in the United States to enact a moratorium. While in St. Louis, Missouri, in January 1999, the pope made an appeal to all nations to end the use of the death penalty.[37] The pope and the church have also been active in urging executive clemency for numerous death row inmates. In one case that same year, the pope persuaded Missouri governor Mel Carnahan, a proponent of the death penalty, to commute the sentence of Darrell Mease. Carnahan claimed that his action was essentially a favor to the pope, calling it a "one-time act of mercy."[38]

Various U.S. branches of the church are independently active in the anti–death penalty movement, as well. The United States–based Catholics Against Capital Punishment, along with the U.S. Catholic bishops, support a moratorium on the death penalty.[39]

Vatican City State
Web: www.vatican.va

National Conference of Catholic Bishops/
   United States Catholic Conference
3211 4th St., NE
Washington, DC 20017-1194
Phone: (202) 541-3000
Fax: (202) 541-3322
Web: www.nccbuscc.org

SOUTHERN CHRISTIAN LEADERSHIP CONFERENCE. The Southern Christian Leadership Conference (SCLC), originally founded by the Reverend Martin Luther King Jr. and other civil rights activists in the late 1950s, describes itself this way:

The SCLC is committed to non-violent action to achieve social, economic, and political justice. Believing in the one-ness of the human family and the efficacy of love in human relations, the SCLC holds that authentic love demands movement against injustice as a moral imperative. With roots grounded in the Black church, SCLC is considered the alter-ego, the social arm of this religious institution.[40]

The SCLC has been involved with the anti–death penalty movement for some time. It organized and cosponsored the 1990 Lighting the Torch of Conscience campaign, which was designed to publicize major religious organizations' opposition to capital punishment and to spur local religious involvement in the issue.[41] The SCLC has been active in forging links between the abolitionist movement and the black community, for whom the organization has considerable historic importance.[42]

Southern Christian Leadership Conference
334 Auburn Ave., NE
Atlanta, GA 30312
Phone: (404) 522-1420
Fax: (404) 659-7390
E-mail: sclchq@bellsouth.net
Web: www.sclcnational.org

OTHER RELIGIOUS GROUPS. The leaders of many religious groups and denominations have declared abolitionist positions or supported a moratorium on executions. While no one of these groups has had a significant impact on the anti–death penalty movement, they are important in combination. For one thing, their messages likely impact the opinions of their congregants. More importantly, perhaps, the overall weight of the combined religious thought on the topic can be quite persuasive. The organizations include, among others:

- Baptist Church
- Christian Church (Disciples of Christ)
- Church of the Brethren
- Episcopal Church
- Evangelical Lutheran Church

- Conference of General Baptists
- Mennonite Church
- Moravian Church in America
- Orthodox Church
- Presbyterian Church
- Rabbinical Assembly
- Reorganized Church of Jesus Christ of Latter-Day Saints
- The Dalai Lama
- Union of American Hebrew Congregations
- Unitarian Universalist Association
- United Church of Christ
- United Methodist Church

Important Abolitionist Individuals

PROFESSOR JAMES S. LIEBMAN. Professor James S. Liebman of the Columbia University School of Law is the author of "A Broken System: Error Rates in Capital Cases, 1973–1995," an influential (and controversial) study released in June 2000 that discusses the number of capital cases in which erroneous convictions or sentences were imposed. Liebman's paper presents an in-depth look at error rates in the nation and in each state over time, and paints a bleak picture about the reliability of the capital justice system in the United States. Among other things, Liebman found that, between 1973 and 1995, 68 percent of all capital sentences reviewed in the United States contained "prejudicial error."[43]

Liebman's evidence about error rates, in combination with other studies about the death penalty, has had an enormous effect on the abolition movement. Anti–death penalty advocates have begun to focus their rhetoric on practical problems with the death penalty, like error rates. These tactics have arguably led to considerable success: Gov. George Ryan, R-Ill., recently called a halt to all executions in his state because of error rates, and other states are at least considering similar moves.

SISTER HELEN PREJEAN. Sister Helen Prejean is a Catholic nun who has devoted much of her career to the abolition of the death penalty. In 1981, while working in New Orleans, she became the pen pal of convicted killer Patrick Sonnier. Soon, she began to visit him regularly in prison and became his spiritual advisor. After his execution, she turned her experience with the Louisiana capital justice system into a Pulitzer Prize–nominated book, *Dead Man Walking: An Eyewitness Account of the Death Penalty in the United States,* which topped the *New York Times* bestseller list for thirty-one weeks and was made into a popular film.[44]

In the years since her encounters with Sonnier, Sister Prejean has become an important voice against the death penalty in the United States. She has witnessed five executions in Louisiana, continues to counsel death row inmates, works to educate the public about this issue, and has served on the board of directors of the National Coalition to Abolish the Death Penalty and as Honorary Chairperson of Moratorium 2000. Among her numerous other awards, Sister Prejean was nominated for the 1998, 1999, and 2000 Nobel Peace Prizes for her work against the death penalty.

Sister Helen Prejean
c/o Moratorium 2000
P.O. Box 13727
New Orleans, LA 70185-3727
Phone: (504) 864-1071
Fax: (504) 864-1654
Contact: Sister Margaret Maggio (504) 948-6557

JOHN PAUL II. The pope has been an important critic of capital punishment in the United States and worldwide. For more information, see the entry for the Catholic Church.

Important Retentionist Groups and Individuals

Overall, there are many fewer organizations that support the death penalty than oppose it. This is almost surely the case because capital punishment is the status quo in the United States. The death penalty is constitutionally permitted and on the books at the federal level and in thirty-eight states; executions are on the rise; and a majority of the U.S. electorate supports the punishment. Capital punishment supporters do not need to form a large network of organizations that work to protect the death penalty.

On the other hand, there are quite a large number of important individual death penalty supporters. Many are politicians in positions of power, whose presence in government ensures the continuation of the death penalty in the United States.

Retentionist Nonprofit Organizations

CRIMINAL JUSTICE LEGAL FOUNDATION. The Criminal Justice Legal Foundation (CJLF) describes itself as "a nonprofit public interest law organization dedicated to restoring a balance between the rights of crime victims and the criminally accused. The Foundation's purpose is to [en]sure that people who are guilty of committing crimes receive swift and certain punishment in an orderly and thoroughly constitutional manner." The foundation pursues a judicial strategy for achieving these goals, bringing certain cases before state and federal appellate courts to encourage precedent-setting decisions and filing amicus curiae briefs in other cases it feels are important.

The CJLF has, through its courthouse strategies, been an important supporter and protector of the death penalty in the United States. For instance, it filed an amicus curiae brief in the important case *Payne v. Tennessee* (1991), in which the Supreme Court decided that prosecutors could present "victim impact" evidence to juries during the sentencing phase of a capital trial (a decision that accorded with CJLF's position). The foundation has also argued several recent Supreme Court cases, including *United States v. Jones* (1999), in which the Court decided not to overturn capital sentences because of possibly faulty jury instructions. Furthermore, the CJLF has been quite active in shaping the several Supreme Court and Federal Appellate Court cases that have addressed the death penalty provisions of the Antiterrorism and Effective Death Penalty Act.

Criminal Justice Legal Foundation
P.O. Box 1199
Sacramento, CA 95816
Phone: (916) 446-0345
Fax: (916) 446-1194
E-mail: rushford@cjlf.org
Web: www.cjlf.org

JUSTICE FOR ALL. Justice for All (JFA) is a Houston-based victims' rights organization headed by Diane Clements, the mother of a murdered boy. JFA describes itself as "an advocate for change in a criminal justice system that is inadequate in protecting the lives and property of law abiding citizens." The organization pursues a variety of legislative ends, including the elimination of probation as a sentencing option for murderers, the extension of the statute of limitations for sexual assault crimes, and the enactment of a law prohibiting felons from "profiting from their notoriety" through book deals and the like.

In addition to its other goals, Justice for All is strongly pro–death penalty. It opposes attempts to impose moratoriums on executions or abolish the death penalty, including for retarded convicts. Although the group operates mostly within Texas, it has a national presence in the death penalty debate—a prominence due in part to the large number of executions that occur in the state. JFA supported the execution of Texas convicted murderer Gary Graham, whose case involved charges of racial discrimination. Clements charged that "Gary Graham is guilty of the capital murder he was tried for,"[45] and she argued that he deserved to be put to death.

Justice For All organizes pro–death penalty demonstrations, lobbies the Texas legislature, publishes a monthly newsletter called "The Voice of Justice," and maintains several Web sites: www.jfa.net, www.prodeathpenalty.com, and www. murder-victims.com.

Justice for All
P.O. Box 55159
Houston, TX 77255
Phone: (713) 935-9300
Fax: (713) 935-9301
E-mail: info@jfa.net
Web: www.jfa.net, www.prodeathpenalty.com, www.murder-victims.com

NATIONAL ASSOCIATION OF POLICE ORGANIZATIONS. The National Association of Police Organizations (NAPO) is "a coalition of police unions and associations from across the United States that serves to advance the interests of America's law enforcement officers through legislative and legal advocacy, political action and education."[46] NAPO, like many police organizations, supports the death penalty.

The association is important in the death penalty debate because of its endorsements of political aspirants. In 1992, for instance, presidential candidate Clinton received the endorsement of NAPO in part because of his support for the death penalty, and he used that endorsement to counter critics.[47] Similarly, Florida chief justice Rosemary Barkett, who was nominated in 1994 for a seat on the Eleventh U.S. Circuit Court of Appeals, defended herself in the Senate against accusations that she would "paralyze the use of the death penalty in [the United States]" by citing her endorsement from NAPO.[48]

National Association of Police Organizations
750 First St., NE
Suite 920
Washington, DC 20002-4241
Phone: (202) 842-4420
Fax: (202) 842-4396
E-mail: napo@erols.com
Web: www.napo.org

NATIONAL CENTER FOR VICTIMS OF CRIME. While the National Center for Victims of Crime (NCVC) is not officially dedicated to death penalty issues, the organization is included in this section because it has been instrumental in the victims' rights movement. Seeking more inclusion in the criminal process for victims of crimes and a legal system that takes victims' interests into account, the victims' rights movement has had an important impact on death penalty policy in the United States. Victims' rights organizations, for instance, lobbied for the use of "victim impact" statements in the penalty phase of capital trials, arguing in their favor in the Supreme Court in *Payne v. Tennessee.*

The NCVC has undertaken two efforts that could affect the capital justice system. The first is an effort to change the way executive clemency works. The organization hopes to push legislation in all fifty states and at the federal level that would require executives empowered to make clemency decisions to notify the criminals' victims of upcoming clemency hearings and to hear statements by the victims.[49] The NCVC is also working on an effort to encourage amendment of all state and the federal constitutions to require that victims be given certain rights, including the right to present victim impact statements during sentencing hearings. This would change the current capital trial procedure of most states from a system in which prosecutors may use victim impact evidence if they wish to one in which prosecutors would be required to use the evidence if the victims so desired.

National Center for Victims of Crime
2000 M St., NW
Suite 480
Washington, DC 20036
Phone: (202) 467-8700
Fax: (202) 467-8701
Web: www.ncvc.org

NATIONAL DISTRICT ATTORNEY ASSOCIATION. The National District Attorney Association (NDAA), the nation's largest organization of prosecuting attorneys, is another important voice in the death penalty debate. The NDAA's support for capital punishment reflects a common position of prosecuting attorneys in the United States, and its presence helps counter the large block of legal organizations that support a moratorium or abolition. In 1997, for instance, when the American Bar Association called for a moratorium on the death penalty, the NDAA was a vocal critic of the resolution, arguing:

> The nation's prosecutors, who are in effect the people's attorneys, faithfully execute these laws, as do our courts. To ask for a moratorium on the execution of any law is to ask that the people's will be thwarted and to denigrate the legislative and criminal justice processes. Whatever the ABA's concerns about capital punishment, this is not the way for any group, and especially the nation's largest association of lawyers, to seek changes in the capital punishment laws.[50]

The NDAA has long been active in answering concerns about the execution of innocent people. The issue's recent prominence has pushed the organization to the forefront of the rhetorical battle. Since Illinois governor Ryan declared a moratorium on executions in his state because of concerns about errors, the national media has focused on that particular aspect of the debate. The NDAA has served as an important bullhorn for the opinions of district attorneys, the lawyers in the United States who prosecute capital crimes on a day-to-day basis.

National District Attorney Association
99 Canal Center Plaza
Alexandria, VA 22314
Telephone: (703) 549-9222

Fax: (703) 836-3195
E-mail: webmaster@ndaa-apri.org
Web: www.ndaa.org

NATIONAL ORGANIZATION FOR VICTIM ASSISTANCE. The National Organization for Victim Assistance (NOVA) is the oldest and one of the most important victims' rights organizations in the country. Although it is not specifically dedicated to death penalty advocacy, it is included in this section because it has been instrumental in the victims' rights movement.

NOVA has worked almost since its inception to convince states and the federal government to allow the use of "victim impact" statements in the penalty phase of capital trials. These are statements by victims of a crime, or their relatives, about the impact the crime has had on their lives. In *Payne*, the Supreme Court considered whether such statements should be allowed in capital trials. NOVA, along with several other victims' rights organizations, submitted a brief arguing that such statements should be allowed, and their position prevailed in the Court. NOVA now works on several efforts relevant to death penalty policy, including an endeavor to pass an amendment to the U.S. Constitution that would guarantee crime victims, among other things, the right to make victim impact statements at various times during the judicial process.

National Organization for Victim Assistance
1730 Park Rd., NW
Washington, DC 20010
Phone: (202) 232-6682
Fax: (202) 462-2255
E-mail: nova@try-nova.org
Web: www.try-nova.org

REPUBLICAN PARTY. The Republican Party in the United States has long supported capital punishment, and its stance is no different today. In its 2000 platform, the party expressed support for the death penalty. Because of the party's importance in national and local-level politics, this issue position can be extremely important in determining federal and state policies about capital punishment.

Like the Democratic Party, the Republican Party has control of large sums of funding for political candidates, and it hands out vital endorsements. The party can easily affect the outcome of many electoral races by withholding money or an endorsement. Although the party has no explicit requirement that candidates running as Republicans have any particular stand on any issue, opposing the death penalty can hurt a hopeful Republican's chance of receiving the party's full support.

One extreme example occurred in Tennessee. In 1996 state supreme court justice Penny White rendered a decision overturning a death sentence on technical grounds, a decision that angered Republican Party officials. In the next election (like many states, Tennessee elects its supreme court justices), the party put its full efforts into opposing White's reelection, withholding its endorsement and sponsoring advertisements criticizing the justice's death penalty record. In the heavily Republican state, the party's tactics worked, and she was not reelected.[51] Although this vehemence is unusual for a judge that generally favored the death penalty, it illustrates the power of the Republican Party to influence elections: a power that the party does on occasion wield to support capital punishment.

Republican National Committee
310 First St., SE
Washington, DC 20003
Phone: (202) 863-8500
Fax: (202) 863-8820
E-mail: info@rnc.org
Web: www.rnc.org

WASHINGTON LEGAL FOUNDATION. The Washington Legal Foundation (WLF) is a "nonprofit public interest law and policy center based in Washington, D.C." Its main goal, according to its literature, is "to defend and promote the principles of free enterprise and individual rights." Among its activities, the foundation advocates and litigates in favor of capital punishment. The WLF pursues this mission through three primary methods: aggressive litigation and policy advocacy, academic legal scholarship, and education of policymakers.

The WLF is not the most visible actor in death penalty politics, though its name sometimes appears in newspaper articles alongside a quote defending capital punishment.[52] The foundation's Web site does not even mention a concern with death penalty policy. Its quiet, behind-the-scenes activities, however, make the WLF a very important player in protecting the death penalty from abolition. The foundation pursues and argues court cases that serve a pro–death penalty position, and it often files amicus curiae briefs in important cases with which it is not directly involved. In fact, the WLF filed briefs in three of the most important Supreme Court cases about capital punishment in the last two decades: *McCleskey v. Kemp* (1987), *Payne v. Tennessee* (1991), and *Davis v. United States* (1994).

Washington Legal Foundation
2009 Massachusetts Ave., NW
Washington, DC 20036
Phone: (202) 588-0302
Fax: (202) 588-0386
E-mail: root@wlf.org
Web: www.wlf.org

Retentionist Religious Groups and Leaders

REVEREND JERRY FALWELL. The Reverend Jerry Falwell, the prominent Baptist minister, leader of the "religious right" in America, and founder of the Moral Majority movement, has long been a strong supporter of the death penalty. "Our Lord [Jesus], who died on the cross, was a victim of capital punishment," he explained in a September 2000 interview. "If Christ ever wanted a platform from which to address the issue, that was it. But he didn't say anything, and I interpret that to mean that he does not consider it wrong."[53]

In April 2000 Falwell entered into a disagreement with religious broadcaster Pat Robertson, who had said he supported a short moratorium on the death penalty to fix some of its problems. Falwell disagreed, saying, "While courts do make mistakes, I do not believe the mistake level is at the point where we need to rethink our whole system, and I personally believe that we need to reduce the time between conviction and execution."[54]

Reverend Jerry Falwell
Lynchburg, VA 24514
Phone: (434) 582-7618
Fax: (434) 582-2625

E-mail: jerry@falwell.com
Web: www.falwell.com

SOUTHERN BAPTIST CONVENTION. The Southern Baptist Convention, an organization of more than 15.8 million in more than 40,000 churches in the United States, fully supports the use of the death penalty. At its annual convention in 2000, church leaders adopted a resolution supporting the use of the punishment.[55] The 11,000 "messengers" to the convention decided that the death penalty is a "legitimate form of punishment for those found guilty of murder or treasonous acts that result in death," but they approved of the punishment only when there is "clear and overwhelming evidence of guilt."[56]

Southern Baptist Convention
Office of Convention Relations
901 Commerce St.
Nashville, TN 37203-3699
Phone: (615) 244-2355
Web: www.sbc.net

PAT ROBERTSON. Pat Robertson, a religious broadcaster, prominent Christian conservative, and sometime presidential candidate, is a strong supporter of the death penalty—at least in principle. He feels that the punishment is a just way to deal with perpetrators of heinous crimes. In recent years, however, Robertson has indicated a willingness to criticize the application of the death penalty in the United States.

In 1998 Robertson was a leading voice calling for clemency for Karla Faye Tucker, a convicted murderer who had become a born-again Christian while on death row. He proclaimed that Tucker had become a different person and now deserved to live.[57] In 2000 Robertson again criticized the death penalty, saying that he supported a temporary moratorium on executions. He felt that the disparities in executions among different races and along socioeconomic class lines indicated problems that needed to be rectified before executions could resume.[58]

Pat Robertson
c/o The Christian Broadcasting Network

Attorney General John Ashcroft
U.S. Department of Justice
950 Pennsylvania Ave., NW
Washington, DC 20530-0001
Phone: (202) 514-2001
Fax: (202) 307-6777
E-mail: askdoj@usdoj.gov
Web: usdoj.gov

PRESIDENT GEORGE W. BUSH. President George W. Bush is a strong supporter of the death penalty. As president of the United States, he is also the only person who can grant clemency to federal prisoners. Although capital punishment was not debated much during the 2000 presidential campaign (Al Gore, Bush's main rival, was also pro–death penalty), Bush's record indicates that he will almost surely be a pro–death penalty president. He was governor of Texas during a four-year span (1996–2000) in which the state executed more people than any other state.

Since, during his tenure as governor, Bush never once granted executive clemency to a capital convict, he is unlikely to do so as president. Since he took office, the federal government has executed two death row inmates—the first federal executions since 1963. Before Bush's term began, supporters of several federal death row inmates made special appeals to President Clinton to intervene in the prisoners' cases, fearing that President Bush would be a less sympathetic target. President Clinton did, in fact, grant David Ronald Chandler executive clemency. He also stayed the execution of Juan Raul Garza for at least six months so that the administration could study "racial and geographic disparities in the federal death penalty system."[64] However, on June 19, 2001, Garza was put to death without further delay by the Bush administration.

The president might also have an opportunity to affect the constitutional questions that surround capital punishment if a Supreme Court justice retires during Bush's term. As president, he is empowered by the Constitution to nominate a new Supreme Court justice to fill the vacancy. Because of the importance of the Supreme Court in this area of public policy, Bush's choice could have an enormous effect on the future of the death penalty in America.

President George W. Bush
White House
1600 Pennsylvania Ave., NW
Washington, DC 20500
Phone: (202) 456-1414
E-mail: president@whitehouse.gov
Web: www.whitehouse.gov

U.S. DEPARTMENT OF JUSTICE. Although the U.S. Department of Justice (DOJ) does not officially advocate for or against capital punishment, it plays an important role in death penalty politics in the United States. Its most direct influence is in the prosecution of federal capital crimes: the U.S. attorneys who prosecute crimes are employed by the DOJ, and the attorney general must authorize them to seek the sentence in any case. (The execution itself is carried out in the state prison system where the trial takes place, or, if that state does not have the death penalty, in another state of the presiding judge's choosing.) Over the course of the 1990s, the several attorneys general seemed to be authorizing more death penalty prosecutions, but this statistic was probably skewed by the passing of new federal death penalty laws. Some observers believe that new attorney general Ashcroft, who had been a vocal supporter of capital punishment during his years as a senator, will make the DOJ more resolute in its prosecution of capital crimes.

The DOJ has also provided anti–death penalty activists with some ammunition. In 2000 it released the results of a statistical analysis of the federal death penalty showing significant disparities in the ways defendants of different races were treated by U.S. attorneys.[65] The report noted that, among other things, between 1995 and 2000, 80 percent of all the cases submitted by federal prosecutors for death penalty review involved minority defendants. Of these, almost half were black. Even after review by the attorney general, 72 percent of cases in which federal prosecutors pushed for capital punishment involved minorities.

The DOJ also plays an important role in the death penalty debate by keeping statistics. Charged with collecting nationwide criminal justice statistics, including ones concerning the death penalty, the DOJ's numbers are used by advocates on both sides of the debate.

U.S. Department of Justice
950 Pennsylvania Ave., NW
Washington, DC 20530-0001
Phone: (202) 514-2001
Fax: (202) 307-6777
E-mail: askdoj@usdoj.gov
Web: www.usdoj.com

Legislative Branch Actors

SEN. RUSSELL FEINGOLD. In January 2001 Sen. Russell Feingold, D-Wis., an important opponent of capital punishment in the Senate, introduced two bills, S. 233 and S. 191. The first would order a moratorium on all federal executions and encourage states to stop executions while a federal commission studies issues of fairness in the application of the death penalty. The second would completely abolish the federal death penalty.

Feingold's actions were prompted in part by a DOJ study showing sharp racial disparities in the application of the federal death penalty. "Just as we feared, the same serious flaws in the administration of the death penalty that have plagued the states also afflict the federal death penalty," he said. "Let's temporarily suspend federal executions and let a thoughtfully chosen commission examine the system. American ideals of justice demand that much."[66]

Feingold is one of the most important anti–death penalty spokespeople in Congress. He has introduced bills similar to S. 191 and S. 233 several times in the past, and he continues to work toward a moratorium.

Sen. Russell Feingold (District of Columbia office)
506 Hart Senate Office Bldg.
Washington, DC 20510-4904
Phone: (202) 224-5323
Fax: (202) 224-2725
E-mail: senator@feingold.senate.gov
Web: feingold.senate.gov

SPEAKER J. DENNIS HASTERT. Rep. J. Dennis Hastert, the Speaker of the House of Representatives, is in a powerful position to affect all manner of public policy issues. As Speaker, Hastert is empowered with agenda-setting authority and majority-party leadership in the House. He is therefore an important player in the death penalty field.[67]

Hastert is a proponent of capital punishment, having voted in favor of several measures to extend the death penalty, including the 1988 bill that reinstated the federal death penalty.[68] He has also indicated a willingness to look carefully at measures designed to prevent innocent persons from being put to death. In 2000 Hastert vowed to ensure that a bill that would ease prisoners' access to DNA evidence would get a full hearing.[69]

Speaker J. Dennis Hastert (District of Columbia office)
2369 Russell House Office Bldg.
Washington, DC 20515
Phone: (202) 225-2976
Fax: (202) 225-0697
E-mail: speaker@mail.house.gov
Web: www.house.gov/hastert

SENATE JUDICIARY COMMITTEE. The Senate Judiciary Committee, chaired by Sen. Patrick J. Leahy, D-Vt., is one of the most important influences on death penalty policy in the federal government. Under Senate bylaws, it has jurisdiction over all bills and matters pertaining to constitutional amendments, judicial proceedings, and federal court appointments. Thus, virtually all bills introduced in the Senate that would impact the application of the death penalty in the United States must pass first through the Judiciary Committee. Moreover, the Senate has power to confirm presidential nominations to the federal courts—including the Supreme Court. All such nominations are sent first to the Judiciary Committee for discussion and recommendation to the full Senate. This power is vitally important to capital punishment policy, since judges—especially Supreme Court justices—can have an enormous impact on the legality of various aspects of death penalty procedure. Nine Republicans and ten Democrats sit on the committee.

Senate Judiciary Committee
United States Senate

224 Senate Office Bldg.
Washington, DC 20510
Phone:(202) 224-5225
Fax:(202) 224-9102
Web: judiciary.senate.gov

Judicial Branch Actors

JUSTICE STEPHEN G. BREYER. U.S. Supreme Court justice Stephen G. Breyer, the most recent Supreme Court nominee, took his seat in 1994. He therefore did not vote in any of the important cases concerning capital punishment that the Court heard in the 1970s and 1980s. He is now, however, an important player in death penalty policy simply because he holds a seat on the Court. Since the Court is empowered to decide the constitutionality of capital punishment and its applications, his is one of nine votes that can fundamentally alter the capital justice system.

Despite his relatively recent appointment to the Court, Breyer has demonstrated an abolitionist streak in his dealings with death penalty issues. In the 1999–2000 term, he dissented from the Court's decisions not to hear two cases, *Knight v. Florida* (1999) and *Moore v. Nebraska* (1999), that concerned the cruelty of long death row stays. Breyer wrote:

> Both of these cases involve astonishingly long delays flowing in significant part from constitutionally defective death penalty procedures. Where a delay, measured in decades, reflects the State's own failure to comply with the Constitution's demands, the claim that time has rendered the execution inhuman is a particularly strong one.

The justice has also dissented in several more ordinary capital appeals, including *Weeks v. Angelone* (2000), in which his dissent was joined by three other justices. In that case, Breyer felt that the sentencing jury was confused about a capital sentencing instruction and that the case should therefore be remanded for another sentencing hearing.

JUSTICE RUTH BADER GINSBURG. U.S. Supreme Court justice Ruth Bader Ginsburg, also a relative newcomer to the Court, was one of the two justices nominated by President Clinton. She took her seat in 1993, so she was not present for the important legal battles over the death penalty that took place in the two previous decades. Her position on the Court now, though, ensures that she will be a vital actor in any future legal struggles.

Ginsburg's stance on the death penalty is fairly liberal compared to many on the Court, tending toward support of a moratorium. In April 2001 she expressed support for a proposed state moratorium on the death penalty in Maryland.[70] Stating her belief that accused murderers with good lawyers usually "do not get the death penalty" while poor people who cannot afford them are more likely to receive the punishment, she criticized the "meager" amount of funding for programs to provide legal representation to the poor.

JUSTICE ANTHONY M. KENNEDY. Since taking his seat on the Supreme Court in 1988, Justice Anthony M. Kennedy has joined the majority of the Court in expressing fairly expansive support for the death penalty and its applications in the United States. Kennedy joined the majority of the Court in *Payne v. Tennessee* (1991), which confirmed the constitutionality of the use of "victim impact" evidence in the sentencing stage of capital trials. He also supported the majority in *Stanford v. Kentucky* (1989), the case that held that defendants may be executed for crimes they committed when they were aged sixteen or older, and the general holding of *Penry v. Lynaugh* (1989), which held that mentally retarded murderers may be executed. Kennedy has also supported the Court's efforts to reduce the number of capital appeals that federal courts must hear.

JUSTICE SANDRA DAY O'CONNOR. Sandra Day O'Connor's voting record as a Supreme Court justice has indicated support for the use of the death penalty. She has opposed doctrines that would limit or threaten the use of capital punishment. For instance, she disagreed with the result in *Ford v. Wainwright* (1986), writing that "the Eighth Amendment does not create a substantive right not to be executed while insane."[71] She has also generally supported holdings that would bolster or expand the use of capital punishment in the United States. O'Connor voted with the majority of the Court in *McCleskey v. Kemp* (1987), the case that announced that evidence about systemic racial disparities in the capital justice system is not sufficient to render a particular death sentence unconstitutional. She also was among the jurists who supported the holdings of *Stanford v. Kentucky* and *Payne v. Tennessee.*

O'Connor has, however, at least verbally indicated some skepticism about the punishment. In a speech in Minneapolis in July 2001, the justice stated that she has "serious questions" about whether the punishment is being applied fairly in the United States. She cited concerns about the quality of defense counsel for many capital defendants, stating, "If statistics are any indication, the system may well be allowing some innocent defendants to be executed."[72]

JUSTICE WILLIAM H. REHNQUIST. William H. Rehnquist, the chief justice of the Supreme Court, has incredible power to influence death penalty policy in the United States. Since the Court is empowered to decide the constitutionality of capital punishment and its applications, Rehnquist's is one of nine votes that can fundamentally alter the capital justice system. Moreover, his position as chief justice gives him a slight institutional edge over the other justices.

In general, Rehnquist has used his power to support the constitutionality of the death penalty and to protect states' rights to apply it as they see fit. He cast one of the seven votes in the 1976 *Gregg* decision that favored reinstituting the death penalty in the United States.[73] Rehnquist also represented a part of the slim majority of the Court that found in *McCleskey* that evidence about systemic racial disparities in the capital justice system is not sufficient to render a particular death sentence unconstitutional.[74]

Rehnquist also dissented in several cases in which the Court limited the permissible scope of the death penalty. In *Emmund v. Florida* (1982), his vote was one of four opposing the majority of the Court's holding that the Eighth Amendment prohibits the imposition of the death penalty for mere participation in a robbery in which an accomplice takes a life. He also dissented from the Court's conclusion in *Ford* that states may not execute the insane.

Rehnquist has led the movement in the Supreme Court to restrict or to allow states to restrict the many post-conviction appeals and writs available to persons upon whom the death sentence has been imposed. He has campaigned vigorously to limit the number of appeals state inmates may bring to the federal courts, voted for changes in the requirements when relevant cases come before the Court, and lobbied Congress for a change in the federal habeas corpus laws.[75]

JUSTICE ANTONIN SCALIA. U.S. Supreme Court justice Antonin Scalia, like Chief Justice Rehnquist, has been a strong supporter of the death penalty since he took his seat on the Court in 1986. His voting record indicates that he has favored a permissive posture toward states' applications of the death penalty and an expansive notion of the constitutionality of the punishment. He voted with the majority in *McCleskey* and *Payne,* and he authored the opinion of the Court in *Stanford* that announced the rule allowing juvenile offenders above the age of fifteen to be executed.

JUSTICE DAVID H. SOUTER. Although U.S. Supreme Court justice David H. Souter did not become a member of the Court until 1990, and therefore did not vote in many of the Court's decisions that shape the application of the death penalty today, it is clear that he supports its use. In *Payne,* a major case in the 1990s, Souter joined the majority in confirming the constitutionality of the use of "victim impact" evidence in the sentencing stage of capital trials. He has also supported the Court's efforts to reduce the number of capital appeals heard by federal courts.

JUSTICE JOHN PAUL STEVENS. U.S. Supreme Court justice John Paul Stevens, who has served on the Court since 1975, is, like the other members of the Court, in a powerful position to affect U.S. death penalty policy. Although he voted in *Gregg* to support the majority holding that the death penalty is constitutional, he has generally used his power as a member of the Supreme Court to limit capital punishment and its application in the states. Stevens was one of the four dissenting justices in *McCleskey,* for example, who would have held that systemic racial disparities ought to be used as evidence in individual death penalty cases. He wrote, "This sort of disparity is constitutionally intolerable."[76]

Stevens dissented in cases like *Payne,* which allowed the introduction of victim impact evidence during the penalty phase of capital trials, and *Stanford,* in which the majority of the Court announced the rule that states may execute murderers who were as young as sixteen when they committed their crime. He has also opposed the Court's recent moves toward limiting access to the federal courts for capital appeals, dissenting in *Kuhlmann v. Wilson* (1986) and *Sawyer v. Whitley* (1992).

JUSTICE CLARENCE THOMAS. Like Souter, Justice Clarence Thomas is a recent nominee to the Court, having joined the bench in 1991. He therefore did not participate in the important legal battles of the 1970s and 1980s. However, his position on the Court now will make him a vital player in any future battles.

Justice Thomas is usually a very conservative jurist, and his votes on death penalty cases are no different. He has often voted in the same manner as Chief Justice Rehnquist on capital punishment cases, and this has meant a strong support for measures that would reduce the number of capital appeals that must be heard by federal courts.

State and Local Government Actors

GOV. GEORGE E. PATAKI.   Gov. George E. Pataki, R-N.Y., one of many state governors who support the use of the death penalty, passed groundbreaking death penalty legislation for his home state in 1995. New York's previous governor, Mario Cuomo, had vetoed a death penalty bill passed by the legislature in every year of his three terms. When Pataki finally defeated Cuomo in 1995, a new bill was quickly passed, and the new governor signed it into law, saying:

> The citizens of New York State have spoken loudly and clearly in their call for justice for those who commit the most serious of crimes by depriving other citizens of their very lives. The citizens of New York State are convinced the death penalty will deter these vicious crimes and I, as their Governor, agree. The legislation I approve today will be the most effective of its kind in the nation. It is balanced to safeguard defendants' rights while ensuring that our state has a fully credible and enforceable death penalty statute. This law significantly buttresses the twin pillars of an effective criminal justice system—deterrence and true justice for those convicted of violent crimes.[77]

His victory made New York the most recent state to readopt capital punishment. Pataki continues to be strongly pro–death penalty, in one instance removing a prosecutor from a case when he refused to seek the punishment.[78]

Gov. George E. Pataki
State Capitol
Albany, NY 12224
E-mail: gov.pataki@chamber.state.ny.us
Web: www.state.ny.us/governor/

GOV. GEORGE RYAN.   In January 2000 Gov. George Ryan, R-Ill., made big news by putting a temporary halt to the use of capital punishment in his state. Although the governor is a supporter of the death penalty in principle, and had long supported its use in practice, on January 31, 2000, he called for a moratorium on further executions.[79] Citing "grave concerns about [Illinois's] shameful record of convicting innocent people and putting them on death row," the governor noted that, since the punishment had been reinstated in Illinois in 1977, thirteen of the twenty-five people who were sentenced to death were later exonerated and set free.[80] He appointed a commission to study the administration of the death penalty in Illinois and to recommend improvements,[81] and he promised not to reinstate the death penalty until he could "be sure with moral certainty that no innocent man or woman is facing lethal injection."[82]

Ryan's move was one of the most important developments in the death penalty debate in the last decade. For one thing, it lent credence to abolitionists' complaints about capital error rates. It also injected the anti–death penalty movement with a new vigor and temporarily shifted its rhetoric away from outright abolitionism to a focus on functional inadequacies in the capital punishment system.[83] Scholars have noted that Illinois's error rate was not unlike those of other states—in fact, its overall error rate (including sentencing and conviction errors) was slightly *less* than the national average.[84] This has allowed abolitionist commentators to argue that other states should follow Illinois's lead in putting a halt to the death penalty until their systems can be fixed.

Perhaps more importantly, Ryan's announcement generated great news coverage and may have started a shift in the way that American voters look at the death penalty. Since Ryan declared the moratorium, five other states have begun the process of reviewing their death penalty systems,[85] and several local city councils have at least considered resolutions supporting a moratorium.[86] Moreover, recent poll data show that many U.S. citizens believe that innocent people have been executed in the past and that certain groups are more likely than others to receive a death sentence.[87]

Gov. George Ryan
Office of the Governor
207 Statehouse
Springfield, IL 62706
Phone: (217) 782-0244
Fax: (217) 524-4049
Web: www.state.il.us/gov/

STEVEN D. STEWART.   Steven D. Stewart, a prosecuting attorney of Clark County, Indiana, has become an important voice in the death penalty debate because he is such a vocal supporter of capital punishment. He is prominent because he is willing to use his position to advocate in favor of the death penalty. The Clark County prosecuting attorney's Web site, for instance, contains a message from Stewart detailing his reasons for supporting the punishment.

Moreover, Stewart is often quoted by national media as an exemplar of the opinions of pro–death penalty prosecutors. In an article on pending congressional bills that would increase access to DNA testing for capital defendants, for instance, *CQ Weekly* quoted him as saying, "Those of us in the business are concerned that our system is an accurate one. . . . I think the claims have been greatly exaggerated. . . . It would be ridiculous for any prosecutor to try to keep out DNA evidence." He did note a fear, however, that "ultimately, any law [Congress] may pass could let a killer back out on the streets."[88]

Steven D. Stewart
Office of the Clark County Prosecuting Attorney
501 East Court Ave.
215 City-County Bldg.
Jeffersonville, IN 47130
Phone: (812) 285-6264
Fax: (812) 285-6259
Web: www.clarkprosecutor.org

Notes

1. ABA Task Force on Death Penalty Habeas Corpus, "Toward a More Just and Effective System of Review in State Death Penalty Cases: A Report Containing the American Bar Association's Recommendations Concerning Death Penalty Habeas Corpus and Related Materials from the American Bar Association Criminal Justice Section's Project on Death Penalty Habeas Corpus," 1990.

2. American Bar Association, "Report Regarding Implementation of the American Bar Association's Recommendations and Resolutions Concerning the Death Penalty and Calling for a Moratorium on Executions," 1996.

3. Ibid.

4. See www.aclu.org/library/FreedomIsWhy.pdf.

5. For a good history of the ACLU's involvement in the anti–death penalty movement, see Herbert H. Haines, *Against Capital Punishment: The Anti–Death Penalty Movement in America, 1972–1994* (Oxford: Oxford University Press, 1996), chs. 1 and 2.

6. Roger Schwed, *Abolition and Capital Punishment: The United States' Judicial, Political, and Moral Barometer* (New York: AMS Press, Incorporated, 1983), 113–114.

7. See Haines, *Against Capital Punishment*, 82.

8. See www.amnesty.org/web/aboutai.nsf.

9. Ibid., 64.

10. See www.amnestyusa.org/rightsforall/dp/index.html.

11. Ibid.

12. Craig Offman, "Benetton Says Ciao to Toscani," *Salon,* May 20, 2000.

13. Craig Offman, "Live From Death Row," *Salon,* April 17, 2000.

14. Offman, "Bennetton," 2000.

15. "Execution Stayed for Inmate in Benetton Ad," *Charleston Gazette,* January 19, 2001, 3C.

16. Ibid.

17. See www.handsoffcain.org.

18. The text of this letter is available at www.hrw.org/campaigns/deathpenalty/gov_letter.htm.

19. See www.hrw.org/reports/2001/ustat/.

20. See www.hrw.org/press/2001/03/mrex0320.htm.

21. See www.moratorium2000.org.

22. Remarks of Secretary General Kofi Annan upon receiving the petition of the Moratorium 2000 campaign, New York, December 18, 2000. Text available online at www.moratorium2000.org/events/annan_statement.lasso.

23. See www.ncadp.org/History.html.

24. Haines, *Against Capital Punishment*, 95, 133–134.

25. Ibid., 100.

26. Ibid., 25–27.

27. Ibid., 72.

28. Ibid., 59.

29. Ibid., 69.

30. See www.afsc.org/about.htm.

31. Haines, *Against Capital Punishment*, 80.

32. Ibid., 105.

33. See www.deathpenaltyreligious.org.

34. Pope John Paul II, Mass in St. Louis, Missouri, January 27, 1999.

35. New Catechism of the Catholic Church, released September 8, 1997, available at www.scborromeo.org/ccc/.

36. Ibid., sect. 2, art. 5, ch. 2, par. 2267.

37. Pope John Paul II, Mass in St. Louis, Missouri, January 27, 1999.

38. Jo Mannies, "Carnahan Gives Details in Commutation of Death Sentence; Governor Acted At Request of Pope," *St. Louis Post-Dispatch*, March 31, 2000, A1.

39. See www.igc.org/cacp/.

40. See www.mindspring.com/~sartor/gradyhs/org_SCLC.html.

41. Haines, *Against Capital Punishment*, 105.

42. Ibid., 106.

43. James S. Liebman, Jeffrey Fagan, and Valerie West, "A Broken System: Error Rates in Capital Cases, 1973–1995," Columbia University School of Law, June 12, 2000.

44. The book was developed into a 1996 film, *Dead Man Walking*, starring Susan Sarandon and Sean Penn.

45. Allan Turner, "Making Life Miserable for Felons; Co-Founder Propels Victims' Rights Group into Heart of Issues," *Houston Chronicle*, June 11, 2000, A35.

46. See www.napo.org/napo1.htm.

47. Bill Nichols, "Clinton Sticks to His Message," *USA Today*, August 21, 1992, 6A.

48. Jeanne Cummings, "Florida Chief Justice Undergoes Quiz for U.S. Appeals Judgeship," *Fresno Bee*, February 4, 1994, A7.

49. Some states already have such provisions.

50. Letter from John Kaye, president, National District Attorneys Association, published in *Legal Times*, February 10, 1997, 26.

51. See Jeff Woods, "Sundquist Admits Early Ballot to Boot White," *Nashville Banner*, July 26, 1996, B2; Jeff Woods, "Public Outrage Nails a Judge," *Nashville Banner*, August 2, 1996, 1A.

52. See, e.g., William Claiborne and Paul Duggan, "Spotlight on Death Penalty; Illinois Ban Ignites a National Debate," *Washington Post*, June 18, 2000, A1.

53. Don Lattin, "WWJD? Once Only the Religious Right Asked That Question—Now Even Democratic Presidential Candidates Say They're Running with God," *San Francisco Chronicle*, September 15, 2000, A1.

54. "Falwell, Robertson Feud over Death Penalty," *Arizona Republic*, April 16, 2000, J3.

55. Steve Kloehn, "Baptists OK Limits on Women's Roles; Southern Sect Cites Bible as Authority," *Chicago Tribune*, June 15, 2000, 1.

56. Gayle White, "Baptists OK Rules on Gays, Women," *Atlanta Journal and Constitution,* June 15, 2000, 1E.

57. "Pat Robertson, ACLU Make Unlikely Allies," *San Antonio Express-News,* April 11, 2000, 6B.

58. Ibid.

59. Isaac Ehrlich, "The Deterrent Effect of Capital Punishment: A Question of Life and Death," *American Economic Review* 65 (1975): 397.

60. *Gregg v. Georgia,* 428 U.S. 153 (1976), 185–186.

61. Ibid.

62. Dan Eggen and David A. Vise, "Ashcroft Sees No Halt in Executions; Death Penalty Appropriate for Those Committing 'Heinous Crimes,' He Says," *Washington Post,* April 28, 2001, A11.

63. Ibid.

64. Ibid.

65. U.S. Department of Justice, "The Federal Death Penalty System: A Statistical Survey (1988–2000)," September 12, 2000. Available online at www.usdoj.gov/dag/pubdoc/dpsurvey.html.

66. Marc Lacey and Raymond Bonner, "Reno Troubled By Death Penalty Statistics," *New York Times,* September 13, 2000, A17.

67. Elizabeth Palmer, "The Death Penalty: Shifting Perspectives," *CQ Weekly,* June 3, 2000, 1324.

68. Ibid.

69. Ibid.

70. "Around the U.S.," *Dallas Morning News,* April 10, 2001, 4A.

71. *Ford v. Wainright* (1986), 477 U.S., 427 (Justice O'Connor concurring in part and dissenting in part).

72. "Justice Questions Death Penalty Fairness," *Chicago Tribune,* July 3, 2001, 10.

73. *Gregg v. Georgia,* 428 U.S. 153 (1976), 226.

74. *McCleskey v. Kemp,* 481 U.S. 279 (1987).

75. Neil A. Lewis, "Four Key Issues in Dispute on Package to Fight Crime," *New York Times,* November 27, 1991, B8.

76. *McCleskey v. Kemp,* 481 U.S. 279 (1987), 366.

77. William C. Donnino, Practice Commentary, N.Y. Penal Law 125.27 (McKinney 1998). Quoting memorandum of New York governor George Pataki on the death penalty.

78. Melissa Block, "New York Governor Removes Bronx D.A. Over Death Penalty," *Morning Edition* (National Public Radio), March 22, 1996, transcript #1830–5.

79. "Governor Ryan Declares Moratorium on Executions, Will Appoint Commission to Review Capital Punishment System," Governor Ryan press release, January 31, 2000, available at www.state.il.us/gov/press/00/jan/morat.htm.

80. Ibid.

81. Illinois Governor's Executive Order Number 4 (2000), Creating the Governor's Commission on Capital Punishment.

82. Governor Ryan press release, 2000.

83. Benjamin Wallace, "States Follow Illinois Lead on Death Penalty," *Boston Globe,* February 9, 2000, A3.

84. Liebman, 2000, ii.

85. "Fixing the Death Penalty," *Chicago Tribune,* December 29, 2000, 22.

86. Benjamin Soskis, "Alive and Kicking," *New Republic,* April 17–24, 2000, 26.

87. Gallup Organization, Gallup poll on the death penalty, released March 2, 2001.

88. Palmer, "The Death Penalty," 1324.

4 International Implications

The United States' continued use of capital punishment stands in pronounced opposition to the international trend. Since World War II the majority of countries worldwide have abolished the sentence for ordinary crimes. This chapter examines this international trend toward abolition, discusses theories about why the United States has not followed the movement, and analyzes the pressure put on the nation by international condemnation of its death penalty policies.

The International Trend

When the U.S. Supreme Court struck down Georgia's capital punishment law in 1972 it seemed to be following in the footsteps of the majority of other countries. Many by then had abandoned the death penalty for ordinary offenses (excluding crimes such as those committed during war and prosecuted under military law), in many cases abolishing the practice despite public support for death penalty statutes. More have abandoned the practice since then. When the Court reinstated the punishment in 1976, the United States set itself in contrast to this international movement.

International Abolition

Although some European countries had abandoned the death penalty by the end of the nineteenth century,[1] the vast majority of nations still used the punishment up until the time of World War II.[2] However, after the war—and the atrocities that accompanied it—the newly formed United Nations (UN) passed the Universal Declaration of Human Rights, a document intended to codify the human rights recognized by civilized nations.[3] Article 3 of that nonbinding agreement among nations proclaims that the "right to life" is a fundamental one. Although the declaration does not say so explicitly, its framers intended that this right represent, in part, a rejection of capital punishment.[4]

Despite the implicit rejection of the death penalty in this seminal piece of international human rights law, the global community did not immediately abandon use of the punishment. Several subsequent treaties and agreements dealing with human rights explicitly made capital punishment an exception to the right to life, including the International Covenant on Civil and Political Rights,[5] which went into force in 1976, and the European and American Conventions on Human Rights, adopted in 1955 and 1979, respectively.[6] The UN even allowed for the imposition of the death penalty for postcapture crimes committed by prisoners-of-war during the Korean War.[7] The Universal Declaration did, however, set a process in motion whereby capital punishment began to lose favor.

Initially, the international legal community, led by the UN, focused its attention on narrowing the scope of the death penalty. Article 6 of the International Covenant on Civil and Political Rights, the drafting of which was completed in 1957, includes a number of procedural requirements for the use of capital punishment, and it mandates that the imposition of the death penalty may not be "arbitrary." Another agreement, the American Convention, which was adopted in 1969 and went into force in 1978, forbids any signatory state from readopting capital punishment once it abandons the practice. Both documents ban the use of capital punishment for juveniles under the age of eighteen, and others protect pregnant women and the elderly from execution.

Over time the international movement has come to show what one scholar termed "inexorable progress towards abolition."[8] In 1982 the European Convention adopted Protocol No. 6 to the European Convention for the Protection of Human Rights and Fundamental Freedoms. This document requires that signatory countries abolish the death penalty during peacetime, unless a nation specifically reserves the right to use the punishment at the time of ratification. Also in the 1980s, the UN promulgated the Second Optional Protocol to the Civil Rights Covenant, which calls for the abolition of the death penalty internationally.[9] In 1990 several South and Central American countries signed a treaty providing for the total abolition of the sentence.[10]

In 1994 the UN considered, but ultimately rejected, a resolution calling for a worldwide ban on executions of any kind by the year 2000.[11] More recently, however, it managed to pass several such resolutions. In 1998, 1999, and 2000, successful resolutions called on retentionist nations "to establish a moratorium to be imposed on all executions, with a view to completely abolishing the death penalty."[12]

As these international agreements were promulgated, individual nations increasingly sought to abandon capital punishment within their own borders. Before 1965, only twenty-three countries had completely abolished the death penalty or abandoned it for peacetime crimes.[13] By 1988 the number had increased to fifty-three, and by 1995 it rose further, to seventy-two.[14] The trend has continued in recent years: in the 1990s an average of three nations per year abolished the sentence for all crimes.[15]

Observers point to four basic categories into which a country might fall with respect to capital punishment. "Complete abolitionist" nations have abolished the death penalty for all crimes. Others have abandoned the punishment for all ordinary crimes. These countries retain the death penalty for offenses committed during war, espionage, or a similar crime, but they do not execute for domestic criminal offenses such as murder. A certain segment of nations worldwide are considered "de facto abolitionist"; they still have statutes allowing for the imposition of the death penalty on the books but have not used the punishment in more than ten years. Finally, a nation—such as the United States—could be "retentionist" and continue to use the death penalty for ordinary crimes.

In 2001 more than half of all nations have abandoned capital punishment in at least a de facto sense. Of the 195 nations in the world, only 87 (or 45 percent) still use the death penalty for ordinary crimes. Seventy-five (almost 39 percent) have completely abolished the sentence for all crimes. Thirteen (about 7 percent) have abolished it for ordinary crimes but retain capital punishment for extraordinary offenses, like crimes committed during wartime or treason. Finally, twenty (almost 10 percent) still have death penalty laws on the books but have not sentenced anyone to death for more than ten years.[16] (See Table 4-1, Figures 4-1 and 4-2, and Appendix for a complete list of nations.)

The United States and Japan are the only completely retentionist first world democracies. The United States is distinct in a geographical sense; while eighty-six other countries are also retentionists, most are concentrated in a few regions of the world: Africa, the Caribbean, and the Middle East. It is among the few countries in the Americas and among Western nations that is fully retentionist.

Almost all of Europe has completely abandoned capital punishment, with the exceptions of Turkey, which is a de facto abolitionist state; Albania, Bosnia-Herzegovina, and Latvia, which allow for the punishment for wartime crimes; and the Russian Federation and Yugoslavia, which are both retentionist. Since 1995, Spain, Belgium, Poland, Bosnia-Herzegovina, Bulgaria, Estonia, Lithuania, Great Britain, Ukraine, Latvia, and Albania all abolished the death penalty completely or for ordinary crimes.[17] Europe's general commitment to abolitionism is further demonstrated by the thirty-nine European nations that ratified and forty-two that signed Protocol No. 6 to the European Convention.[18]

Several South and Central American countries have been leaders in the international abolitionist movement. In fact, nine Latin American nations abolished the death penalty before 1965.[19] Almost all countries in the region have by now abandoned the death penalty in at least a de facto sense; Paraguay, the latest to do so, abolished the sentence for all crimes in 1992. Belize, Chile, Guatemala, and Guyana have retained capital punishment, as have most Caribbean nations.[20]

Many African nations, most countries with predominantly Muslim populations, and a large number of Asian nations retain the death penalty for ordinary crimes.[21] However, some have begun to move toward abolition as well. Since 1990, twelve African and six Asian nations have wholly or partially abandoned the death penalty.[22] Moreover, the abolitionist movement seems to have gained steam in several countries in those regions, including Kenya, Mongolia, South Korea, Taiwan, Tanzania, and Zimbabwe.[23]

Table 4-1 International Capital Punishment Practices in 2001

Category	Number of Nations	Percentage of Nations
Abolitionist nations, total	105	55.4%
Complete abolitionist	75	38.5%
Abolitionist for ordinary crimes	13	6.7%
De facto abolitionist	20	10.2%
Retentionist	87	44.6%

Source: Amnesty International, "Abolitionist and Retentionist Countries," available at www.web.amnesty.org/rmp/dplibrary.

Number of nations

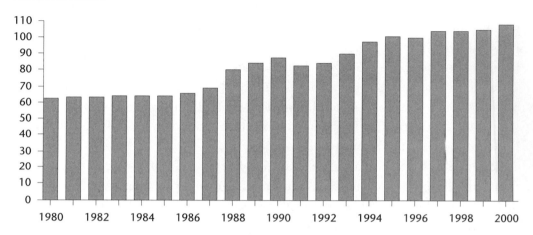

Source: Amnesty International, "Abolitionist and Retentionist Countries," available at www.web.amnesty.org/rmp/dplibrary.

Figure 4-1 Abolitionist Nations in Law or Practice

Number of nations

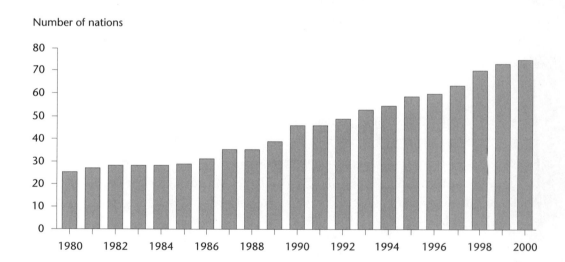

Source: Amnesty International, "Abolitionist and Retentionist Countries," available at www.web.amnesty.org/rmp/dplibrary.

Figure 4-2 Number of Nations Abolitionist for All Crimes

The Middle East and North Africa represent the areas with the strongest adherence to capital punishment. All nations in these areas, with the exception of Israel, use the death penalty. Some countries, like Lebanon in 1994, have recently moved out of the ranks of de facto abolitionists by holding one or more executions.[24] Few report any significant movement toward abolition, though Col. Mu'ammar Gadhafi of Libya in 1988 pronounced an intention to move in the direction of that goal.[25] Scholars consider the strong support for capital punishment in these countries to be connected to the growing influence of Islamic law in the region, which supports the use of death as a punishment. Some Middle Eastern and North African nations have even expressed religious opposition to abolition at the United Nations.[26]

Overall, the worldwide trend is clearly toward abolition. Since 1985, forty nations have completely abolished the death penalty. During that same period, only four have reintroduced capital punishment. One of those countries, Nepal, subsequently abolished it again, and two others have not yet conducted an execution.[27]

Meanwhile, the death penalty has seen an increase in the United States. Since 1985, the number of U.S. executions has jumped from eighteen to nearly one hundred per year—putting the United States among the top six countries in the world to use this sentence. The United States, China, Iran, Saudi Arabia, and the Democratic Republic of Congo conducted 85 percent of all known executions worldwide in 1999.[28]

The United States does not display signs that it is moving toward abolition. Most countries go through a period of de facto abolitionism, where executions are allowed under the law but not carried out, before legislatively abolishing capital punishment. An extreme example is Brazil, which did not officially abandon the death penalty for ordinary crimes until 1979 but has not executed anyone since 1855.[29] More common is Greece, which legally abolished the death penalty in 1993 after a period of twenty-one years of de facto abolition.[30] The United States seemed to be entering a de facto abolitionist period in the 1960s, when most states ceased to carry out executions.[31] Now, however, the numbers of executions are on the rise.

It is important to note that the United States has signed and ratified most of the international agreements discussed above. Under international law, the American states are obligated to follow the strictures set forth in treaties and agreements that the nation ratifies. However, in certain cases a nation may sign on to a treaty while maintaining a "reservation" from a certain clause. This means that the nation agrees to all the terms of the agreement except for those contained in that certain clause. The United States, for instance, has signed and ratified the International Covenant on Civil and Political Rights, which, among other things, forbids capital punishment for crimes the defendant committed as a juvenile. The United States, though, made a "reservation" to the juvenile-crime clause, meaning that it reserved the right to execute criminals for their juvenile crimes.

The United States, at least according to U.S. interpretation of often complicated international legal questions, has never agreed to a treaty or covenant that completely forbids capital punishment without making some kind of reservation. This tendency has provoked some controversy. Some nations argue that a country may not make a reservation with respect to a clause of an international agreement that is fundamental to the purpose of the overall agreement. Thus, in the case of the International Covenant on Civil and Political Rights, some nations have argued that its juvenile-crime clause is so central that the United States may not simply reserve the right to ignore it. Sweden objected to the reservation, stating, "Reservations of this nature contribute to undermining the basis of international treaty law. All parties share a common interest in the respect for the object and purpose of the treaty to which they have chosen to become parties."[32] Thus, it is unclear whether or not the United States is in full compliance with the formal tenets of international law.

Abolition in Great Britain

As a contrast to the development of death penalty policy in the United States, and an example of the abolitionist trend, it is useful to briefly examine the history of abolition in another nation. Great Britain makes for a good comparison with the United States, since both are English speaking, have democratic systems of government, are predominantly non-Catholic Christian, and have legal systems that are closely tied to one another.

Like many European nations and the United States, the abolition movement in Britain grew steadily after World War II. In the years just after the war, abolitionist sentiments made the most headway in the House of Lords, the unelected and largely powerless "upper house" of Britain's Parliament.[33] Anglican bishops were important opponents of the death penalty in the House of Lords, and they pressed for abolition. By 1957 the movement had grown to the point that Parliament enacted legislation on the issue that was meant to be a compromise between abolitionist and retentionist factions. The Homicide Act of 1957 attempted to distinguish between capital and noncapital homicide by defining as capital only those crimes that might be deterred by the death penalty.[34]

This clumsy legislation was widely criticized as being ambiguous and lacking in moral underpinnings—so much so, in fact, that it aided the abolitionists in their attempts to throw out the death penalty completely.[35] Many commentators believed that the legislation would lead to confusing jury instructions in capital cases, compounding concerns about a rash of questionable executions. These problems, and the growing strength of abolitionist legislators, eventually led to the passage of the Murder Act of 1965, which abolished the death penalty for a five-year trial period, except in cases of treason, piracy, and certain offenses under military law.[36] The provisions of the Murder Act were later made permanent.

Notably, this largely abolitionist legislation was passed by the legislature despite overwhelming public support for retaining the death penalty. A 1964 Gallup poll found that only 21 percent of British respondents favored abolition. A 1966 Gallup poll found that 76 percent supported full reinstatement. This support rose even higher—to 82 percent—by 1975.[37] Yet Britain never reinstated capital punishment.

Between 1965 and 1998, no executions were carried out in Britain. During that time, at least ten attempts were made in the British Parliament to reinstate the death penalty.[38] They were all defeated, though, by increasingly large margins. Abolitionists also failed in their attempts to completely abolish the death penalty in Britain during most of that time. In 1990 Parliament considered a bill that would abandon all the remaining death penalty laws by replacing the words "hanged by the neck until he be severely dead" with "sentenced to imprisonment for life" in each of the old statutes that imposed capital punishment.[39] This proposed amendment failed.

Although the voting on death penalty legislation in Parliament was based less on party lines than on "votes of conscience," the people who voted for reinstatement of capital punishment were almost all members of the Conservative or Ulster Unionist Parties.[40] When the Labour Party won a landslide election in 1997, ousting many Conservatives, a door was opened to the abolition movement. In 1998, the British government completely abolished the death penalty.[41] The House of Commons voted to incorporate Protocol No. 6 into domestic law, thus repealing the remaining laws providing for capital punishment for domestic crimes. That same year, the House of Commons passed the Human Rights Act, which abolished the death penalty in military law.

The U.S. Trend

It is obvious that the United States' position on the death penalty is fairly unusual. Commonly considered a leader in the promotion of human rights worldwide, the United States is often criticized on this issue. As one commentator put it, "Not only does the United States retain the death penalty, but she pursues it with such tenacity as to place herself in very suspect company."[42] Given this oft-noted discrepancy, there is surprisingly little scholarship on the question *why* the nation is going in such a different direction than that of the international community.[43]

One writer, Kristi Prinzo, recently posited two theories about the discrepancy. First, she noted that the United States has a long history of enforcing the death penalty and suggested that this record plays a partial role in its continued use.[44] Second, she argued that the strong public popularity of capital punishment contributes to its resistance to abolition in the United States. She noted that in some other countries, like France, policy changes concerning the death penalty were supported by majorities of voters.[45]

These theories, however, raise more questions than they answer. Although the United States does in fact have a long history of using capital punishment, many abolitionist countries had much longer traditions behind them when they abandoned the sentence. Britain, for instance, had recognized the death penalty for many centuries when it finally completely abolished the sentence in 1998.

The theory about political popularity is slightly more illuminating, but it also falls short. Many nations have abolished the death penalty even though their populaces supported its continued use.[46] In Britain, for instance, the Murder Act of 1965 temporarily suspended the use of the death penalty despite strong backing for capital punishment among British voters in 1964 and 1966.[47] In Germany, the death penalty was abolished in 1949, though 74 percent of German citizens favored retention of the sentence in 1948.

Moreover, in many nations where the death penalty is abolished, it remains popular among the populace for several years.[48] In Germany most voters favored capital punishment until 1967, when support began to fall precipitously. By 1980 55 percent of Germans opposed the death penalty, while only 27 percent favored its use.[49] Interestingly, the experience of the United States in the 1970s is not necessarily inconsistent with this model: when the Supreme Court struck down the death penalty as applied in 1972, support for the sentence was high among American voters and continued until 1976, when the Court reinstated capital punishment. It is not impossible that Americans, like the citizens of many abolitionist nations, would eventually have begun to change their minds if the Court's abolition had remained in place.

Even leaving these considerations aside, and assuming that the strength of public pressure *is* a primary difference between abolitionist nations and the United States, the public opinion thesis is not satisfactory. It begs a vital question: Why would the U.S. populace hold stronger opinions on capital punishment than the voters in other countries do? No clear reason has been posited, but one idea can be gleaned from criminology literature.

In their book *Crime Is Not the Problem: Lethal Violence in America*, Franklin Zimring and Gordon Hawkins point out that the levels of lethal crime in the United States differ drastically from those in other first world nations:

> Other industrial democracies have rates of crime comparable to those found in the United States. Even rates of violent crime in European and Commonwealth nations are closer to U.S. levels than had been thought. But the death rates from all forms of violence are many times greater in the United States than in other comparable nations. Lethal violence is the distinctive American problem.[50]

The rates of lethal violence in the United States, in fact, are similar to those found in many third world nations. According to the World Health Organization, the homicide rate in the United States in the late 1980s was 9.4 homicides per 100,000 citizens. The homicide rate of Britain was just 1.5, Japan's 0.6, and Canada's 2.1.[51] It might be argued, then, that U.S. citizens have strong preferences for the death penalty because the society is more dangerously violent.[52]

This idea has some problems, however. For one thing, some nations with high murder rates have abandoned the death penalty. At 17.1 homicides per 100,000 citizens, Mexico, for instance, has a homicide rate significantly higher than that of the United States, but it has abandoned the death penalty for peacetime crimes. Furthermore, as Zimring and Hawkins note in another work, U.S. citizens' preferences for the death penalty do not seem to be correlated to the crime rates of their home states.[53] South Dakota, a state with a very low crime rate, has the death penalty. New York, on the other hand, remained abolitionist throughout the 1980s and early 1990s, during which time its crime rates were famously high (especially in New York City).

Zimring and Hawkins suggest another reason for the difference between the United States and the international community. They connect the abolition movement in Europe to the "cataclysmic lessons of the Nazi regime," which they claim led governments to shy away from the use of their full power.[54] Perhaps, they intimate, the lack of such an experience in the United States has allowed for the continued use of capital punishment. This explanation cannot, however, account for the strong abolitionism of Latin America nor the recent abolitionist trends in Africa. Why is the United States different from countries in these regions, which also did not directly experience the Holocaust? This is another question that has not been fully answered.

Perhaps the most satisfactory idea was propounded by Joshua Marshall, former editor of *American Prospect,* who pointed out that the United States has a different political infrastructure than do most other democratic nations, including many abolitionist ones. He observed, "Europeans and Canadians crave executions almost as much as their American counterparts do. It's just that their politicians don't listen to them."[55] Even in Italy, whose government is decidedly anti–capital punishment, about half of the population favors the death penalty.[56] In Britain, too, two-thirds or three-quarters of poll respondents routinely support the punishment.[57]

Marshall argues that political elites in these countries have managed to abolish the death penalty, while American politicians have not, for two reasons. First, in some countries, like Germany and Italy, the post–World War II constitutions ban the death penalty. Such structural roadblocks to capital punishment legislation put the issue "effectively out of public reach."[58] Second, the other European nations' electoral and political systems are in several ways "less democratic" than that of the United States, allowing politicians to ignore the will of the people on certain issues.

For one thing, European nations (and most others) lack "American-style federalism, which in [the United States] allows ardently pro–death penalty regions like the South to proceed without regard for opinion in other parts of the country."[59] Also, in the parliamentary systems common in most world democracies, voters choose among parties, not individual candidates. This allows legislators to withstand public pressure on various issues, as long as political elites remain intellectually united—which Marshall claims they are on the topic of capital punishment. In the United States, on the other hand, voters select among candidates, who "serve as a much more direct conduit between raw public opinion and actual political action."[60] According to Marshall's account, then, the American political system, since it is "more democratic" than those of Europe, is more susceptible to the will of the people. While public support for the death penalty in European abolitionist states (and, one can assume, parliamentary democracies in other areas of the world) can be overlooked by politicians there, that same pressure is more powerfully felt by elites in the United States, and so the death penalty remains in full effect.[61]

International Criticism of the United States' Death Penalty Policies

International bodies have not shied away from expressing their displeasure with what they perceive as the United States' reticence to conform with the human rights standards of the modern world. Criticism has come from four major sources: supra-national bodies like the United Nations, governments of individual nations, nonprofits and other nongovernmental organizations concerned with human rights, and international religious organizations.

Supra-National Bodies

The United States' variance from international norms regarding capital punishment has drawn criticism from supra-national bodies that attempt to enforce the norms. The two main critics have been the United Nations and the European Union (EU).

The United Nations has criticized the United States both implicitly and explicitly. As already noted, the UN has encouraged all nations that retain the death penalty to consider a moratorium on executions. Moreover, various UN agreements and treaties have established standards for the death penalty, like those forbidding capital punishment for crimes committed by juvenile defendants. The United States acts counter to these demands and even specifically reserved the right to execute people for juvenile crimes when it ratified the International Covenant on Civil and Political Rights. Thus, the international norms promulgated by the UN implicitly censure the United States by generally condemning the types of policies followed in U.S. jurisdictions.

In addition to this implicit criticism the UN has specifically singled out the United States for disapproval, for example with a 1998 report on capital punishment in America. (See Appendix.) From September 21 to October 9, 1997, Bacre Waly Ndiaye, a Senegalese lawyer with the UN Human Rights Commission, visited the United States to research the imposition of capital punishment. Although many federal and state officials refused to meet with him, Ndiaye felt that he was able to gather enough information to formulate a bluntly critical report.[62]

The account called the death penalty, as it was practiced in the United States, a "step backwards in the protection of the right to life." Ndiaye noted, with evident disapproval, "a tendency to increase the scope of the death penalty both at the state level, either by reinstating the death penalty or by increasing the number of aggravating circumstances, and at the federal level, where the scope of this punishment has recently been dramatically extended." The report strongly criticized U.S. jurisdictions for sentencing juvenile and mentally retarded offenders to death in contravention of international law.

The report also expressed concerns about the application of death penalty laws. Ndiaye found "a significant degree of unfairness and arbitrariness" in the states' imposition of capital punishment. The report stated that "race, ethnic origin, and economic status appear to be key determinants of who will, and who will not, receive a death penalty," though it cited no direct evidence of racial discrimination. Instead, Ndiaye referred to the largely white racial composition of the judiciary and the prosecutors in the states where most death sentences are imposed, and to "allegations of racial discrimination."

Ndiaye concluded by making several recommendations. First, he suggested that the United States establish a moratorium on executions. Second, he urged the nation to "discontinue the practice of imposing death sentences on juvenile offenders and mentally retarded persons." He also advocated a continuation of the de facto moratorium on the execution of women (which has since ended with the 1998 execution of Karla Faye Tucker in Texas); restriction of the number of offenses punishable by death; changes in the way judges are selected and in the states' public defender systems; and various training programs to educate judicial officials about international human rights obligations. Overall, Ndiaye questioned the U.S. government's commitment to international human rights standards in this area and suggested that the U.S. ratification of the International Covenant on Civil and Political Rights be voided.

The EU has also criticized the United States both implicitly and explicitly. The implicit condemnation has come in two forms: First, through agreements like Protocol No. 6 to the European Convention, which requires signatory countries to abandon the death penalty during peacetime (although such documents do not di-

rectly discuss U.S. laws, they do indicate that European nations find capital punishment a violation of human rights in most instances); and second, by sponsoring
resolutions to the UN calling for a moratorium on executions.[63] Again, the resolutions do not directly mention the United States, but the implication is clear that
EU members find death penalty policies like those employed in the United States
to be out of step with international human rights norms.

International courts in Europe have supported the actions of individual nations
in refusing to extradite persons facing trials for capital crimes in the United States.
In one highly publicized case in 1989, Britain refused to extradite to the United
States a man accused of a double homicide in Virginia. The man, a German national named Jans Soering, sued in the European Court of Human Rights to prevent
the extradition, arguing that the death penalty as administered in the United States
violated his right to avoid inhumane and degrading punishment. The Court
agreed, ruling that the six-to-eight year stay on death row that likely awaited him
in Virginia violated Article III of the European Human Rights Charter.[64]

The EU has also attempted in various direct ways to convince the United States
to change its death penalty policies by pressuring the federal government. For instance, in 2000, the EU presented Frank Loy, the U.S. assistant secretary of state for
human rights, with a memorandum asking the United States to join the ranks of
abolitionist nations worldwide.[65]

Recognizing the limits of the federal government's power to change state policy,
however, the EU has also directly contacted state government officials. Since 1998,
the EU has made numerous appeals to various U.S. states for clemency or stays of
execution on behalf of convicted felons with imminent execution dates.[66] For instance, in February 2001, the EU asked Gov. Bob Holden, D-Mo., to "exercise all
powers invested in your office to commute the sentence of [convicted murderer
Antonio] Richardson to life imprisonment or such other penalty as is compatible
with international law."[67] That same month, the EU issued a plea to all governors
of states enforcing capital punishment in the United States "follow the example of
. . . Governor George Ryan, of Illinois, who has recently imposed a moratorium on
the use of capital punishment."[68]

The UN and the EU are the institutions that enforce international law. No such
organizations have ever imposed any real sanctions on the United States regarding
death penalty policy. This is due to the power of the United States in world politics
and also to the somewhat ambiguous nature of international law itself. Still, it is

clear that these organizations want to exert some kind of pressure on the United States to change its ways.

Individual Nations

In addition to the supra-national institutions that represent many member countries, individual nations have also attempted to influence U.S. behavior. Much of this activity has concerned plans in various states to execute foreign nationals. Often the convict's home country strenuously objects to his or her execution. Executing foreign nationals without informing them of their right to confer with their consulate is a contravention of international norms, but it has occurred in the United States from time to time. Twice in 1999, a U.S. state ignored an order from the International Court of Justice and executed a foreign national.[69] In one case a German official described Arizona's execution of two German brothers as "barbaric and unworthy of a state based on the rule of law."[70] In the past few years other states have ignored similar appeals and suits from the governments of Paraguay and Canada on behalf of their citizens.[71]

In some cases nations have attempted to pressure the United States to stop all executions or certain categories of executions, not just those of their own citizens. By one count, for instance, as many as ten countries formally objected to the United States' reservation to the clause of the International Covenant on Civil and Political Rights that forbids capital punishment for juvenile crimes.[72] In June 1995 the Venezuelan representative to the UN cautioned that the United States was in danger of being the "last country in the world to ensure the fundamental right to life."[73]

The Italian government has made a special effort to convince U.S. officials to abolish the death penalty altogether. In January 1998 the Italian senate unanimously voted to entreat all death penalty states within the United States to consider imposing a moratorium on executions.[74] It also appealed to Italian companies not to invest in U.S. death penalty states.[75] In March 2000 Giancarlo Tavoli, a member of the Italian Parliament's ruling coalition, petitioned the United States and Texas in particular to stop the upcoming execution of Odell Barnes, a Texas black man convicted of murdering his lover. He said, "America is a leader in so many ways, and yet this is as shocking to us as if the country were condoning slavery or torture."[76] The Italian government also started beaming lights of "protest" onto the Roman Coliseum on nights when executions were being carried out anywhere in the world.[77]

The French government has also appealed directly to the United States to abolish capital punishment. In August 2000, while on a visit to the United States, the president of the French National Assembly held a news conference urging abolition.[78] He also took time to visit Mumia Abu-Jamal, a death row inmate convicted of killing a Philadelphia police officer, whose case, for some, represents many of the problems of the American capital justice system.[79]

Earlier, this chapter alluded to another method by which some nations indirectly pressure the United States: by refusing to extradite criminals accused of capital crimes in the United States without guarantees that the death penalty would not be imposed. International treaties have long included exceptions to extradition agreements for cases of capital offences—as early as 1889, the South American Convention allowed one country to refuse to deport a person who might be executed in the requesting nation.[80] Now, these exceptions are fairly commonplace. Most European and many Latin American nations will not extradite persons accused of capital crimes to the United States without assurances that the death penalty will not be sought.[81] Italy's constitution forbids the extradition of a fugitive to a nation that has charged him or her with a capital crime, regardless of any assurances.[82]

This reluctance to extradite has helped spur U.S. action on capital punishment. Recently, Los Angeles County district attorney Steve Cooley announced that his office would seek life imprisonment, rather than the death penalty, in some cases in which an accused murderer has fled to another country that presents extradition obstacles.[83] Cooley's office often must deal with Mexico, a nation that refuses to extradite in death penalty cases. Previously, the office had a strict policy of not deciding on the punishment to seek until the fugitive was in U.S. police custody. As more and more fugitives were kept in Mexico and other nations because of death penalty disagreements, however, Cooley felt that a change was needed. He said, "There are a number of cases where justice is not being done because of our office's historic policy," adding, "If we get life without possibility of parole, there is serious justice."[84]

The nations that do retain the death penalty tend not to be close allies of the United States. Most executions not performed in the United States in the 1990s were enforced in China, Iran, Saudi Arabia, or the Democratic Republic of Congo. China has almost certainly executed the most people in the past decade, although, because of difficulties in gathering information, analysts cannot be sure exactly how many executions took place. Amnesty International knows that China executed at least 1,077 people in 1999 and 18,000 in the 1990s, but it believes the true figures to be substantially higher.[85]

China has drawn heavy international criticism for its methods. According to Amnesty International, executions in China often take place within hours of the sentence being delivered. The appellate process, when defendants have an opportunity to make use of it, rarely overturns a death sentence. Moreover, China has sometimes carried out mass executions on major public holidays or events and around those times hands out death sentences for relatively minor crimes.[86] Most other executions are performed by a shot to the convict's head.[87]

Other retentionist nations that execute large numbers of people suffer from similar problems. Because of this, they are not useful allies in the international debate about capital punishment. In fact, their behavior hurts the United States' case, since abolitionist commentators can rhetorically link it to these other countries.

International Human Rights Organizations

Quite a large portion of the criticism of the United States on capital punishment comes from human rights organizations. Many international nonprofits regard the sentence as a violation of human rights and therefore criticize the United States simply for employing the death penalty. Others condemn what they regard as human rights violations in the application of the death penalty—executions of minors or mentally retarded defendants, racial disparities, and so on.

The most prominent such critic is Amnesty International, an organization dedicated to promoting the human rights declared in the UN's Universal Declaration of Human Rights and similar international agreements and standards.[88] The Universal Declaration includes an assertion of every person's right to life, and thus implicitly condemns the death penalty.

In 1999, for the first time, Amnesty International put the United States on its list of human rights violators.[89] This list usually includes about six nations Amnesty feels are the worst violators of human rights, which it lobbies the UN to censure. The use of the death penalty in the United States, and particularly its use against juveniles and the mentally retarded, formed an important reason that Amnesty included the United States on the list. Amnesty's conviction that the application of the death penalty in America is racist also played a large role in the decision.

In its 2000 recent annual report, which examined worldwide human rights abuses the previous year, Amnesty devoted a good deal of attention to U.S. death penalty activity.[90] The report listed the United States as one of six nations that conducted 85 percent of all executions in 1999, and it chastised the nation for continuing to use the punishment. Amnesty paid special attention to what it considers to be a U.S. violation of international law: the continued use of the death penalty for crimes committed by children under eighteen years of age. It also criticized the nation for denying foreigners charged with capital crimes the right to seek assistance from their home-nation's consulate in the United States and for racial disparities in the application of the death penalty.

Amnesty has even created the Program to Abolish the Death Penalty, currently headed by a U.S. citizen, Sam Jordan.[91] The organization routinely objects to upcoming U.S. executions, often calling for stays of execution or executive clemency. A March 2001 press release attacks the planned execution of Thomas Nevius, a man scheduled to die in Nevada after almost two decades on death row.[92] Amnesty issued a report on Nevius's case, detailing allegations of ineffective counsel, racial discrimination in jury selection, and inaccurate testimony at trial. In 1999 Amnesty released four special reports on capital punishment in the United States.[93]

Amnesty also plays an important role in international criticism of the United States by simply keeping track of death penalty statistics. Amnesty has an extensive and up-to-date database of statistics on the death penalty worldwide and in the United States.[94] These statistics help international observers to track the progress of the international abolition trend and to observe the degree to which the United States acts counter to that trend.

Other major international human rights organizations also attempt to pressure the United States on the death penalty. Human Rights Watch (HRW), for instance, opposes the use of capital punishment by any nation "because of its inherent cruelty."[95] The organization worries about arbitrary application of the death penalty, disparate impacts on vulnerable communities, and the execution of the innocent. HRW tracks U.S. capital cases, pleading with governors for executive clemency. In cases that the organization deems "particularly egregious," HRW attempts to raise the profile of the case with United States and international media sources. At times, the group has also issued special reports on certain aspects of the application death penalty in America, such as a 1995 report on the execution of juvenile defendants.[96]

Some international organizations are devoted specifically to the abolition of the death penalty. One influential group of this kind is Hands off Cain, an organization of citizens and parliamentarians, originally founded in Italy, dedicated to achieving a worldwide moratorium on executions. Hands off Cain was a driving force behind Italy's 1994 proposal that the UN support a ban on capital punishment. The proposal did not win the support of the UN that year, but similar resolutions against the death penalty have been adopted every year since 1997. Hands off Cain has also organized several regional and international conferences on death penalty abolition, including the first pan-Arab conference on the death penalty.

Another international group specifically dedicated to the abolition of capital punishment is Moratorium 2000. A "campaign to obtain an immediate moratorium on the death penalty," the organization's primary mode of action is a global petition drive.[97] According to its Web site, by March 2001 Moratorium 2000 had collected 3.2 million signatures demanding a halt to the death penalty. The group also helped generate public pressure on President Bill Clinton in his last months in office to commute the death sentence of David Ronald Chandler. In 1999 Chandler, an Alabama marijuana farmer, had been sentenced to death under the federal "drug kingpin" statute for hiring an accomplice to kill another man. After his conviction and sentencing, many of the government's witnesses in his case recanted their testimony. A federal court had temporarily overturned his death sentence in October 1999 but reinstated it two months later. In his final hours in office, Clinton did grant Chandler executive clemency.

Other international human rights groups dedicated solely to opposing the death penalty include Derechos, originally founded in Spain, and Lifespark, initially established in Switzerland as a "pen pal" group connecting U.S. death row inmates and European citizens, but now dedicated to anti–capital punishment activism.

Another anti–death penalty organization of interest, though not a human rights group per se, is the Italian clothing manufacturer Benetton. The company, following the lead of photographer Oliviero Toscani, mounted a controversial advertising campaign that featured sympathetic photographs of U.S. death row inmates.[98] The images lacked any accompanying text about their subjects' crimes or victims, outraging victims' rights groups.[99] Although the company ended the campaign in March 2000 and severed its ties with Toscani, the advertisements may have been effective at drumming up some anti–death penalty sentiments.[100] One of the twenty-six inmates featured in the advertisements, Bobbie Lee Harris, received a stay of execution from the North Carolina Supreme Court.[101] The campaign also moved one major client— Sears, Roebuck & Co.—to stop selling Benetton products.[102]

Religious Organizations

Other types of nongovernmental organizations that pressure the United States are religious and faith-based groups. Like human rights organizations, some religious groups have formed associations specifically aimed at the abolition of the death penalty. In other cases, the death-penalty position is simply a part of the group's overall message.

The Catholic Church, led by Pope John Paul II, has called for a moratorium on the death penalty.[103] The church's new Catechism, published by the Vatican in 1997, also indicates the sceptical view with which the church approaches capital punishment.[104] The teaching does allow for the death penalty "if this is the only possible way of effectively protecting human lives against the unjust aggressor." The Catechism, however, pronounces the church's belief that such cases are "practically nonexistent" in today's world, and that governments should limit themselves to nonlethal punishments if they would be effective in protecting society. Nonlethal punishments, according to official church doctrine, are "more in keeping with the concrete conditions of the common good and more in conformity with the dignity of the human person."[105]

The Catholic Church has put direct pressure on the United States to enact a moratorium. While in St. Louis, Missouri, in January 1999, the pope appealed to all nations to end the use of the death penalty.[106] John Paul and the church have also urged executive clemency for numerous death row inmates, including Karla Faye Tucker of Texas, Darrell Mease of Missouri, and Mark Gardner and Alan Willett of Arkansas. In the Arkansas case, Archbishop Gabriel Montalvo, the pope's spokesperson, wrote to Arkansas legislators, "The Holy Father, while praying and expressing deep sympathy for the victims, for their families and friends, prays nevertheless that the life of Mr. Gardner and Mr. Willett themselves may be saved through your compassion and magnanimity."[107]

Many world Jewish organizations have also called for the abolition of capital punishment in the United States. The Reform Jewish movement, centered in North America, has urged a moratorium.[108] It has appealed directly to governors to grant clemency to capital convicts. On February 3, 2001, Rabbis Eric Yoffie and David Saperstein wrote on behalf of the movement to Gov. Frank Keating, R-Okla., asking him to stay the sentence of Sean Sellers:

Jewish Tradition, which in theory allows capital punishment, regulated its legal system so stringently in this area as to make it almost nonexistent. . . . Our prophets teach that God does not seek vengeance but rather that the sinner should repent. Based on these values, we join with the myriad of American and international religious and political leaders in saying that, beyond our opposition to capital punishment generally, the execution of a person who committed a crime as a minor and/or who suffered from mental illness is particularly abhorrent.[109]

Other Jewish groups, too, have condemned the death penalty. The International Rabbinical Assembly has called the practice "repugnant" and urged its abolition. Israel, a nation whose laws are heavily influenced by the Jewish faith, is the only nation in the Middle East that lacks a death penalty statute.

The Dalai Lama, the leader of Tibetan Buddhism, has joined these voices. In a 1999 statement he wrote, "I wholeheartedly support an appeal to those countries who at present employ the death penalty to observe an unconditional moratorium."[110] Many Protestant Christian groups also oppose the death penalty on moral grounds. In March 2000, for instance, the Reverend J. Philip Wogaman of the Foundry United Methodist Church in Washington, D.C., joined with other religious leaders to urge President Clinton to adopt a moratorium on executions. Many other denominations, or their U.S. affiliates, have expressed similar sentiments, including the Episcopal, Evangelical Lutheran, Orthodox, and United Methodist Churches.

It is important to note, however, that not all religious bodies oppose the death penalty. In fact, many Muslim leaders worldwide (especially those from the more fundamentalist regions of the Middle East and North Africa) have vocally supported capital punishment. The Koran, Islam's most holy text, expresses explicit support for the use of the death penalty. In the Koran Allah reminds Mohammad, "We laid it down for the Israelites that whoever killed a human being, *except as punishment for murder or other wicked crimes,* should be looked upon as though he had killed all mankind."[111]

Representatives of many Muslim states in the Middle East and North Africa have fought on religious grounds against international standards condemning the death penalty. For example, during debate over the Second Optional Protocol, the

Sudanese delegate argued that abolition was "incompatible with the criminal code and legislation of Sudan based on the divine and sacred laws of Islam which were immutable."[112]

Collaboration between International and National Abolitionists

The international critics of U.S. capital punishment policy do not act alone. To some degree, they collaborate with groups within the United States to attempt to push the nation toward abolition. This section examines the degree to which these groups have joined forces.

In general, the supra-national bodies and the governments of critical nations discussed earlier do not explicitly collaborate with internal U.S. organizations. This would be unseemly behavior in international politics. Rather, they use diplomatic channels to communicate their discontent to the various levels of U.S. government. International nonprofit and religious organizations, on the other hand, collaborate extensively with U.S. groups.

Many international abolitionist organizations have wings or affiliates that operate solely within the United States. Amnesty International, for instance, maintains Amnesty International USA (AIUSA), which tracks human rights developments within the United States. The U.S. branch has taken the lead in Amnesty's effort to end capital punishment within the United States: it collects statistics, issues periodic reports about perceived problems with the nation's capital justice system, and leads Amnesty International's efforts to encourage executive clemency for death row inmates.

Recently, AIUSA led Amnesty International's efforts with respect to Stanley Lingar, a gay man convicted of killing a teenage girl in Missouri. Amnesty charged that prosecutors used Lingar's sexual orientation in an inflammatory manner, rendering his trial unfair. On February 5, 2001, AIUSA hand delivered a letter to the office of Gov. Bob Holden, D-Mo., pleading for clemency for Lingar, who was scheduled to die on February 7.[113] When the effort failed and Lingar was put to death, AIUSA spearheaded Amnesty International's response, issuing statements and press releases.[114]

Human Rights Watch also maintains a Special Initiative on the United States, which monitors human rights problems within the United States and undertakes advocacy efforts to reform what it believes to be abusive practices by U.S. government bodies.[115] The Special Initiative carefully tracks death penalty developments within the nation, working toward abolition.

National affiliates of a number of religious groups are active in opposing the death penalty, as well. The United States–based Catholics Against Capital Punishment, along with the U.S. Catholic bishops and those bishops of a great many states, support a moratorium on the death penalty.[116] As noted in Chapter 3, many U.S. Protestant churches oppose the death penalty, too, as do several Jewish organizations based in the United States. These groups pass resolutions opposing the death penalty, appeal to executives to grant clemency to capital convicts, and press for a moratorium on executions.

International nonprofits and religious organizations that oppose the death penalty also collaborate with organizations with which they are not affiliated. Amnesty International is a good example, since the group is so active in death penalty abolition. Amnesty very often works alongside the American Civil Liberties Union (ACLU) for abolitionist causes. In May 2000 the two organizations together pressed Gov. Mike Huckabee, R-Ark., to intervene in the execution of Christina Riggs, who was convicted of murdering her own children.[117] In 1999 they formed a coalition to protest executions in Virginia.[118] In 1998 the two issued a joint statement condemning an Oklahoma execution.[119] Other examples of such collaboration abound. Amnesty International has also cooperated with the National Association for the Advancement of Colored People (NAACP), with which it united to back a bill to end the federal death penalty, and Human Rights Watch, with which Amnesty has jointly condemned several executions in the past few years.[120]

Religious organizations also routinely team up to fight for abolitionist causes. In December 2000, for instance, several clerics from diverse religious organizations—including Catholics, Jews, Protestants, Buddhists, and Muslims—met with New Jersey governor Christine Whitman to urge her to impose a temporary moratorium on executions.[121] Also, beginning in 1987, Catholic and Jewish leaders have met to form the National Jewish/Catholic Consultation, a forum for discussing important social issues. In 1999 the groups published "To End the Death Penalty," a report about the reasons their respective faiths reject the death penalty in the modern era and a call for abolition.[122]

The United States' Response to International Criticism

Much of the international criticism discussed in the preceding section is aimed at persuading the United States to adopt an abolitionist position toward the death penalty. Obviously, in a fundamental sense the critics have failed in their goal, since the United States not only continues to execute murderers but is doing so at an increasing rate. Still, the U.S. government is a complicated entity, consisting of several branches—executive, legislative, and judicial—and existing on several different levels—federal, state, and local. This section examines the ways in which governmental actors in those many areas have responded to international criticism about the death penalty.

The Federal Government

The federal government, of course, is deeply involved with death penalty policy in the United States. Moreover, that level of government has the most contact with other nations and supra-national groups because of diplomatic ties, treaty-making responsibilities, and so on. One might guess, then, that international criticism of the U.S. stance on the death penalty would have the most potential to move agents of the federal government. This has not been, however, borne out in fact: international criticism has made very little impact on the federal government.

The sector of the U.S. government that arguably has the most potential to change the nation's capital punishment policy is at the head of the judicial branch: the Supreme Court of the United States. This is because the Court is the final arbiter of the constitutionality of capital punishment. As discussed in Chapter 2, many of the constitutional questions surrounding the death penalty rest on issues involving the Eighth Amendment, which prohibits "cruel and unusual punishment." The Court has ruled that whether a punishment is cruel or unusual depends upon " the evolving standards of decency that mark the progress of a maturing society."[123]

If the Supreme Court decided that these "standards of decency" should be determined by looking at the norms prevalent throughout the world rather than only in the United States, it might strike down all death penalty legislation. It is clear that the worldwide trend, especially in developed democracies, is toward abolition. In the 1980s, American abolitionists held out hope that this tendency would sway the Court, causing it to find that modern standards of decency now precluded the use of the death penalty. In several death penalty appeals cases, abolitionist groups and defense lawyers submitted briefs arguing that the international trend showed that capital punishment had become "cruel and unusual." Eventually the Court addressed these arguments directly, and it expressly rejected them. In a footnote in the case *Stanford v. Kentucky* (1989) the Court stated:

> We emphasize that it is American conceptions of decency that are dispositive, rejecting the contention of petitioners and their various amici . . . that the sentencing practices of other countries are relevant. While "the practices of other nations, particularly other democracies, can be relevant to determining whether a practice uniform among our people is not merely an historical accident, but rather so 'implicit in the concept of ordered liberty' that it occupies a place not merely in our mores, but, text permitting, in our Constitution as well," [citation omitted] they cannot serve to establish the first Eighth Amendment prerequisite, that the practice is accepted among our people.[124]

Thus, the Supreme Court's jurisprudence regarding the death penalty has remained completely unaffected by international criticism.

Recent presidents and members of Congress have also apparently been largely unmoved by international disapproval. Most U.S. politicians believe that the United States is not in violation of any human rights standards and assert that the nation has the "right, subject to its Constitutional constraints, to impose capital punishment on any person (other than a pregnant woman) duly convicted under existing or future laws permitting the imposition of capital punishment, including such punishment for crimes by persons below eighteen years of age."[125] Moreover, as the sole "superpower" remaining in the modern world, the United States is in some respects immune from the harshest effects of international criticism: it is unlikely that many nations would impose trade embargoes or other such sanctions on the United States.

Several commentators have remarked upon the U.S. government's indifference to international criticism. David Cole of the Georgetown University Law Center wrote an opinion piece in 1998 describing the "typical" U.S. response "to the growing international legal condemnation of our administration of the death penalty: We violate international law and simply ignore the consequences."[126] While it is debatable whether the United States is in fact in violation of international laws, Cole's main point, that the nation "couldn't care less" about international criticism, is echoed by others. Richard Dieter, executive director of the Death Penalty Information Center, an anti–death penalty organization in Washington, D.C., put it this way: "The over-all U.S. response to this criticism has been to ignore it."[127] Perhaps Jim Willett, the warden at the Huntsville, Texas, death chamber facility, summed up the general attitude best by saying, "Europeans don't vote in this country."[128]

The federal government's fiery response to the 1998 UN report on U.S. death penalty policy is instructive. The U.S. ambassador to the United Nations in Geneva, George Moose, called the report "severely flawed" and denied that the United States was violating international law. He accused Ndiaye, the author of the report, of excluding "valuable and extensive information" that would have supported the United States' position. Sen. Jesse Helms, R-N.C., chair of the Senate Foreign Relations Committee, described the mission as "an absurd UN charade." Helms's spokesman said, "With all the abuses in places like Burma, China, Cuba and Iraq, to be wasting time and money to investigate the freest country in the world shows what a strange and distant planet the United Nations inhabits."[129] Bill Richardson, the U.S. ambassador to the UN, suggested that the report would merely "collect a lot of dust."[130]

There was one case, though, in which international actors may have had some limited effect on a federal government official. In late 2000 the European Union, the pope, and French president Jacques Chirac were part of a large chorus calling for President Clinton to stay or commute the execution of Juan Raul Garza, who was to become the first federal prisoner executed since 1963.[131] The president did, in fact, stay the execution for at least six months so that the administration could study "racial and geographic disparities in the federal death penalty system."[132] However, the move was less final than some abolitionists had hoped, given the impending change of administrations. Clinton's successor, George W. Bush, was thought of as a vigorously pro–death penalty politician (under whom, in fact, Garza was executed in June 2001).[133]

Also, some executive branch officials have demonstrated worry over certain states' violations of an international law that requires that foreign nationals charged with capital crimes be allowed to consult with the consulate from their home nation. The U.S. State Department has expressed concern that, if U.S. states continue to deny this right, U.S. nationals in foreign countries may be treated the same way.[134] Even Madeleine Albright, the U.S. secretary of state at the time, was moved to express this concern.[135] However, these words have had little practical effect on the behavior of the states.

State Governments

There is little evidence that international pressure has much effect on state government actors. State courts almost never deal with issues of international law in deciding death penalty cases.[136] Usually, when an accused brings up a defense based on international law, the court simply dismisses it as ungrounded or irrelevant.[137] In the few cases in which state courts have addressed issues of international death penalty law, they have been almost uniformly unwilling to give it precedence over state laws and practices.[138] In one 1992 appeal in Ohio, for instance, a capital convict argued that international law prohibited his execution.[139] The court responded that the defendant had not showed that the U.S. government, in signing various international agreements, had meant to alter any state practices with respect to the application of the death penalty, and it rejected his arguments.[140] Even in cases of capital punishment of foreign nationals and persons who committed murders as juveniles, where clear international norms are in place, courts have not given precedence to international standards or international court decisions.

Nor have state governors or legislators been much moved by international pressure. In no case except one has international pressure succeeded in convincing a state executive to grant mercy to a person sentenced to death. In fact, most governors will not even meet with representatives from supra-national bodies or other nations to speak about death penalty issues.[141] The April 1998 execution of Angel Breard in Virginia is a good example of gubernatorial disinterest in international complaints. The execution of Breard, a Paraguayan citizen who was not informed of his right to consult with the Paraguayan consulate upon his arrest for murder, went ahead despite a ruling of the International Court of Justice demanding that it be stopped. Gov. James S. Gilmore, R-Va., did nothing to prevent the execution, despite requests from the international community.[142]

Of all the commuted death sentences since 1976, just one has resulted from international pressure.[143] In 1999 Gov. Mel Carnahan of Missouri, a proponent of the death penalty, commuted the sentence of Darrell Mease. In a 2000 speech Carnahan revealed that his action came at the direct request of Pope John Paul II in a "one-time act of mercy."[144] Although international actors have called for leniency in many cases, these appeals usually have little effect: executives normally commute sentences for reasons of internal U.S. politics, like disproportionate sentencing, questionable trial procedures, and the like.

Similarly, there is little evidence that state legislatures debating death penalty legislation give much thought to the concerns of the international community. During the recent attempt by the New Hampshire legislature to abolish the death penalty, politicians' rhetoric was centered on morality and effectiveness but did not make significant mention of international concerns. The same was true of New York State's reinstatement of the penalty in 1995 and the several successful abolition movements of the 1980s.

An exception came in 1991, when a state legislator in Massachusetts joined Amnesty International in attacking the governor's new death penalty proposal, which would have allowed execution for juvenile crimes.[145] Even then, however, the focus of the criticism had more to do with the Massachusetts constitution than with international sentiment about capital punishment. Put simply, state government actors in the United States mostly do not seem concerned about international condemnation: their worries lie with the opinion of the U.S. electorate.

Local Governments

The one area of U.S government on which international condemnation of the death penalty seems to have had some small effect is local: specifically, local prosecutors. As mentioned above, individual nations can be effective in getting prosecutors to drop capital charges by refusing to extradite accused criminals to the United States. The chief prosecutor in Los Angeles, for instance, recently stated that he would be willing to forgo seeking the death penalty in cases where doing so would prevent the return of the accused to U.S. authorities.[146]

Even those cases are rare, though. The most common policy of prosecutors is that which had been used by the Los Angeles district attorney's office prior to the change: authorities will not rule out seeking any punishment until the accused is in U.S. custody. Moreover, the extradition blocks do not affect prosecutors' use of the death penalty in cases in which the accused did not manage to flee the country. Although individual nations can sometimes change the behaviour of local government agents with respect to capital punishment in a few isolated cases, international pressure is mostly as powerless on the local level as it is on the state and national levels.

Notes

1. Roger Hood, "The Death Penalty: The USA in World Perspective," *Journal of Transnational Law and Policy* 6 (1997): 518.

2. William A. Schabas, *The Abolition of the Death Penalty in International Law* (Cambridge: Cambridge University Press, 1993), 1.

3. UN Doc. A/810 (1948).

4. Schabas, *The Abolition of the Death Penalty in International Law,* 25–50.

5. 999 U.N.T.S. 17.

6. 213 U.N.T.S. 221; 1144 U.N.T.S. 123.

7. Schabas, *The Abolition of the Death Penalty,* 1.

8. Ibid., 18.

9. G.A. Res. 44/128 (1990).

10. Protocol to the American Convention on Human Rights.

11. Ariane M. Schreiber, "States that Kill: Discretion and the Death Penalty—A Worldwide Perspective," *Cornell International Law Journal* 29 (1996): 278.

12. Status of the International Covenants on Human Rights, Question of the Death Penalty, UN ESCOR, Comm. on Human Rights, 5413. Sess., Agenda Item 13, UN Doc. E/CN.4/1998/L.12 (1998).

13. Hood, "The Death Penalty," 7.

14. Ibid., 8–9.

15. "Facts and Figures on the Death Penalty," Amnesty International, available at www.web.amnesty.org/rmp/dplibrary.

16. "Abolitionist and Retentionist Countries," Amnesty International, available at www.web.amnesty.org/rmp/dplibrary.

17. Ibid.

18. Hood, "The Death Penalty," 11–12.

19. Ibid.

20. "Abolitionist and Retentionist Countries," Amnesty International, available at www.web.amnesty.org/rmp/dplibrary.

21. Ibid.

22. Ibid.

23. Hood, "The Death Penalty,"29–34.

24. Ibid., 24.

25. Ibid.

26. Ibid., 25–26.

27. "Facts and Figures on the Death Penalty," Amnesty International, available at www.web. amnesty.org/rmp/dplibrary.

28. Ibid. This figure excludes the large number of executions that likely occurred in Iraq because of lack of data.

29. William A. Schabas, ed.,*The International Sourcebook on Capital Punishment* (Boston: Northeastern University Press, 1997), 241.

30. Ibid., 240.

31. Hood, "The Death Penalty," 47.

32. See Richard C. Dieter, "International Perspectives on the Death Penalty: A Costly Isolation for the U.S.," Death Penalty Information Center, October 1999, available at www. deathpenaltyinfo.org/internationalreport.html.

33. Peter Hodgkinson, "The United Kingdom and the European Union," in *Capital Punishment: Global Issues and Prospects,* ed. Peter Hodgkinson and Andrew Rutherford (Oxford: Waterside Press, 1996), 194.

34. Ibid.

35. Ibid., 194–95.

36. Ibid., 194.

37. Franklin E. Zimring and Gordon Hawkins, *Capital Punishment and the American Agenda* (Cambridge: Cambridge University Press, 1987), 12.

38. Hodgkinson, "The United Kingdom and the European Union," 195–196.

39. Ibid., 195.

40. Ibid., 198–199.

41. Peter Hodgkinson, "Europe—A Death Penalty Free Zone: Commentary and Critique of Abolitionist Strategies, " *Ohio Northern University Law Review* (2000): 661.

42. Cheryl Aviva Amitay, "Justice or 'Just Us': The Anomalous Retention of the Death Penalty in the United States," *Maryland Journal of Contemporary Legal Issues* 7 (1996): 545.

43. Kristi Tumminello Prinzo, "The United States—'Capital' of the World: An Analysis of Why the United States Practices Capital Punishment While the International Trend Is towards Its Abolition," *Brooklyn Journal of International Law* 24 (1999): 855.

44. Ibid., 866–873.

45. Ibid., 878–889.

46. Zimring and Hawkins, *Capital Punishment and the American Agenda,* 3.

47. Ibid., 12.

48. Ibid., 13–14.

49. Ibid.

50. Franklin Zimring and Gordon Hawkins, *Crime Is Not the Problem: Lethal Violence in America* (Oxford: Oxford University Press, 1997), 51.

51. Ibid., 53.

52. Note that Zimring and Hawkins do not make this argument.

53. Zimring and Hawkins, *Capital Punishment and the American Agenda*, 149–150.

54. Ibid., 164.

55. Joshua Micah Marshall, "Over There, a Capital Disconnect," *Pittsburgh Post-Gazette,* September 3, 2000, E4.

56. Ibid.

57. Ibid.

58. Ibid.

59. Ibid.

60. Ibid.

61. Ibid.

62. *Historic Documents of 1998* (Washington, D.C.: CQ Press, 1999).

63. Toni M. Fine, "Moratorium 2000: An International Dialogue toward a Ban on Capital Punishment," *Columbia Human Rights Law Review* 30 (1999): 430.

64. Jessica Feldman, "Comment: A Death Row Incarceration Calculus: When Prolonged Death Row Imprisonment Becomes Unconstitutional," *Santa Clara Law Review* 40 (1999): 204–205.

65. EU Demarche on the Death Penalty, February 25, 2000. Text available at www.eurunion.org/legislat/deathpenalty/Demarche.htm.

66. See www.eurunion.org/legislat/deathpenalty/deathpenhome.htm.

67. See www.eurunion.org/legislat/deathpenalty/Richardson.htm.

68. See www.eurunion.org/legislat/deathpenalty/governors.htm.

69. R. Cohen, "U.S. Execution of German Stirs Anger," *New York Times,* March 5, 1999.

70. Ibid.

71. See M. Jimenez, "Texas Rules Alberta Man Will Die but Canadian Momentum Builds to Save His Life," *National Post* (Canada), November 24, 1998; Richard Dieter, "International Perspectives on the Death Penalty: A Costly Isolation for the U.S.," Death Penalty Information Center, October 1999, available at www.deathpenaltyinfo.org/internationalreport.html.

72. The Right Honourable the Lord Scarman and Philip Sapsford, QC, "The Death Penalty: Can Delay Render Execution Lawful?" *Anglo-American Law Review* 25 (1996): 282.

73. Frank Ching, "U.S. Role on Rights Reversed: UN Committee Members Criticize Washington's Record," *Far East Economic Review* (June 22, 1995): 40.

74. Fine, "Moratorium 2000," 428.

75. Ibid.

76. Eric J. Lyman, "Killers Embodied as Victims of U.S. Justice; Italians Are the Most Vocal in Europe to Speak Out Against Capital Punishment," *Houston Chronicle*, March 5, 2000, A1.

77. Ibid.

78. Anjali Sachdeva, "French Leader Says U.S. Should Abolish Death Penalty," *Pittsburgh Post-Gazette*, August 29, 2000, D-6.

79. Ibid.

80. See William A. Schabas, "International Law and Abolition of the Death Penalty," *Washington and Lee Law Review* 55 (summer 1998): 837–838.

81. Ibid. See also Elana Mintz, "The Fight To Extradite," *CQ Weekly*, October 10, 1998; and Nadine Cohodas, "Fights Over Death Penalty, Gun Control Likely to Mark House Drug Bill Debate," *CQ Weekly*, September 3, 1988.

82. Constitution of Italy, Article 2, 27.

83. Ted Rohrlich, "D.A. to Stop Seeking Death in Some Cases to Ease Extraditions; Justice: Cooley Instead Will Aim for Life Sentences in Hopes of Getting Nations that Oppose Capital Punishment to Cooperate in Sending Back Fugitives," *Los Angeles Times*, January 9, 2001, B3.

84. Ibid.

85. Amnesty International, annual report 2000.

86. Ibid.

87. Mark Curriden, "Inmate's Last Wish Is to Donate Kidney," *American Bar Association Journal* 82 (1996): 26.

88. "About Amnesty International," available at www.web.amnesty.org/web/aboutai.nsf.

89. Elizabeth Olson, "Good Friends Join Enemies to Criticize U.S. on Rights," *New York Times*, March 28, 1999, 9.

90. Amnesty International, Annual Report 2000, available at www.amnesty.org.

91. Maya Bell, "U.S. Comes Under Fire for Killing Teen Killers," *Orlando Sentinel*, January 10, 2000, A1.

92. Amnesty International, "USA: Serious Allegations of Racism and Injustice in Nevada Death Penalty Case," March 3, 2001.

93. Amnesty International, annual report 2000, section on United States.

94. Available at www.web.amnesty.org/rmp/dplibrary.nsf.

95. Human Rights Watch, "The Death Penalty," available at www.hrw.org/about/initiatives/deathpen.htm.

96. Human Rights Watch, "United States: World Leader in Executing Juveniles," March 1995 report.

97. See www.moratorium2000.org.

98. Craig Offman, "Benetton Says Ciao to Toscani," *Salon,* May 20, 2000.

99. Craig Offman, "Live From Death Row," *Salon,* April 17, 2000.

100. Offman, "Benetton," 2000.

101. "Execution Stayed for Inmate in Benetton Ad," *Charleston Gazette,* January 19, 2001, 3C.

102. Ibid.

103. Pope John Paul II, Mass in St. Louis, Missouri, January 27, 1999.

104. New Catechism of the Catholic Church, released September 8, 1997, available at www.scborromeo.org/ccc/.

105. Ibid., at sect. 2, art. 5, chap. 2, par. 2267.

106. Pope John Paul II, Mass in St. Louis, Missouri, January 27, 1999.

107. "Pope Seeks Clemency for Two Arkansas Death-Row Inmates," *Catholic News Service,* August 27, 1999.

108. Statement of Rabbi Eric Yoffie, president, Union of American Hebrew Congregations, March 9, 2000. Text available at www.deathpenaltyreligious.org.

109. Letter reprinted in "Largest Jewish Organization Calls on Oklahoma Governor to Grant Clemency for Crimes Prisoner Committed as a Boy," *U.S. Newswire,* February 3, 2001.

110. Statement read by Kobutsu Malone, April 9, 1999. Text reprinted at www.deathpenaltyreligious.org.

111. Koran, trans. N. J. Dawood (London: Penguin, 1988), 390. Emphasis added.

112. 34 UN GAOR 3d. comm., 37115. Sess., 67116. Mtg., 46, UN Doc. A/C.3/37/SR.67 (1982).

113. Bill Bell Jr., "Group Urges Holden to Halt Man's Execution; Inmate's Sexual Orientation Was Used Against Him, Amnesty International Says," *St. Louis Post-Dispatch,* February 6, 2001, B2.

114. "Amnesty International Condemns Execution of Missouri Inmate," Amnesty International press release, February 7, 2001, available at www.amnestyusa.org/abolish/index.html.

115. See www.hrw.org/about/initiatives/us.html.

116. See www.igc.org/cacp/.

117. Emily Yellin, "Arkansas Executes Woman Who Killed Both Her Children," *New York Times,* May 3, 2000, A22.

118. Joan Biskupic and Donald Baker, "Supreme Court Delays Va. Execution To Consider Standards for Appeals," *Washington Post,* April 6, 1999, A13.

119. Tim Hoover and Joe Robertson, "Killer Is Executed for Wife's Slaying," *Tulsa World,* December 17, 1998.

120. Jenny Staletovich, "The Electric Chair Power Struggle; Florida's 'Old Sparky' Endures Despite Inefficiency," *Palm Beach Post,* January 2, 2000, 1A.

121. Jeff Pillets, "Death Penalty Foes Visit Whitman," *The Record* (Bergen County, New Jersey), December 12, 2000, A3.

122. For text, see www.deathpenaltyreligious.org.

123. *Gregg v. Georgia,* 428 U.S. 153 (1976).

124. *Stanford v. Kentucky,* 492 U.S. 361 (1989), 370.

125. United States' reservation to Article 6 of the International Covenant on Human Rights, 1992.

126. David Cole, "We've Long Been Death Penalty Outlaws," *Legal Times,* April 27, 1998, 23.

127. Richard Dieter, "International Perspectives on the Death Penalty: A Costly Isolation for the U.S.," October 1999, available at www.deathpenaltyinfo.org/internationalreport.html.

128. Kevin Johnson and Guillermo X. Garcia, "Europeans Keep Vigil at Texas' Death Row," *USA Today,* December 14, 2000, 21A.

129. Elif Kaban, "U.S. Rejects UN Executions Charge as 'Severely Flawed,'" AP Newsfeed, April 15, 1998.

130. Ibid.

131. Henry Weinstein and Eric Tichtblau, "Clinton Stays Execution for Racial Study," *Los Angeles Times,* December 8, 2000, A1.

132. Ibid.

133. Ibid.

134. "U.S. Gets Criticism for Rights Practices; World Court's Rebuff Is Cited in Execution," *Sun-Sentinel* (Fort Lauderdale, Florida), April 16, 1998, 14A.

135. Ibid.

136. Ronan Doherty, "Foreign Affairs v. Federalism: How State Control of Criminal Law Implicates Federal Responsibility Under International Law," *Virginia Law Review* 82 (October 1996): 315. See also Erica Templeton, "Killing Kids: The Impact of *Dominguez v. Nevada* on the Juvenile Death Penalty As a Violation of International Law," *Boston College Law Review* 41 (September 2000): 1214–1215.

137. Doherty, "Foreign Affairs v. Federalism," 1315.

138. Ibid.

139. *Ohio v. Williams*, Ohio App. LEXIS 5529 (1992).

140. Ibid. See also Doherty, "Foreign Affairs v. Federalism," 1315.

141. Ibid., 1329–1330.

142. Asha Rangappa, "The Power to Pardon, the Power to Gain," *New York Times*, February 3, 2001, A13.

143. See Michael Radelet and Barbara Zsembik, "Executive Clemency in post-*Furman* Capital Cases," *University of Richmond Law Review* 27 (winter 1993); and www.deathpenaltyinfo.org/clemency.html.

144. Jo Mannies, "Carnahan Gives Details in Commutation of Death Sentence; Governor Acted at Request of Pope," *St. Louis Post-Dispatch*, March 31, 2000, A1.

145. Frederic M. Biddle, "As Rights Group Raps Youth Death Penalty, Weld Limits Its Scope," *Boston Globe*, October 9, 1991, 28.

146. Ted Rohrlich, "D.A. to Stop Seeking Death in Some Cases to Ease Extraditions; Justice: Cooley instead Will Aim for Life Sentences in Hopes of Getting Nations that Oppose Capital Punishment to Cooperate in Sending Back Fugitives," *Los Angeles Times*, January 9, 2001, B3.

Appendix

Further Research and Chronology 195

    Bibliography of Print Sources   195

    Bibliography of Internet Sources   206

    Chronology   208

Facts, Policies, and Commentary 212

    U.S. Jurisdictions that Lack the Death Penalty   212

    An Example of Aggravating Factors: Alabama's Murder Statute   215

    Limiting Proportionality Review   216

    Capital Punishment Policies in Nations Worldwide   217

    Notable Quotes on Capital Punishment   221

Encyclopedia Articles 223

    Capital Punishment   223

    International Bill of Human Rights   224

    Universal Declaration of Human Rights   226

Primary Documents 229

    Fact Sheet: The International Bill of Human Rights   229

    UN Report on the Use of the Death Penalty in the United States   242

    Selected Supreme Court Cases   250

Further Research and Chronology

Bibliography of Print Sources

"ACLU Joins Lawsuit Against County With High Execution Rate." *Chicago Tribune,* October 1, 2000, 12C.

"Against the American System of Capital Punishment." *Harvard Law Review* 99 (1986): 1687.

American Bar Association. "Report Regarding Implementation of the American Bar Association's Recommendations and Resolutions Concerning the Death Penalty and Calling for a Moratorium on Executions," 1998.

———. "Toward a More Just and Effective System of Review in State Death Penalty Cases: A Report Containing the American Bar Association's Recommendations Concerning Death Penalty Habeas Corpus and Related Materials From the American Bar Association Criminal Justice Section's Project on Death Penalty Habeas Corpus." ABA Task Force on Death Penalty Habeas Corpus, 1990.

American Convention on Human Rights, 1144 U.N.T.S. 123 (1979).

American Ethical Union. Resolution on Capital Punishment. Adopted September 17, 1976.

Amitay, Cheryl Aviva. "Justice or 'Just Us': The Anomalous Retention of the Death Penalty in the United States." *Maryland Journal of Contemporary Legal Issues* 7 (1996): 545.

Amnesty International. "Abolitionist and Retentionist Countries." Available at www.web.amnesty.org/rmp/dplibrary.

———. "About Amnesty International." Available at www.web.amnesty.org/web/aboutai.nsf.

———. "Amnesty International Condemns Execution of Missouri Inmate." February 7, 2001. Available at www.amnestyusa.org/abolish/index.html.

———. Annual report 2000. Available at www.amnesty.org.

———. "Facts and Figures on the Death Penalty." Available at www.web.amnesty.org/rmp/dplibrary.

———. "USA: Serious Allegations of Racism and Injustice in Nevada Death Penalty Case." March 3, 2001.

Annan, Kofi. Remarks upon receiving the petition of the Moratorium 2000 campaign, New York. December 18, 2000. Text available online at www.moratorium2000.org/events/annan_statement.lasso.

"Around the U.S." *Dallas Morning News,* April 10, 2001, 4A.

Bedeau, Hugo, ed. *The Death Penalty in America.* 3d ed. Oxford: Oxford University Press, 1982, 95.

Bell, Bill, Jr. "Group Urges Holden to Halt Man's Execution; Inmate's Sexual Orientation Was Used Against Him, Amnesty International Says." *St. Louis Post-Dispatch,* February 6, 2001, B2.

Bell, Maya. "U.S. Comes Under Fire for Killing Teen Killers." *Orlando Sentinel,* January 10, 2000, A1.

Berry, Jason. "Is Justice Forgiving?" *Dallas Morning News,* August 15, 1993, 1J.

Biddle, Frederic M. "As Rights Group Raps Youth Death Penalty, Weld Limits Its Scope." *Boston Globe,* October 9, 1991, 28.

Bienen, Leigh B. "Criminal Law: The Proportionality Review of Capital Cases by State High Courts After *Gregg:* Only the 'Appearance of Justice'?" *Northwestern School of Law Journal of Criminal Law and Criminology* 87 (fall 1996): 130, 170.

Biskupic, Joan, and Donald Baker. "Supreme Court Delays Virginia Execution to Consider Standards for Appeals." *Washington Post,* April 6, 1999, A13.

Block, Melissa. "New York Governor Removes Bronx D.A. Over Death Penalty." *Morning Edition* (National Public Radio), March 22, 1996. Transcript #1830-5.

Bowers, William J. *Legal Homicide: Death as Punishment in America, 1864–1982.* Boston: Northeastern University Press, 1984.

Bright, S. "Judges and the Politics of Death: Deciding Between the Bill of Rights and the Next Election in Capital Cases." *Boston University Law Review* 75 (1995): 779.

Brooks, Elizabeth A. "Thou Shalt Not Quote the Bible: Determining the Propriety of Attorney Use of Religious Philosophy and Themes in Oral Arguments." *Georgia Law Review* 30 (summer 1999).

Bureau of Justice Statistics. http://www.ojp.usdoj.gov/bjs/id.htm.

Cabana v. Bullock, 474 U.S. 376 (1986).

Catholic Church. New Catechism. Released September 8, 1997.

Ching, Frank. "U.S. Role on Rights Reversed: UN Committee Members Criticize Washington's Record." *Far East Economic Review* (June 22, 1995): 40.

Claiborne, William, and Paul Duggan. "Spotlight on Death Penalty; Illinois Ban Ignites a National Debate." *Washington Post,* June 18, 2000, A1.

Cohen, R. "U.S. Execution of German Stirs Anger." *New York Times,* March 5, 1999.

Cohodas, Nadine. "Fights over Death Penalty, Gun Control Likely to Mark House Drug Bill Debate." *CQ Weekly,* September 3, 1988.

Coker v. Georgia, 433 U.S. 584 (1977).

Cole, David. "We've Long Been Death Penalty Outlaws." *Legal Times,* April 27, 1998, 23.

Collins, Rachel. "N.H. to Begin Hearings on Death Penalty Today—Dozens to Testify about Bill Revisited By N.H. Legislators." *Boston Globe,* January 30, 2001, B8.

Constitution of Italy. Art. 2, 27.

Cummings, Jeanne. "Florida Chief Justice Undergoes Quiz for U.S. Appeals Judgeship." *Fresno Bee,* February 4, 1994, A7.

Curriden, Mark. "Inmate's Last Wish Is to Donate Kidney." *American Bar Association Journal* 82 (1996): 26.

Davenport, P. "Death Row Inmates Losing Key Source of Legal Help." *Dallas Morning News,* February 19, 1996.

"Death Penalty in the Legislature: Some Thoughts About Money, Myth, and Morality." *University of Kansas Law Review* 37 (1989): 457.

Death Penalty Information Center. "The Death Penalty in 2000: Year End Report." December 2000. Available online at www.deathpenaltyinfo.org/yrendrpt00.html.

———. "Race of Defendants Executed Since 1976." Available at www.deathpenaltyinfo. org/dpicrace.html.

"Death Row USA." NAACP Legal Defense and Educational Fund, January, 2001.

"Death Row USA: Winter 2000." *Death Row USA Reporter.* NAACP Legal Defense and Educational Fund.

Debate on Second Optional Protocol to the International Covenant on Civil and Political Rights. 34 UN GAOR 3d Comm., 37th sess., 67th mtg., 46. UN Doc. A/C.3/37/SR.67 (1982).

Denning, Lord Justice. Royal Commission on Capital Punishment. Minutes of evidence, December 1, 1949. 1950, 207.

Dieter, Richard C. "International Perspectives on the Death Penalty: A Costly Isolation for the U.S." Death Penalty Information Center, October, 1999. Available at www. deathpenaltyinfo.org/internationalreport.html.

District Attorney v. Watson, 381 Mass. 648 (1980).

Doherty, Ronan. "Foreign Affairs v. Federalism: How State Control of Criminal Law Implicates Federal Responsibility Under International Law." *Virginia Law Review* 82 (October 1996): 1315.

Donnino, William C. Practice Commentary, N.Y. Penal Law 125.27 (McKinney 1998).

Douglas v. California, 372 U.S. 353 (1963).

Duggan, Paul. "Second Conviction in Dragging Death: Former Leader of White Supremacist Prison Group Faces Death Penalty in Texas." *Washington Post,* September 21, 1999, A2.

Dwyer, Jim, Barry Scheck, and Peter Neufeld. *Actual Innocence: Five Days to Execution and Other Dispatches from the Wrongly Convicted.* New York: Doubleday, 2000.

Eddings v. Oklahoma, 455 U.S. 104 (1982).

Eggen, Dan, and David A. Vise. "Ashcroft Sees No Halt in Executions; Death Penalty Appropriate for Those Committing 'Heinous Crimes,' He Says." *Washington Post,* April 28, 2001, A11.

Ehrlich, Isaac. "The Deterrent Effect of Capital Punishment: A Question of Life and Death." *American Economic Review* 65 (1975): 397.

Ellsworth, Phoebe C., and Lee Ross. "Public Opinion and Capital Punishment: A Close Examination of the Views of Abolitionists and Retentionists." *Crime & Delinquency* 29 (1983): 145.

Enmund v. Florida, 458 U.S. 782 (1982).

Epstein, Lee, and Thomas G. Walker. *Constitutional Law for a Changing America: Rights, Liberties and Justice.* Washington, D.C.: CQ Press, 2001.

EU Demarche on the Death Penalty, February 25, 2000. Available at www.eurunion.org/legislat/deathpenalty/Demarche.htm.

European Convention of Human Rights, 213 U.N.T.S. 221 (1955).

"Execution Stayed for Inmate in Benetton Ad." *Charleston Gazette,* January 19, 2001, 3C.

Exodus 21:24.

"Falwell, Robertson Feud over Death Penalty." *Arizona Republic,* April 16, 2000, J3.

Feldman, Jessica. "Comment: A Death Row Incarceration Calculus: When Prolonged Death Row Imprisonment Becomes Unconstitutional." *Santa Clara Law Review* 40 (1999): 204–205.

Fierro v. Gomez, 77 F.3d 301 (1996).

Finckenauer, James O. "Public Support for the Death Penalty: Retribution as Just Deserts or Retribution as Revenge?" *Justice Quarterly* 5 (1988): 90.

Fine, Toni M. "Moratorium 2000: An International Dialogue Toward a Ban on Capital Punishment." *Columbia Human Rights Law Review* 30 (1999): 430.

Fisher, Joan M. "Expedited Review of Capital Post-Conviction Claims: Idaho's Flawed Process." *Journal of Appellate Practice and Process* 2 (winter 2000): 85.

"Fixing the Death Penalty." *Chicago Tribune.* December 29, 2000, 22.

Ford v. Wainwright, 477 U.S. 399 (1986).

Fox, James Alan, and Michael L. Radelet. "Persistent Flaws in Econometric Studies of the Deterrent Effect of the Death Penalty." *Loyola Los Angeles Law Review* 23 (1989): 29.

Frost, Brian. "Capital Punishment and Deterrence: Conflicting Evidence?" *Journal of Criminal Law and Criminology* 74 (1983): 927.

Furman v. Georgia, 408 U.S. 238 (1972).

G.A. Res. 44/128 (1990).

Gallup, Alec, and Frank Newport. "Death Penalty Support Remains Strong." *Gallup Poll Monthly* (June 1991): 40.

Gallup Organization. "Gallup Report: The Death Penalty" (1985): 3.

———. Polls on capital punishment. Released June 16, 1991, and March 2, 2001.

———. Press release. February 24, 2000.

———. "Seven in 10 Favor Death Penalty for Murder." *Gallup Report* (January–February 1986): 10.

Gideon v. Wainwright, 372 U.S. 335 (1963).

Gleik, E. "Rich Justice, Poor Justice." *Time,* June 19, 1995, 40.

Gray v. Lucas, 710 F.2d 1048 (5th Cir. 1983).

Greene, Norman L. "Sparing Cain: Executive Clemency in Capital Cases." *Capital University Law Review* 28 (2000): 571.

Gregg v. Georgia, 428 U.S. 153 (1976).

Haines, Herbert H. *Against Capital Punishment: The Anti–Death Penalty Movement in America, 1972–1994.* Oxford: Oxford University Press, 1996.

Haney, Craig. "Riding the Punishment Wave: On the Origins of Our Devolving Standards of Decency." *Hastings Women's Law Journal* 9 (winter 1998): 48–49.

Hansen, M. "Politics and the Death Penalty." *Palm Beach Review,* February 25, 1991, 10B.

Heflin v. United States, 358 U.S. 415, 420 (1959). (Justice Stewart concurring.)

Higgins, Sean. "Death Penalty Is Still Popular in U.S., Despite Growing Campaign to End It." *Investor's Business Daily,* December 29, 2000, A22.

Historic Documents of 1998. Washington, D.C.: CQ Press, 1999.

Hodgkinson, Peter. "Europe—A Death Penalty Free Zone: Commentary and Critique of Abolitionist Strategies." *Ohio Northern University Law Review* (2000): 661.

———. "The United Kingdom and the European Union." In *Capital Punishment: Global Issues and Prospects,* ed. Peter Hodgkinson and Andrew Rutherford. Oxford: Waterside Press, 1996, 194.

Hood, Roger. *The Death Penalty: A Worldwide Perspective.* Oxford: Oxford University Press, 1996.

———. "The Death Penalty: The USA in World Perspective." *Journal of Transnational Law and Policy* 6 (1997): 518.

Hoover, Tim, and Joe Robertson. "Killer Is Executed for Wife's Slaying." *Tulsa World,* December 17, 1998.

Hoyt, Jennifer. "Death Penalty Opponents Ask Clinton for Moratorium." *Houston Chronicle,* November 22, 2000, A9.

Human Rights Watch. "The Death Penalty." Available at www.hrw.org/about/initiatives/deathpen.htm.

———. "United States: World Leader in Executing Juveniles" (March 1995).

Hunt v. Nuth, 57 F.3d 1327 (4th Cir. 1995).

"Ideas & Trends; Death and the White House." *New York Times,* December 17, 2000.

International Covenant on Civil and Political Rights, 999 U.N.T.S. 17.

Janicik, Doug. "Allowing Victims' Families to View Executions: The Eighth Amendment and Society's Justifications for Punishment." *Ohio State Law Journal* 61 (2000): 967–969.

Jimenez, M. "Texas Rules Alberta Man Will Die but Canadian Momentum Builds to Save His Life." *National Post* (Canada), November 24, 1998.

John Paul II (pope). Mass in St. Louis, Missouri, January 27, 1999.

Johnson, Dirk. "Illinois, Citing Faulty Verdicts, Bars Executions." *New York Times,* February 1, 2000, 1.

Johnson, Kevin, and Guillermo X. Garcia. "Europeans Keep Vigil at Texas' Death Row." *USA Today,* December 14, 2000, 21A.

Jordan, Sandra D. "Death for Drug Related Killings: Revival of the Federal Death Penalty." *Chicago-Kent Law Review* 67 (1991): 92.

Kadish, Sanford H., and Stephen J. Schulhofer. *Criminal Law and Its Processes.* 6th ed. Gaithersburg, Md.: Aspen, 1995, 544.

Kahan, Dan M. "The Secret Ambition of Deterrence." *Harvard Law Review* 113 (December 1999): 436.

Kannar, George. "Federalizing Death." *Buffalo Law Review* 44 (spring 1996): 325.

Kaplan, John. "The Problem of Capital Punishment." *University of Illinois Law Review* (1983): 561.

Kaye, John. Letter, published in *Legal Times,* February 10, 1997, 26.

Klein, Lawrence L., et al. "The Deterrent Effect of Capital Punishment: An Assessment of the Estimates." In *Deterrence and Incapacitation: Estimating the Effects of Criminal Sanctions on Crime Rates,* ed Alfred Blumstein et al. Washington, D.C.: National Academy of Sciences Press, 1978.

Klein, R., and R. Spangenburg. *The Indigent Defense Crisis.* Prepared for the American Bar Association Section of Criminal Justice Ad Hoc Committee on the Indigent Defense Crisis, 1993, 7.

Klein, Stephen J., and John E. Rolph. "Relationship of Offender and Victim Race to Death Penalty Sentences in California." *Jurimetrics* 32 (1991): 33.

Kloehn, Steve. "Baptists OK Limits on Women's Roles; Southern Sect Cites Bible as Authority." *Chicago Tribune,* June 15, 2000, 1.

Koenig, Sarah. "Racial Aspect Complicates Execution Issue; General Assembly Debates Moratorium, End to Death Penalty; Bills Compete for Support." *Baltimore Sun,* February 3, 2001, 1A.

Koran. N.J. Dawood, trans. London: Penguin, 1988, 390.

Kuhlmann v. Wilson, 477 U.S. 436, 454 (1986).

Lacey, Marc, and Raymond Bonner. "Reno Troubled by Death Penalty Statistics." *New York Times,* September 13, 2000, A17.

Lattin, Don. "WWJD? Once Only the Religious Right Asked That Question—Now Even Democratic Presidential Candidates Say They're Running with God." *San Francisco Chronicle,* September 15, 2000, A1.

Latzer, Barry, and James N.G. Cauthen. "Capital Appeals Revisited." *Judicature* 84, no. 2 (September–October 2000).

Layson, Stephen K. "Homicide and Deterrence: A Reexamination of the United States Time-Series Evidence." S. Econ. Journal 52 (1985): 80.

Lewis, John (Rep.). Press release. "Crime Bill." *Congressional Press Releases,* August 17, 1994.

Lewis, Neil A. "Four Key Issues in Dispute on Package to Fight Crime." *New York Times,* November 27, 1991, B8.

Liebman, James S., Jeffrey Fagan, and Valerie West. "A Broken System: Error Rates in Capital Cases, 1973–1995." Columbia University School of Law, June 12, 2000.

Linder, Craig. "Calling for New Abu-Jamal Trial, Activists Meet with Justice Department." *States New Service,* December 11, 2000.

Lockett v. Ohio, 438 U.S. 586 (1978).

Louisiana ex rel. Francis v. Resweber, 329 U.S. 459 (1947).

Lyman, Eric J. "Killers Embodied as Victims of U.S. Justice; Italians Are the Most Vocal in Europe to Speak Out Against Capital Punishment." *Houston Chronicle,* March 5, 2000, A1.

Malone, Kobutsu. Statement read on April 9, 1999. Available at www.deathpenalty religious.org.

Mannies, Jo. "Carnahan Gives Details in Commutation of Death Sentence; Governor Acted at Request of Pope." *St. Louis Post-Dispatch,* March 31, 2000, A1.

Marshall, Joshua Micah. "Over There, A Capital Disconnect." *Pittsburgh Post-Gazette,* September 3, 2000, E4.

Martin, Earl F. "Tessie Hutchinson and the American System of Capital Punishment." *Maryland Law Review* 59 (2000): 585–588.

Marx, Gary. "Fear Takes Spotlight in Governor's Race." *Chicago Tribune,* October 19, 1994, A1.

McCleskey v. Kemp, 481 U.S. 279 (1987).

"Meting Death to Juvenile Criminals." *Washington Post,* December 8, 2000, A54.

Mills, Steve. "Texas Criticized on Death Penalty; Study by Defenders Group Says System Is Deeply Flawed, Biased." *Chicago Tribune,* October 16, 2000, 3.

Mintz, Elana. "The Fight to Extradite." *CQ Weekly,* October 10, 1998.

Mintz, Howard. "Killer Wants Death but San Francisco DA Says 'No,'" *San Jose Mercury News,* January 9, 2001.

Minzesheimer, Bob. "Executioner's Song Heard in Gubernatorial Races." *USA Today,* October 27, 1994, 9A.

Mooney, Christopher Z., and Mei-Hsien Lee. "Morality Policy Reinvention: State Death Penalties." *The Annals of the American Academy of Political and Social Science* 566 (1999): 84.

Murray v. Carrier, 477 U.S. 478 (1986).

National Center for Policy Analysis. "Myth of Racism in Death Penalty." Available at www.ncpa.org/pi/crime/pd111998d.html.

National Coalition to Abolish the Death Penalty. "Death Penalty Profile." January 1, 2001. Available at www.ncadp.org/stats.html.

"National Perspective; The Law; Attorney's Dozing at Center of Texas Murder Case Challenge; Defendant Facing the Death Penalty Contends His Lawyer in 1984 Trial Was No More Aware 'Than A Potted Plant.'" *Los Angeles Times,* January 23, 2001, A1.

New York Times, July 29, 1994, A1.

Nichols, Bill. "Clinton Sticks to His Message." *USA Today,* August 21, 1992, 6A.

Nossiter, Adam. "Balking Prosecutors: A Door Opens to Death Row Challenges." *New York Times,* March 11, 1995, sect. 1, 27.

O'Connor, Paul. "Racial Bias in Death Penalty Cases Gets a Closer Look." *Asheville Citizen-Times,* September 24, 2000, A10.

"Officials Hear Call for Moratorium on Death Penalty." *South Bend Tribune,* D4.

Offman, Craig. "Benetton Says Ciao to Toscani." *Salon,* May 20, 2000. Available at www.salon. com.

———. "Live from Death Row." *Salon,* April 17, 2000. Available at www.salon.com.

Ohio v. Williams, 1992 Ohio App. LEXIS 5529, 1992.

Palmer, Elizabeth A. "Congress Considers Taking a Role in Improving Quality of Counsel." *CQ Weekly,* June 3, 2000, 1324.

———. "The Death Penalty: Shifting Perspectives." *CQ Weekly,* June 3, 2000, 1324.

Paternoster, Raymond. *Capital Punishment in America,* 1991.

"Pat Robertson, ACLU Make Unlikely Allies." *San Antonio Express-News,* April 11, 2000, 6B.

Payne v. Tennessee, 501 U.S. 808 (1991).

Pennsylvania Coalition to Abolish the Death Penalty. "Pennsylvania Death Penalty Legislative Alert." July 1, 1996.

Penry v. Lynaugh, 492 U.S. 302 (1989).

People v. Anderson, 6 Cal. 3d 628 (1972).

Pillets, Jeff. "Death Penalty Foes Visit Whitman." *The Record* (Bergen County, New Jersey), December 12, 2000, A3.

"Pope Seeks Clemency for Two Arkansas Death-Row Inmates." *Catholic News Service,* August 27, 1999.

Prinzo, Kristi Tumminello. "The United States—'Capital' of the World: An Analysis of Why the United States Practices Capital Punishment While the International Trend Is Towards Its Abolition." *Brooklyn Journal of International Law* 24 (1999): 855.

Protocol to the American Convention on Human Rights.

Provenzano v. Moore, 120 S. Ct. 1222, cert. denied 2000 U.S. LEXIS 1439.

Provenzano v. Moore, 744 So. 2d 413 (Fla. 1999).

Pulley v. Harris, 465 U.S. 37 (1984).

Radelet, Michael L., and Barbara Zsembik. "Executive Clemency in Post-*Furman* Capital Cases." *University of Richmond Law Review* 27 (winter 1993); and www.deathpenaltyinfo.org/clemency.html.

Radelet, Michael L., and Ronald L. Akers. "Policy and Perspective: Deterrence and the Death Penalty: The Views of the Experts." *Northwestern School of Law Journal of Criminal Law and Criminology* 87 (fall 1996).

Radin. "Cruel Punishment and Respect for Persons: Super Due Process for Death." *Southern California Law Review* 53 (1980): 1143.

Rangappa, Asha. "The Power to Pardon, the Power to Gain." *New York Times,* February 3, 2001, A13.

Reinert, Patty, and Richard Stewart. "Doctor Details 'Devastating Pain' of Dragging: Prosecutors Finish Case with Gruesome Testimony." *Houston Chronicle,* September 17, 1999, A33.

Renaud, Trisha. "Killer Asks Jurors, 'Why Take the Risk?' of Letting Him Live." *Fulton County Daily Report,* October 7, 1998.

Roberts v. Louisiana, 431 U.S. 633 (1977).

Rohrlich, Ted. "D.A. to Stop Seeking Death in Some Cases to Ease Extraditions"; "Justice: Cooley Instead Will Aim for Life Sentences in Hopes of Getting Nations That Oppose Capital Punishment to Cooperate in Sending Back Fugitives." *Los Angeles Times,* January 9, 2001, B3.

Ryan, George (Gov.). Executive Order Number 4 (2000), creating the governor's commission on capital punishment.

———. Press release. "Governor Ryan Declares Moratorium on Executions, Will Appoint Commission to Review Capital Punishment System." January 31, 2000. Available at www.state.il.us/gov/press/00/jan/morat.htm.

Sachdeva, Anjali. "French Leader Says U.S. Should Abolish Death Penalty." *Pittsburgh Post-Gazette,* August 29, 2000, D6.

Sawyer v. Whitley, 505 U.S. 333, 339 (1992).

Scarman, Right Honourable Lord, and Philip Sapsford, QC. "The Death Penalty: Can Delay Render Execution Lawful?" *Anglo-American Law Review* 25 (1996): 282.

Schabas, William A. *The Abolition of the Death Penalty in International Law.* Cambridge: Cambridge University Press, 1993, 1.

———. "International Law and Abolition of the Death Penalty." *Washington and Lee Law Review* 55 (summer 1998): 837–838.

———., ed. *The International Sourcebook on Capital Punishment.* Boston: Northeastern University Press, 1997, 241.

Schlup v. Delo, 513 U.S. 298, 314 (1995).

Schreiber, Ariane M. "States That Kill: Discretion and the Death Penalty—A Worldwide Perspective." *Cornell International Law Journal* 29 (1996): 278.

Schwed, Roger. *Abolition and Capital Punishment: The United States' Judicial, Political and Moral Barometer,* 1983.

Sharpe, Dudley. "Death Penalty and Sentencing Information in the United States." Justice for All. Available at www.prodeathpenalty,com/DP.html#C.

———. "Pro & Con: The Death Penalty in Black and White." Justice for All. Available at www.prodeathpenalty.com/racism.htm.

Sheridan v. State, 852 S.W.2d 772, 780 (Ark. 1993).

Sherrell, George Wesley Jr. "Note: Successive Chances for Life: *Kuhlmann v. Wilson,* Federal Habeas Corpus, and the Capital Petitioner." *New York University Law Review* 64 (1989): 478.

Snell, Tracy L., and James J. Stephan. "Capital Punishment 1994." United States Department of Justice, Office of Justice Programs, February, 1996, 8.

Snell, Tracy L. "Capital Punishment 1995." United States Department of Justice, Office of Justice Programs, February, 1997, 8.

———. "Capital Punishment 1996." United States Department of Justice, Office of Justice Programs, December, 1997, 8.

———. "Capital Punishment 1997." United States Department of Justice, Office of Justice Programs, December, 1998, 9.

———. "Capital Punishment 1998." United States Department of Justice, Office of Justice Programs, December, 1999, 9.

Soskis, Benjamin. "Alive and Kicking." *New Republic,* April 17–24, 2000, 26.

Staletovitch, Jenny. "The Electric Chair Power Struggle; Florida's 'Old Sparky' Endures Despite Inefficiency." *Palm Beach Post,* January 2, 2000, 1A.

Stanford v. Kentucky, 492 U.S. 361 (1989).

Status of the International Covenants on Human Rights, Question of the Death Penalty, U.N. ESCOR, Comm. on Hum. Rts., 54th Sess., Agenda Item 13, U.N. Doc. E/CN.4/1998/L.12 (1998).

Stephan, James J., and Peter Brien. "Capital Punishment 1993." United States Department of Justice, Office of Justice Programs, December 1994.

Streib, Victor L. "Death Penalty for Female Offenders: January 1, 1973–June 30, 2000." Available at http://www.law.onu.edu/faculty/streib/femdeath.htm or http://www.law.onu.edu/faculty/streib/femdeath.pdf.

Templeton, Erica. "Killing Kids: The Impact of *Dominguez v. Nevada* on the Juvenile Death Penalty as a Violation of International Law." *Boston College Law Review* 41 (September 2000): 1214–1215.

Tison v. Arizona, 481 U.S. 137 (1987).

Turner, Allan. "Making Life Miserable for Felons; Co-Founder Propels Victims' Rights Group into Heart of Issues." *Houston Chronicle,* June 11, 2000, A35.

UN Doc. A/810 (1948).

U.S. Census Bureau. "Resident Population Estimates of the United States by Sex, Race, and Hispanic Origin." Population Estimates Program, Population Division. April 1, 1990–July 1, 1999, with short-term projection to November 1, 2000.

U.S. Constitution. Amendment V.

———. Amendment XIV.

———. Art. I, § 9, cl. 2.

U.S. Department of Justice. "The Federal Death Penalty System: A Statistical Survey (1988–2000)." September 12, 2000. Available online at www.usdoj.gov/dag/ pubdoc/dp-survey.html.

U.S. General Accounting Office. "Death Penalty Sentencing," 1990, 5–6.

"U.S. Gets Criticism for Rights Practices; World Court's Rebuff Is Cited in Execution." *Sun-Sentinel* (Fort Lauderdale, Florida), April 16, 1998, 14A.

United States v. Cooper, 754 F. Supp. 617, 627 (N.D. Ill. 1990).

United States v. Pitera, 795 F. Supp. 546, 569-70 (E.D.N.Y. 1992).

United States' reservation to Article 6 of the International Covenant on Human Rights, 1992.

Van den Haag, Ernest. "Refuting Reiman and Nathanson." In *Punishment and the Death Penalty,* ed. Robert M. Baird and Stuart E. Rosenbaum. Buffalo: Prometheus Books, 1995, 207, 214.

Vandiver, M. "The Quality of Mercy: Race and Clemency in Florida Death Penalty Cases, 1924–1966." *University of Richmond Law Review* 27 (1993): 315.

Verhovek, Sam Howe. "AK-47's, Battery Acid; Dead Women Waiting: Who's Who on Death Row." *New York Times,* February 8, 1998, sect. 4, 1.

Vilbig, Peter. "Innocent on Death Row; Cases of Innocent People Sentenced to Die." *New York Times Upfront* 2, vol. 133 (September 18, 2000): 10.

Wallace, Benjamin. "States Follow Illinois Lead on Death Penalty." *Boston Globe,* February 9, 2000, A3.

Weinstein, Henry, and Eric Tichtblau. "Clinton Stays Execution for Racial Study." *Los Angeles Times,* December 8, 2000, A1.

Weinstein, Henry. "Issue of Clemency Is Davis's Most Difficult as Governor." *Los Angeles Times,* February 6, 1991, A1.

White, Gayle. "Baptists OK Rules on Gays, Women." *Atlanta Journal and Constitution,* June 15, 2000, 1E.

"Why Won't They Give the New President a Chance?" *Daily Telegraph* (London), December 15, 2000, 31.

Willing, Richard, and Gary Fields. "Geography of the Death Penalty. *USA Today,* December 20, 1999, 1A.

Woods, Jeff. "Public Outrage Nails a Judge." *Nashville Banner,* July 15, 1996, A1.

———. "Sundquist Admits Early Ballot to Boot White." *Nashville Banner,* July 26, 1996, B2.

Yellin, Emily. "Arkansas Executes Woman Who Killed Both her Children." *New York Times,* May 3, 2000, A22.

Yoffie, Eric, and David Saperstein. Letter to Gov. Frank Keating. Reprinted in "Largest Jewish Organization Calls on Oklahoma Governor to Grant Clemency for Crimes Prisoner Committed as a Boy." *U.S. Newswire,* February 3.

Yoffie, Eric. President, Union of American Hebrew Congregations. Statement made Thursday, March 9, 2000. Available at www.deathpenaltyreligious.org.

Zimring, Franklin E., and Gordon Hawkins. *Capital Punishment and the American Agenda.* Cambridge: Cambridge University Press, 1987, 12.

———. *Crime Is Not the Problem: Lethal Violence in America.* Oxford: Oxford University Press, 1997.

Bibliography of Internet Sources

Abolitionist Action Committee   http//www.abolition.org

American Bar Association   http://www.abanet.org

American Civil Liberties Union   http://www.aclu.org

American Friends Service Committee   http://www.afsc.org

Amnesty International   http://www.web.amnesty.org

Amnesty International—Rights for All: Death Penalty in the USA   http://www.amnestyusa.org/rightsforall/dp/index.html

". . . and Justice for All" (sponsored by the National Association of Criminal Defense Lawyers)   http://www.criminaljustice.org

Catholics Against Capital Punishment   http://www.igc.org/cacp/

Christian Broadcasting Network   http://www.cbn.com
Citizens United for Alternatives to the Death Penalty   http://www.cuadp.org
Criminal Justice Legal Foundation   http://www.cjlf.org
Death Penalty Information   http://www.dpinfo.com
Death Penalty Information Center   http://www.deathpenaltyinfo.org
Equal Justice USA—a project of the Quixote Center http://www.quixote.org/ej/
European Union—Delegation of the European Commission to the United States
    http://www.eurunion.org/legislat/deathpenalty/deathpenhome.htm
Hands off Cain   http://www.handsoffcain.org
Human Rights Watch   http://www.hrw.org
Jerry Falwell Ministries   http://www.falwell.com
Justice for All   http://www.jfa.net
Moratorium Campaign   http://www.moratorium2000.org
MurderVictims.com   http://www.murdervictims.com
National Association for the Advancement of Colored People   http://www.naacp.org
National Association of Criminal Defense Lawyers   http://www.nacdl.org
National Association of Police Organizations   http://www.napo.org
National Center for Victims of Crime   http://www.ncvc.org
National Coalition to Abolish the Death Penalty   http://www.ncadp.org
National Conference of Catholic Bishops/United States Catholic Conference
    http://www.nccbuscc.org
National District Attorneys Association   http://www.ndaa.org
National Organization for Victim Assistance   http://www.try-nova.org
Office of the Clark County (Indiana) Prosecuting Attorney
    http://www.clarkprosecutor.org
Office of the Governor of Illinois   http://www.state.il.us/gov/
Office of the Governor of New York   http://www.state.ny.us/governor/
Pat Robertson (official site)   http://www.patrobertson.com
Pro–Death Penalty.com   http://www.prodeathpenalty.com
Religious Organizing Against the Death Penalty Project
    http://www.deathpenaltyreligious.org
Republican National Committee   http://www.rnc.org
Southern Baptist Convention   http://www.sbc.net
Southern Christian Leadership Conference
    http://www.mindspring.com/~sartor/gradyhs/org_SCLC.html
United Nations Office of the High Commissioner for Human Rights
    http://www.unhchr.ch/

United States Department of Justice   http://www.usdoj.gov
United States Senate Committee on the Judiciary   http://www.senate.gov/~judiciary/
Vatican: The Holy See   http://www.vatican.va
Washington Legal Fund   http://www.wlf.org
United Colors of Benetton   http://www.benetton.com
White House   http://www.whitehouse.gov

Chronology

July 2, 1976   U.S. Supreme Court decides *Gregg v. Georgia,* holding that U.S. jurisdictions may impose capital punishment.

June 29, 1977   In *Coker v. Georgia* Supreme Court rules that states may not execute for the crime of rape of an adult woman.

July 2, 1982   Supreme Court decides *Enmund v. Florida,* holding that the Eighth Amendment prohibits the imposition of the death penalty for mere participation in a robbery in which an accomplice takes a life.

January 23, 1984   Supreme Court justices decide *Pulley v. Harris,* ruling that automatic review of death sentences and proportionality review are not constitutional requirements.

June 26, 1986   In *Murray v. Carrier* Supreme Court holds that state prisoners must first exhaust all state court remedies before filing federal habeas corpus writs.

June 26, 1986   Supreme Court decides *Ford v. Wainwright,* ruling that the government may not execute an insane person.

April 21, 1987   Supreme Court decides *Tison v. Arizona,* holding that the Eighth Amendment does not necessarily prohibit the death penalty when the defendant lacked an outright intent to kill; a person who knowingly engages in a crime that is likely to cause the death of another may be executed.

April 22, 1987   In *McCleskey v. Kemp* Supreme Court rules that a death sentence imposed by a system containing racial disparities does not contravene the tenets of the Constitution if the defendant can prove no discrimination in his or her particular case.

June 26, 1989   Supreme Court decides *Penry v. Lynaugh,* holding that the government may constitutionally execute a mentally retarded person.

June 26, 1989   Supreme Court decides *Stanford v. Kentucky,* holding that the government may execute people for crimes they committed at age sixteen or older.

June 27, 1991   In *Payne v. Tennessee* Supreme Court rules that the Eighth Amendment does not prohibit juries from hearing "victim impact" evidence during the sentencing phase of a trial.

June 8, 1992   The United States accedes to the International Covenant on Civil and Political Rights but reserves the right to execute criminals for offenses committed when they were juveniles.

February 16, 1995   U.S. representative to the United Nations Madeleine Albright signs the Convention on the Rights of the Child on behalf of President Bill Clinton. Among other things, the agreement forbids ratifying nations from executing people for crimes they commit before the age of eighteen. The Senate never ratifies the accord.

March 7, 1995   New York becomes most recent state to re-adopt a capital punishment statute. New governor George Pataki signs the law, ending a string of twelve years during which former governor Mario Cuomo had vetoed death penalty legislation each year.

September 13, 1995   Congress passes the Federal Death Penalty Act, which requires U.S. attorneys to submit for review by a committee of senior Justice Department attorneys all cases in which a defendant is charged with a capital-eligible offense. The attorney general now makes a final decision in every case about whether or not to seek the death penalty. The act also changes the appellate procedure for federal death sentences.

June 27, 1995   The Fourth Circuit Court of Appeals decides *Hunt v. Nuth,* ruling that electrocution as a method of execution is permissible under the Constitution.

December 5, 1995   The Ninth Circuit Court of Appeals decides *Fierro v. Gomez,* holding that electrocution is unconstitutional because it is "cruel and unusual" and therefore violates the Eighth Amendment.

April 24, 1996   President Clinton signs the 1996 Anti-Terrorism and Effective Death Penalty Act into law. The law, drafted as a response to the bombing of a federal building in Oklahoma City, was in part intended to reduce the time between the sentencing and execution of capital criminals.

February 3, 1997   The Individual Rights and Responsibilities and the Litigation Sections of the House of Delegates of the American Bar Association (ABA) votes to issue a resolution calling for a moratorium on executions in the United States. The ABA, while taking no position on the death penalty in theory, argues that capital defendants in the United States are not guaranteed adequate legal representation and that racial discrimination causes the death penalty to be unfairly applied.

April 3, 1997   The UN, for the first time, adopts a resolution supporting a worldwide ban on executions.

September 8, 1997   The Catholic Church releases the new Catholic Catechism, which pronounces that instances in which the death penalty should be used are "practically nonexistent" in today's world.

February 3, 1998   Karla Faye Tucker is executed—the first woman to be executed in Texas since the Civil War. Celebrated death penalty opponents including Bianca Jagger, televangelist Pat Robertson, and Pope John Paul II called for clemency but failed in their efforts.

April 3, 1998   The UN releases a report authored by Senegalese lawyer Bacre Waly Ndiaye criticizing U.S. death penalty policies. The report focuses especially on racial disparities, the increasing scope of capital laws, and sentences for juvenile offenders and the mentally retarded.

March 27, 1999   Amnesty International, for the first time, places the United States on its list of international human rights violators. The organization cites U.S. death penalty policy as a major reason for the move.

January 30, 2000   Gov. George Ryan of Illinois makes national headlines by instituting a moratorium on executions in his state until he can "be sure with moral certainty that no innocent man or woman is facing lethal injection." The move, according to Gov. Ryan, was prompted by "grave concerns about [Illinois's] shameful record of convicting innocent people and putting them on death row," noting that, since the punishment had been reinstated in Illinois in 1977, thirteen of the twenty-five people who were sentenced to death were later exonerated and set free.

February 24, 2000   Gallup reveals that 66 percent of respondents to a recent poll support the death penalty as a punishment for murder.

April 7, 2000   Conservative televangelist Pat Robertson calls for a nationwide moratorium on capital punishment, saying the death penalty is administered in a discriminatory way.

June 12, 2000   James Liebman and his colleagues release their influential and controversial study showing high error rates in capital sentencing in jurisdictions across the United States.

June 15, 2000   The Southern Baptist Convention adopts a resolution supporting use of the death penalty.

September 12, 2000   The U.S. Department of Justice releases the results of a statistical analysis of the federal death penalty showing significant disparities in the way defendants of different races were treated by U.S attorneys. Among other things, the report notes that, between 1995 and 2000, 80 percent of all the cases submitted by federal prosecutors for death penalty review involved minority defendants.

September 31, 2000   ACLU joins lawsuit seeking better legal aid for capital defendants in Harris County, Texas.

December 8, 2000   President Clinton stays the execution of Juan Raul Garza, once scheduled to be the first federal prisoner executed since the 1960s, for six months so that the administration can study "racial and geographic disparities in the federal death penalty system."

December 18, 2000   UN secretary general Kofi Annan accepts a petition, gathered by Moratorium 2000, of 3.2 million signatures supporting a moratorium on executions.

April 27, 2001   Recently appointed attorney general John Ashcroft pronounces his opposition to a moratorium on executions.

June 11, 2001   Timothy J. McVeigh is executed.

June 19, 2001   Juan Raul Garza is executed.

Facts, Policies, and Commentary

U.S. Jurisdictions that Lack the Death Penalty

For obvious reasons, there is less variation in related policy among the thirteen U.S. jurisdictions that do not enforce capital punishment than in those that do. Yet these jurisdictions—Alaska, Hawaii, Iowa, Maine, Massachusetts, Michigan, Minnesota, North Dakota, Rhode Island, Vermont, West Virginia, Wisconsin, and the District of Columbia—differ in some important ways. They came to their positions in different manners and at different times, and they have diverse approaches to punishment for very serious crimes in the absence of capital punishment.

How the Jurisdictions Came to Abstinence

There have been essentially three methods for jurisdictions to rid themselves of the death penalty: state constitutional amendment, statutory abolition, and inaction after an old death penalty statute is struck down by the courts. A fourth method, state supreme court abolition, has been tried twice but each time failed to achieve a lasting ban.

Constitutional amendment is the most final method of abolishing the death penalty and the most difficult to overcome—and it is rare. Only one jurisdiction has taken this route. In 1846 Michigan adopted Title 1, Chapter 1, Article IV, § 46 to its state constitution, becoming the first government in the English-speaking world to ban the punishment.[1] Under the state's constitution, the legislature may not pass any law providing for the death penalty.

Statutory abolition of capital punishment by the jurisdiction's legislature has been the most common method of ending the practice. In ten of the death penalty–free jurisdictions, legislatures have affirmatively banned the sentence by statute, or simply repealed all laws that call for the punishment. These jurisdictions are Alaska, Hawaii, Iowa, Maine, Massachusetts, Minnesota, North Dakota, Vermont, West Virginia, Wisconsin, and the District of Columbia.

Alaska is an interesting case; its state legislature has never passed a law about the death penalty. Rather, the territorial government banned the punishment in 1957, before Alaska became a state, and the state congress has never reinstated the practice. The legislature has considered seven death penalty bills in recent years, but none have yet passed.

The final method by which some of the thirteen jurisdictions have successfully eschewed capital punishment also takes on an aspect of inaction. In one state, Rhode Island, the legislature passed a death penalty statute in 1973, after *Furman*, but it was struck down by the state supreme court in 1979. The court did not attempt to rule that capital punishment is intrinsically unconstitutional; rather, it struck down the law under the U.S. Supreme Court's death penalty jurisprudence. The court felt that Rhode Island's law did not meet the demands of *Gregg* and other U.S. constitutional decisions. Thus, though the Rhode Island court struck down the state's law, it left open the possibility that the legislature would pass a new acceptable statute. This has not happened. The legislature has failed to reenact a death penalty statute, so the state does not practice the punishment.

In California and Massachusetts, the state supreme courts at one point ruled that capital punishment is intrinsically a violation of the respective state's constitution. Theoretically, this would be another method by which jurisdictions could ban the death penalty. However, in neither case did the rulings have a lasting impact, since state constitutional amendments overrode the courts' decisions. Both California and Massachusetts now have constitutional provisions allowing capital punishment. In Massachusetts, however, the state legislature has since opted not to employ the sentence.

The Date Capital Punishment Was Abolished

Another difference among jurisdictions not practicing the death penalty regards the date when they actually abolished the sentence. This factor could be important, since it reveals whether a jurisdiction's anti–death penalty stance is a long-standing one or more recent, and therefore might shed some light on the probability of a policy change. Many states have waffled considerably on the issue.

A fair number of states and jurisdictions abolished the death penalty at some point. By the time of *Furman* eighteen states had completely abandoned capital punishment for some period in their history[2] and another eight had partially abolished it in some way. Many of the states in each of these groups fully reestablished the practice even before 1972.

Michigan was the first state to ban capital punishment, in 1846, and it has never used it since. From that date until 1887, a small wave of states—Iowa, Maine, Rhode Island, and Wisconsin—partially or fully abandoned the sentence.[3] Despite the fact that none of these states use the death penalty now, however, this period of abolition did not always result in a lasting ban. Both Iowa and Rhode Island had reinstated the sentence by 1882; Maine and Wisconsin never reestablished it.

Another wave of abolition activity occurred between 1897 and 1939.[4] In this period, nine states fully or partially abolished the death penalty. Of these, only two abolitions resulted in permanent and complete bans. Minnesota abandoned capital punishment in 1911 and North Dakota discarded it in 1915; neither has yet reestablished the practice.

A third wave occurred between 1957 and 1969, just before *Furman* was decided.[5] During this span, nine states fully or partially banned capital punishment. Two of them, Iowa and Oregon, had previously banned and then reestablished the practice during an earlier wave. Of the abolitions that transpired in the third wave, Alaska and Hawaii in 1957 and Iowa and West Virginia in 1965 represented the only complete bans that have lasted to this day.

A final wave has occurred since *Gregg* was decided in 1976. Rhode Island's death penalty statute was struck down in 1979 and the legislature has never passed a new one. The District of Columbia abolished the punishment in 1981 and Massachusetts in 1984. Finally, Vermont, which had mostly abandoned the sentence in 1964, removed all lingering statutes in 1987. Since 1987 no jurisdiction in the United States has completely abandoned capital punishment.

Alternative Punishment: Life without Parole?

A final important difference among the jurisdictions that do not use the death penalty concerns their alternative strategies for punishing very serious crimes. Most of these jurisdictions punish serious offenders with a sentence of life imprisonment without the possibility of parole. But not every jurisdiction has such a sentence.

Hawaii, Iowa, Maine, Massachusetts, Michigan, Rhode Island, West Virginia, and the District of Columbia each provide for the sentence of life imprisonment without parole. In Alaska and Wisconsin, though statutes do not explicitly delineate such a sentence, the sentencing judge has discretion over when to set the parole date. In these states, when a criminal receives a very long sentence for committing a serious crime, the judge may simply set the parole date far enough in the future that, practically speaking, the convict cannot be released before his or her death.

Minnesota and North Dakota lack the sentence of life imprisonment without the possibility of parole, and they do not give sentencing judges parole discretion. In these states every criminal, even perpetrators of heinous crimes, may eventually have the possibility of parole. In Minnesota, a person convicted of murder is eligible for parole in twenty-five years at a maximum. Under North Dakota law, any convict displaying good behavior may earn five days of time-served credit each month, regardless of his or her crime.[6]

Notes

1. See www.deathpenaltyinfo.org/nodp.html.

2. William J. Bowers, *Legal Homicide: Death as Punishment in America,* 1864–1982 (Boston: Northeastern University Press, 1984), 9.

3. Christopher Z. Mooney and Mei-Hsein Lee, "Morality Policy Reinvention: State Death Penalties," *Annals of the American Academy of Political and Social Science* 566 (November 1999): 87.

4. Ibid.

5. Ibid.

6. N.D. Cent. Code, § 12-54.101.

An Example of Aggravating Factors—Alabama's Murder Statute

The following circumstances are counted as "aggravating factors" under Alabama law—one of these must be true in order for a jury to impose the death penalty. (Ala Stat. Ann. 13A-5-40.)

1. Murder by the defendant during a kidnapping in the first degree or an attempt thereof committed by the defendant.
2. Murder by the defendant during a robbery in the first degree or an attempt thereof committed by the defendant.
3. Murder by the defendant during a rape in the first or second degree or an attempt thereof committed by the defendant; or murder by the defendant during sodomy in the first or second degree or an attempt thereof committed by the defendant.
4. Murder by the defendant during a burglary in the first or second degree or an attempt thereof committed by the defendant.
5. Murder of any police officer, sheriff, deputy, state trooper, federal law enforcement officer, or any other state or federal peace officer of any kind, or prison or jail guard, while such officer or guard is on duty, regardless of whether the defendant knew or should have known the victim was an officer or guard on duty, or because of some official or job-related act or performance of such officer or guard.
6. Murder committed while the defendant is under sentence of life imprisonment.
7. Murder done for a pecuniary or other valuable consideration or pursuant to a contract or for hire.
8. Murder by the defendant during sexual abuse in the first or second degree or an attempt thereof committed by the defendant.
9. Murder by the defendant during arson in the first or second degree committed by the defendant, or murder by the defendant by means of explosives or explosion.
10. Murder wherein two or more persons are murdered by the defendant by one act or pursuant to one scheme or course of conduct.
11. Murder by the defendant when the victim is a state or federal public official or former

public official and the murder stems from or is caused by or is related to his official position, act, or capacity.

12. Murder by the defendant during the act of unlawfully assuming control of any aircraft by use of threats or force with intent to obtain any valuable consideration for the release of said aircraft or any passenger or crewmen thereon or to direct the route or movement of said aircraft, or otherwise exert control over said aircraft.

13. Murder by a defendant who has been convicted of any other murder in the 20 years preceding the crime; provided that the murder which constitutes the capital crime shall be murder as defined in subsection (b) of this section; and provided further that the prior murder conviction referred to shall include murder in any degree as defined at the time and place of the prior conviction.

14. Murder when the victim is subpoenaed, or has been subpoenaed, to testify, or the victim had testified, in any preliminary hearing, grand jury proceeding, criminal trial or criminal proceeding of whatever nature, or civil trial or civil proceeding of whatever nature, in any municipal, state, or federal court, when the murder stems from, is caused by, or is related to the capacity or role of the victim as a witness.

15. Murder when the victim is less than fourteen years of age.

16. Murder committed by or through the use of a deadly weapon fired or otherwise used from outside a dwelling while the victim is in a dwelling.

17. Murder committed by or through the use of a deadly weapon while the victim is in a vehicle.

18. Murder committed by or through the use of a deadly weapon fired or otherwise used within or from a vehicle.

Limiting Proportionality Review

As discussed in Chapter 2, the states approach proportionality review of death sentences in different ways, in many cases acting to limit or eliminate the practice. This section sheds more light on the manner in which specific jurisdictions have limited proportionality review. The information comes from Leigh B. Bienen, "Criminal Law: The Proportionality Review of Capital Cases by State High Courts after *Gregg*: Only the 'Appearance of Justice'?" *Northwestern School of Law Journal of Criminal Law and Criminology* 87 (fall 1996): 130.

Thirteen states have no systematic proportionality review at all. In six—Connecticut, Idaho, Maryland, Nevada, Oklahoma, Tennessee, and Wyoming—the legislature has repealed a previous proportionality review policy. (Tennessee also repealed its requirement once, but it reinstated the practice in 1992.)

In Alabama, Kentucky, Louisiana, Mississippi, Nebraska, New Jersey, Ohio, South Carolina, and Virginia courts compare a death sentence only against other cases in which the

Table A-1 States with No Systematic Proportionality Review

Arizona	Indiana	Oregon
Colorado	Kansas	Tennessee
Connecticut	Maryland	Texas
Idaho	Nevada	Wyoming
Illinois	Oklahoma	

death penalty has actually been imposed, rather than against all cases in which it might have been imposed.

In Delaware, Georgia, Idaho, Maryland, Missouri, Montana, New Mexico, North Carolina, and Washington courts limit the pool of comparison to all cases that resulted in a conviction for capital murder.

Capital Punishment Policies in Nations Worldwide

This section details the approach to capital punishment in each nation in the world. The material is reprinted from Amnesty International, www.web.amnesty. org/rmp/dplibrary. nsf.

Abolitionist and Retentionist Countries

As of March 29, 2001, more than half the countries in the world had abolished capital punishment in law or practice. The numbers are as follows:

Abolitionist for all crimes: 75
Abolitionist for ordinary crimes only: 13
Abolitionist in practice: 20
Total abolitionist in law or practice: 108
Retentionist: 87

Following are lists of countries in the four categories: abolitionist for all crimes, abolitionist for ordinary crimes only, abolitionist in practice, and retentionist. (The lists include a few territories whose laws on capital punishment differ significantly from those of the country with which they are associated.)

At the end is a list of countries that have abolished capital punishment since 1976. It shows that, in the past decade, an average of over three countries a year have abolished capital punishment in law or, having done so for ordinary crimes, have gone on to abolish it for all offences.

Abolitionist for All Crimes

Countries whose laws do not provide for capital punishment for any crime:

Andorra
Angola
Australia
Austria
Azerbaijan
Belgium
Bulgaria
Cambodia
Canada
Cape Verde
Colombia
Costa Rica
Cote D'Ivoire
Croatia
Czech Republic
Denmark
Djibouti
Dominican Republic
East Timor
Ecuador
Estonia
Finland
France
Georgia
Germany
Great Britain

Greece
Guinea-Bissau
Haiti
Honduras
Hungary
Iceland
Ireland
Italy
Kiribati
Liechtenstein
Lithuania
Luxembourg
Macedonia
  (former Yugoslav Republic)
Malta
Marshall Islands
Mauritius
Micronesia
  (federated states)
Moldova
Monaco
Mozambique
Namibia
Nepal
Netherlands
New Zealand

Nicaragua
Norway
Palau
Panama
Paraguay
Poland
Portugal
Romania
San Marino
Sao Tome and
  Principe
Seychelles
Slovak Republic
Slovenia
Solomon Islands
South Africa
Spain
Sweden
Switzerland
Turkmenistan
Tuvalu
Ukraine
Uruguay
Vanuatu
Vatican City State
Venezuela

Abolitionist for Ordinary Crimes Only

Countries whose laws provide for capital punishment only for exceptional crimes such as crimes under military law or crimes committed in exceptional circumstances:

Albania	Bosnia-Herzegovina	Cyprus	Israel	Peru
Argentina	Brazil	El Salvador	Latvia	
Bolivia	Cook Islands	Fiji	Mexico	

Abolitionist in Practice

Countries that retain capital punishment for ordinary crimes such as murder but can be considered abolitionist in practice in that they have not executed anyone during the past ten years and are believed to have a policy or established practice of not carrying out executions. The list also includes countries that have made an international commitment not to use capital punishment:

Bhutan	Nauru	Sri Lanka
Brunei Darussalam	Niger	Suriname
Burkina Faso	Papua New Guinea	Togo
Central African Republic	Samoa	Tonga
Congo (Republic)	Senegal	Turkey

Retentionist

Countries that retain capital punishment for ordinary crimes:

Afghanistan	Dominica	Laos
Algeria	Egypt	Lebanon
Antigua and Barbuda	Equatorial Guinea	Lesotho
Armenia	Eritrea	Liberia
Bahamas	Ethiopia	Libya
Bahrain	Gabon	Malawi
Bangladesh	Ghana	Malaysia
Barbados	Guatemala	Mauritania
Belarus	Guinea	Mongolia
Belize	Guyana	Morocco
Benin	India	Myanmar
Botswana	Indonesia	Nigeria
Burundi	Iran	North Korea
Cameroon	Iraq	Oman
Chad	Jamaica	Pakistan
Chile	Japan	Palestinian Authority
China	Jordan	Philippines
Comoros	Kazakstan	Qatar
Congo	Kenya	Russian Federation
(Democratic Republic)	Kuwait	Rwanda
Cuba	Kyrgyzstan	Saint Christopher and Nevis

Retentionist *continued*

Countries that retain capital punishment for ordinary crimes:

Saint Lucia	Syria	United States
Saint Vincent and Grenadines	Taiwan	Uzbekistan
Saudi Arabia	Tajikistan	Vietnam
Sierra Leone	Tanzania	Yemen
Singapore	Thailand	Yugoslavia
Somalia	Trinidad and Tobago	(federal republic)
South Korea	Tunisia	Zambia
Sudan	Uganda	Zimbabwe
Swaziland	United Arab Emirates	

Countries That Have Abolished Capital Punishment Since 1976

1976   Portugal for all crimes.

1978   Denmark for all crimes.

1979   Luxembourg, Nicaragua, and Norway for all crimes. Brazil, Fiji, and Peru for ordinary crimes.

1981   France and Cape Verde for all crimes.

1982   The Netherlands for all crimes.

1983   Cyprus and El Salvador for ordinary crimes.

1984   Argentina for ordinary crimes.

1985   Australia for all crimes.

1987   Haiti, Liechtenstein, and the German Democratic Republic for all crimes.[1]

1989   Cambodia, New Zealand, Romania, and Slovenia for all crimes.[2]

1990   Andorra, Croatia, the Czech and Slovak Federal Republic,[3] Hungary, Ireland, Mozambique, Namibia, and Sao Tome and Príncipe for all crimes.

1992   Angola, Paraguay, and Switzerland for all crimes.

1993   Greece, Guinea-Bissau, Hong Kong,[4] and Seychelles for all crimes.

1994   Italy for all crimes.

1995   Djibouti, Mauritius, Moldova, and Spain for all crimes.

1996   Belgium for all crimes.

1997   Georgia, Nepal, Poland, and South Africa for all crimes. Bolivia and Bosnia-Herzegovina for ordinary crimes.

1998   Azerbaijan, Bulgaria, Canada, Estonia, Great Britain, and Lithuania for all crimes.

1999   East Timor, Turkmenistan, and Ukraine for all crimes. Latvia abolished
        capital punishment for ordinary crimes.[5]
2000   Albania for ordinary crimes.[6] Malta and Cote D'Ivoire for all crimes.

Notes

1. In 1990 the German Democratic Republic became unified with the Federal Republic of Germany, where capital punishment had been abolished in 1949.

2. Slovenia and Croatia abolished capital punishment while they were still republics of the Socialist Federal Republic of Yugoslavia. The two republics became independent in 1991.

3. In 1993 the Czech and Slovak Federal Republic divided into two states: the Czech Republic and Slovakia.

4. Hong Kong was returned to Chinese rule in 1997 as a special administrative region of China. Amnesty International understands that Hong Kong will remain abolitionist.

5. In 1999 the Latvian parliament voted to ratify Protocol No. 6 to the European Convention on Human Rights, abolishing capital punishment for peacetime offences.

6. Albania ratified Protocol No. 6 in 2000, abolishing capital punishment for peacetime offences.

Notable Quotes on Capital Punishment

Pope John Paul II

The new evangelization calls for followers of Christ who are unconditionally pro-life: who will proclaim, celebrate and serve the Gospel of life in every situation. A sign of hope is the increasing recognition that the dignity of human life must never be taken away, even in the case of someone who has done great evil. Modern society has the means of protecting itself, without definitively denying criminals the chance to reform. I renew the appeal I made most recently at Christmas for a consensus to end the death penalty, which is both cruel and unnecessary.[1]

Reverend Bernice A. King (daughter of Martin Luther King Jr.)

Those who thirst for revenge may experience the illusion of satisfaction, but this never lasts long in people of conscience, because every act of violence leaves in its wake the seeds of more violence. We don't redeem the loss of our loved ones by adding to the misery of our society and the callousness of our government. In the short term, the death penalty may satisfy the very human impulse to seek revenge. In the long run, however, compounding acts of brutality add to the suffering of the loved ones of offenders and victims alike.[2]

Ernest van den Haag (expert on capital punishment)

If and when discrimination occurs it should be corrected. Not, however, by letting the guilty blacks escape the death penalty because guilty whites do, but by making sure that the guilty white offenders suffer it as the guilty blacks do. . . . However, even if . . . this cannot be done, I do not see any good reason to let any guilty murderer escape his penalty. It does happen in the administration of criminal justice that one person gets away with murder and another is executed. Yet the fact that one gets away with it is no reason to let another one escape.[3]

Notes

1. Pope John Paul II, Mass in St. Louis, Missouri, January 27, 1999.

2. Reverend Bernice A. King, "Uprooting the Seeds of Violence, the Other Side," September–December 1997, 36.

3. Ernest van den Haag, "Refuting Reiman and Nathanson," in *Punishment and the Death Penalty,* ed. Robert M. Baird and Stuart E. Rosenbaum (Buffalo: Prometheus Books, 1995), 207, 214.

Encyclopedia Articles

Following are entries related to capital punishment that appeared in the International Encyclopedia of Human Rights: Freedoms, Abuses, and Remedies, *by Robert L. Maddex, adviser on constitutional issues and former chief counsel of the Foreign Claims Settlement Commission of the United States.*

Capital Punishment

Although the death penalty is denounced or prohibited in some international and regional human rights documents as well as in some national constitutions and laws, ninety countries, including the United States and China, still do not consider capital punishment a violation of human rights. Its use, however, is generally limited to certain types of crimes involving heinous offenses or the murder of law enforcement officers. The severity and finality of the death penalty, which make it impossible to correct a judicial error once a sentence of death has been carried out, have led to efforts to ensure that capital punishment is restricted to extreme crimes and that those accused of capital offenses receive a fair trial.

For at least as long as recorded history, the penalty for certain crimes has been capital punishment, a term derived from the Latin *caput* (head) that was used in England as early as the sixteenth century. Plato, the Greek philosopher of the fourth century b.c.e., devotes a section of his *Laws* to capital offenses—crimes that call for the death penalty—and includes among them robbery of temples, political subversion, and treason. The eighteenth-century French philosopher Jean-Jacques Rousseau argued that the death penalty was based on the consent of the people, because some citizens are asked to risk death in the defense of their country. Another French jurist and philosopher, Montesquieu, believed that the death penalty was too harsh a punishment for some crimes and could result in a reluctance by humane judges to impose it.

Cesare Beccaria, an eighteenth-century Italian jurist and criminologist, questioned the appropriateness of the death penalty in his *Treatise on Crimes and Punishment* (1764). The debate over the acceptability of capital punishment in an enlightened society has continued ever since, especially in the United States. In 1998, according to Amnesty International, eighty-six percent of all executions took place in China, the Democratic Republic of Congo, Iran, and the United States.

The arguments for and against capital punishment were summarized in a study requested by the UN General Assembly in 1959. The death penalty can be supported on the basis that it deters further crimes by the same offender, it punishes extreme antisocial behavior against which the state has the right to protect itself, it provides atonement for particularly heinous crimes, and it is an economical alternative to maintaining a criminal at government expense for a long period of time. Arguments against capital punishment include that it is a violation of the sanctity of life; the aim of penalties for crimes should be punishment and prevention (rather than atonement), which can be accomplished by means other than the death penalty; it is generally not an effective deterrent to crime; and it is a form of cruelty and inhumanity unworthy of a humane civilization. A tangential reasoning is that the death penalty often falls disproportionately on minorities or those charged with political crimes.

The International Covenant on Civil and Political Rights, adopted by the UN General Assembly in 1966, clearly supports abolition of capital punishment. Acknowledging the many countries that still allow it, however, article 6 sets out criteria for protecting the rights of persons sentenced to death for crimes. These include the right to due process and to seek a pardon or commutation of the sentence and a prohibition on capital punishment for pregnant women and anyone under eighteen years of age.

Reviewing the issue two decades later, the UN General Assembly in 1989 adopted the Second Optional Protocol to the 1966 covenant, Aiming at the Abolition of the Death Penalty. The introduction to the protocol enunciates the states parties' belief that "the abolition of the death penalty contributes to enhancement of human dignity and progressive development of human rights. . . ." Article 1 mandates: "1. No one within the jurisdiction of a State Party to the present Protocol shall be executed. 2. Each State Party shall take all necessary measures to abolish the death penalty within its jurisdiction."

International Bill of Human Rights

The International Bill of Human Rights is the collective term for the Universal Declaration of Human Rights (1948); International Covenant on Civil and Political Rights (1966), including its two optional protocols adopted in 1966 and 1989; and International Covenant on Economic, Social and Cultural Rights (1966). This trio was formally referred to as the International Bill of Human Rights in the Limburg Principles on the Implementation of the International Covenant on Economic, Social and Cultural Rights (1986).

The notion of creating an international bill of rights after World War II was inspired by the first bill of rights, drafted by George Mason for the Virginia constitution (1776), as well as by France's Declaration of the Rights of Man and of the Citizen (1789) and the U.S. Bill of Rights (1791). Inspiration also came from President Franklin Roosevelt's "four freedoms"—freedom of speech and worship and freedom from want and fear—which were included in the text of the Atlantic Charter (1941), a precursor of the United Nations. British prime minister Winston Churchill also hoped that the war would end "with the enthronement of human rights."

The Charter of the United Nations (1945) called for "promoting and encouraging respect for human rights and for fundamental freedoms for all without distinction as to race, sex, language or religion." During the San Francisco conference at which the charter was drafted, a proposal was made that a Declaration on the Essential Rights of Man also be drawn up; however, time constraints made this impossible. The idea nonetheless took root that the charter itself implied that an international bill of human rights would be promulgated by the UN.

At its first session in 1946, the UN General Assembly considered a draft Declaration on Fundamental Human Rights and Freedoms and sent it to its human rights agency, the Economic and Social Council (ECOSOC), with a request that it be forwarded to ECOSOC's Commission on Human Rights for consideration "in the preparation of an international bill of rights." The next year the commission decided to apply the concept of an international bill of human rights to several documents being prepared by working groups under its direction, among them a declaration of human rights, a covenant, and an implementing document.

In 1948 the commission produced the Universal Declaration of Human Rights, which, although not binding, was the first comprehensive statement of human rights ever proclaimed on a global level. On the same day that it was adopted by the General Assembly, the UN requested that the commission, as a matter of priority, draft a covenant on human rights and measures for implementing it. It would be eighteen years, however, before these documents were actually adopted.

Although the General Assembly in 1950 resolved that "the enjoyment of civic and political freedoms and of economic, social and cultural rights are interconnected and interdependent," it later decided to draft two separate covenants for these rights. The International Covenant on Civil and Political Rights, together with a protocol that provided for its implementation, and the International Covenant on Economic, Social and Cultural Rights were both adopted by the General Assembly on December 16, 1966. A second protocol to the civil covenant urging abolition of the death penalty was adopted on December 15, 1989.

Although the Universal Declaration of Human Rights was and still is a significant statement, the two covenants that followed added teeth to the international community's lofty goals. By providing that nations had to ratify the covenants and implement their provisions through domestic laws and policies, as well as through bodies such as the Human Rights Committee set up under the civil and political covenant, these instruments made great strides in the enforcement of human rights around the world. The International Bill of Human Rights stands today as a beacon of hope for all victims of human rights abuses. While the provisions of the component documents may not be adequately observed in many countries, they nevertheless represent milestones in how far the ideals of human rights have come and set out the goals yet to be reached.

Universal Declaration of Human Rights

One of the most significant human rights documents, the Universal Declaration of Human Rights (1948) was drafted to carry out the mandate of the Charter of the United Nations (1945): "promoting and encouraging respect for human rights and fundamental freedoms." The first attempt to establish a universal standard of human and fundamental rights for every person, the declaration was adopted by the UN General Assembly on December 10, 1948, by a vote of forty-eight in favor, none opposed, with eight abstentions (December 10 is now observed internationally as Human Rights Day). The declaration became the first document of what is now referred to as the International Bill of Human Rights, which also includes the International Covenant on Civil and Political Rights (1966) and its two optional protocols as well as the International Covenant on Economic, Social and Cultural Rights (1966).

Under the chairmanship of Eleanor Roosevelt, the widow of President Franklin D. Roosevelt, the declaration was produced by the Commission on Human Rights, created in 1946. She believed that the world "could not have peace, or an atmosphere in which peace could grow, unless we [recognize] the rights of individual human beings . . . their importance, their . . . dignity. . . ." Others who made significant contributions to the document include Alexandre Bogomolov and Alexei Pavlov of the Soviet Union, René Cassin of France, Peng Chun Chang of China, Lord Dukeston and Geoffrey Wilson of the United Kingdom, William Hodgson of Australia, John Humphrey of Canada, Charles Malik of Lebanon, and Hernán Santa Cruz of Chile.

The declaration, as proclaimed by the General Assembly, is to serve "as a common standard of achievement for all peoples and all nations, to the end that every individual and every organ of society, keeping this Declaration constantly in mind, shall strive by teaching and education to promote respect for these rights and freedoms and by progressive measures, national and international, to secure their universal and effective recognition and observance, both among the peoples of Member States themselves and among the peoples of territories under their jurisdiction."

The declaration consists of a preamble and thirty articles. The preamble begins with a series of seven clauses providing justification for the document. According to the fifth clause, "the peoples of the United Nations have in the Charter reaffirmed their faith in fundamental human rights, in the dignity and worth of the human person and in the equal rights of men and women and have determined to promote social progress and better standards of life in larger freedom[.]"

Article 1 sets forth the declaration's basic philosophy: "All human beings are born free and equal in dignity and rights. They are endowed with reason and conscience and should act towards one another in a spirit of brotherhood."

Fundamental rights and remedies for violations of those rights are described in articles 2 through 8. Fundamental rights, the document states, may not be denied on the basis of "race, color, sex, language, religion, political or other opinion, national origin, property, birth or other status." Any distinction based on territorial jurisdiction is also prohibited. Each person has the rights to life, liberty, and personal security; torture and "cruel, inhuman or degrading treatment or punishment" are prohibited; each person must be recognized as a person before the law; all people are equal before the law; and "[e]veryone has the right to an effective remedy by the competent national tribunals for acts violating the fundamental rights granted him by the constitution or by law."

Articles 9, 10, and 11 address basic rights for persons accused of crimes. "No one shall be subjected to arbitrary interference with his privacy, family, home or correspondence, nor to attacks upon his honor and reputation," provides article 12 in part. Articles 13 through 20 enumerate additional rights, including freedom of movement and residence; the rights to asylum, nationality, marriage and family, and property ownership; freedom of thought, conscience, and religion; freedom of opinion and expression; and the right of peaceful assembly.

The right of each person to participate in the government and equal access to public services of his or her country is extended in article 21. Article 22 states that everyone has the right to social security, and article 23 endorses equal pay for equal work, a just and favorable rate of pay, and the right to form and join trade unions. Articles 24 through 27 provide for the right to rest and leisure; an adequate standard of living, clothing, housing, and medical care as well as "special assistance" for motherhood and childhood; education; and participation in the community's cultural life, the benefit of "scientific advancement and its benefits," and protection of interests of scientific and artistic creations.

According to article 28, "Everyone is entitled to a social and international order in which the rights and freedoms set forth in this Declaration can be fully realized." Article 29 notes that, as well as rights, everyone has "duties to the community" and that rights and freedoms have limitations. The final article, article 30, states: "Nothing in this Declaration may be interpreted as implying for any State, group or person any right to engage in any activity or to perform any act aimed at the destruction of any rights and freedoms set forth herein."

In an address at the University of Tehran, Iran, on December 10, 1997, UN Secretary General Kofi Annan noted: "The growth in support for the Declaration of Human Rights over the past fifty years has given it new life and reaffirmed its universality. The basic principles of the Declaration have been incorporated into national laws of countries from all cultural traditions."

Primary Documents

Following are texts of selected documents, resolutions, and Supreme Court cases that have played prominent roles in capital punishment in the United States during the past two decades.

Fact Sheet: International Bill of Human Rights (1986)

This fact sheet on the International Bill of Human Rights, formally named in the Limburg Principles on the Implementation of the International Covenant on Economic, Social and Cultural Rights in 1986, was printed in Geneva, Switzerland, by the Office of the United Nations High Commissioner for Human Rights.

Background

The International Bill of Human Rights consists of the Universal Declaration of Human Rights, the International Covenant on Economic, Social and Cultural Rights; and the International Covenant on Civil and Political Rights and its two Optional Protocols.

Human rights had already found expression in the Covenant of the League of Nations, which led, inter alia, to the creation of the International Labour Organisation. At the 1945 San Francisco Conference, held to draft the Charter of the United Nations, a proposal to embody a "Declaration on the Essential Rights of Man" was put forward but was not examined because it required more detailed consideration than was possible at the time. The Charter clearly speaks of "promoting and encouraging respect for human rights and for fundamental freedoms for all without distinction as to race, sex, language or religion" (Art. 1, para. 3). The idea of promulgating an "international bill of rights" was also considered by many as basically implicit in the Charter.

The Preparatory Commission of the United Nations, which met immediately after the closing session of the San Francisco Conference, recommended that the Economic and Social Council should, at its first session, establish a commission for the promotion of human rights as envisaged in Article 68 of the Charter. Accordingly, the Council established the Commission on Human Rights early in 1946.

At its first session, in 1946, the General Assembly considered a draft Declaration on Fundamental Human Rights and Freedoms and transmitted it to the Economic and Social Council "for reference to the Commission on Human Rights for consideration ... in its preparation of an international bill of rights" (resolution 43 (I)). The Commission, at its first session early in 1947, authorized its officers to formulate what it termed "a preliminary draft International Bill of Human Rights". Later the work was taken over by a formal drafting committee, consisting of members of the Commission from eight States, selected with due regard for geographical distribution.

Towards the Universal Declaration

In the beginning, different views were expressed about the form the bill of rights should take. The Drafting Committee decided to prepare two documents: one in the form of a declaration, which would set forth general principles or standards of human rights; the other in the form of a convention, which would define specific rights and their limitations. Accordingly, the Committee transmitted to the Commission on Human Rights draft articles of an international declaration and an international convention on human rights. At its second session, in December 1947, the Commission decided to apply the term "International Bill of Human Rights" to the series of documents in preparation and established three working groups: one on the declaration, one on the convention (which it renamed "covenant") and one on implementation. The Commission revised the draft declaration at its third session, in May/June 1948, taking into consideration comments received from Governments. It did not have time, however, to consider the covenant or the question of implementation. The declaration was therefore submitted through the Economic and Social Council to the General Assembly, meeting in Paris.

By its resolution 217 A (III) of 10 December 1948, the General Assembly adopted the Universal Declaration of Human Rights as the first of these projected instruments.

Towards the International Covenants

On the same day that it adopted the Universal Declaration, the General Assembly requested the Commission on Human Rights to prepare, as a matter of priority, a draft covenant on human rights and draft measures of implementation. The Commission examined the text of the draft covenant in 1949 and the following year it revised the first 18 articles, on the basis of comments received from Governments. In 1950, the General Assembly declared that "the enjoyment of civic and political freedoms and of economic, social and cultural rights are interconnected and interdependent" (resolution 421 (V), sect. E). The Assembly thus decided to include in the covenant on human rights economic, social and cultural rights and an explicit recognition of the equality of men and women in related rights, as set forth in the Charter. In 1951, the Commission drafted 14 articles on economic, social and cultural rights on the basis of proposals made by Governments and suggestions by specialized agencies. It also formulated 10 articles on measures for implementation of those rights under which States parties to the covenant would submit periodic reports. After a long debate at its sixth session, in 1951/1952, the General Assembly requested the Commission "to draft two Covenants on Human Rights, . . . one to contain civil and political rights and the other to contain economic, social and cultural rights" (resolution 543 (VI), para. 1). The Assembly specified that the two covenants should contain as many similar provisions as possible. It also decided to include an article providing that "all peoples shall have the right of self-determination" (resolution 545 (VI)).

The Commission completed preparation of the two drafts at its ninth and tenth sessions, in 1953 and 1954. The General Assembly reviewed those texts at its ninth session, in 1954, and decided to give the drafts the widest possible publicity in order that Governments might study them thoroughly and that public opinion might express itself freely. It recommended that its Third Committee start an article-by-article discussion of the texts at its tenth session, in 1955. Although the article-by-article discussion began as scheduled, it was not until 1966 that the preparation of the two covenants was completed.

The International Covenant on Economic, Social and Cultural Rights and the International Covenant on Civil and Political Rights were adopted by the General Assembly by its resolution 2200 A (XXI) of 16 December 1966. The first Optional Protocol to the International Covenant on Civil and Political Rights, adopted by the same resolution, provided international machinery for dealing with communications from individuals claiming to be victims of violations of any of the rights set forth in the Covenant.

Universal Declaration of Human Rights

The Universal Declaration of Human Rights was adopted and proclaimed by the General Assembly

> as a common standard of achievement for all peoples and all nations, to the end that every individual and every organ of society, keeping this Declaration constantly in mind, shall strive by teaching and education to promote respect for these rights and freedoms and by progressive measures, national and international, to secure their universal and effective recognition and observance, both among, the peoples of Member States themselves and among the peoples of territories under their jurisdiction.

Forty-eight States voted in favour of the Declaration, none against, with eight abstentions. In a statement following the voting, the President of the General Assembly pointed out that adoption of the Declaration was "a remarkable achievement, a step forward in the great evolutionary process". It was the first occasion on which the organized community of nations had made a Declaration of human rights and fundamental freedoms. The instrument was backed by the authority of the body of opinion of the United Nations as a whole, and millions of people—men, women and children all over the world—would turn to it for help, guidance and inspiration.

The Declaration consists of a preamble and 30 articles, setting forth the human rights and fundamental freedoms to which all men and women, everywhere in the world, are entitled, without any discrimination.

Article 1, which lays down the philosophy on which the Declaration is based, reads:

> All human beings are born free and equal in dignity and rights. They are endowed with reason and conscience and should act towards one another in a spirit of brotherhood.

The article thus defines the basic assumptions of the Declaration: that the right to liberty and equality is man's birthright and cannot be alienated: and that, because man is a rational and moral being, he is different from other creatures on earth and therefore entitled to certain rights and freedoms which other creatures do not enjoy.

Article 2, which sets out the basic principle of equality and non discrimination as regards the enjoyment of human rights and fundamental freedoms, forbids "distinction of any kind, such as race, colour, sex, language, religion, political or other opinion, national or social origin, property, birth or other status".

Article 3, the first cornerstone of the Declaration, proclaims the right to life, liberty and security of person[s]—a right essential to the enjoyment of all other rights. This article introduces articles 4 to 21, in which other civil and political rights are set out, including: freedom from slavery and servitude; freedom from torture and cruel, inhuman or degrading treatment or punishment; the right to recognition everywhere as a person before the law; the right to an effective judicial remedy; freedom from arbitrary arrest, detention or exile; the right to a fair trial and public hearing by an independent and impartial tribunal; the right to be presumed innocent until proved guilty; freedom from arbitrary interference with privacy, family, home or correspondence; freedom of movement and residence; the right of asylum; the right to a nationality; the right to marry and to found a family; the right to own property; freedom of thought, conscience and religion; freedom of opinion and expression; the right to peaceful assembly and association; and the right to take part in the government of one's country and to equal access to public service in one's country.

Article 22, the second cornerstone of the Declaration, introduces articles 23 to 27, in which economic, social and cultural rights—the rights to which everyone is entitled "as a member of society"—are set out. The article characterizes these rights as indispensable for human dignity and the free development of personality, and indicates that they are to be realized "through national effort and international cooperation". At the same time, it points out the limitations of realization, the extent of which depends on the resources of each State.

The economic, social and cultural rights recognized in articles 22 to 27 include the right to social security; the right to work; the right to equal pay for equal work; the right to rest and leisure; the right to a standard of living adequate for health and well-being; the right to education; and the right to participate in the cultural life of the community.

The concluding articles, articles 28 to 30, recognize that everyone is entitled to a social and international order in which the human rights and fundamental freedoms set forth in the Declaration may be fully realized, and stress the duties and responsibilities which each individual owes to his community. Article 29 states that "in the exercise of his rights and freedoms, everyone shall be subject only to such limitations as are determined by law solely for the purpose of securing due recognition and respect for the rights and freedoms of others and of meeting the just requirements of morality, public order and the general welfare in a democratic society". It adds that in no case may human rights and fundamental freedoms be exercised contrary to the purposes and principles of the United Nations. Article 30 emphasizes that no State, group or person may claim any right, under the Declaration, "to engage in any activity or to perform any act aimed at the destruction of any of the rights and freedoms set forth" in the Declaration.

Importance and Influence of the Declaration

Conceived as "a common standard of achievement for all peoples and all nations", the Universal Declaration of Human Rights has become just that: a yardstick by which to measure the degree of respect for, and compliance with, international human rights standards.

Since 1948 it has been and rightly continues to be the most important and far-reaching of all United Nations declarations, and a fundamental source of inspiration for national and international efforts to promote and protect human rights and fundamental freedoms. It has set the direction for all subsequent work in the field of human rights and has provided the basic philosophy for many legally binding international instruments designed to protect the rights and freedoms which it proclaims.

In the Proclamation of Teheran, adopted by the International Conference on Human Rights held in Iran in 1968, the Conference agreed that "the Universal Declaration of Human Rights states a common understanding of the peoples of the world concerning the inalienable and inviolable rights of all members of the human family and constitutes an obligation for the members of the international community". The Conference affirmed its faith in the principles set forth in the Declaration, and urged all peoples and Governments "to dedicate themselves to [those] principles . . . . and to redouble their efforts to provide for all human beings a life consonant with freedom and dignity and conducive to physical, mental, social and spiritual welfare".

In recent years, there has been a growing tendency for United Nations organs, in preparing international instruments in the filed of human rights, to refer not only to the Universal Declaration, but also to other parts of the International Bill of Human Rights.

International Covenants on Human Rights

The preambles and articles 1, 3 and 5 of the two International Covenants are almost identical. The preambles recall the obligation of States under the Charter of the United Nations to promote human rights; remind the individual of his responsibility to strive for the promotion and observance of those rights; and recognize that, in accordance with the Universal Declaration of Human Rights, the ideal of free human beings enjoying civil and political freedom and freedom from fear and want can be achieved only if conditions are created whereby everyone may enjoy his civil and political rights, as well as his economic, social and cultural rights.

Article 1 of each Covenant states that the right to self-determination is universal and calls upon States to promote the realization of that right and to respect it. The article provides that "All peoples have the right of self-determination" and adds that "By virtue of that right they freely determine their political status and freely pursue their economic, social and cultural development". Article 3, in both cases, reaffirms the equal right of men and women to the enjoyment of all human rights, and enjoins States to make that principle a reality. Article 5, in both cases, provides safeguards against the destruction or undue limitation of any human right or fundamental freedom, and against misinterpretation of any provision of the Covenants as a means of justifying infringement of a right or freedom or its restriction to a greater extent than provided for in the Covenants. It also prevents States from limiting rights already enjoyed within their territories on the ground that such rights are not recognized, or recognized to a lesser extent, in the Covenants.

Articles 6 to 15 of the International Covenant on Economic, Social and Cultural Rights recognize the rights to work (art. 6); to the enjoyment of just and favourable conditions of work (art. 7); to form and join trade unions (art. 8); to social security, including social insurance (art. 9); to the widest possible protection and assistance for the family, especially mothers, children and young persons (art. 10); to an adequate standard of living (art. 11); to the enjoyment of the highest attainable standard of physical and mental health (art. 12); to education (arts. 13 and 14); and to take part in cultural life (art. 15).

In its articles 6 to 27, the International Covenant on Civil and Political Rights protects the right to life (art. 6) and lays down that no one is to be subjected to torture or to cruel, inhuman or degrading treatment or punishment (art. 7); that no one is to be held in slavery; that slavery and the slave-trade are to be prohibited; and that no one is to be held in servitude or required to perform forced or compulsory labour (art. 8); that no one is to be subjected to arbitrary arrest or detention (art. 9); that all persons deprived of their liberty are to be treated with humanity (art. 10); and that no one is to be imprisoned merely on the ground of inability to fulfil a contractual obligation (art. 11).

The Covenant provides for freedom of movement and freedom to choose a residence (art. 12) and for limitations to be placed on the expulsion of aliens lawfully in the territory of a State party (art. 13). It makes provision for the equality of all persons before the courts and tribunals and for guarantees in criminal and civil proceedings (art. 14). It prohibits retroactive criminal legislation (art. 15); lays down the right of everyone to recognition everywhere as a person before the law (art. 16); and calls for the prohibition of arbitrary or unlawful interference with an individual's privacy, family, home or correspondence, and of unlawful attacks on his honour and reputation (art. 17).

The Covenant provides for protection of the rights to freedom of thought, conscience and religion (art. 18) and to freedom of opinion and expression (art. 19). It calls for the prohibition by law of any propaganda for war and of any advocacy of national, racial or religious hatred that constitutes incitement to discrimination, hostility or violence (art. 20). It recognizes the right of peaceful assembly (art. 21) and the right to freedom of association (art. 22). It also recognizes the right of men and women of marriageable age to marry and to found a family, and the principle of equality of rights and responsibilities of spouses as to marriage, during marriage and at its dissolution (art. 23). It lays down measures to protect the rights of children (art. 24), and recognizes the right of every citizen to take part in the conduct of public affairs, to vote and to be elected, and to have access, on general terms of equality, to public service in his country (art. 25). It provides that all persons are equal before the law and are entitled to equal protection of the law (art. 26). It also calls for protection of the rights of ethnic, religious and linguistic minorities in the territories of States parties (art. 27).

Finally, article 28 provides for the establishment of a Human Rights Committee responsible for supervising implementation of the rights set out in the Covenant.

Conditions

The Universal Declaration of Human Rights affirms that the exercise of a person's rights and freedoms may be subject to certain limitations, which must be determined by law, solely for the purpose of securing due recognition of the rights and freedoms of others and of meeting the just requirements of morality, public order and the general welfare in a democratic society. Rights may not be exercised contrary to the purposes and principles of the United Nations, or if they are aimed at destroying any of the rights set forth in the Declaration (arts. 29 and 30).

The International Covenant on Economic, Social and Cultural Rights states that the rights provided for therein may be limited by law, but only in so far as it is compatible with the nature of the rights and solely to promote the general welfare in a democratic society (art. 4).

Unlike the Universal Declaration and the Covenant on Economic, Social and Cultural Rights, the International Covenant on Civil and Political Rights contains no general provision applicable to all the rights provided for in the Covenant authorizing restrictions on their exercise. However, several articles in the Covenant provide that the rights being dealt with shall not be subject to any restrictions except those which are prescribed by law and are necessary to protect national security, public order, or the rights and freedoms of others.

Certain rights, therefore, may never be suspended or limited, even in emergency situations. These are the rights to life, to freedom from torture, to freedom from enslavement or servitude, to protection from imprisonment for debt, to freedom from retroactive penal laws, to recognition as a person before the law, and to freedom of thought, conscience and religion.

The Covenant on Civil and Political Rights allows a State to limit or suspend the enjoyment of certain rights in cases of officially proclaimed public emergencies which threaten the life of the nation. Such limitations or suspensions are permitted only "to the extent strictly required by the exigencies of the situation" and may never involve discrimination solely on the ground of race, colour, sex, language, religion or social origin (art. 4). The limitations or suspensions must also be reported to the United Nations.

First Optional Protocol

The first Optional Protocol to the International Covenant on Civil and Political Rights enables the Human Rights Committee, set up under that Covenant, to receive and consider communications from individuals claiming to be victims of violations of any of the rights set forth in the Covenant.

Under article I of the Optional Protocol, a State party to the Covenant that becomes a party to the Protocol recognizes the competence of the Human Rights Committee to receive and consider communications from individuals subject to its jurisdiction who claim to be victims of a violation by that State of any of the rights set forth in the Covenant. Individuals who make such a claim, and who have exhausted all available domestic remedies, are entitled to submit a written communication to the Committee (art. 2).

Such communications as are determined to be admissible by the Committee (in addition to article 2, articles 3 and 5 (2) lay down conditions for admissibility) are brought to the attention of the State party alleged to be violating a provision of the Covenant. Within six months, that State must submit to the Committee written explanations or statements clarifying the matter and indicating the remedy, if any, that it may have applied (art. 4).

The Human Rights Committee considers the admissible communications, at closed meetings, in the light of all written information made available to it by the individual and the State party concerned. It then forwards its views to the State party and to the individual (art. 5).

A summary of the Committee's activities under the Optional Protocol is included in the report which it submits annually to the General Assembly through the Economic and Social Council (art. 6).

Second Optional Protocol

The Second Optional Protocol to the International Covenant on Civil and Political Rights, aiming at the abolition of the death penalty, was adopted by the General Assembly by its resolution 44/128 of 15 December 1989. Under its article 1, no one within the jurisdiction of a State party to the Protocol may be executed.

Under article 3 of the Protocol, States parties must include in the reports which they submit to the Human Rights Committee information on measures taken to give effect to the Protocol.

Article 5 of the Second Optional Protocol provides that, with respect to any State party to the first Optional Protocol, the competence of the Human Rights Committee to receive and consider communications from individuals subject to that State's jurisdiction shall extend to the provisions of the Second Optional Protocol, unless the State party concerned has made a statement to the contrary at the moment of ratification or accession.

Under article 6, the provisions of the Second Optional Protocol apply as additional provisions to the Covenant.

Entry into Force of the Covenants and the Optional Protocols

The International Covenant on Economic, Social and Cultural Rights entered into force on 3 January 1976, three months after the date of deposit with the Secretary-General of the thirty-fifth instrument of ratification or accession, as provided in article 27. As at 30 September 1995, the Covenant had been ratified or acceded to by 132 States:

Afghanistan, Albania, Algeria, Angola, Argentina, Armenia, Australia, Austria, Azerbaijan, Barbados, Belarus, Belgium, Benin, Bolivia, Bosnia and Herzegovina, Brazil, Bulgaria, Burundi, Cambodia, Cameroon, Canada, Cape Verde, Central African Republic, Chad, Chile, Colombia, Congo, Costa Rica, Côte d'Ivoire, Croatia, Cyprus, Czech Republic,

Democratic People's Republic of Korea, Denmark, Dominica, Dominican Republic, Ecuador, Egypt, El Salvador, Equatorial Guinea, Estonia, Ethiopia, Finland, France, Gabon, Gambia, Georgia, Germany, Greece, Grenada, Guatemala, Guinea, Guinea-Bissau, Guyana, Haiti, Hungary, Iceland, India, Iran (Islamic Republic of), Iraq, Ireland, Israel, Italy, Jamaica, Japan, Jordan, Kenya, Kyrgyzstan, Latvia, Lebanon, Lesotho, Libyan Arab Jamahiriya, Lithuania, Luxembourg, Madagascar, Malawi, Mali, Malta, Mauritius, Mexico, Mongolia, Morocco, Mozambique, Namibia, Nepal, Netherlands, New Zealand, Nicaragua, Niger, Nigeria, Norway, Panama, Paraguay, Peru, Philippines, Poland, Portugal, Republic of Korea, Republic of Moldova, Romania, Russian Federation, Rwanda, Saint Vincent and the Grenadines, San Marino, Senegal, Seychelles, Slovakia, Slovenia, Somalia, Spain, Sri Lanka, Sudan, Suriname, Sweden, Switzerland, Syrian Arab Republic, The former Yugoslav Republic of Macedonia, Togo, Trinidad and Tobago, Tunisia, Ukraine, United Kingdom, United Republic of Tanzania, United States of America, Uruguay, Venezuela, Viet Nam, Yemen, Yugoslavia, Zaire, Zambia and Zimbabwe.

The International Covenant on Civil and Political Rights entered into force on 23 March 1976, three months after the date of deposit with the Secretary-General of the thirty-fifth instrument of ratification or accession, as provided in article 49. As at 30 September 1995, the Covenant had been ratified or acceded to by 132 States:

Afghanistan, Albania, Algeria, Angola, Argentina, Armenia, Australia, Austria, Azerbaijan, Barbados, Belarus, Belgium, Benin, Bolivia, Bosnia and Herzegovina, Brazil, Bulgaria, Burundi, Cambodia, Cameroon, Canada, Cape Verde, Central African Republic, Chad, Chile, Colombia, Congo, Costa Rica, Côte d'Ivoire, Croatia, Cyprus, Czech Republic, Democratic People's Republic of Korea, Denmark, Dominica, Dominican Republic, Ecuador, Egypt, El Salvador, Equatorial Guinea, Estonia, Ethiopia, Finland, France, Gabon, Gambia, Georgia, Germany, Grenada, Guatemala, Guinea, Guyana, Haiti, Hungary, Iceland, India, Iran (Islamic Republic of), Iraq, Ireland, Israel, Italy, Jamaica, Japan, Jordan, Kenya, Kyrgyzstan, Latvia, Lebanon, Lesotho, Libyan Arab Jamahiriya, Lithuania, Luxembourg, Madagascar, Malawi, Mali, Malta, Mauritius, Mexico, Mongolia, Morocco, Mozambique, Namibia, Nepal, Netherlands, New Zealand, Nicaragua, Niger, Nigeria, Norway, Panama, Paraguay, Peru, Philippines, Poland, Portugal, Republic of Korea, Republic of Moldova, Romania, Russian Federation, Rwanda, Saint Vincent and the Grenadines, San Marino, Senegal, Seychelles, Slovakia, Slovenia, Somalia, Spain, Sri Lanka, Sudan, Suriname, Sweden, Switzerland, Syrian Arab Republic, The former Yugoslav Republic of Macedonia, Togo, Trinidad and Tobago, Tunisia, Uganda, Ukraine, United Kingdom, United Republic of Tanzania, United States of America, Uruguay, Uzbekistan, Venezuela, Viet Nam, Yemen, Yugoslavia, Zaire, Zambia and Zimbabwe.

[As of 30 September] 44 States parties to the International Covenant on Civil and Political Rights had made the declaration under its article 41, recognizing the competence of the Human Rights Committee "to receive and consider communications to the effect that a State Party claims that another State Party is not fulfilling its obligations" under the Covenant. The provisions of article 41 entered into force on 28 March 1979 in accordance with paragraph 2 of that article.

The first Optional Protocol to the International Covenant on Civil and Political Rights entered into force simultaneously with the Covenant, having received the minimum 10 ratifications or accessions required. As at 30 September 1995, 85 States parties to the Covenant had also become parties to the first Optional Protocol:

Algeria, Angola, Argentina, Armenia, Australia, Austria, Barbados, Belarus, Belgium, Benin, Bolivia, Bosnia and Herzegovina, Bulgaria, Cameroon, Canada, Central African Republic, Chad, Chile, Colombia, Congo, Costa Rica, Cyprus, Czech Republic, Denmark, Dominican Republic, Ecuador, El Salvador, Equatorial Guinea, Estonia, Finland, France, Gambia, Georgia, Germany, Guinea, Guyana, Hungary, Iceland, Ireland, Italy, Jamaica, Kyrgyzstan, Latvia, Libyan Arab Jamahiriya, Lithuania, Luxembourg, Madagascar, Malta, Mauritius, Mongolia, Namibia, Nepal, Netherlands, New Zealand, Nicaragua, Niger, Norway, Panama, Paraguay, Peru, Philippines, Poland, Portugal, Republic of Korea, Romania, Russian Federation, Saint Vincent and the Grenadines, San Marino, Senegal, Seychelles, Slovakia, Slovenia, Somalia, Spain, Suriname, Sweden, The former Yugoslav Republic of Macedonia, Togo, Trinidad and Tobago, Ukraine, Uruguay, Uzbekistan, Venezuela, Zaire and Zambia.

The Second Optional Protocol to the International Covenant on Civil and Political Rights, aiming at the abolition of the death penalty, entered into force on 11 July 1991, having received the minimum 10 ratifications or accessions required. As at 30 September 1995, the Protocol had been ratified or acceded to by 28 States:

Australia, Austria, Denmark, Ecuador, Finland, Germany, Hungary, Iceland, Ireland, Italy, Luxembourg, Malta, Mozambique, Namibia, Netherlands, New Zealand, Norway, Panama, Portugal, Romania, Seychelles, Slovenia, Spain, Sweden, Switzerland, The former Yugoslav Republic of Macedonia, Uruguay and Venezuela.

Worldwide Influence of the International Bill of Human Rights

From 1948, when the Universal Declaration of Human Rights was adopted and proclaimed, until 1976, when the International Covenants on Human Rights entered into force, the Declaration was the only completed portion of the International Bill of Human Rights. The Declaration, and at a later stage the Covenants, exercised a profound influence on the thoughts and actions of individuals and their Governments in all parts of the world.

The International Conference on Human Rights, which met at Teheran from 22 April to

13 May 1968 to review the progress made in the 20 years since the adoption of the Universal Declaration and to formulate a programme for the future, solemnly declared in the Proclamation of Teheran:

1 . It is imperative that the members of the international community fulfill their solemn obligations to promote and encourage respect for human rights and fundamental freedoms for all without distinctions of any kind such as race, colour, sex, language, religion, political or other opinions;

2. The Universal Declaration of Human Rights states a common understanding, of the peoples of the world concerning the inalienable and inviolable rights of all members of the human family and constitutes an obligation for the members of the international community;

3. The International Covenant on Civil and Political Rights, the International Covenant on Economic, Social and Cultural Rights, the Declaration on the Granting of Independence to Colonial Countries and Peoples, the International Convention on the Elimination of All Forms of Racial Discrimination as well as other conventions and declarations in the field of human rights adopted under the auspices of the United Nations, the specialized agencies and the regional intergovernmental organizations, have created new standards and obligations to which States should conform. . . .

Thus, for more than 25 years, the Universal Declaration on Human Rights stood alone as an international "standard of achievement for all peoples and all nations". It became known and was accepted as authoritative both in States which became parties to one or both of the Covenants and in those which did not ratify or accede to either. Its provisions were cited as the basis and justification for many important decisions taken by United Nations bodies; they inspired the preparation of a number of international human rights instruments, both within and outside the United Nations system; they exercised a significant influence on a number of multilateral and bilateral treaties; and they had a strong impact as the basis for the preparation of many new national constitutions and national laws.

The Universal Declaration came to be recognized as a historic document articulating a common definition of human dignity and values. The Declaration is a yardstick by which to measure the degree of respect for, and compliance with, international human rights standards everywhere on earth.

The coming into force of the Covenants, by which States parties accepted a legal as well as a moral obligation to promote and protect human rights and fundamental freedoms, did not in any way diminish the widespread influence of the Universal Declaration. On the contrary, the very existence of the Covenants, and the fact that they contain the measures of implementation required to ensure the realization of the rights and freedoms set out in the Declaration, gives greater strength to the Declaration.

Moreover, the Universal Declaration is truly universal in scope, as it preserves its validity for every member of the human family, everywhere, regardless of whether or not Governments have formally accepted its principles or ratified the Covenants. On the other hand, the Covenants, by their nature as multilateral conventions, are legally binding only on those States which have accepted them by ratification or accession.

In many important resolutions and decisions adopted by United Nations bodies, including the General Assembly and the Security Council, the Universal Declaration of Human Rights and one or both Covenants have been cited as the basis for action.

Nearly all the international human rights instruments adopted by United Nations bodies since 1948 elaborate principles set out in the Universal Declaration of Human Rights. The International Covenant on Economic, Social and Cultural Rights states in its preamble that it developed out of recognition of the fact that

> in accordance with the Universal Declaration of Human Rights, the ideal of free human beings enjoying freedom from fear and want can only be achieved if conditions are created whereby everyone may enjoy his economic, social and cultural rights, as well as his civil and political rights.

A similar statement is made in the preamble to the International Covenant on Civil and Political Rights.

The Declaration on the Protection of All Persons from Being Subjected to Torture and Other Cruel, Inhuman or Degrading Treatment or Punishment, adopted by the General Assembly in 1975 (resolution 3452 (XXX)), spells out the meaning of article 5 of the Universal Declaration of Human Rights and article 7 of the International Covenant on Civil and Political Rights, both of which provide that no one may be subjected to torture or to cruel, inhuman or degrading treatment or punishment. This prohibition was further reinforced by the adoption in 1984 of the Convention against Torture and Other Cruel, Inhuman or Degrading Treatment or Punishment (General Assembly resolution 39/46). Similarly, the Declaration on the Elimination of All Forms of Intolerance and of Discrimination Based on Religion or Belief, proclaimed by the General Assembly in 1981 (resolution 36/55); clearly defines the nature and scope of the principles of non-discrimination and equality before the law and the right to freedom of thought, conscience, religion and belief contained in the Universal Declaration and the International Covenants.

A similar situation prevails as regards international human rights instruments adopted outside the United Nations system. For example, the preamble to the Convention for the Protection of Human Rights and Fundamental Freedoms, adopted by the Council of Europe at Rome in 1950, concludes with the following words:

Being resolved, as the Governments of European countries which are like-minded and have a common heritage of political traditions, ideals, freedom and the rule of law, to take the first steps for the collective enforcement of certain of the rights stated in the Universal Declaration;

Article II of the Charter of the Organization of African Unity, adopted at Addis Ababa in 1963, provides that one of the purposes of the Organization is "to promote international cooperation, having due regard to the Charter of the United Nations and the Universal Declaration of Human Rights". The American Convention on Human Rights, signed at San José, Costa Rica, in 1969, states in its preamble that the principles to which it gives effect are those set forth in the Charter of the Organization of American States, in the American Declaration of the Rights and Duties of Man, and in the Universal Declaration of Human Rights.

Judges of the International Court of Justice have occasionally invoked principles contained in the International Bill of Human Rights as a basis for their decisions. National and local tribunals have frequently cited principles set out in the International Bill of Human Rights in their decisions. Moreover, in recent years, national constitutional and legislative texts have increasingly provided measures of legal protection for those principles; indeed, many recent national and local laws are clearly modelled on provisions set forth in the Universal Declaration of Human Rights and the International Covenants, which remain a beacon for all present and future efforts in the field of human rights, both nationally and internationally.

Finally, the World Conference on Human Rights, held at Vienna in June 1993, adopted by acclamation the Vienna Declaration and Programme of Action, in which it welcomed the progress made in the codification of human rights instruments and urged the universal ratification of human rights treaties. In addition, all States were encouraged to avoid, as far as possible, the resort to reservations (part 1, para. 26).

Thus the International Bill of Human Rights represents a milestone in the history of human rights, a veritable Magna Carta marking mankind's arrival at a vitally important phase: the conscious acquisition of human dignity and worth.

UN Report on the Use of the Death Penalty in the United States (1998)

Following are excerpts from a report on use of the death penalty in the United States, as prepared by Senegalese lawyer Bacre Waly Ndiaye, special rapporteur for the United Nations Commission on Human Rights. Ndiaye claimed that imposition of capital punishment was often arbitrary and discriminatory in the United States, and he called for a U.S. moratorium on executions—a position echoed by the commission itself, which also suggested that all countries move to abolish the death penalty.

[Section I omitted]

II. The General Context of the Death Penalty in the United States

37. Currently, 40 jurisdictions in the United States of America have death penalty statutes. Thirteen other jurisdictions do not. According to the information received, 3,269 persons are on death row, of whom 47.05 per cent are White, 40.99 per cent are Black, 6.94 per cent are Hispanic, 1.41 per cent are Native American, and 0.70 per cent are Asian. Of the total death row population, more than 98 per cent are male.

38. Since the death penalty was reinstated in 1976, 403 persons have been executed. There have been no federal executions since 1963. Out of these 403 executions, only 6 white persons have reportedly been executed for the murder of a black person. Texas has been responsible for more than 30 per cent of the executions, followed by Virginia (10.17 per cent) and Florida (9.68 per cent). It is reported that since the reinstatement of death penalty statutes, more than 47 persons have been released from death row because of later evidence of their innocence. . . .

39. One hundred and fourteen women have reportedly been sentenced to death from 1973 to June 1997. Of them 47 are on death row and 66 had their sentences either reversed or commuted to life imprisonment. Florida, North Carolina and Texas account for the highest imposition of female death sentences. Female executions have been rare. The last woman executed was in 1984 in North Carolina.

40. Nine juvenile offenders, individuals aged less than 18 at the time they committed the crime for which they were convicted, have been executed. . . .

III. Findings of the Special Rapporteur
A. Current practices in the application of the death penalty
1. Reintroduction of death penalty statutes and extension of the scope

44. The Special Rapporteur has observed a tendency to increase the application of the death penalty both at the state level, either by reinstating the death penalty or by increasing the number of aggravating circumstances, and at the federal level, where the scope of this punishment has recently been dramatically extended. . . .

2. Execution of juveniles

49. International law prohibits the imposition of a death sentence on juvenile offenders (those who committed the crime while under 18 years of age). The consensus of the international community in this respect is reflected in the wide range of international legal instruments. . . .

51. Out of the 38 states with death penalty statutes, 14 provide that 18 is the minimum

age for execution. In 4 states, 17 is the minimum age, while in 21 other states, 16 is the minimum age. According to the information received, 47 offenders who committed the crimes before the age of 18 are currently on death row. At the federal level, the imposition of the death penalty on juvenile offenders is not permitted.

52. In *Thompson v. Oklahoma* (1988), the Supreme Court ruled that it was unconstitutional to impose the death penalty on a person who was under 16 years of age at the time of commission of the crime. In *Stanford v. Kentucky,* the Supreme Court ruled that it was constitutional to impose the death penalty on an offender who was aged 16 at the time of commission of the crime.

53. Although the United States of America has not executed any juvenile offenders while still under 18, it is one of the few countries, together with the Islamic Republic of Iran, Pakistan, Saudi Arabia and Yemen, to execute persons who were under 18 years of age at the time they committed the crime. Charles Rumbaugh was the first juvenile offender executed in the United States since the reinstatement of the death penalty in 1976. He was executed in Texas in September 1985. The last one, Christopher Burger, was executed in Georgia in December 1993. . . .

3. Executions of persons with mental retardation

57. According to information received from non-governmental sources, at least 29 persons with severe mental disabilities have been executed in the United States since the death penalty was reinstated in 1976. Twenty-eight capital jurisdictions are said to permit the execution of mentally retarded defendants. Eleven death penalty states, and the Federal Government, prohibit the execution of mentally retarded persons.

58. Because of the nature of mental retardation, mentally retarded persons are much more vulnerable to manipulation during arrest, interrogation and confession. Moreover, mental retardation appears not to be compatible with the principle of full criminal responsibility. The Special Rapporteur believes that mental retardation should at least be considered as a mitigating circumstance. . . .

B. The administration of the death penalty

61. A death sentence may be imposed both at the federal and state levels. The majority of death penalty sentences are imposed at the state level. Each capital punishment state has its own statute and each state determines how the death penalty will be administrated within the state. However, only a very small proportion of murders result in a sentence of death.

62. It is to be noted that the small percentage of defendants who receive a death sentence are not necessarily those who committed the most heinous crimes. Many factors, other

than the crime itself, appear to influence the imposition of a death sentence. Class, race and economic status, both of the victim and the defendant, are said to be key elements. It is alleged that those who are able to afford good legal representation have less chance of being sentenced to death. The influence of public opinion and political pressure cannot be disregarded either. In addition, racial attitudes of lawyers, prosecutors, juries and judges, although not necessarily conscious, are also believed to play a role in determining who will, or who will not, receive a death sentence. Supreme Court Justice Blackmun, in his dissenting opinion in *Callins v. Collins* (1994), made reference to this problem stating that "(. . .) the death penalty remains fraught with arbitrariness, discrimination, caprice and mistake". He also stated that "Even under the most sophisticated death penalty statutes, race continues to play a major role in determining who shall live and who shall die".

63. Allegations of racial discrimination in the imposition of death sentences are particularly serious in southern states, such as Alabama, Florida, Louisiana, Mississippi, Georgia and Texas, known as the "death penalty belt". The Special Rapporteur was informed that a discriminatory imposition of capital sentences may be favoured by the composition of the judiciary: in Alabama, only 1 of the 67 elected district attorneys is said to be black, and none of Georgia's 159 counties is reported to have a black district attorney. The majority of judges in these states are also reported to be white. . . .

1. The judiciary

69. Federal judges are appointed for life. At the state level, in only 6 of the 38 death penalty states are judges appointed for life by the state governor. In the other 32 states, judges are subject to election.

70. The possibility of elected or appointed judges is recognized in principle 12 of the Basic Principles on the Independence of the Judiciary, adopted by the Seventh United Nations Congress on the Prevention of Crime and the Treatment of Offenders in 1985 and endorsed by the General Assembly in resolutions 40/32 of 29 November 1985 and 40/146 of 13 December 1985. No matter what system is being used, the judiciary shall decide matters impartially, without any restrictions, improper influences, inducements, pressures, threats or interferences, direct or indirect (principle 2).

71. Many sources have expressed concern as to whether the election of judges puts their independence at risk. In its concluding observations to the United States report, the Human Rights Committee expressed its concern about the impact which the current system of election of judges may, in a few states, have on the implementation of the rights provided under article 14 of the ICCPR [International Covenant on Civil and Political Rights]. . . .

V. Conclusions and Recommendations

"Where, after all, do universal rights begin? In small places, close to home—so close and so small that they cannot be seen on any maps of the world. . . . Unless these rights have meaning there, they have little meaning anywhere. Without concerned citizen action to uphold them close to home, we shall look in vain for progress in the larger world."—*Eleanor Roosevelt*

A. Concerning the use of the death penalty

140. The Special Rapporteur shares the view of the Human Rights Committee and considers that the extent of the reservations, declarations and understandings entered by the United States at the time of ratification of the ICCPR are intended to ensure that the United States has only accepted what is already the law of the United States. He is of the opinion that the reservation entered by the United States on the death penalty provision is incompatible with the object and purpose of the treaty and should therefore be considered void.

141. Not only do the reservations entered by the United States seriously reduce the impact of the ICCPR, but its effectiveness nationwide is further undermined by the absence of active enforcement mechanisms to ensure its implementation at state level.

142. The Special Rapporteur is of the view that a serious gap exists between federal and state governments, concerning implementation of international obligations undertaken by the United States Government. He notes with concern that the ICCPR appears not to have been disseminated to state authorities and that knowledge of the country's international obligations is almost non-existent at state level. Further, he is of the opinion that the Federal Government cannot claim to represent the states at the international level and at the same time fail to take steps to implement international obligations accepted on their behalf.

143. The Special Rapporteur is aware of the implications of the United States system of federalism as set out in the Constitution and the impact that it has on the laws and practices of the United States. At the same time, it is clear that the Federal Government in undertaking international obligations also undertakes to use all of its constitutionally mandated powers to ensure that the human rights obligations are fulfilled at all levels.

144. The Special Rapporteur questions the overall commitment of the Federal Government to enforce international obligations at home if it claimed not to be in a position to ensure the access of United Nations experts such as special rapporteurs to authorities at state level. He is concerned that his visit revealed little evidence of such a commitment at the highest levels of the Federal Government.

145. The Special Rapporteur believes that the current practice of imposing death sen-

tences and executions of juveniles in the United States violates international law. He further believes that the reintroduction of the death penalty and the extension of its scope, both at federal and at state level, contravene the spirit and purpose of article 6 of the ICCPR, as well as the international trend towards the progressive restriction of the number of offences for which the death penalty may be imposed. He is further concerned about the execution of mentally retarded and insane persons which he considers to be in contravention of relevant international standards.

146. The Special Rapporteur deplores these practices and considers that they constitute a step backwards in the promotion and protection of the right to life.

147. Because of the definitive nature of a death sentence, a process leading to its imposition must comply fully with the highest safeguards and fair trial standards, and must be in accordance with restrictions imposed by international law. The Special Rapporteur notes with concern that in the United States, guarantees and safeguards, as well as specific restrictions on capital punishment, are not being fully respected. Lack of adequate counsel and legal representation for many capital defendants is disturbing. The enactment of the 1996 Anti-terrorism and Effective Death Penalty Act and the lack of funding of PCDOs [post-conviction defender organizations] have further jeopardized the implementation of the right to a fair trial as provided for in the ICCPR and other international instruments.

148. Despite the excellent reputation of the United States judiciary, the Special Rapporteur observes that the imposition of death sentences in the United States seems to continue to be marked by arbitrariness. Race, ethnic origin and economic status appear to be key determinants of who will, and who will not, receive a sentence of death. As Justice Marshall stated in *Godfrey v. Georgia*, "The task of eliminating arbitrariness in the infliction of capital punishment is proving to be one which our criminal justice system—and perhaps any criminal justice system—is unable to perform".

149. The politics behind the death penalty, particularly during election campaigns, raises doubts as to the objectivity of its imposition. The Special Rapporteur believes that the system of election of judges to relatively short terms of office, and the practice of requesting financial contributions particularly from members of the bar and the public, may risk interfering with the independence and impartiality of the judiciary. Further, the discretionary power of the prosecutor as to whether or not to seek the death penalty raises serious concern regarding the fairness of its administration.

150. The process of jury selection may also be tainted by racial factors and unfairness. The Special Rapporteur notes with concern that people who are opposed to or have hesitations about the death penalty are unlikely to sit as jurors and believes that a "death qualified" jury will be predisposed to apply the harshest sentence. He fears that the right to a fair trial before an impartial tribunal may be jeopardized by such juries. Moreover, he is convinced that

a "death qualified" jury does not represent the community conscience as a whole, but only the conscience of that part of the community which favours capital punishment.

151. The high level of support for the death penalty, even if studies have shown that it is not as deep as is claimed, cannot justify the lack of respect for the restrictions and safe-guards surrounding its use. In many countries, mob killings and lynchings enjoy public support as a way to deal with violent crime and are often portrayed as "popular justice". Yet they are not acceptable in any civilized society.

152. While acknowledging the difficulties that authorities face in fighting violent crime, he believes that solutions other than the increasing use of the death penalty need to be sought. Moreover, the inherent cruelty of executions might only lead to the perpetuation of a culture of violence.

153. The Special Rapporteur is particularly concerned by the current approach to vic-tims' rights. He considers that while victims are entitled to respect and compassion, access to justice and prompt redress, these rights should not be implemented at the expenses of those of the accused. Courts should not become a forum for retaliation. The duty of the State to provide justice should not be privatized and brought back to victims, as it was be-fore the emergence of modern States.

154. While the Special Rapporteur would hope that the United States would join the movement of the international community towards progressively restricting the use of the death penalty as a way to strengthen the protection of the right to life, he is concerned that, to the contrary, the United States is carrying out an increasing number of executions, in-cluding of juveniles and mentally retarded persons. He also fears that executions of women will resume if this trend is not reversed.

155. The Special Rapporteur wishes to emphasize that the use of the death penalty in vi-olation of international standards will not help to resolve social problems and build a more harmonious society but, on the contrary, will contribute to exacerbated tensions between races and classes, particularly at a moment when the United States is proclaiming its inten-tion to combat racism more vigorously.

156. In view of the above, the Special Rapporteur recommends the following to the Government of the United States:

(a) To establish a moratorium on executions in accordance with the recommendations made by the American Bar Association and resolution 1997/12 of the Commission on Hu-man Rights;

(b) To discontinue the practice of imposing death sentences on juvenile offenders and mentally retarded persons and to amend national legislation in this respect to bring it into conformity with international standards;

(c) Not to resume executions of women and respect the de facto moratorium in existence since 1984;

(d) To review legislation, both at federal and state levels, so as to restrict the number of offences punishable by death. In particular, the growing tendency to reinstate death penalty statutes and the increase in the number of aggravating circumstances both at state and federal levels should be addressed in order not to contravene the spirit and purpose of article 6 of the ICCPR and the goal expressed by the international community to progressively restrict the number of offences for which the death penalty is applied;

(e) To encourage the development of public defender systems so as to ensure the right to adequate legal representation for indigent defendants; to reinstate funding for legal resource centres in order to guarantee a more appropriate representation of death row inmates, particularly in those states where a public defender system does not exist. This would also help to diminish the risk of executing innocent persons;

(f) To take steps to disseminate and educate government officials at all levels as well as to develop monitoring and appropriate enforcement mechanisms to achieve full implementation of the provisions of the ICCPR, as well as other international treaties, at state level;

(g) To include a human rights component in training programmes for members of the judiciary. A campaign on the role of juries could further aim at informing the public about the responsibilities of jurors;

(h) To review the system of election of members of the judiciary at state level, in order to ensure a degree of independence and impartiality similar to that of the federal system. It is recommended that in order to provide a greater degree of independence and impartiality that judges be elected for longer terms, for instance 10 years or for life;

(i) In view of the above, to consider inviting the Special Rapporteur on the independence of judges and lawyers to undertake a visit to the United States;

(j) To develop an intensive programme aimed at informing state authorities about international obligations undertaken by the United States and at bringing national laws into conformity with these standards; to increase the cooperation between the Department of Justice and the Department of State to disseminate and enforce the human rights undertakings of the United States;

(k) To lift the reservations, particularly on article 6, and the declarations and understandings entered to the ICCPR. The Special Rapporteur also recommends that the United States ratify the Convention on the Rights of the Child. He further recommends that the United States consider ratifying the first and second Optional Protocols to the ICCPR.

B. Concerning killings by the police

157. The Special Rapporteur is concerned by the reports of violations of the right to life as a result of excessive use of force by law enforcement officials which he received during his mission, and he will continue to monitor the situation closely.

158. While acknowledging that the police face extremely difficult situations in their daily work, authorities have an obligation to ensure that the police respect the right to life.

159. Preliminary recommendations to the Government of the United States include the following:

(a) All alleged violations of the right to life should be investigated, police officials responsible brought to justice and compensation provided to the victims. Further, measures should be taken to prevent recurrence of these violations;

(b) Patterns of use of lethal force should be systematically investigated by the Justice Department;

(c) Training on international standards on law enforcement and human rights should be included in police academies. This is particularly relevant because the United States has taken a leading role in training police forces in other countries;

(d) Independent organs, outside the police departments, should be put in place to investigate all allegations of violations of the right to life promptly and impartially, in accordance with principle 9 of the Principles on the Effective Prevention and Investigation of Extra-legal, Arbitrary and Summary Executions;

(e) In order to avoid conflict of interest with the local district attorney's office, special prosecutors should be appointed more frequently in order to conduct investigations into allegations of violations of the right to life, to identify perpetrators and bring them to justice. . . .

Selected Supreme Court Cases

Following are discussions of and excerpts from five Supreme Court cases discussed in this book: Furman v. Georgia, Gregg v. Georgia, McCleskey v. Kemp, Stanford v. Kentucky, *and* Payne v. Tennessee.

Furman v. Georgia (1972)

In Furman v. Georgia, *in a close 5–4 decision, the Court struck down as unconstitutional a Georgia death penalty law that gave the jury in capital cases complete discretion in deciding whether to impose the death penalty, claiming that it violated the Eighth Amendment's protections against cruel and unusual punishment. Following is a discussion of the case and its implications by Professors Lee Epstein of Washington University and Thomas G. Walker of Emory University in their book* Constitutional Law for a Changing America: Rights, Liberties, and Justice, *4th ed.*

This case involved William Furman, a black man accused of murdering a white man, the father of five children. Under Georgia law, it was completely up to the jury to determine whether a convicted murderer should be put to death. This system, the LDF [Legal Defense Fund] argued, led to unacceptable disparities in sentencing; specifically, blacks convicted of murdering whites were far more likely to receive the death penalty than whites convicted of the same crime.

A divided Supreme Court agreed with the LDF. In a short per curiam opinion, deciding *Furman* and two companion cases, the justices said, "The Court holds that the imposition and carrying out of the death penalty in these cases constitutes cruel and unusual punishment." [A per curiam opinion is one in which each justice writes his or her own opinion.] But there was little else on which the justices agreed. Each took the opportunity to write his own opinion. [Table A-2] summarizes them, and, as you can see, only Brennan and Marshall stated that the death penalty constituted cruel and unusual punishment. Three others agreed only on the unconstitutionality of the Georgia system; the remaining four dissented.

Taking cues from the justices' opinions in *Furman,* Georgia legislators devised a new plan for the administration of the death penalty. At the heart of this law was the "bifurcated trial," which consisted of two stages—the trial and the sentencing phase. The trial would proceed as usual, with a jury or judge finding the defendant guilty or innocent. If the verdict was guilty, the prosecution could seek the death penalty at the sentencing stage, in which the defense attorney presents the mitigating facts and the prosecution, the aggravating. Mitigating facts include the individual's age, record, family responsibility, psychiatric reports, and chances for rehabilitation. Such data are not specified in law. The prosecution, on the other hand, has to demonstrate that at least one codified aggravating factor exists. The Georgia law specified ten, including: murders committed "while the offender was engaged in the commission of another capital offense" and the murder of "a judicial officer . . . or . . . district attorney because of the exercise of his official duty." After hearing arguments in mitigation and aggravation, the jury determines whether the individual receives the death penalty. By spelling out the conditions that must be present before a death penalty can be imposed, the law sought to reduce the jury's discretion and eliminate the arbitrary application of the death penalty that the Court in *Furman* found unacceptable. As a further safeguard, the Georgia Supreme Court was to review all jury determinations of death.

Table A-2 Summary of Justices' Opinions and Modes of Analysis, *Furman v. Georgia* (1972)

Justice	Major Points	Modes of Analysis
Douglas	1. Equal Protection: discriminates against poor and minorities 2. arbitrary because of selective usage	1. reliance on studies, qualitative and quantitative 2. historical analysis of English Bill of Rights and U.S. debates
Brennan	1. Eighth Amendment: does not "comport with human dignity" 2. fails four-pronged test of acceptable punishment (cannot be degrading, arbitrary, unacceptable to contemporary society, excessive) 3. responsibility of courts to apply rights	1. historical analysis of debates over capital punishment 2. statistics on infrequency of use and national trends
Stewart	1. need not deal with Eighth Amendment question per se 2. cruel and unusual as currently applied because it is "wantonly and so freakishly" and rarely imposed	1. citations to statistical studies 2. citations to other justices' opinions
White	1. so infrequently imposed that it is not a "credible" deterrent 2. so infrequently imposed as to be of little service to the administration of criminal justice 3. no "discernible social or political purpose"	1. personal experience with state criminal cases
Marshall	1. evolving standards of decency 2. death penalties are cruel and unusual if they are physically intolerable, inhumane, have no valid legislative purpose, abhorred by "popular sentiment" 3. "morally unacceptable"	1. historical analysis of debates, history, and usage 2. analysis of precedent 3. examination of bases for punishment 4. statistics on deterrence, usage
Burger	1. not judicial terrain	1. Framers' intent

Table A-2 *continued*

Justice	Major Points	Modes of Analysis
	2. punishment does not offend Americans 3. suggests changes in existing laws to comply with Court's opinions	2. public opinion polls, state laws and application 3. analysis of other justices' views
Blackmun	1. expresses personal antipathy, but no judicial function 2. inconsistent with past precedent 3. inconsistent with congressional intent	1. analysis of precedent 2. Framers' intent
Powell	1. encroachment of legislative function 2. death penalty has not been "repudiated" by Americans 3. discrimination probably occurs in all areas of criminal sentencing 4. deterrence value is unclear 5. not disproportionate for rape	1. analysis of precedent 2. federal data, public opinion polls 3. state court opinions 4. deterrence studies
Rehnquist	1. contradicts precedent 2. defer to legislatures	1. precedent

In 1976 the Supreme Court reviewed the constitutionality of this law in *Gregg v. Georgia.* Did this law reduce the chance for "wanton and freakish punishment" of the sort the Court found so distasteful in *Furman?*

Gregg v. Georgia (1976)

Professors Epstein and Walker also discuss Gregg v. Georgia, *the 1976 case in which the Supreme Court rejected the notion that the death penalty invariably violates the Eighth Amendment and claimed that the Constitution discusses the use of capital punishment in the Fifth and Fourteenth Amendments.*

Troy Gregg and a friend were hitchhiking north in Florida. Two men picked them up, and later the foursome was joined by another passenger who rode with them as far as Atlanta. The four then continued to a rest stop on the highway. The next day, the bodies of the two drivers were found in a nearby ditch. The individual let off in Atlanta identified Gregg and his friend as possible assailants. Gregg was tried under Georgia's new death penalty system. He was convicted of murder and sentenced to death, a penalty the state's highest court upheld.

Justice Stewart announced the judgment of the Court:
The issue in this case is whether the imposition of the sentence of death for the crime of murder under the law of Georgia violates the Eighth and Fourteenth Amendments. . . .

We address initially the basic contention that the punishment of death for the crime of murder is, under all circumstances, "cruel and unusual" in violation of the Eighth and Fourteenth Amendments of the Constitution. . . . [W]e will [also] consider the sentence of death imposed under the Georgia statutes at issue in this case.

The Court on a number of occasions has both assumed and asserted the constitutionality of capital punishment. In several cases that assumption provided a necessary foundation for the decision, as the Court was asked to decide whether a particular method of carrying out a capital sentence would be allowed to stand under the Eighth Amendment. But until *Furman v. Georgia* (1972), the Court never confronted squarely the fundamental claim that the punishment of death always, regardless of the enormity of the offense or the procedure followed in imposing the sentence, is cruel and unusual punishment in violation of the Constitution. Although this issue was presented and addressed in *Furman,* it was not resolved by the Court. Four Justices would have held that capital punishment is not unconstitutional *per se;* two Justices would have reached the opposite conclusion; and three Justices, while agreeing that the statutes then before the Court were invalid as applied, left open the question whether such punishment may ever be imposed. We now hold that the punishment of death does not invariably violate the Constitution.

The history of the prohibition of "cruel and unusual" punishment already has been reviewed at length. The phrase first appeared in the English Bill of Rights of 1689, which was drafted by Parliament at the accession of William and Mary. The English version appears to have been directed against punishments unauthorized by statute and beyond the jurisdiction of the sentencing court, as well as those disproportionate to the offense involved. The American draftsmen, who adopted the English phrasing in drafting the Eighth Amendment, were primarily concerned, however, with proscribing "tortures" and other "barbarous" methods of punishment.

In the earliest cases raising Eighth Amendment claims, the Court focused on particular methods of execution to determine whether they were too cruel to pass constitutional muster. The constitutionality of the sentence of death itself was not at issue, and the criterion used to evaluate the mode of execution was its similarity to "torture" and other "barbarous" methods.

But the Court has not confined the prohibition embodied in the Eighth Amendment to "barbarous" methods that were generally outlawed in the 18th century. Instead, the Amendment has been interpreted in a flexible and dynamic manner. The Court early recognized that "a principle to be vital must be capable of wider application than the mischief which gave it birth." *Weems v. United States* (1910). Thus the Clause forbidding "cruel and unusual" punishments "is not fastened to the obsolete but may acquire meaning as public opinion becomes enlightened by a humane justice." . . .

It is clear from . . . these precedents that the Eighth Amendment has not been regarded as a static concept. As Mr. Chief Justice Warren said, in an oft-quoted phrase, "[t]he Amendment must draw its meaning from the evolving standards of decency that mark the progress of a maturing society." Thus, an assessment of contemporary values concerning the infliction of a challenged sanction is relevant to the application of the Eighth Amendment. As we develop below more fully, this assessment does not call for a subjective judgment. It requires, rather, that we look to objective indicia that reflect the public attitude toward a given sanction.

But our cases also make clear that public perceptions of standards of decency with respect to criminal sanctions are not conclusive. A penalty also must accord with "the dignity of man," which is the "basic concept underlying the Eighth Amendment." This means, at least, that the punishment not be "excessive." When a form of punishment in the abstract (in this case, whether capital punishment may ever be imposed as a sanction for murder) rather than in the particular (the propriety of death as a penalty to be applied to a specific defendant for a specific crime) is under consideration, the inquiry into "excessiveness" has two aspects. First, the punishment must not involve the unnecessary and wanton infliction of pain. Second, the punishment must not be grossly out of proportion to the severity of the crime.

Of course, the requirements of the Eighth Amendment must be applied with an awareness of the limited role to be played by the courts. This does not mean that judges have no role to play, for the Eighth Amendment is a restraint upon the exercise of legislative power. . . .

But, while we have an obligation to insure that constitutional bounds are not overreached, we may not act as judges as we might as legislators. . . .

Therefore, in assessing a punishment selected by a democratically elected legislature against the constitutional measure, we presume its validity. We may not require the legislature to select the least severe penalty possible so long as the penalty selected is not cruelly inhumane or disproportionate to the crime involved. And a heavy burden rests on those who would attack the judgment of the representatives of the people. . . .

In the discussion to this point we have sought to identify the principles and considerations that guide a court in addressing an Eighth Amendment claim. We now consider specifically whether the sentence of death for the crime of murder is a *per se* violation of the Eighth and Fourteenth Amendments to the Constitution. We note first that history and precedent strongly support a negative answer to this question.

The imposition of the death penalty for the crime of murder has a long history of acceptance both in the United States and in England. . . .

It is apparent from the text of the Constitution itself that the existence of capital punishment was accepted by the Framers. At the time the Eighth Amendment was ratified, capital punishment was a common sanction in every State. . . . The Fifth Amendment, adopted at the same time as the Eighth, contemplated the continued existence of the capital sanction by imposing certain limits on the prosecution of capital cases:

"No person shall be held to answer for a capital, or otherwise infamous crime, unless on a presentment or indictment of a Grand Jury . . . ; nor shall any person be subject for the same offense to be twice put in jeopardy of life or limb; . . . nor be deprived of life, liberty, or property, without due process of law. . . ."

And the Fourteenth Amendment, adopted over three quarters of a century later, similarly contemplates the existence of the capital sanction in providing that no State shall deprive any person of "life, liberty, or property" without due process of law.

For nearly two centuries, this Court, repeatedly and often expressly, has recognized that capital punishment is not invalid *per se*. . . .

Four years ago, the petitioners in *Furman* and its companion cases predicated their argument primarily upon the asserted proposition that standards of decency had evolved to the point where capital punishment no longer could be tolerated. The petitioners in those cases said, in effect, that the evolutionary process had come to an end, and that standards of decency required that the Eighth Amendment be construed finally as prohibiting capital punishment for any crime regardless of its depravity and impact on society. This view was accepted by two Justices. Three other Justices were unwilling to go so far; focusing on the procedures by which convicted defendants were selected for the death penalty rather than on the actual punishment inflicted, they joined in the conclusion that the statutes before the Court were constitutionally invalid.

The petitioners in the capital cases before the Court today renew the "standards of decency" argument, but developments during the four years since *Furman* have undercut substantially the assumptions upon which their argument rested. Despite the continuing debate, dating back to the 19th century, over the morality and utility of capital punishment, it is now evident that a large proportion of American society continues to regard it as an appropriate and necessary criminal sanction.

The most marked indication of society's endorsement of the death penalty for murder is the legislative response to *Furman*. The legislatures of at least 35 States have enacted new statutes that provide for the death penalty for at least some crimes that result in the death of another person. And the Congress of the United States, in 1974, enacted a statute providing the death penalty for aircraft piracy that results in death. These recently adopted statutes have attempted to address the concerns expressed by the Court in *Furman* primarily (i) by specifying the factors to be weighed and the procedures to be followed in deciding when to impose a capital sentence, or (ii) by making the death penalty mandatory for specified crimes. But all of the post-*Furman* statutes make clear that capital punishment itself has not been rejected by the elected representatives of the people.

In the only statewide referendum occurring since *Furman* and brought to our attention, the people of California adopted a constitutional amendment that authorized capital punishment, in effect negating a prior ruling by the Supreme Court of California that the death penalty violated the California Constitution.

The jury also is a significant and reliable objective index of contemporary values because it is so directly involved. . . . It may be true that evolving standards have influenced juries in recent decades to be more discriminating in imposing the sentence of death. But the relative infrequency of jury verdicts imposing the death sentence does not indicate rejection of capital punishment *per se*. Rather, the reluctance of juries in many cases to impose the sentence may well reflect the humane feeling that this most irrevocable of sanctions should be reserved for a small number of extreme cases. Indeed, the actions of juries in many States since *Furman* are fully compatible with the legislative judgments, reflected in the new statutes, as to the continued utility and necessity of capital punishment in appropriate cases. At the close of 1974 at least 254 persons had been sentenced to death since *Furman*, and by the end of March 1976, more than 460 persons were subject to death sentences.

As we have seen, however, the Eighth Amendment demands more than that a challenged punishment be acceptable to contemporary society. The Court also must ask whether it comports with the basic concept of human dignity at the core of the Amendment. Although we cannot "invalidate a category of penalties because we deem less severe penalties adequate to serve the ends of penology," the sanction imposed cannot be so totally without penological justification that it results in the gratuitous infliction of suffering.

The death penalty is said to serve two principal social purposes: retribution and deterrence of capital crimes by prospective offenders.

In part, capital punishment is an expression of society's moral outrage at particularly offensive conduct. This function may be unappealing to many, but it is essential in an ordered society that asks its citizens to rely on legal processes rather than self-help to vindicate their wrongs. . . . "Retribution is no longer the dominant objective of the criminal law," but neither is it a forbidden objective nor one inconsistent with our respect for the dignity of men. . . .

Statistical attempts to evaluate the worth of the death penalty as a deterrent to crimes by potential offenders have occasioned a great deal of debate. The results simply have been inconclusive. . . .

Although some of the studies suggest that the death penalty may not function as a significantly greater deterrent than lesser penalties, there is no convincing empirical evidence either supporting or refuting this view. We may nevertheless assume safely that there are murderers, such as those who act in passion, for whom the threat of death has little or no deterrent effect. But for many others, the death penalty undoubtedly is a significant deterrent. There are carefully contemplated murders, such as murder for hire, where the possible penalty of death may well enter into the cold calculus that precedes the decision to act. And there are some categories of murder, such as murder by a life prisoner, where other sanctions may not be adequate.

The value of capital punishment as a deterrent of crime is a complex factual issue the resolution of which properly rests with the legislatures, which can evaluate the results of statistical studies in terms of their own local conditions and with a flexibility of approach that is not available to the courts. Indeed, many of the post-*Furman* statutes reflect just such a responsible effort to define those crimes and those criminals for which capital punishment is most probably an effective deterrent.

In sum, we cannot say that the judgment of the Georgia Legislature that capital punishment may be necessary in some cases is clearly wrong. Considerations of federalism, as well as respect for the ability of a legislature to evaluate, in terms of its particular State, the moral consensus concerning the death penalty and its social utility as a sanction, require us to conclude, in the absence of more convincing evidence, that the infliction of death as a punishment for murder is not without justification and thus is not unconstitutionally severe.

Finally, we must consider whether the punishment of death is disproportionate in relation to the crime for which it is imposed. There is no question that death as a punishment is unique in its severity and irrevocability. When a defendant's life is at stake, the Court has been particularly sensitive to insure that every safeguard is observed. But we are concerned here only with the imposition of capital punishment for the crime of murder, and when a life has been taken deliberately by the offender, we cannot say that the punishment is invariably disproportionate to the crime. It is an extreme sanction, suitable to the most extreme of crimes.

We hold that the death penalty is not a form of punishment that may never be imposed, regardless of the circumstances of the offense, regardless of the character of the offender, and regardless of the procedure followed in reaching the decision to impose it.

We now consider whether Georgia may impose the death penalty on the petitioner in this case.

While *Furman* did not hold that the infliction of the death penalty *per se* violates the Constitution's ban on cruel and unusual punishments, it did recognize that the penalty of death is different in kind from any other punishment imposed under our system of criminal justice. Because of the uniqueness of the death penalty, *Furman* held that it could not be imposed under sentencing procedures that created a substantial risk that it would be inflicted in an arbitrary and capricious manner. . . .

Furman mandates that where discretion is afforded a sentencing body on a matter so grave as the determination of whether a human life should be taken or spared, that discretion must be suitably directed and limited so as to minimize the risk of wholly arbitrary and capricious action. . . .

Jury sentencing has been considered desirable in capital cases in order "to maintain a link between contemporary community values and the penal system—a link without which the determination of punishment could hardly reflect 'the evolving standards of decency that mark the progress of a maturing society.'" But it creates special problems. Much of the information that is relevant to the sentencing decision may have no relevance to the question of guilt, or may even be extremely prejudicial to a fair determination of that question. This problem, however, is scarcely insurmountable. Those who have studied the question suggest that a bifurcated procedure—one in which the question of sentence is not considered until the determination of guilt has been made—is the best answer. . . . When a human life is at stake and when the jury must have information prejudicial to the question of guilt but relevant to the question of penalty in order to impose a rational sentence, a bifurcated system is more likely to ensure elimination of the constitutional deficiencies identified in *Furman*.

But the provision of relevant information under fair procedural rules is not alone sufficient to guarantee that the information will be properly used in the imposition of punishment, especially if sentencing is performed by a jury. Since the members of a jury will have had little, if any, previous experience in sentencing, they are unlikely to be skilled in dealing with the information they are given. To the extent that this problem is inherent in jury sentencing, it may not be totally correctable. It seems clear, however, that the problem will be alleviated if the jury is given guidance regarding the factors about the crime and the defendant that the State, representing organized society, deems particularly relevant to the sentencing decision.

The idea that a jury should be given guidance in its decision making is also hardly a novel proposition. Juries are invariably given careful instructions on the law and how to apply it before they are authorized to decide the merits of a lawsuit. It would be virtually unthinkable to follow any other course in a legal system that has traditionally operated by following prior precedents and fixed rules of law. When erroneous instructions are given, retrial is often required. It is quite simply a hallmark of our legal system that juries be carefully and adequately guided in their deliberations.

While some have suggested that standards to guide a capital jury's sentencing deliberations are impossible to formulate, the fact is that such standards have been developed. . . . While such standards are by necessity somewhat general, they do provide guidance to the sentencing authority and thereby reduce the likelihood that it will impose a sentence that fairly can be called capricious or arbitrary. Where the sentencing authority is required to specify the factors it relied upon in reaching its decision, the further safeguard of meaningful appellate review is available to ensure that death sentences are not imposed capriciously or in a freakish manner.

In summary, the concerns expressed in *Furman* that the penalty of death not be imposed in an arbitrary or capricious manner can be met by a carefully drafted statute that ensures that the sentencing authority is given adequate information and guidance. As a general proposition these concerns are best met by a system that provides for a bifurcated proceeding at which the sentencing authority is apprised of the information relevant to the imposition of sentence and provided with standards to guide its use of the information.

We do not intend to suggest that only the above-described procedures would be permissible under *Furman* or that any sentencing system constructed along these general lines would inevitably satisfy the concerns of *Furman*, for each distinct system must be examined on an individual basis. Rather, we have embarked upon this general exposition to make clear that it is possible to construct capital-sentencing systems capable of meeting *Furman*'s constitutional concerns.

We now turn to consideration of the constitutionality of Georgia's capital-sentencing procedures. In the wake of *Furman*, Georgia amended its capital punishment statute, but chose not to narrow the scope of its murder provisions. Thus, now as before *Furman*, in Georgia "[a] person commits murder when he unlawfully and with malice aforethought, either express or implied, causes the death of another human being." All persons convicted of murder "shall be punished by death or by imprisonment for life."

Georgia did act, however, to narrow the class of murderers subject to capital punishment by specifying 10 statutory aggravating circumstances, one of which must be found by the jury to exist beyond a reasonable doubt before a death sentence can ever be imposed. In addition, the jury is authorized to consider any other appropriate aggravating or mitigating circumstances. The jury is not required to find any mitigating circumstance in order to make a recommendation of mercy that is binding on the trial court, but it must find a *statutory* aggravating circumstance before recommending a sentence of death.

These procedures require the jury to consider the circumstances of the crime and the criminal before it recommends sentence. No longer can a Georgia jury do as *Furman's* jury did: reach a finding of the defendant's guilt and then, without guidance or direction, decide whether he should live or die. Instead, the jury's attention is directed to the specific circumstances of the crime. . . . In addition, the jury's attention is focused on the characteristics of the person who committed the crime. . . . As a result, while some jury discretion still exists, "the discretion to be exercised is controlled by clear and objective standards so as to produce nondiscriminatory application."

As an important additional safeguard against arbitrariness and caprice, the Georgia statutory scheme provides for automatic appeal of all death sentences to the State's Supreme Court. That court is required by statute to review each sentence of death and determine whether it was imposed under the influence of passion or prejudice, whether the evidence supports the jury's finding of a statutory aggravating circumstance, and whether the sentence is disproportionate compared to those sentences imposed in similar cases.

In short, Georgia's new sentencing procedures require as a prerequisite to the imposition of the death penalty, specific jury findings as to the circumstances of the crime or the character of the defendant. Moreover, to guard further against a situation comparable to that presented in *Furman,* the Supreme Court of Georgia compares each death sentence with the sentences imposed on similarly situated defendants to ensure that the sentence of death in a particular case is not disproportionate. On their face these procedures seem to satisfy the concerns of *Furman.* No longer should there be "no meaningful basis for distinguishing the few cases in which [the death penalty] is imposed from the many cases in which it is not." . . .

The basic concern of *Furman* centered on those defendants who were being condemned to death capriciously and arbitrarily. Under the procedures before the Court in that case, sentencing authorities were not directed to give attention to the nature or circumstances of the crime committed or to the character or record of the defendant. Left unguided, juries imposed the death sentence in a way that could only be called freakish. The new Georgia sentencing procedures, by contrast, focus the jury's attention on the particularized nature of the crime and the particularized characteristics of the individual defendant. While the jury is permitted to consider any aggravating or mitigating circumstances, it must find and identify at least one statutory aggravating factor before it may impose a penalty of death. In this way the jury's discretion is channeled. No longer can a jury wantonly and freakishly impose the death sentence; it is always circumscribed by the legislative guidelines. In addition, the review function of the Supreme Court of Georgia affords additional assurance that the concerns that prompted our decision in *Furman* are not present to any significant degree in the Georgia procedure applied here.

For the reasons expressed in this opinion, we hold that the statutory system under which Gregg was sentenced to death does not violate the Constitution. Accordingly, the judgment of the Georgia Supreme Court is affirmed.

McCleskey v. Kemp (1987)

In their discussion of McCleskey v. Kemp, *the case in which the Court directly addressed a petitioner's argument that defendants of any race who killed white victims were more likely to receive the death penalty than were defendants of any race who killed nonwhites, Professors Epstein and Walker claim that the Court ruled that capital defendants may not present evidence about systemic discrimination during their trial.*

On May 13, 1978, Warren McCleskey, a black man, and three accomplices attempted to rob a furniture store in Atlanta, Georgia. One of the employees hit a silent alarm button, which was answered by a white, thirty-one-year-old police officer. As the officer entered the store, he was shot and killed. Several weeks later, when police arrested McCleskey on another charge, he confessed to the robbery. At his trial, McCleskey was identified by one of the accomplices as the individual who killed the officer. The prosecution also entered evidence indicating that McCleskey had bragged about the shooting.

Three months after the robbery, a jury of eleven whites and one black convicted McCleskey and sentenced him to death. At that point, the NAACP LDF took over his defense. The LDF based its appeal in the federal courts on a 1986 study showing that blacks convicted of murdering whites received death sentences at disproportionately high rates. The study centered on a statistical examination by several professors of the application of Georgia's death penalty. Named for one of the researchers, David Baldus, the study examined 2,484 Georgia murder cases from 1973 to 1979, coded for some 230 variables. To analyze this mammoth amount of data, Baldus used a multivariate technique, which allows researchers to demonstrate the effects of possible explanatory variables (such as the race of the defendant or victim) on outcomes (such as the decision to sentence to death).

Baldus's conclusions were dramatic. Among the most noteworthy were the following:

- The chances of receiving a death sentence were 4.3 times greater for defendants whose victims were white than for defendants whose victims were black.
- Of the 128 cases in which death was imposed, 108 or 87 percent involved white victims.
- Prosecutors sought the death penalty in 70 percent of cases involving black defendants and white victims, but in only 32 percent in which both the defendant and victim were white.

- Black defendants were 1.1 times more likely than other defendants to receive death sentences.

Armed with this study the LDF tried to convince the justices once and for all that the disparate application of death penalty laws led to unacceptable violations of the Equal Protection, Due Process, and Cruel and Unusual Punishment Clauses.

Justice Powell delivered the opinion of the Court:

This case presents the question whether a complex statistical study that indicates a risk that racial considerations enter into capital sentencing determinations proves that petitioner McCleskey's capital sentence is unconstitutional under the Eighth or Fourteenth Amendment. . . .

Our analysis begins with the basic principle that a defendant who alleges an equal protection violation has the burden of proving "the existence of purposeful discrimination." A corollary to this principle is that a criminal defendant must prove that the purposeful discrimination "had a discriminatory effect" on him. Thus, to prevail under the Equal Protection Clause, McCleskey must prove that the decision makers in *his* case acted with discriminatory purpose. He offers no evidence specific to his own case that would support an inference that racial considerations played a part in his sentence. Instead, he relies solely on the Baldus study. McCleskey argues that the Baldus study compels an inference that his sentence rests on purposeful discrimination. McCleskey's claim that these statistics are sufficient proof of discrimination, without regard to the facts of a particular case, would extend to all capital cases in Georgia, at least where the victim was white and the defendant is black.

The Court has accepted statistics as proof of intent to discriminate in certain limited contexts. First, this Court has accepted statistical disparities as proof of an equal protection violation in the selection of the jury venire in a particular district. Although statistical proof normally must present a "stark" pattern to be accepted as the sole proof of discriminatory intent under the Constitution, "[b]ecause of the nature of the jury-selection task, . . . we have permitted a finding of constitutional violation even when the statistical pattern does not approach [such] extremes." Second, this Court has accepted statistics in the form of multiple regression analysis to prove statutory violations under Title VII.

But the nature of the capital sentencing decision, and the relationship of the statistics to that decision, are fundamentally different from the corresponding elements in the venire-selection or Title VII cases. Most importantly, each particular decision to impose the death penalty is made by a petit jury selected from a properly constituted venire. Each jury is unique in its composition, and the Constitution requires that its decision rest on consideration of innumerable factors that vary according to the characteristics of the individual defendant and the facts of the particular capital offense. Thus, the application of an inference drawn from the general statistics to a specific decision in a trial and sentencing simply is not comparable to the application of an inference drawn from general statistics to a specific venire-selection or Title VII case. In those cases, the statistics relate to fewer entities, and fewer variables are relevant to the challenged decisions.

Another important difference between the cases in which we have accepted statistics as proof of discriminatory intent and this case is that, in the venire-selection and Title VII contexts, the decision maker has an opportunity to explain the statistical disparity. Here, the State has no practical opportunity to rebut the Baldus study. . . .

Finally, McCleskey's statistical proffer must be viewed in the context of his challenge. McCleskey challenges decisions at the heart of the State's criminal justice system. "[O]ne of society's most basic tasks is that of protecting the lives of its citizens and one of the most basic ways in which it achieves the task is through criminal laws against murder." Implementation of these laws necessarily requires discretionary judgments. Because discretion is essential to the criminal justice process, we would demand exceptionally clear proof before we would infer that the discretion has been abused. The unique nature of the decisions at issue in this case also counsel against adopting such an inference from the disparities indicated by the Baldus study. Accordingly, we hold that the Baldus study is clearly insufficient to support an inference that any of the decision makers in McCleskey's case acted with discriminatory purpose. . . .

McCleskey also argues that the Baldus study demonstrates that the Georgia capital sentencing system violates the Eighth Amendment. . . .

Two principal decisions guide our resolution of McCleskey's Eighth Amendment claim. In *Furman v. Georgia* (1972), the Court concluded that the death penalty was so irrationally imposed that any particular death sentence could be presumed excessive. . . .

In *Gregg,* the Court specifically addressed the question left open in *Furman*—whether the punishment of death for murder is "under all circumstances, 'cruel and unusual' in violation of the Eighth and Fourteenth Amendments of the Constitution." . . . We noted that any punishment might be unconstitutionally severe if inflicted without penological justification, but concluded:

"Considerations of federalism, as well as respect for the ability of a legislature to evaluate, in terms of its particular State, the moral consensus concerning the death penalty and its social utility as a sanction, require us to conclude, in the absence of more convincing evidence, that the infliction of death as a punishment for murder is not without justification and thus is not unconstitutionally severe." . . .

In light of our precedents under the Eighth Amendment, McCleskey cannot argue successfully that his sentence is "disproportionate to the crime in the traditional sense." He does not deny that he committed a murder in the course of a planned robbery, a crime for which this Court has determined that the death penalty constitutionally may be imposed. His disproportionality claim "is of a different sort." McCleskey argues that the sentence in his case is disproportionate to the sentences in other murder cases.

On the one hand, he cannot base a constitutional claim on an argument that his case differs from other cases in which defendants did receive the death penalty. On automatic appeal, the Georgia Supreme Court found that McCleskey's death sentence was not disproportionate to other death sentences imposed in the State. . . .

On the other hand, absent a showing that the Georgia capital punishment system operates in an arbitrary and capricious manner, McCleskey cannot prove a constitutional violation by demonstrating that other defendants who may be similarly situated did not receive the death penalty. In *Gregg*, the Court confronted the argument that "the opportunities for discretionary action that are inherent in the processing of any murder case under Georgia law," specifically, the opportunities for discretionary leniency, rendered the capital sentences imposed arbitrary and capricious. We rejected this contention. . . .

Because McCleskey's sentence was imposed under Georgia's sentencing procedures that focus discretion "on the particularized nature of the crime and the particularized characteristics of the individual defendant," we lawfully may presume that McCleskey's death sentence was not "wantonly and freakishly" imposed, and thus that the sentence is not disproportionate within any recognized meaning under the Eighth Amendment.

Although our decision in *Gregg* as to the facial validity of the Georgia capital punishment statute appears to foreclose McCleskey's disproportionality argument, he further contends that the Georgia capital punishment system is arbitrary and capricious in *application*, and therefore his sentence is excessive, because racial considerations may influence capital sentencing decisions in Georgia. We now address this claim.

To evaluate McCleskey's challenge, we must examine exactly what the Baldus study may show. Even Professor Baldus does not contend that his statistics prove that race enters into any capital sentencing decisions or that race was a factor in McCleskey's particular case. Statistics at most may show only a likelihood that a particular factor entered into some decisions. There is, of course, some risk of racial prejudice influencing a jury's decision in a criminal case. There are similar risks that other kinds of prejudice will influence other criminal trials. The question "is at what point that risk becomes constitutionally unacceptable." McCleskey asks us to accept the likelihood allegedly shown by the Baldus study as the constitutional measure of an unacceptable risk of racial prejudice influencing capital sentencing decisions. This we decline to do.

Because of the risk that the factor of race may enter the criminal justice process, we have engaged in "unceasing efforts" to eradicate racial prejudice from our criminal justice system. Our efforts have been guided by our recognition that "the inestimable privilege of trial by jury . . . is a vital principle, underlying the whole administration of criminal justice." Specifically, a capital sentencing jury representative of a criminal defendant's community assures a "'diffused impartiality'" in the jury's task of "express[ing] the conscience of the community on the ultimate question of life or death."

Individual jurors bring to their deliberations "qualities of human nature and varieties of human experience, the range of which is unknown and perhaps unknowable." The capital sentencing decision requires the individual jurors to focus their collective judgment on the unique characteristics of a particular criminal defendant. It is not surprising that such collective judgments often are difficult to explain. But the inherent lack of predictability of jury decisions does not justify their condemnation. . . .

McCleskey's argument that the Constitution condemns the discretion allowed decision makers in the Georgia capital sentencing system is antithetical to the fundamental role of discretion in our criminal justice system. Discretion in the criminal justice system offers substantial benefits to the criminal defendant. Not only can a jury decline to impose the death sentence, it can decline to convict, or choose to convict of a lesser offense. Whereas decisions against a defendant's interest may be reversed by the trial judge or on appeal, these discretionary exercises of leniency are final and unreviewable. Similarly, the capacity of prosecutorial discretion to provide individualized justice is "firmly entrenched in American law." As we have noted, a prosecutor can decline to charge, offer a plea bargain, or decline to seek a death sentence in any particular case. Of course, "the power to be lenient [also] is the power to discriminate," but a capital-punishment system that did not allow for discretionary acts of leniency "would be totally alien to our notions of criminal justice."

At most, the Baldus study indicates a discrepancy that appears to correlate with race. Apparent disparities in sentencing are an inevitable part of our criminal justice system. . . . Despite these imperfections, our consistent rule has been that constitutional guarantees are met when "the mode [for determining guilt or punishment] itself has been surrounded with safeguards to make it as fair as possible." Where the discretion that is fundamental to our criminal process is involved, we decline to assume that what is unexplained is invidious. In light of the safeguards designed to minimize racial bias in the process, the fundamental value of jury trial in our criminal justice system, and the benefits that discretion provides to criminal defendants, we hold that the Baldus study does not demonstrate a constitutionally significant risk of racial bias affecting the Georgia capital-sentencing process.

Two additional concerns inform our decision in this case. First, McCleskey's claim, taken to its logical conclusion, throws into serious question the principles that underlie our entire criminal justice system. The Eighth Amendment is not limited in application to capital punishment, but applies to all penalties. Thus, if we accepted McCleskey's claim that racial bias has impermissibly tainted the capital sentencing decision, we could soon be faced with similar claims as to other types of penalty. Moreover, the claim that his sentence rests on the irrelevant factor of race easily could be extended to apply to claims based on unexplained discrepancies that correlate to membership in other minority groups, and even to gender. Similarly, since McCleskey's claim relates to the race of his victim, other claims could apply with equally logical force to statistical disparities that correlate with the race or sex of other actors in the criminal justice system, such as defense attorneys or judges. Also, there is no logical reason that such a claim need be limited to racial or sexual bias. If arbitrary and capricious punishment is the touchstone under the Eighth Amendment, such a claim could—at least in theory—be based upon any arbitrary variable, such as the defendant's facial characteristics, or the physical attractiveness of the defendant or the victim, that some statistical study indicates may be influential in jury decision making. As these examples illustrate, there is no limiting principle to the type of challenge brought by McCleskey. The Constitution does not require that a State eliminate any demonstrable disparity that correlates with a potentially irrelevant factor in order to operate a criminal justice system that includes capital punishment. As we have stated specifically in the context of capital punishment, the Constitution does not "plac[e] totally unrealistic conditions on its use." Second, McCleskey's arguments are best presented to the legislative bodies. It is not the responsibility—or indeed even the right—of this Court to determine the appropriate punishment for particular crimes. . . . Legislatures also are better qualified to weigh and "evaluate the results of statistical studies in terms of their own local conditions and with a flexibility of approach that is not available to the courts." Capital punishment is now the law in more than two thirds of our States. It is the ultimate duty of courts to determine on a case-by-case basis whether these laws are applied consistently with the Constitution. Despite McCleskey's wide ranging arguments that basically challenge the validity of capital punishment in our multiracial society, the only question before us is whether in his case the law of Georgia was properly applied. We agree with the District Court and the Court of Appeals for the Eleventh Circuit that this was carefully and correctly done in this case.

Accordingly, we affirm the judgment of the Court of Appeals for the Eleventh Circuit.

It is so ordered.

Stanford v. Kentucky (1989)

In Stanford v. Kentucky *the Court concluded that the Eighth Amendment does not prohibit the government from executing juveniles who committed crimes at ages sixteen or seventeen.*

Justice Scalia wrote the opinion of the Court:
These two consolidated cases require us to decide whether the imposition of capital pun-

ishment on an individual for a crime committed at 16 or 17 years of age constitutes cruel and unusual punishment under the Eighth Amendment. . . .

The thrust of both [defendants] Wilkins' and Stanford's arguments is that imposition of the death penalty on those who were juveniles when they committed their crimes falls within the Eighth Amendment's prohibition against "cruel and unusual punishments." . . .

Neither petitioner asserts that his sentence constitutes one of "those modes or acts of punishment that had been considered cruel and unusual at the time that the Bill of Rights was adopted." Ford v. Wainwright, 477 U.S. 399, 405 (1986). Nor could they support such a contention. At that time, the common law set the rebuttable presumption of incapacity to commit any felony at the age of 14, and theoretically permitted capital punishment to be imposed on anyone over the age of 7. . . In accordance with the standards of this common-law tradition, at least 281 offenders under the age of 18 have been executed in this country, and at least 126 under the age of 17. See V. Streib, Death Penalty for Juveniles 57 (1987).

Thus petitioners are left to argue that their punishment is contrary to the "evolving standards of decency that mark the progress of a maturing society," Trop v. Dulles, 356 U.S. 86, 101 (1958) (plurality opinion). They are correct in asserting that this Court has "not confined the prohibition embodied in the Eighth Amendment to 'barbarous' methods that were generally outlawed in the 18th century," but instead has interpreted the Amendment "in a flexible and dynamic manner." Gregg v. Georgia, 428 U.S. 153, 171 (1976) (opinion of Stewart, Powell, and Stevens, JJ.). In determining what standards have "evolved," however, we have looked not to our own conceptions of decency, but to those of modern American society as a whole. As we have said, "Eighth Amendment judgments should not be, or appear to be, merely the subjective views of individual Justices; judgment should be informed by objective factors to the maximum possible extent." Coker v. Georgia, 433 U.S. 584, 592 (1977) (plurality opinion). See also Penry v. Lynaugh, ante, at 331; Ford v. Wainwright, supra, at 406; Enmund v. Florida, 458 U.S. 782, 788–789 (1982); Furman v. Georgia, 408 U.S. 238, 277–279 (1972) (Brennan, J., concurring). This approach is dictated both by the language of the Amendment—which proscribes only those punishments that are both "cruel and unusual"—and by the "deference we owe to the decisions of the state legislatures under our federal system," Gregg v. Georgia, supra, at 176.

"First" among the "'objective indicia that reflect the public attitude toward a given sanction'" are statutes passed by society's elected representatives. McCleskey v. Kemp, 481 U.S. 279, 300 (1987), quoting Gregg v. Georgia, supra, at 173. Of the 37 States whose laws permit capital punishment, 15 decline to impose it upon 16-year-old offenders and 12 decline to impose it on 17-year-old offenders. [Footnote omitted]. This does not establish the degree of national consensus this Court has previously thought sufficient to label a particular punishment cruel and unusual. In invalidating the death penalty for rape of an adult woman, we stressed that Georgia was the *sole* jurisdiction that authorized such a punishment. See *Coker* v. *Georgia, supra,* at 595–596. In striking down capital punishment for participation in a robbery in which an accomplice takes a life, we emphasized that only eight jurisdictions authorized similar punishment. *Enmund* v. *Florida, supra,* at 792. In finding that the Eighth Amendment precludes execution [of] the insane and thus requires an adequate hearing on the issue of sanity, we relied up[on] (in addition to the common-law rule) the fact that "no State in the Union" permitted [such] punishment. *Ford* v. *Wainwright,* 477 U.S., at 408. And in striking down a life sentence [with]out parole under a recidivist statute, we stressed that "it appears that [petitioner] [was] treated more severely than he would have been in any other State." *Solem* v. *Helm,* 46[3] [U.S.] 277, 300 (1983).

Since a majority of [the] [states] that permit capital punishment authorize it for crimes committed at age 16 [or] 7 (1987), than *Coker, Enmund, Ford,* and *Solem.* In *Tison,* which upheld Arizona's i[mposition] of the death penalty for major participation in a felony with reckless indiff[erence to] human life, we noted that only 11 of those jurisdictions imposing capital punis[hment] [reje]cted its use in such circumstances. *Id.,* at 154. As we noted earlier, here the n[umber] [is] 15 for offenders under 17, and 12 for offenders under 18. We think the same con[sensus] in *Tison* is required in this case.

Petit[ioners] [make] much of the recently enacted federal statute providing capital punishment [for] drug-related offenses, but limiting that punishment to offenders 18 and over [(Anti-]Drug Abuse Act of 1988, Pub. L. 100-690, 102 Stat. 4390, § 7001(1), 21 U. S. C. [(1988] ed.). That reliance is entirely misplaced. To begin with, the statute in question [does no]t embody a judgment by the Federal Legislature that *no* murder is heinous [enough to] warrant the execution of such a youthful offender, but merely that the narrow [off]ense it defines is not. The congressional judgment on the broader question, if applicable at all, is to be found in the law that permits 16- and 17-year-olds (after appropriate [proceeding]s) to be tried and punished as adults for *all* federal offenses, including those bearing [a capi]tal penalty that is not limited to 18-year-olds. [Footnote omitted]. See 18 U. S. C. § [5032] (1982 ed., Supp. V). Moreover, even if it were true that no federal statute permitted the [exe]cution of persons under 18, that would not remotely establish—in the face of a substan[ti]al number of state statutes to the contrary—a national consensus that such punishment is inhumane, any more than the absence of a federal lottery establishes a national consensus that lotteries are socially harmful. . . .

Wilkins and Stanford argue, however, that even if the laws themselves do not establish a settled consensus, the application of the laws does. That contemporary society views capital punishment of 16- and 17-year-old offenders as inappropriate is demonstrated, they say, by the reluctance of juries to impose, and prosecutors to seek, such sentences. Petitioners are quite correct that a far smaller number of offenders under 18 than over 18 have been sentenced to death in this country. From 1982 through 1988, for example, out of 2,106 total death sentences, only 15 were imposed on individuals who were 16 or under when they committed their crimes, and only 30 on individuals who were 17 at the time of the crime. See Streib, *Imposition of Death Sentences For Juvenile Offenders, January 1, 1982, Through April 1, 1989*, p. 2 (paper for Cleveland-Marshall College of Law, April 5, 1989). And it appears that actual executions for crimes committed under age 18 accounted for only about two percent of the total number of executions that occurred between 1982 and 1986. See Streib, *Death Penalty for Juveniles*, at 55, 57. As Wilkins points out, the last execution of a person who committed a crime under 17 years of age occurred in 1959. These statistics, however, carry little significance. Given the undisputed fact that a far smaller percentage of capital crimes are committed by persons under 18 than over 18, the discrepancy in capital sentences is much less than might seem. Granted, however, that a substantial discrepancy that does not establish the requisite proposition that the death sentence for offenders under 18 is categorically unacceptable to prosecutors and juries. To the contrary, it is not only possible, but overwhelmingly probable, that the very considerations which induce petitioners and their supporters to believe that death should *never* be imposed on offenders under 18 lead their prosecutors and juries to believe that it should *rarely* be imposed.

This last point suggests why there is also no relevance to the laws cited by petitioners and their *amici* which set 18 or more as the legal age for engaging in various activities, ranging from driving to drinking alcoholic beverages to voting. It is, to begin with, absurd to think that one must be mature enough to drive carefully, to drink responsibly, or to vote intelligently, in order to be mature enough to understand that murdering another human being is profoundly wrong, and to conform one's conduct to that most minimal of all civilized standards. But even if the requisite degrees of maturity were comparable, the age statutes in question would still not be relevant. They do not represent a social judgment that all persons under the designated ages are not responsible enough to drive, to drink, or to vote, but at most a judgment that the vast majority are not. . . .

Having failed to establish a consensus against capital punishment for 16- and 17-year-old offenders through state and federal statutes and the behavior of prosecutors and juries, petitioners seek to demonstrate it through other indicia, including public opinion polls, the views of interest groups, and the positions adopted by various professional associations. We decline the invitation to rest constitutional law upon such uncertain foundations. A revised national consensus so broad, so clear, and so enduring as to justify a permanent prohibition upon all units of democratic government must appear in the operative acts (laws and the application of laws) that the people have approved. . . .

we stressed that Georgia was the *sole* jurisdiction that authorized such a punishment. See *Coker* v. *Georgia, supra,* at 595–596. In striking down capital punishment for participation in a robbery in which an accomplice takes a life, we emphasized that only eight jurisdictions authorized similar punishment. *Enmund* v. *Florida, supra,* at 792. In finding that the Eighth Amendment precludes execution of the insane and thus requires an adequate hearing on the issue of sanity, we relied upon (in addition to the common-law rule) the fact that "no State in the Union" permitted such punishment. *Ford* v. *Wainwright,* 477 U.S., at 408. And in striking down a life sentence without parole under a recidivist statute, we stressed that "it appears that [petitioner] was treated more severely than he would have been in any other State." *Solem* v. *Helm,* 463 U.S. 277, 300 (1983).

Since a majority of the States that permit capital punishment authorize it for crimes committed at age 16 or above, [footnote omitted] petitioners' cases are more analogous to *Tison* v. *Arizona,* 481 U.S. 137 (1987), than *Coker, Enmund, Ford,* and *Solem.* In *Tison,* which upheld Arizona's imposition of the death penalty for major participation in a felony with reckless indifference to human life, we noted that only 11 of those jurisdictions imposing capital punishment rejected its use in such circumstances. *Id.,* at 154. As we noted earlier, here the number is 15 for offenders under 17, and 12 for offenders under 18. We think the same conclusion as in *Tison* is required in this case.

Petitioners make much of the recently enacted federal statute providing capital punishment for certain drug-related offenses, but limiting that punishment to offenders 18 and over. The Anti-Drug Abuse Act of 1988, Pub. L. 100-690, 102 Stat. 4390, § 7001(1), 21 U. S. C. § 848(l) (1988 ed.). That reliance is entirely misplaced. To begin with, the statute in question does not embody a judgment by the Federal Legislature that *no* murder is heinous enough to warrant the execution of such a youthful offender, but merely that the narrow class of offense it defines is not. The congressional judgment on the broader question, if apparent at all, is to be found in the law that permits 16- and 17-year-olds (after appropriate findings) to be tried and punished as adults for *all* federal offenses, including those bearing a capital penalty that is not limited to 18-year-olds. [Footnote omitted]. See 18 U. S. C. § 5032 (1982 ed., Supp. V). Moreover, even if it were true that no federal statute permitted the execution of persons under 18, that would not remotely establish—in the face of a substantial number of state statutes to the contrary—a national consensus that such punishment is inhumane, any more than the absence of a federal lottery establishes a national consensus that lotteries are socially harmful. . . .

Wilkins and Stanford argue, however, that even if the laws themselves do not establish a settled consensus, the application of the laws does. That contemporary society views capital punishment of 16- and 17-year-old offenders as inappropriate is demonstrated, they say, by the reluctance of juries to impose, and prosecutors to seek, such sentences. Petitioners are quite correct that a far smaller number of offenders under 18 than over 18 have been sentenced to death in this country. From 1982 through 1988, for example, out of 2,106 total death sentences, only 15 were imposed on individuals who were 16 or under when they committed their crimes, and only 30 on individuals who were 17 at the time of the crime. See Streib, *Imposition of Death Sentences For Juvenile Offenses, January 1, 1982, Through April 1, 1989,* p. 2 (paper for Cleveland-Marshall College of Law, April 5, 1989). And it appears that actual executions for crimes committed under age 18 accounted for only about two percent of the total number of executions that occurred between 1642 and 1986. See Streib, *Death Penalty for Juveniles,* at 55, 57. As Wilkins points out, the last execution of a person who committed a crime under 17 years of age occurred in 1959. These statistics, however, carry little significance. Given the undisputed fact that a far smaller percentage of capital crimes are committed by persons under 18 than over 18, the discrepancy in treatment is much less than might seem. Granted, however, that a substantial discrepancy exists, that does not establish the requisite proposition that the death sentence for offenders under 18 is categorically unacceptable to prosecutors and juries. To the contrary, it is not only possible, but overwhelmingly probable, that the very considerations which induce petitioners and their supporters to believe that death should *never* be imposed on offenders under 18 cause prosecutors and juries to believe that it should *rarely* be imposed.

This last point suggests why there is also no relevance to the laws cited by petitioners and their *amici* which set 18 or more as the legal age for engaging in various activities, ranging from driving to drinking alcoholic beverages to voting. It is, to begin with, absurd to think that one must be mature enough to drive carefully, to drink responsibly, or to vote intelligently, in order to be mature enough to understand that murdering another human being is profoundly wrong, and to conform one's conduct to that most minimal of all civilized standards. But even if the requisite degrees of maturity were comparable, the age statutes in question would still not be relevant. They do not represent a social judgment that all persons under the designated ages are not responsible enough to drive, to drink, or to vote, but at most a judgment that the vast majority are not. . . .

Having failed to establish a consensus against capital punishment for 16- and 17-year-old offenders through state and federal statutes and the behavior of prosecutors and juries, petitioners seek to demonstrate it through other indicia, including public opinion polls, the views of interest groups, and the positions adopted by various professional associations. We decline the invitation to rest constitutional law upon such uncertain foundations. A revised national consensus so broad, so clear, and so enduring as to justify a permanent prohibition upon all units of democratic government must appear in the operative acts (laws and the application of laws) that the people have approved. . . .

We discern neither a historical nor a modern societal consensus forbidding the imposition of capital punishment on any person who murders at 16 or 17 years of age. Accordingly, we conclude that such punishment does not offend the Eighth Amendment's prohibition against cruel and unusual punishment.

Payne v. Tennessee (1991)

In Payne v. Tennessee *the Court ruled that the Eighth Amendment does not bar juries from hearing "victim impact evidence"—or evidence relating to the victim's personal characteristics or the impact of the crime on the victim's family—during the sentencing phase of a capital trial.*

Chief Justice Rehnquist delivered the opinion of the Court:
In this case we reconsider our holdings in *Booth* v. *Maryland*, 482 U.S. 496, 96 L. Ed. 2d 440, 107 S. Ct. 2529 (1987), and *South Carolina v. Gathers*, 490 U.S. 805, 104 L. Ed. 2d 876, 109 S. Ct. 2207 (1989), that the Eighth Amendment bars the admission of victim impact evidence during the penalty phase of a capital trial. Petitioner, Pervis Tyrone Payne, was convicted by a jury on two counts of first-degree murder and one count of assault with intent to commit murder in the first degree. He was sentenced to death for each of the murders and to 30 years in prison for the assault. . . .

During the sentencing phase of the trial, Payne presented the testimony of four witnesses: his mother and father, Bobbie Thomas, and Dr. John T. Hutson, a clinical psychologist specializing in criminal court evaluation work. Bobbie Thomas testified that she met Payne at church, during a time when she was being abused by her husband. She stated that Payne was a very caring person, and that he devoted much time and attention to her three children, who were being affected by her marital difficulties. She said that the children had come to love him very much and would miss him, and that he "behaved just like a father that loved his kids." She asserted that he did not drink, nor did he use drugs, and that it was generally inconsistent with Payne's character to have committed these crimes.

Dr. Hutson testified that based on Payne's low score on an IQ test, Payne was "mentally handicapped." Hutson also said that Payne was neither psychotic nor schizophrenic, and that Payne was the most polite prisoner he had ever met. Payne's parents testified that their son had no prior criminal record and had never been arrested. They also stated that Payne had no history of alcohol or drug abuse, he worked with his father as a painter, he was good with children, and he was a good son.

The State presented the testimony of Charisse's mother, Mary Zvolanek. When asked how Nicholas had been affected by the murders of his mother and sister, she responded:
"He cries for his mom. He doesn't seem to understand why she doesn't come home. And

he cries for his sister Lacie. He comes to me many times during the week and asks me, Grandmama, do you miss my Lacie. And I tell him yes. He says, I'm worried about my Lacie." . . .

In arguing for the death penalty during closing argument, the prosecutor commented on the continuing effects of Nicholas' experience, stating:

"But we do know that Nicholas was alive. And Nicholas was in the same room. Nicholas was still conscious. His eyes were open. He responded to the paramedics. He was able to follow their directions. He was able to hold his intestines in as he was carried to the ambulance. So he knew what happened to his mother and baby sister." *Id.*, at 9.

There is nothing you can do to ease the pain of any of the families involved in this case. There is nothing you can do to ease the pain of Bernice or Carl Payne, and that's a tragedy. There is nothing you can do basically to ease the pain of Mr. and Mrs. Zvolanek, and that's a tragedy. They will have to live with it the rest of their lives. There is obviously nothing you can do for Charisse and Lacie Jo. But there is something that you can do for Nicholas.

"Somewhere down the road Nicholas is going to grow up, hopefully. He's going to want to know what happened. And he is going to know what happened to his baby sister and his mother. He is going to want to know what type of justice was done. He is going to want to know what happened. With your verdict, you will provide the answer." *Id.*, at 12.

In the rebuttal to Payne's closing argument, the prosecutor stated:

"You saw the videotape this morning. You saw what Nicholas Christopher will carry in his mind forever. When you talk about cruel, when you talk about atrocious, and when you talk about heinous, that picture will always come into your mind, probably throughout the rest of your lives. . . .

". . . No one will ever know about Lacie Jo because she never had the chance to grow up. Her life was taken from her at the age of two years old. So, no there won't be a high school principal to talk about Lacie Jo Christopher, and there won't be anybody to take her to her high school prom. And there won't be anybody there—there won't be her mother there or Nicholas' mother there to kiss him at night. His mother will never kiss him good night or pat him as he goes off to bed, or hold him and sing him a lullaby. . . .

"[Petitioner's attorney] wants you to think about a good reputation, people who love the defendant and things about him. He doesn't want you to think about the people who love Charisse Christopher, her mother and daddy who loved her. The people who loved little Lacie Jo, the grandparents who are still here. The brother who mourns for her every single day and wants to know where his best little playmate is. He doesn't have anybody to watch cartoons with him, a little one. These are the things that go into why it is especially cruel, heinous, and atrocious, the burden that that child will carry forever." *Id.*, at 13–15.

The jury sentenced Payne to death on each of the murder counts. . . .

We granted certiorari, 498 U.S. 1080 (1991), to reconsider our holdings in *Booth* and *Gathers* that the Eighth Amendment prohibits a capital sentencing jury from considering "victim impact" evidence relating to the personal characteristics of the victim and the emotional impact of the crimes on the victim's family.

In *Booth*, the defendant robbed and murdered an elderly couple. As required by a state statute, a victim impact statement was prepared based on interviews with the victims' son, daughter, son-in-law, and granddaughter. The statement, which described the personal characteristics of the victims, the emotional impact of the crimes on the family, and set forth the family members' opinions and characterizations of the crimes and the defendant, was submitted to the jury at sentencing. The jury imposed the death penalty. The conviction and sentence were affirmed on appeal by the State's highest court.

This Court held by a 5-to-4 vote that the Eighth Amendment prohibits a jury from considering a victim impact statement at the sentencing phase of a capital trial. The Court made clear that the admissibility of victim impact evidence was not to be determined on a case-by-case basis, but that such evidence was *per se* inadmissible in the sentencing phase of a capital case except to the extent that it "related directly to the circumstances of the crime." 482 U.S. at 507, n. 10. In *Gathers*, decided two years later, the Court extended the rule announced in *Booth* to statements made by a prosecutor to the sentencing jury regarding the personal qualities of the victim. . . .

Booth and *Gathers* were based on two premises: that evidence relating to a particular victim or to the harm that a capital defendant causes a victim's family do not in general reflect on the defendant's "blameworthiness," and that only evidence relating to "blameworthiness" is relevant to the capital sentencing decision. However, the assessment of harm caused by the defendant as a result of the crime charged has understandably been an important concern of the criminal law, both in determining the elements of the offense and in determining the appropriate punishment. Thus, two equally blameworthy criminal defendants may be guilty of different offenses solely because their acts cause differing amounts of harm. "If a bank robber aims his gun at a guard, pulls the trigger, and kills his target, he may be put to death. If the gun unexpectedly misfires, he may not. His moral guilt in both cases is identical, but his responsibility in the former is greater." *Booth*, 482 U.S. at 519 (Scalia, J., dissenting). The same is true with respect to two defendants, each of whom participates in a robbery, and each of whom acts with reckless disregard for human life; if the robbery in which the first defendant participated results in the death of a victim, he may be subjected to the death penalty, but if the robbery in which the second defendant participates does not result in the death of a victim, the death penalty may not be imposed. *Tison v. Arizona*, 481 U.S. 137, 148, 95 L. Ed. 2d 127, 107 S. Ct. 1676 (1987). . . .

Wherever judges in recent years have had discretion to impose sentence, the consideration of the harm caused by the crime has been an important factor in the exercise of that discretion:

"The first significance of harm in Anglo-American jurisprudence is, then, as a prerequisite to the criminal sanction. The second significance of harm—one no less important to judges—is as a measure of the seriousness of the offense and therefore as a standard for determining the severity of the sentence that will be meted out." S. Wheeler, K. Mann, & A. Sarat, *Sitting in Judgment: The Sentencing of White-Collar Criminals* 56 (1988).

Whatever the prevailing sentencing philosophy, the sentencing authority has always been free to consider a wide range of relevant material. *Williams* v. *New York,* 337 U.S. 241, 93 L. Ed. 1337, 69 S. Ct. 1079 (1949). In the federal system, we observed that "a judge may appropriately conduct an inquiry broad in scope, largely unlimited either as to the kind of information he may consider, or the source from which it may come." *United States* v. *Tucker,* 404 U.S. 443, 446, 30 L. Ed. 2d 592, 92 S. Ct. 589 (1972). Even in the context of capital sentencing, prior to *Booth* the joint opinion of Justices Stewart, Powell, and Stevens in *Gregg* v. *Georgia,* 428 U.S. 153, 203-204, 49 L. Ed. 2d 859, 96 S. Ct. 2909 (1976), had rejected petitioner's attack on the Georgia statute because of the "wide scope of evidence and argument allowed at presentence hearings."

. . .We have held that a State cannot preclude the sentencer from considering "any relevant mitigating evidence" that the defendant proffers in support of a sentence less than death. . . . Thus we have, as the Court observed in *Booth,* required that the capital defendant be treated as a "'uniquely individual human being,'" 482 U.S. at 504 (quoting *Woodson* v. *North Carolina,* 428 U.S. at 304). But it was never held or even suggested in any of our cases preceding *Booth* that the defendant, entitled as he was to individualized consideration, was to receive that consideration wholly apart from the crime which he had committed. The language quoted from *Woodson* in the *Booth* opinion was not intended to describe a class of evidence that *could not* be received, but a class of evidence which *must* be received. Any doubt on the matter is dispelled by comparing the language in *Woodson* with the language from *Gregg* v. *Georgia,* quoted above, which was handed down the same day as *Woodson.* This misreading of precedent in *Booth* has, we think, unfairly weighted the scales in a capital trial; while virtually no limits are placed on the relevant mitigating evidence a capital defendant may introduce concerning his own circumstances, the State is barred from either offering "a quick glimpse of the life" which a defendant "chose to extinguish," *Mills* v. *Maryland,* 486 U.S. 367, 397, 100 L. Ed. 2d 384, 108 S. Ct. 1860 (1988) (Rehnquist, C.J., dissenting), or demonstrating the loss to the victim's family and to society which has resulted from the defendant's homicide.

Within the constitutional limitations defined by our cases, the States enjoy their traditional latitude to prescribe the method by which those who commit murder shall be punished." *Blystone* v. *Pennsylvania*, 494 U.S. 299, 309, 108 L. Ed. 2d 255, 110 S. Ct. 1078 (1990). The States remain free, in capital cases, as well as others, to devise new procedures and new remedies to meet felt needs. Victim impact evidence is simply another form or method of informing the sentencing authority about the specific harm caused by the crime in question, evidence of a general type long considered by sentencing authorities. We think the *Booth* Court was wrong in stating that this kind of evidence leads to the arbitrary imposition of the death penalty. In the majority of cases, and in this case, victim impact evidence serves entirely legitimate purposes. In the event that evidence is introduced that is so unduly prejudicial that it renders the trial fundamentally unfair, the Due Process Clause of the Fourteenth Amendment provides a mechanism for relief. See *Darden* v. *Wainwright*, 477 U.S. 168, 179-183, 91 L. Ed. 2d 144, 106 S. Ct. 2464 (1986). Courts have always taken into consideration the harm done by the defendant in imposing sentence, and the evidence adduced in this case was illustrative of the harm caused by Payne's double murder. . . .

We are now of the view that a State may properly conclude that for the jury to assess meaningfully the defendant's moral culpability and blameworthiness, it should have before it at the sentencing phase evidence of the specific harm caused by the defendant. . . .

We thus hold that if the State chooses to permit the admission of victim impact evidence and prosecutorial argument on that subject, the Eighth Amendment erects no *per se* bar. A State may legitimately conclude that evidence about the victim and about the impact of the murder on the victim's family is relevant to the jury's decision as to whether or not the death penalty should be imposed. There is no reason to treat such evidence differently than other relevant evidence is treated.

Index

Note: *f* refers to figures and *t* refers to tables.

Abolitionist Action Committee
(AAC), 115–116
Abolitionist Directories, 126, 127
Abolitionist-for-ordinary-crimes
countries, 160, 161*t*
Abolition movement, U.S., 16–17.
See also International abolition
movement
about, 114–115
on executions of women, 77
individuals, 131–132
international, 158–164
Nazi regime and, 168
nonprofit groups, 115–127
religious organizations, 127–131
Abu-Jamal, Mumia, 99–100, 173
Accomplice takes life during rob-
bery, 48, 50
Actual Innocence, 84
Africa, 161, 163
Aggravated circumstances, 24, 26,
57–58
Agreements, international
extradition exceptions in, 173
reservations from, 163–164, 169
Aircraft hijackers, 44
Akers, Ronald L., 109*n*165,
110*nn*182, 183
Alabama, 71, 83
Alaskans Against the Death
Penalty, 127
Albright, Madeleine, 183
American Bar Association, 25, 30,
116, 153*nn*1, 2, 3
calls for moratorium on execu-
tions, 4, 19, 28

indigent criminal defense report by, 62–63
National District Attorney Association and, 136
American Civil Liberties Union
(ACLU), 116–117, 127, 154*n*5,
180
of Texas, 62
American Convention on Human
Rights, 159
American Ethical Union, 94,
110*n*194
American Friends Service Committee (AFSC), 127–128
Amitay, Cheryl Aviva, 187*n*42
Amnesty International,
186*nn*15–17, 20–22, 187*nn*26–28,
189*nn*85, 86, 88, 90, 92, 93,
190*n*114
American Civil Liberties Union
and, 180
Amnesty International USA
and, 179
on China, 173–174
on death penalty data, 115
description and contact information, 117–119
humanitarian standards of, 94
state and local chapters of, 127
on U.S. executions, 174–175
Amnesty International USA, 26,
31*nn*2, 13, 179
on abolishing the death
penalty, 26
description and contact information, 118–119

on executions in United States,
21*n*3, 22*nn*3, 4, 5
on Universal Declaration of
Human Rights, 22
Anaya, Tony, 85
Annan, Kofi, 123–124, 154*n*22
Anti-Terrorism and Effective
Death Penalty Act (1996), 4, 19,
24–25, 28
Criminal Justice Legal Foundation and, 133
on execution appeals process,
5
on expedited capital appeals, 7
habeas corpus and, 52
Appeals process, 49–53
conservatives on meritless
claims during, 24–25
introduction of use for death
sentences, 15
jurisdictional variations in, 63
Rehnquist, William H., on, 149
under state laws, 7
Supreme Court restrictions on,
4–5, 18, 19
system for, 81–84
Arab nations, 122
Arguments against capital punishment, 90–101
deterrence, 91–93
error rates, 100–101
morality, 93–96
racism, 96–100
Arizona, 85
Article 1, Section 9, U.S. Constitution, 4

Ashcroft, John, 142–143
Asia, capital punishment in, 161
Assault of superior officer during war, 58
Assigned counsel systems, 61, 62
Attorneys general. *See* Justice, U.S. Department of
Automatic proportionality review, 51, 63
Automatic review, 50, 51, 63, 68

Baker, Donald, 191*n*118
Baldus, David C., 20, 32*n*23
Baptist Church, 130
Barkett, Rosemary, 135
Barnes, Odell, 172
Bedau, Hugo Adam, 31*n*9, 32*n*21, 110*n*178
Beiser, Vince, 31*n*3
Bell, Bill, Jr., 190*n*113
Bell, Maya, 189*n*91
Benetton, 119, 176. *See also* Offman, Craig
Berry, Jason, 109*n*164
Bible, on retribution, 95
Biddle, Frederic M., 192*n*145
Bienen, Leigh B., 67–68, 102*n*32, 104*nn*68, 71–75, 106*nn*107–109, 107*n*131
Bifurcated trials, 44, 47
Bill of Rights, 15
Biskupic, Joan, 191*n*118
Blackmun, Harry A., 18, 20, 32*n*26, 43
Black people. *See also* Racism
    on death row, 77
    executions of, 96
    as murder victims, 98
    in U.S. population, 97
Block, Melissa, 108*n*158, 156*n*78
Board of pardons, clemency authority of, 68–69
Bonner, Raymond, 156*n*66
Bork, Robert, 91
Bowers, William J., 101*nn*5, 6
Bragg, Rick, 106*n*111
Brazil, 163
Breard, Angel, 184

Brennan, William J., 43, 47, 95–96
Breyer, Stephen G., 147
Brien, Peter, 105*n*95
Bright, S., 109*n*168
British criminal justice system, 15, 55, 58
Bronx, New York, sentiments on death penalty, 88
Brooks, Elizabeth A., 111*n*205
Brown, Joseph Green, 11
Brown, Pat, 85
Buckley, William F., Jr., 12, 31*n*12
Burdine, Calvin J., 62
Burger, Warren E., 43
Bush, George H.W., 17, 52
Bush, George W., 143–144
    Abu-Jamal, Mumia, case and, 100
    application of death penalty by, 85–86
    Citizens United for Alternatives to the Death Penalty on, 120
    Garza, Juan Raul, case and, 183
    on state death penalty systems, 87
    Tucker, Karla Faye, case and, 8, 12, 19
Butler, Sabrina, 10
Byrd, James, 95

Cabana v. Bullock (1986), 48, 50, 58, 102*n*15
California
    clemency procedures in, 69
    death penalty backlog in, 7
    execution choices in, 73–74
    executions in, 78–79
    People v. Anderson (California, 1972), 103*n*47
    referendum on constitution of, 54–55
    state amendment on capital punishment, 47
    state high court on death penalty in, 54, 55
Cannon, Joe Frank, 62
Capital punishment. *See also* Appeals process; Death penalty;

International Covenant on Civil and Political Rights; Laws on capital punishment; Life sentences
    as American political symbol, 89–90
    distribution of, 6
    for juvenile offenders, 13–14
    offenses qualifying for, 15–16
    in U.S., theories on, 166–169
Carnahan, Mel, 129, 184
Catholic Church, 128–129, 177, 190*nn*104, 105
Catholics Against the Death Penalty, 129, 180
Cauthen, James N.G., 107*nn*119–123, 113*n*239
Celeste, Richard, 85
Central America, 161
Chandler, David Ronald, 123, 143, 176
China, 21, 22, 163, 174
Ching, Frank, 189*n*73
Chirac, Jacques, 183
Christian Church (Disciples of Christ), 130
Church of the Brethren, 130
Church Women United of Indiana, 99
Citizens United for Alternatives to the Death Penalty (CUADP), 115, 119–120
Civil Rights Covenant, UN Second Optional Protocol, 159
Civil rights offenses, 58
Cizik, Richard, 9
Claiborne, William, 155*n*52
Clark, Charles S., 32*n*22
Clemency, 9, 20, 85. *See also* Governors; Presidents, U.S.
    alternative punishments and, 69–70
    authority across jurisdictions, 69–70*t*, 71
    jurisdictional variations in, 63, 68–69
    National Center for Victims of Crime and, 135

Clements, Diane, 11, 12, 23, 29, 133–134
Clinton, Bill
  Abu-Jamal, Mumia, case and, 100
  appeals to impose moratorium on executions, 99
  Chandler, David Ronald, case and, 143, 176
  Garza, Juan Raul, case and, 143
  Moratorium 2000 and, 123
  NAPO endorsement and, 134–135
  Rector, Ricky Ray, case and, 60–61
  on state death penalty systems, 87
  UN Convention on the Rights of the Child, 61
Cohen, R., 188nn69, 70
Coker v. Georgia (1977), 48, 50, 102n13
Cole, David, 182, 191n130
Collins, Rachel, 108n143
Colwell, Daniel M., 91
Common law, 55
Complete abolitionist nations, 160, 161t
Conference of General Baptists, 130
Congo, Democratic Republic of, 163, 173
Congress, U.S., 54
Constitution, U.S., 54. See also specific amendments
  Article 1, Section 9, 4
  suspension clause, 28–29
Contract attorneys, 61, 62
Convictions, appeals of, 82
Cooley, Steve, 173
Council of Europe, Amnesty International and, 118
Counsel, right to assistance of, 52–53, 61–63
Countersign misuse during war, 58
Court rulings, 54
Cousin, Shareef, 12
Crime Bill (1994), 100

Crime Is Not the Problem: Lethal Violence in America (Zimring and Hawkins), 167
Criminal Justice Legal Foundation (CJLF), 30, 133
Criminal justice systems, 15
Cruel and unusual punishment, 43, 47, 73, 181–182. See also Eighth Amendment
Cruz, Rolando, 1–2
Cuomo, Mario, 94, 151
Curriden, Mark, 189n87

Dalai Lama, 131, 178
D'Alema, Massimo, 21
Davenport, P., 103n45
Davis, "Tiny," 74
Davis v. United States (1994), 139
Dawson v. Nevada (1987), 82, 107n118
Dead Man Walking: An Eyewitness Account of the Death Penalty in the United States (Prejean), 23, 124, 132
Death penalty. See also Appeals process; Deterrence
  abolition movement, 16–17
  aggravated circumstances leading to, 24
  as American political symbol, 89–90
  arguments to abolish, 26
  arguments to retain, 27
  chronology of, 18–19
  criticism of U.S. applications of, 2
  early U.S. history of, 15–16, 43
  fairness questions, 20, 23–24
  global trends for, 21–22
  Justice for All support for, 134
  retroactive application of, 28
  ruled unconstitutional, 17, 18
  support for, 17, 20
Death Penalty, The: A Debate (van den Haag), 141
Death Penalty Information Center (DPIC), 30, 31nn6, 17, 101n8, 103nn48–50, 52, 104n66, 105nn91,

94, 95, 106n104, 111nn212, 215, 115
  description and contact information, 120–121
  map of nationwide executions since 1976, 6f
Death row population
  appeals delays and, 4–5
  demographics of, 77–78, 96–97
  DNA testing access for, 84
  foreign nationals in United States, 172
  growth in, 16, 75, 76f
  jurisdictional differences in executions of, 78–79
Death Row USA, 98, 115, 124
De facto abolitionist countries, 160, 161t
Defense lawyers, 52–53, 61–63
Delahunt, Bill, 84
Delaware, 15, 79
Democracy, abolition and, 168–169
Denning, Lord Justice, 110n196
Derechos, 176
Desertion during war, 58
Deterrence, 91–93
Dieter, Richard C., 2, 3, 5, 7, 9, 11, 24, 31n5, 32n24, 105n89, 106nn101, 102, 183, 187n32, 188n71, 191n127
Discrimination, systemic, 48–49, 50. See also Racism
Disobedience of superior officer during war, 58
District attorneys, 87–88, 136
District Attorney v. Watson (Massachusetts, 1980), 103n47
DNA testing, 2, 84, 124, 146
Doherty, Ronan, 191nn136–138, 140
Domestic violence, 29
Donnino, William C., 109n174, 156n77
Douglas, William O., 43
Douglas v. California (1963), 103n44
Drug kingpin statute, 54, 89
Drug-related offenses, 20, 58
Drug trafficking, 20
Due process, 42, 49

Dugan, Brian, 2
Duggan, Paul, 111*n*201, 155*n*52
DuPage County, Illinois, 1
Dwyer, Jim, 107*n*132

Eddings v. Oklahoma (1982), 50, 102*n*12
Edgar, Jim, 90
Educational level of death row population, 77, 78
Eggen, Dan, 156*nn*62, 63, 64
Ehrlich, Isaac, 91, 110*n*177, 141, 156*n*59
Eighth Amendment, U.S., 3, 15, 17, 47, 48. *See also* Cruel and unusual punishment; *Gregg v. Georgia* (1976)
Elderly convicts. *See also* Senior citizens
    international agreements on, 159
Electric chair, 15
Electrocution, 71, 73
Ellsworth, Phoebe C., 109*n*171
Emergency personnel murder, 24
Enmund v. Florida (1982), 48, 50, 102*n*14, 149
Episcopal Church, 130, 178
Equal Justice USA, 121
Error rates, 82–84, 86, 100–101
Espionage, 20, 58
Europe, 158, 160–161
European Convention for the Protection of Human Rights and Fundamental Freedoms, Protocol No. 6, 159, 170–171
European Union (EU), 122, 170–172, 183
Evangelical Christians, 9. *See also* Falwell, Jerry; Robertson, Pat
Evangelical Lutheran Church, 130, 178
Evidence, 48, 50, 133
Execution methods, 71, 72*t*, 73–74
Executions. *See also* Appeals process; Error rates; Innocent prisoners; Moratorium on executions

Baltimore City versus Baltimore County, Maryland, 87
    decrease in, 16
    distribution of, 6
    Hamilton versus Franklin Counties, Ohio, 87–88
    increase in, 24, 75, 76*f*
    jurisdictional differences in, 78–79, 80–81*t*
    prison behavior and, 8–9, 12
    public, 15
    as state-sponsored suicide, 91
    in United States, 6*f*, 162*t*, 163
Extradition exceptions, 173

Fagan, Jeffrey, 102*n*35, 106*nn*113, 114, 155*n*43
Falwell, Jerry, 139–140, 155*n*54
Federal appeals courts, 15, 25
Federal Death Penalty Act (1994), 16, 51
Federal government, U.S. *See also* United States
    capital punishment laws of, 2, 46*t*
    execution regulations of, 71
    executions by, 79
    executive branch actors, 142–145
    judicial branch actors, 147–151
    legislative branch actors, 145–147
    response to international criticism, 181–183
Federalism, abolition movement and, 168–169
Feguer, Victor, 106*n*110
Feingold, Russell, 145
Feldman, Jessica, 188*n*64
Fields, Gary, 108*nn*154–156
Fierro, David, 73–74
Fierro v. Gomez (1996), 73, 104*n*77
Fifth Amendment, U.S., 42, 49. *See also Gregg v. Georgia*
Fifth U.S. Circuit Court of Appeals, 25
Finckenauer, James O., 111*n*199
Fine, Toni M., 188*n*63, 189*nn*74, 75

Firefighter murder, 24
Firing squads, 71, 74
Fisher, Joan M., 104*nn*67, 76
Florida, 74, 79, 83
Ford v. Wainwright (1986), 50, 102*n*17, 156*n*71
Forgiveness, healing and, 23
Fourteenth Amendment, U.S., 42, 49. *See also Gregg v. Georgia*
Fourth U.S. Circuit Court of Appeals, 25
Fox, James Alan, 110*n*186
France, on U.S. policies, 173
Francis v. Resweber (1947), 104*n*78
Frost, Brian, 91, 110*nn*180, 181
Furman, William, 43, 124
Furman v. Georgia (1972), 101*n*10, 102*n*29, 111*nn*207, 208
    ACLU and, 117
    effect on clemency of, 85
    politics and, 43–44
    on unconstitutionality of death penalty, 17, 18, 49

Gadhafi, Mu'ammar, 163
Gallup, Alec, 110*n*192
Garcia, Guillermo X., 191*nn*128, 129
Gardner, Mark, 177
Garza, Juan Raul, 81, 99, 143, 183
Gas chambers, 15
Gelernter, David, 27
General Accounting Office, U.S., 97
Georgia, 71, 74
Gerardi, Michael, 12
Germany, 166, 172
Gideon v. Wainwright (1963), 103*nn*43, 58
Gilmore, Gary Mark, 74
Gilmore, James S., III, 13, 184
Ginsburg, Ruth Bader, 147–148
Gleik, E., 104*n*64
Goldsmith, Kenneth, 28
Gonzalez, John W., 32*n*20
Goshko, John M., 22*n*6
Gottlieb, David, 96
Governors. *See also* Gilmore, James S., III; Pataki, George E.; Ryan, George

application of capital punish-
    ment and, 84–86
clemency authority of, 68–69
death penalty symbolism and,
    90
EU plea for moratoriums to, 171
important voices among,
    151–152
legislative agendas of, 86–87
local prosecutors and, 88
Graham, Gary, 134
Gray v. Lucas (1983), 104*n*79
Great Britain, 164–165, 166. *See also*
    British criminal justice system
Greece, 163
Greenberg, Jack, 96
Greene, Norman L., 107*n*135,
    108*n*139
Gregg, Troy, 44, 47
Gregg v. Georgia (1976), 102*nn*26,
    30, 109*n*172, 110*nn*187–189, 190,
    197, 156*nn*60, 61, 73, 191*n*123
    Ehrlich, Isaac, and, 141
    executions after, 75
    politics and, 44, 47
    Rehnquist, William H., on, 149
    on retribution, 95
    on revised state capital punish-
        ment laws, 17, 49
    Stevens, John Paul, on, 150
Griffin, Patrick, 31*n*15

Habeas corpus
    appeals under, 51–52
    restrictions on, 4, 5, 19
    suspension clause and, 28–29
Habeas Corpus Act (1867), 29
Haines, Herbert H., 105*n*84,
    154*nn*5, 6, 25–29, 31, 32, 155*nn*41,
    42
Hallinan, Terence, 88
Hamilton, Lee, 93–94
Hammer, Paul David, 120
Hands off Cain, 122, 175–176
Haney, Craig, 109*n*160
Hanging, 15, 71, 74
Hansen, M., 108*n*140
Harris, Bobbie Lee, 119, 176

Hastert, J. Dennis, 145–146
Hatch, Orrin, 13
Hawkins, Gordon, 167, 187*n*37,
    188*nn*50–54
Heflin v. United States (1959),
    103*n*42
Helms, Jesse, 22, 183
Henninger, Brian, 14, 28, 29
Hernandez, Alejandro, 1–2
Higgins, Sean, 108*n*153
Hijackers, 44
Hispanics. *See also* Latinos
    executions of, 96
    in U.S. population, 97
Hodgkinson, Peter, 187*nn*33–36,
    38–41
Holden, Bob, 171, 179
Homicide, 58. *See also* Murder
    as prior crime of death row
        population, 78
    societal preferences and rates
        of, 167
Homicide Act (Great Britain,
    1957), 164–165
Hood, Roger, 186*nn*1, 13, 14, 18, 19,
    23–25, 187*n*31
Hoover, Tim, 191*n*119
Hoyt, Jennifer, 112*nn*230, 231
Huckabee, Mike, 180
Human Rights, Universal Declara-
    tion of, 22, 117
Human Rights Act (Great Britain,
    1999), 165
Human Rights Watch (HRW),
    122–123, 175, 179–180, 190*nn*95, 96
Hunt v. Nuth (1995), 104*n*79
Hyde, Henry, 101

Illinois, 79, 86
Indiana, 99
Indigent convicts, 53, 61–63
Innocence Protection Act, 125
Innocent prisoners, 2, 7–8, 26
    conference on, 10–11, 19
    O'Connor, Sandra Day, on,
        149
    van den Haag, Ernest, on,
        141–142

Insane murderers, 48, 50. *See also*
    Mentally ill convicts
Intent to kill, 48, 50
International abolition move-
    ment, 158–164. *See also* Abolition
    movement
    British development of, 164–165
    countries by degree of commit-
        ment to, 161*t*
    and criticism of U.S. policies by
        human rights organizations,
        174–176
    and criticism of U.S. policies by
        individual countries, 172–174
    and criticism of U.S. policies by
        religious organizations,
        177–179
    and criticism of U.S. policies by
        supra-national bodies,
        169–172
    growth in, 162*t*
    U.S. abolitionists and, 179–180
    U.S. aversion to, 166–169
International Court of Justice, 184
International Covenant on Civil
    and Political Rights, 13, 18, 22,
    159, 164, 169
International Rabbinical Assem-
    bly, 178
Iran, 13, 22, 163, 173
Islamic law, 163
Italy, 21, 172

Jackson, Jesse, 94
Jagger, Bianca, 77
Jamaica, 21
Janicik, Doug, 111*n*203
Japan, death penalty in, 160
Jewish groups, on U.S. policies,
    177–178, 180
Jimenez, M., 188*n*71
Jimerson, Verneal, 10
John Paul II (pope), 132, 155*nn*34,
    36, 190*nn*103, 106
    Garza, Juan Raul, case and, 183
    Mease, Darrell, case and, 184
    on moratorium for death
        penalty, 128

on Tucker, Karla Faye, case, 8, 77
on U.S. policies, 177
Johnson, Dirk, 108*n*152
Johnson, Kevin, 191*nn*128, 129
Johnson, Robert T., 88
Jordan, Sam, 175
Jordan, Sandra D., 109*n*162
Judaism, Reform, 177
Judges, 63, 90
Juries, 15, 26
    faulty instructions to, 133
    Furman v. Georgia on, 43
    jurisdictional variations in sen-
      tencing by, 63
    racial composition of sentenc-
      ing, 99
Justice, U.S. Department of,
    144–145
Justice for All (JFA), 8, 30, 31*n*10,
    133–134
Juvenile offenders
    death penalty for, 12–14, 24, 48
    on death row, 77
    execution of, 50
    international agreements on,
      159
    jurisdictional variations in
      penalties for, 58, 60–61
    punishment for, 12–14
    states allowing execution of,
      59–60*t*

Kaczynski, Theodore, 1, 3, 19
Kadish, Sanford, 113*n*233
Kahan, Dan M., 109*n*173
Kannar, George, 109*nn*162, 163
Kaplan, John, 91, 109*n*175
Kaye, John, 155*n*50
Keating, Frank, 177
Kendall, George, 15
Kennedy, Anthony M., 148
Kentucky, 24, 83
Kidnapping, 58
King, Martin Luther, Jr., 129
Klein, Lawrence L., 110*n*179
Klein, R., 104*n*65
Klein, Stephen J., 98, 112*nn*219, 220
Kloehn, Steve, 155*n*55

Knight v. Florida (1999), 147
Koenig, Sarah, 112*nn*224, 225, 226
Koran, 178, 190*n*111
Korean War postcapture crimes,
    159
Kuhlman v. Wilson (1986), 103*n*38,
    150

Lacey, Marc, 156*n*66
LaHood, Ray, 84
Latinos, 77. *See also* Hispanics
Lattin, Don, 155*n*53
Latzer, Barry, 107*nn*119–123,
    113*n*239
Laws on capital punishment,
    53–74
    appeals and clemency, 63
    application of, 74–90
    crimes punished, 57–58
    decision-making methods on,
      54–55
    defendants eligible for, 58–61
    defense lawyers, 61–63
    execution methods, 71, 73–74
    jurisdictional variations in,
      56*t*
    on punishment methods, 55
Layson, Stephen K., 91, 110*nn*184,
    185
LDF. *See* NAACP Legal Defense
    and Educational Fund
Leahy, Patrick J., 84, 146
Lee, Mei-Hsien, 101*nn*3, 4, 102*n*24
Legal aid services, 62
Lethal gas, 71, 74
Lethal injection, 15, 71, 74
Levinson, Arlene, 31*n*16, 32*n*18
Lewis, John, 94, 110*n*195
Lewis, Neil A., 102*n*36, 156*n*75
Liebman, James S., 81–83, 101,
    102*n*35, 106*nn*113, 114,
    107*nn*115–117, 124–131, 108*n*151,
    155*n*43, 157*n*84
Lifelines, 126
Life sentences, 15, 69
Lifespark, 176
Lighting the Torch of Conscience
    campaign, 130

Linder, Craig, 112*n*232
Lindh v. Murphy (1997), 7
Lingar, Stanley, 179
Local abolitionist organizations,
    127
Local politicians, 89–90
Local prosecutors. *See* Prosecutors
Lockett v. Ohio (1978), 50, 102*n*12
Los Angeles, California, prosecutor,
    173, 185
Louisiana, 62, 83
Louisiana ex rel. Francis v. Resweber
    (1947), 73
Lyman, Eric J., 189*nn*76, 77

Macey, Bob, 90
Mailing explosives, causing death
    by, 20
Malone, Kobutsu, 190*n*110
Mannies, Jo, 155*n*38, 192*n*144
Marital status of death row popula-
    tion, 78
Marshall, Joshua Micah, 168–169,
    188*nn*55–61
Marshall, Thurgood, 43, 47, 95–96
Martin, Earl F., 111*nn*206, 209
Martinez, Bob, 85
Marx, Gary, 109*n*167
Maryland, 83, 98–99
Massachusetts, 54, 55, 103*n*47, 185
McCarver v. North Carolina (2001), 61
McCleskey, Warren, 48–49
McCleskey v. Kemp (1987), 50, 102*n*23,
    156*nn*74, 76
    on discrimination in death sen-
      tence application, 18, 20,
      48–49, 100
    O'Connor, Sandra Day, on, 148
    Rehnquist, William H., on, 149
    Scalia, Antonin, on, 150
    Washington Legal Foundation
      and, 139
McVeigh, Timothy J., 2–3, 18, 79, 81,
    89
Mease, Darrell, 129, 177, 184
Mennonite Church, 131
Mentally ill convicts, 3–4, 18. *See
    also* Insane murderers

Mentally retarded convicts, 48, 50
    executions of, 4
    jurisdictional variations, 58–59
    Rector, Ricky Ray, case, 60–61
    states allowing execution of,
        59–60t
Mexico, 173
Michigan, 54, 55
Middle East, 163
Military
    on capital punishment, 2, 46t
    court's regulations on execu-
        tion, 71
    executions by, 79
Mills, Steve, 112n229
Minors, 58. See also Juvenile of-
    fenders
Mintz, Howard, 109n159
Minzesheimer, Bob, 109n166
Mississippi, 83
Missouri, 83
Mitigating factors, 47
Montalvo, Gabriel, 177
Mooney, Christopher Z., 101nn3,
    4, 102n24
Moore v. Nebraska (1999), 147
Moose, George, 183
Morality of capital punishment,
    93–96
Moratorium 2000, 123–124, 132,
    176, 190n97
Moratorium on executions. See
    also Ryan, George
    American Bar Association call
        for, 4, 19, 28
    in Illinois, 86
    racism and calls for, 98–99
    UN call for, 159–160
Moravian Church in America, 131
Morris, Debbie, 23, 32n27
Murder. See also Deterrence
    by death row prisoners, 77–78
    as dispute resolution method,
        91
    felony, 58
    first degree, 57
    premeditated, 15
    punishment for, 27

white victims, death penalty
    for perpetrators of, 48–49, 78
Murder Act (Great Britain, 1965),
    165, 166
Murray v. Carrier (1986), 50, 52
Muslim states, on death penalty,
    178–179
Mutilation and torture, 24

NAACP Legal Defense and Educa-
    tional Fund, 43, 98, 105nn88, 90,
    106nn103, 105, 111n213, 124
National Association for the Ad-
    vancement of Colored People
    (NAACP), 124, 180
National Association of Criminal
    Defense Lawyers (NACDL), 125
National Association of Evangeli-
    cals, 30
National Association of Police Or-
    ganizations (NAPO), 134–135
National Center for Victims of
    Crime (NCVC), 135–136
National Coalition to Abolish the
    Death Penalty (NCADP), 30,
    107n138, 125–126, 132
National District Attorney Associ-
    ation (NDAA), 136–137
National Execution Alert, 126
National Jewish/Catholic Consul-
    tation, 180
National Organization for Victim
    Assistance (NOVA), 137
Native Americans, 77
Nazi regime, abolitionists and, 168
Ndiaye, Bacre Waly, 169–170, 183
Nebraska, 71, 87
Neufeld, Peter, 107n132
Nevius, Thomas, 175
New Hampshire, 86, 106n110, 185
Newport, Frank, 110n192
New York, 185. See also Pataki,
    George E.
New York Times, 74
Nicarico, Jeanine, 1, 2
Nichols, Bill, 155n47
Nichols, Terry, 18
Nigeria, 13

Ninth U.S. Circuit Court of Ap-
    peals, San Francisco, 25, 73
Nonprofit groups
    abolitionist, 115–127
    retentionist, 133–139
North Africa, 163
North Carolina, 83, 99
Northwestern University Law
    School, conference on wrongful
    convictions, 10–11, 19
Nossiter, Adam, 108n157

Ocalan, Abdullah, 21
O'Connor, Paul, 112n228
O'Connor, Sandra Day, 148–149
Offman, Craig, 154nn12–14,
    190nn98–100
Ohio, 79, 184
Ohio v. Williams (1992), 191nn139,
    140, 192n141
Oklahoma, 79, 85
Olson, Elizabeth, 189n89
On Deterrence and the Death Penalty
    (van den Haag), 141
Opponents, death penalty. See
    Abolition movement
Orthodox Church, 131, 178

Pakistan, 13
Palmer, Elizabeth A., 107nn133,
    134, 108n142, 113nn237, 238,
    156nn67–69, 157n88
Paramedic murder, 24
Parole, 69, 78
Pataki, George E., 84, 88, 91, 151
Patterson, Raymond, 88
Payne v. Tennessee (1991),
    102nn20–22
    Criminal Justice Legal Founda-
        tion and, 133
    Kennedy, Anthony M., on, 148
    National Organization for Vic-
        tim Assistance and, 137
    O'Connor, Sandra Day, on, 148
    on victim impact evidence, 48,
        50
    Washington Legal Foundation
        and, 139

Pennsylvania, 79
Pennsylvania Coalition to Abolish
    the Death Penalty, 108n141
Penry, John Paul, 61
Penry v. Lynaugh (1989), 48, 50,
    102n18, 103n56, 148
Perjury that led to execution, 58
Perpetrators, gender differences
    of, 9
Perry, Rick, 61
Perry, Tony, 32n29
Pillets, Jeff, 191n121
Pitts, Jim, 14
Plantz, Marilyn, 77
Political endorsements
    by National Association of
        Police Organizations, 134–135
    by Republican Party, 138
Political infrastructure, abolition
    and, 168–169
Political pressure, state courts' er-
    ror detection and, 83
Powell, Lewis F., Jr., 43
Powell v. Alabama (1932), 15
Pregnant women, 159
Prejean, Sister Helen, 23, 123–124,
    131–132
Prejudicial errors, 81–82
Presbyterian Church, 131
Presidents, U.S.
    appeals to impose moratorium
        on executions, 99
    application of capital punish-
        ment and, 84–86
    clemency authority of, 71
    death penalty cases and elec-
        tions of, 60–61
    on international criticism,
        182
    legislative agenda of, 86–87
    military death penalty cases
        and, 58
Prinzo, Kristi Tumminello, 166,
    187nn43–47, 188nn48, 49
Prior criminal convictions of
    death row population, 78
Prison behavior, 8–9, 12
Probation, 78

Program to Abolish the Death
    Penalty, 175
Proportionality principle, 47–48
Proportionality review, 50, 51
    jurisdictional variations in, 65,
        66–67t
    narrow definitions for com-
        parison and, 67–68
Prosecutors, 87–88, 95, 97, 153, 185
Provenzano v. Moore (1999),
    105nn82, 83
Public defender offices, 61–62
Public opinion
    after abolition of death penalty,
        166–167
    on death penalty, 1, 2–3, 85–86,
        89–90
    on deterrence, 93
    retribution rationale and, 95
Pulanski, Charles, 32n23
Pulley v. Harris (1984), 50, 65, 67,
    102n31, 104n70
*Punishing Criminals: Concerning a
    Very Old and Painful Question* (van
    den Haag), 141

Quakers, 15
Quixote Center, 121

Rabbinical Assembly, 131
Racial Justice Act (Kentucky,
    1998), 19
Racism, 20, 23–24, 26
    as argument against capital
        punishment, 96–100
    retribution rationale and, 96
    statistics on, 3
    white victims and, 48–49, 78
Radelet, Michael L., 31n9, 109n165,
    110nn182, 183, 186, 192n143
Rangappa, Asha, 192n142
Rape, 15, 48, 50, 58
Reagan, Ronald, 17
Rector, Ricky Ray, 60–61
Referendum systems, 54–55
Reform Jewish movement, 177
Rehabilitation, clemency proceed-
    ings and, 9

Rehnquist, William H., 4–5, 43,
    149
Reinert, Patty, 111n200
Religious groups and leaders
    abolitionist, 93–94, 127–131, 180
    retentionist, 95, 139–141
Religious Organizing Against the
    Death Penalty Project, 128
Renaud, Trisha, 110n176
Reno, Janet, 10, 97
Reorganized Church of Jesus
    Christ of Latter-Day Saints, 131
Reprieves, 69
Republican Party, 137–138
Retentionist countries, 160, 161t,
    173–174
Retentionists, U.S., 132–142
    about, 132–133
    nonprofit organizations,
        133–139
    rationale of, 23, 94–96
    religious groups and leaders,
        95, 139–141
Richardson, Antonio, 171
Richardson, Bill, 183
Richardson, James, 10
Ridge, Tom, 85
Riggs, Christina, 180
Robbins, Ira, 5, 28–29
Robertson, James, 90
Robertson, Joe, 191n119
Robertson, Pat, 8, 9, 77, 139–141,
    155n54, 156nn57, 58
Roberts v. Louisiana (1977), 47, 50,
    101n11
Rohrlich, Ted, 189nn83, 84,
    192n146
Rohter, Larry, 21n2
Rolph, John E., 98, 112nn219, 220
Ross, Lee, 109n171
Rush, Benjamin, 15
Ryan, George, 108nn143–145, 147,
    131, 151–152, 157nn79, 80, 82, 86,
    100–101

Sachdeva, Anjali, 189nn78, 79
Saperstein, David, 177–178
Sapsford, Philip, 188n72

Saudi Arabia, 13, 22, 163, 173
Sawyer v. Whitley (1992), 103n40, 150
Scalia, Antonin, 149–150
Scarman, Lord, 188n72
Schabas, William A., 186nn2, 4, 7, 8, 187nn29, 30, 189nn80, 81
Scheck, Barry, 2, 107n132
Scheidegger, Kent S., 3, 7, 9, 25
Schlup v. Delo, 103n39
Schoolyard shootings, 13–14
Schreiber, Ariane M., 186n11
Schulhofer, Stephen J., 113n233
Schwed, Roger, 154n6
Scottsboro Boys rape case, 15
Sears, Roebuck & Co., 119, 176
Second Optional Protocol to Civil Rights Covenant, 159, 178–179
Sellers, Sean, 177–178
Senate Judiciary Committee, 146–147
Senior citizens, 29. *See also* Elderly convicts
Sentences
    adequate information and guidance for, 49, 51
    responsibility for, 63, 64–65t
    statistics 1984 to 1999, 105n85
    variations in, 26
Sentinel misbehavior during war, 58
Sessions, Jeff, 13
Shaheen, Jeanne, 86
Sharpe, Dudley, 112nn221, 222
Sherrell, George Wesley, Jr., 102n28
Smith, Andrew, 24
Smith, Susan, 3, 18
Snell, Tracy L., 31n7, 32n28, 102n25, 105nn86, 87, 95, 106nn96–100
Sonnier, Patrick, 131–132
Soskis, Benjamin, 108n149, 157n86
Souter, David H., 150
South America, 161
South Carolina, 83
Southern Baptist Convention, 140
Southern Christian Leadership Conference (SCLC), 129–130

Southern Coalition on Jails and Prisons (SCJP), 126–127
Southern states, 79
Spangenburg, R., 104n65
Sprenger, Steven M., 104n75
Spying during war, 58
Staletovitch, Jenny, 191n120
Stanford v. Kentucky (1989), 102n19, 191n124
    on cruel and unusual punishment, 182
    on juvenile offender executions, 48, 50
    Kennedy, Anthony M., on, 148
    O'Connor, Sandra Day, on, 148
    Scalia, Antonin, on, 150
Stark, Michael, 99
State abolitionist organizations, 127
State courts, 54, 55, 83
State governments
    appeals process, 7
    capital punishment laws of, 2, 45–46t
    first-degree murder only, 57t
    habeas corpus relief, 29, 50, 52
    response to international criticism by, 184–185
State politicians, 89–90
Statute of limitations, 5, 50, 103n41
Stephan, James J., 105n95
Stevens, John Paul, 150
Stewart, Potter, 43, 49, 95
Stewart, Richard, 111n200
Stewart, Steven D., 153
Streib, Victor L., 11, 13, 14, 23, 31n14, 105n92
Sudan, 178–179
Suicide, state sponsored, 91
Supreme Court, U.S. *See also specific cases*
    on Anti-Terrorism law scope, 19
    on appeals process, 25, 49
    appointments to, 143
    on constitutionality of capital punishment, 42–44, 47–49
    on deterrence, 92–93

electrocution law challenges and, 73, 74
    on execution delays, 4–5, 19
    on execution of insane prisoners, 3
    major decisions since *Gregg,* 50t
    on mentally retarded convicts, 61
    on proportionality review, 65, 67
    response to international criticism by, 181
Suro, Roberto, 32n25
Suspension clause, U.S. Constitution, 28–29
Sweden, 164
Szymanski, Linda, 31n15

Tavoli, Giancarlo, 172
Tennessee, 83
Terrorism, 20
Texas, 8, 61, 62, 79, 99. *See also* Tucker, Karla Faye
Texas Defender Service, 99
Thiessen, Marc, 22
Thomas, Andrew Peyton, 7, 25, 31n8, 32n30
Thomas, Clarence, 150–151
Thompson, Thomas, 5, 25
Tichtblau, Eric, 191nn131, 132, 133
Tison v. Arizona (1987), 48, 50, 58, 102n16
Torbet, Patricia, 31n15
Torture and mutilation, 24
Toscani, Oliviero, 119, 176
Treadway, Jonathan, 11
Treason, 20, 58
Treaties
    extradition exceptions in, 173
    reservations from, 163–164, 169
Trinidad and Tobago, 21
Tucker, Karla Faye, 8–9, 19, 77, 140, 177
Turkey, 21
Turner, Allan, 155n45

Unabomber, 1, 13, 19
Union of American Hebrew Congregations, 131

Unitarian Universalist Association, 131
United Church of Christ, 131
United Methodist Church, 131, 178
United Nations. *See also* International Covenant on Civil and Political Rights; Universal Declaration of Human Rights
    Amnesty International and, 118
    Commission on Human Rights, 22
    Convention on the Rights of the Child, 61
    criticism of U.S. policies by, 169–170
    Economic and Social Council, 22
    Hands off Cain and, 122
    Moratorium 2000 and, 123
    Second Optional Protocol to Civil Rights Covenant, 159
United States
    Amnesty International on, 174–175
    EU on policies of, 170–172
    executions in, 6f, 21, 22, 162t, 163
    extradition cases for, 173
    federal government response to international criticism, 181–183
    federalism and abolition movement, 168–169
    foreign nationals on death row in, 172
    human rights organizations on policies of, 174–176
    individual countries on policies of, 172–174
    local government response to international criticism, 185
    military code on wartime crimes, 58
    public opinion on death penalty in, 166–167

religious organizations on policies of, 177–179
    reservations to treaties and agreements by, 164, 191nn124, 125
    as retentionist country, 160
    state government response to international criticism, 184–185
    supra-national bodies on policies of, 169–172
    theories on capital punishment in, 166–169
    UN on policies of, 169–170, 171–172
United States v. Cooper (1990), 109n162
United States v. Jones (1999), 133
United States v. Pitera (1992), 109n162
Universal Declaration of Human Rights, 22, 117, 158–159, 174
Utah, 79

Van den Haag, Ernest, 98, 112n223, 141–142
Vandiver, M., 107n137
Venezuela, 172
Verhovek, Sam Howe, 105n93
Victim impact evidence, 48, 50, 133
Victims' rights movement, 23, 135, 137
Vilbig, Peter, 104n80, 105n81
Violent Crime Control and Law Enforcement Act (1994), 71
Violent crime punishable by death, 17, 18
Virginia, 79, 83
Vise, David A., 156nn62–64
"Voice of Justice, The," 134

Wallace, Benjamin, 108n150, 157n83

Washington Coalition to Abolish the Death Penalty, 127
Washington Legal Foundation (WLF), 138–139
Waters, Maxine, 100
Weeks v. Angelone (2000), 147
Weinstein, Henry, 107n136, 191nn131–133
West, Valerie, 102n35, 106nn113, 114, 155n43
White, Byron R., 43
White, Gayle, 156n56
White, Penny, 90, 138
White murder victims, 48–49, 78, 97, 98
White people, 77, 96, 97, 98
Whitman, Christine, 180
Willett, Alan, 177
Willett, Jim, 183
Williams, Dennis, 10
Willie, Robert, 23
Willing, Richard, 106n112, 108nn154, 155, 156
Witness murder, 24
Wogaman, J. Philip, 178
Women on death row, 77
Woods, Jeff, 109nn169, 170, 155n51
Woodworth, George, 32n23
World War II, 158
Worsnop, Richard L., 32n21
Wright, Dwayne, 12–13
Wrongful convictions, 2, 7–8. *See also* Innocent prisoners conference on, 10–11, 19
Wyoming, 83

Yellin, Emily, 190n117
Yemen, 13
Yoffie, Eric, 177–178, 190n108

Zimring, Franklin E., 167, 187n37, 188nn50–54
Zsembik, Barbara, 192n143

C. S. LEWIS

The Last Battle

Illustrated by
Pauline Baynes

Grafton

First published in Great Britain by The Bodley Head in 1956
First published by Collins in paperback in 1980

This edition published by Grafton 2002
Grafton is an imprint of
HarperCollins*Publishers*
77-85 Fulham Palace Road, Hammersmith
London, W6 8JB

1 3 5 7 9 10 8 6 4 2

ISBN 0 00 765008 6 (DMG Ltd.)
ISBN 0 26 167052 2 (Remainders Ltd.)

Printed and bound in Great Britain by
Bookmarque Ltd, Croydon, Surrey

CONTENTS

1. By Caldron Pool   7
2. The rashness of the King   17
3. The Ape in its glory   27
4. What happened that night   38
5. How help came to the King   47
6. A good night's work   58
7. Mainly about Dwarfs   68
8. What news the Eagle brought   79
9. The great meeting on Stable Hill   89
10. Who will go into the stable?   99
11. The pace quickens   109
12. Through the stable door   119
13. How the Dwarfs refused to be taken in   129
14. Night falls on Narnia   141
15. Further up and further in   152
16. Farewell to Shadowlands   162

CHAPTER ONE

BY CALDRON POOL

IN the last days of Narnia, far up to the west beyond Lantern Waste and close beside the great waterfall, there lived an Ape. He was so old that no one could remember when he had first come to live in those parts, and he was the cleverest, ugliest, most wrinkled Ape you can imagine. He had a little house, built of wood and thatched with leaves, up in the fork of a great tree, and his name was Shift. There were very few Talking Beasts or Men or Dwarfs, or people of any sort, in that part of the wood, but Shift had one friend and neighbour who was a donkey called Puzzle. At least they both said they were friends, but from the way things went on you might have thought Puzzle was more like Shift's servant than his friend. He did all the work. When they went together to the river, Shift filled the big skin bottles with water but it was Puzzle who carried them back. When they wanted anything from the towns further down the river it was Puzzle who went down with empty panniers on his back and came back with the panniers full and heavy. And all the nicest things that Puzzle brought back were eaten by Shift; for as Shift said, "You see, Puzzle, I can't eat grass and thistles like you, so it's only fair I should make it up in other ways." And Puzzle always said, "Of course, Shift, of course. I see that." Puzzle never complained, because he knew that Shift was far cleverer than himself and he thought it was very kind of Shift to be friends with him at all. And if ever Puzzle did try to argue about anything, Shift would always say, "Now, Puzzle, I understand what needs to be done better than you. You know you're not clever, Puzzle." And Puzzle

always said, "No, Shift. It's quite true. I'm *not* clever."
Then he would sigh and do whatever Shift had said.

One morning early in the year the pair of them were out
walking along the shore of Caldron Pool. Caldron Pool is
the big pool right under the cliffs at the western end of
Narnia. The great waterfall pours down into it with a noise
like everlasting thunder, and the River of Narnia flows out
on the other side. The waterfall keeps the Pool always
dancing and bubbling and churning round and round as if
it were on the boil, and that of course is how it got its name
of Caldron Pool. It is liveliest in the early spring when the
waterfall is swollen with all the snow that has melted off
the mountains from up beyond Narnia in the Western Wild
from which the river comes. And as they looked at Caldron
Pool Shift suddenly pointed with his dark, skinny finger
and said,

"Look! What's that?"

"What's what?" said Puzzle.

"That yellow thing that's just come down the waterfall.
Look! There it is again, it's floating. We must find out
what it is."

"Must we?" said Puzzle.

"Of course we must," said Shift. "It may be something
useful. Just hop into the Pool like a good fellow and fish it
out. Then we can have a proper look at it."

"Hop into the Pool?" said Puzzle, twitching his long
ears.

"Well how are we to get it if you don't?" said the Ape.

"But — but," said Puzzle, "wouldn't it be better if *you*
went in? Because, you see, it's you who wants to know
what it is, and I don't much. And you've got hands, you
see. You're as good as a Man or a Dwarf when it comes to
catching hold of things. I've only got hoofs."

"Really, Puzzle," said Shift, "I didn't think you'd ever say a thing like that. I didn't think it of you, really."

"Why, what have I said wrong?" said the Ass, speaking in rather a humble voice, for he saw that Shift was very deeply offended. "All I meant was —"

"Wanting *me* to go into the water," said the Ape. "As if you didn't know perfectly well what weak chests Apes always have and how easily they catch cold! Very well. I *will* go in. I'm feeling cold enough already in this cruel wind. But I'll go in. I shall probably die. Then you'll be sorry." And Shift's voice sounded as if he was just going to burst into tears.

"Please don't, please don't, please don't," said Puzzle, half braying, and half talking. "I never meant anything of the sort, Shift, really I didn't. You know how stupid I am and how I can't think of more than one thing at a time. I'd forgotten about your weak chest. Of course I'll go in. You mustn't think of doing it yourself. Promise me you won't, Shift."

So Shift promised, and Puzzle went cloppety-clop on his four hoofs round the rocky edge of the Pool to find a place where he could get in. Quite apart from the cold it was no joke getting into that quivering and foaming water, and Puzzle had to stand and shiver for a whole minute before he made up his mind to do it. But then Shift called out from behind him and said: "Perhaps I'd better do it after all, Puzzle." And when Puzzle heard that he said, "No, no. You promised. I'm in now," and in he went.

A great mass of foam got him in the face and filled his mouth with water and blinded him. Then he went under altogether for a few seconds, and when he came up again he was in quite another part of the Pool. Then the swirl caught him and carried him round and round and faster and faster till it took him right under the waterfall itself, and the force of the water plunged him down, deep down, so that he thought he would never be able to hold his breath till he came up again. And when he had come up and when at last he got somewhere near the thing he was trying to catch, it sailed away from him till it too got under the fall and was forced down to the bottom. When it came up again it was further from him than ever. But at last, when he was almost tired to death, and bruised all over and numb with cold, he succeeded in gripping the thing with his teeth. And out he came carrying it in front of him and getting his front hoofs tangled up in it, for it was as big as a large hearthrug, and it was very heavy and cold and slimy.

He flung it down in front of Shift and stood dripping and shivering and trying to get his breath back. But the Ape never looked at him or asked him how he felt. The Ape was too busy going round and round the Thing and spreading it out and patting it and smelling it. Then a wicked gleam came into his eye and he said:

"It is a lion's skin."

"Ee – auh – auh – oh, is it?" gasped Puzzle.

"Now I wonder . . . I wonder . . . I wonder," said Shift to himself, for he was thinking very hard.

"I wonder who killed the poor lion," said Puzzle presently. "It ought to be buried. We must have a funeral."

"Oh, it wasn't a Talking Lion," said Shift. "You needn't bother about *that*. There are no Talking Beasts up beyond the Falls, up in the Western Wild. This skin must have belonged to a dumb, wild lion."

This, by the way, was true. A Hunter, a Man, had killed and skinned this lion somewhere up in the Western Wild several months before. But that doesn't come into this story.

"All the same, Shift," said Puzzle, "even if the skin only belonged to a dumb, wild lion, oughtn't we to give it a decent burial? I mean, aren't all lions rather – well, rather solemn? Because of you know Who. Don't you see?"

"Don't you start getting ideas into your head, Puzzle," said Shift. "Because, you know, thinking isn't your strong point. We'll make this skin into a fine warm winter coat for you."

"Oh, I don't think I'd like that," said the Donkey. "It

would look – I mean, the other Beasts might think – that is to say, I shouldn't feel –"

"What are you talking about?" said Shift, scratching himself the wrong way up as Apes do.

"I don't think it would be respectful to the Great Lion, to Aslan himself, if an ass like me went about dressed up in a lion-skin," said Puzzle.

"Now don't stand arguing, please," said Shift. "What does an ass like you know about things of that sort? You know you're no good at thinking, Puzzle, so why don't you let me do your thinking for you? Why don't you treat me as I treat you? I don't think I can do everything. I know you're better at some things than I am. That's why I let you go into the Pool; I knew you'd do it better than me. But why can't I have my turn when it comes to something I *can* do and you can't? Am I never to be allowed to do anything? Do be fair. Turn and turn about."

"Oh, well, of course, if you put it that way," said Puzzle.

"I tell you what," said Shift. "You'd better take a good brisk trot down river as far as Chippingford and see if they have any oranges or bananas."

"But I'm so tired, Shift," pleaded Puzzle.

"Yes, but you are very cold and wet," said the Ape. "You want something to warm you up. A brisk trot would be just the thing. Besides, it's market day at Chippingford today." And then of course Puzzle said he would go.

As soon as he was alone Shift went shambling along, sometimes on two paws and sometimes on four, till he reached his own tree. Then he swung himself up from branch to branch, chattering and grinning all the time, and went into his little house. He found needle and thread and a big pair of scissors there; for he was a clever Ape and the

Dwarfs had taught him how to sew. He put the ball of thread (it was very thick stuff, more like cord than thread) into his mouth so that his cheek bulged out as if he were sucking a big bit of toffee. He held the needle between his lips and took the scissors in his left paw. Then he came down the tree and shambled across to the lion-skin. He squatted down and got to work.

He saw at once that the body of the lion-skin would be too long for Puzzle and its neck too short. So he cut a good piece out of the body and used it to make a long collar for Puzzle's long neck. Then he cut off the head and sewed the collar in between the head and the shoulders. He put threads on both sides of the skin so that it would tie up under Puzzle's chest and stomach. Every now and then a bird would pass overhead and Shift would stop his work, looking anxiously up. He did not want anyone to see what he was doing. But none of the birds he saw were Talking Birds, so it didn't matter.

Late in the afternoon Puzzle came back. He was not trotting but only plodding patiently along, the way donkeys do.

"There weren't any oranges," he said, "and there weren't any bananas. And I'm very tired." He lay down.

"Come and try on your beautiful new lion-skin coat," said Shift.

"Oh bother that old skin," said Puzzle. "I'll try it on in the morning. I'm too tired tonight."

"You *are* unkind, Puzzle," said Shift. "If *you're* tired what do you think I am? All day long, while you've been having a lovely refreshing walk down the valley, I've been working hard to make you a coat. My paws are so tired I can hardly hold these scissors. And you won't say thank

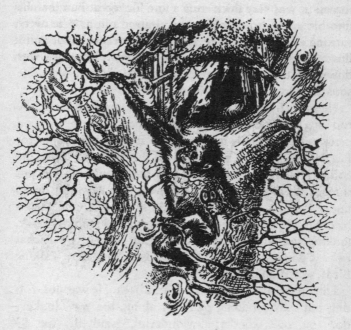

you – and you won't even look at the coat – and you don't
care – and – and –"

"My dear Shift," said Puzzle getting up at once, "I am so
sorry. I've been horrid. Of course I'd love to try it on. And it
looks simply splendid. Do try it on me at once. Please do."

"Well, stand still then," said the Ape. The skin was very
heavy for him to lift, but in the end, with a lot of pulling
and pushing and puffing and blowing, he got it on to the
donkey. He tied it underneath Puzzle's body and he tied the
legs to Puzzle's legs and the tail to Puzzle's tail. A good deal
of Puzzle's grey nose and face could be seen through the
open mouth of the lion's head. No one who had ever seen a

real lion would have been taken in for a moment. But if someone who had never seen a lion looked at Puzzle in his lion-skin he just might mistake him for a lion, if he didn't come too close, and if the light was not too good, and if Puzzle didn't let out a bray and didn't make any noise with his hoofs.

"You look wonderful, wonderful," said the Ape. "If anyone saw you now, they'd think you were Aslan, the Great Lion, himself."

"That would be dreadful," said Puzzle.

"No it wouldn't," said Shift. "Everyone would do whatever you told them."

"But I don't want to tell them anything."

"But you think of the good we could do!" said Shift. "You'd have me to advise you, you know. I'd think of sensible orders for you to give. And everyone would have to obey us, even the King himself. We would set everything right in Narnia."

"But isn't everything right already?" said Puzzle.

"What!" cried Shift. "Everything right? – when there are no oranges or bananas?"

"Well, you know," said Puzzle, "there aren't many people – in fact, I don't think there's anyone but yourself – who wants those sort of things."

"There's sugar too," said Shift.

"H'm yes," said the Ass. "It would be nice if there was more sugar."

"Well then, that's settled," said the Ape. "You will pretend to be Aslan, and I'll tell you what to say."

"No, no, no," said Puzzle. "Don't say such dreadful things. It would be wrong, Shift. I may be not very clever but I know that much. What would become of us if the real Aslan turned up?"

"I expect he'd be very pleased," said Shift. "Probably he sent us the lion-skin on purpose, so that we could set things to right. Anyway, he never *does* turn up, you know. Not nowadays."

At that moment there came a great thunderclap right overhead and the gound trembled with a small earthquake. Both the animals lost their balance and were flung on their faces.

"There!" gasped Puzzle, as soon as he had breath to speak. "It's a sign, a warning. I knew we were doing something dreadfully wicked. Take this wretched skin off me at once."

"No, no," said the Ape (whose mind worked very quickly). "It's a sign the other way. I was just going to say that if the real Aslan, as you call him, meant us to go on with this, he would send us a thunderclap and an earth-tremor. It was just on the tip of my tongue, only the sign itself came before I could get the words out. You've *got* to do it now, Puzzle. And please don't let us have any more arguing. You know you don't understand these things. What could a donkey know about signs?"

CHAPTER TWO

THE RASHNESS OF THE KING

ABOUT three weeks later the last of the Kings of Narnia sat under the great oak which grew beside the door of his little hunting lodge, where he often stayed for ten days or so in the pleasant spring weather. It was a low, thatched building not far from the Eastern end of Lantern Waste and some way above the meeting of the two rivers. He loved to live there simply and at ease, away from the state and pomp of Cair Paravel, the royal city. His name was King Tirian, and he was between twenty and twenty-five years old; his shoulders were already broad and strong and his limbs full of hard muscle, but his beard was still scanty. He had blue eyes and a fearless, honest face.

There was no one with him that spring morning except his dearest friend, Jewel the Unicorn. They loved each other like brothers and each had saved the other's life in the wars. The lordly beast stood close beside the King's chair, with its neck bent round polishing its blue horn against the creamy whiteness of its flank.

"I cannot set myself to any work or sport today, Jewel," said the King. "I can think of nothing but this wonderful news. Think you we shall hear any more of it today?"

"They are the most wonderful tidings ever heard in our days or our fathers' or our grandfathers' days, Sire," said Jewel, "if they are true."

"How can they choose but be true?" said the King. "It is more than a week ago that the first birds came flying over us saying, Aslan is here, Aslan has come to Narnia again. And after that it was the squirrels. They had not seen him, but they said it was certain he was in the woods. Then came the Stag. He said he had seen him with his own eyes, a great way off, by moonlight, in Lantern Waste. Then came that dark Man with the beard, the merchant from Calormen. The Calormenes care nothing for Aslan as we do; but the man spoke of it as a thing beyond doubt. And there was the Badger last night; he too had seen Aslan."

"Indeed, Sire," answered Jewel, "I believe it all. If I seem not to, it is only that my joy is too great to let my belief settle itself. It is almost too beautiful to believe."

"Yes," said the King with a great sigh, almost a shiver, of delight. "It is beyond all that I ever hoped for in all my life."

"Listen!" said Jewel, putting his head on one side and cocking his ears forward.

"What is it?" asked the King.

"Hoofs, Sire," said Jewel. "A galloping horse. A very heavy horse. It must be one of the Centaurs. And look, there he is."

A great, golden bearded Centaur, with man's sweat on his forehead and horse's sweat on his chestnut flanks, dashed up to the King, stopped, and bowed low. "Hail, King," it cried in a voice as deep as a bull's.

"Ho, there!" said the King, looking over his shoulder towards the door of the hunting lodge. "A bowl of wine for the noble Centaur. Welcome, Roonwit. When you have found your breath you shall tell us your errand."

A page came out of the house carrying a great wooden bowl, curiously carved, and handed it to the Centaur. The Centaur raised the bowl and said,

"I drink first to Aslan and truth, Sire, and secondly to your Majesty."

He finished the wine (enough for six strong men) at one draught and handed the empty bowl back to the page.

"Now, Roonwit," said the King. "Do you bring us more news of Aslan?"

Roonwit looked very grave, frowning a little.

"Sire," he said. "You know how long I have lived and studied the stars; for we Centaurs live longer than you Men, and even longer than your kind, Unicorn. Never in

all my days have I seen such terrible things written in the skies as there have been nightly since this year began. The stars say nothing of the coming of Aslan, nor of peace, nor of joy. I know by my art that there have not been such disastrous conjunctions of the planets for five hundred years. It was already in my mind to come and warn your Majesty that some great evil hangs over Narnia. But last night the rumour reached me that Aslan is abroad in Narnia. Sire, do not believe this tale. It cannot be. The stars never lie, but Men and Beasts do. If Aslan were really coming to Narnia the sky would have foretold it. If he were really come, all the most gracious stars would be assembled in his honour. It is all a lie."

"A lie!" said the King fiercely. "What creature in Narnia or all the world would dare to lie on such a matter?" And, without knowing it, he laid his hand on his sword hilt.

"That I know not, Lord King," said the Centaur. "But I know there are liars on earth; there are none among the stars."

"I wonder," said Jewel, "whether Aslan might not come though all the stars foretold otherwise. He is not the slave of the stars but their Maker. Is it not said in all the old stories that He is not a tame lion."

"Well said, well said, Jewel," cried the King. "Those are the very words: *not a tame lion*. It comes in many tales."

Roonwit had just raised his hand and was leaning forward to say something very earnestly to the King when all three of them turned their heads to listen to a wailing sound that was quickly drawing nearer. The wood was so thick to the West of them that they could not see the newcomer yet. But they could soon hear the words.

"Woe, woe, woe!" called the voice. "Woe for my brothers and sisters! Woe for the holy trees! The woods are laid waste. The axe is loosed against us. We are being felled. Great trees are falling, falling, falling."

With the last "falling" the speaker came in sight. She was like a woman but so tall that her head was on a level with the Centaur's yet she was like a tree too. It is hard to explain if you have never seen a Dryad but quite unmistakable once you have – something different in the colour, the voice, and the hair. King Tirian and the two Beasts knew at once that she was the nymph of a beech tree.

"Justice, Lord King!" she cried. "Come to our aid. Protect your people. They are felling us in Lantern Waste.

Forty great trunks of my brothers and sisters are already on the ground."

"What, Lady! Felling Lantern Waste? Murdering the talking trees?" cried the King, leaping to his feet and drawing his sword. "How dare they? And who dares it? Now by the Mane of Aslan –"

"A-a-a-h," gasped the Dryad shuddering as if in pain – shuddering time after time as if under repeated blows. Then all at once she fell sideways as suddenly as if both her feet had been cut from under her. For a second they saw her lying dead on the grass and then she vanished. They knew what had happened. Her tree, miles away, had been cut down.

For a moment the King's grief and anger were so great that he could not speak. Then he said:

"Come, friends. We must go up river and find the villains who have done this, with all the speed we may. I will leave not one of them alive."

"Sire, with a good will," said Jewel.

But Roonwit said, "Sire, be wary in your just wrath. There are strange doings on foot. If there should be rebels in arms further up the valley, we three are too few to meet them. If it would please you to wait while –"

"I will not wait the tenth part of a second," said the King. "But while Jewel and I go forward, do you gallop as hard as you may to Cair Paravel. Here is my ring for your token. Get me a score of men-at-arms, all well mounted, and a score of Talking Dogs, and ten Dwarfs (let them all be fell archers), and a Leopard or so, and Stonefoot the Giant. Bring all these after us as quickly as may be."

"With a good will, Sire," said Roonwit. And at once he turned and galloped Eastward down the valley.

The King strode on at a great pace, sometimes muttering to himself and sometimes clenching his fists. Jewel walked beside him, saying nothing; so there was no sound between them but the faint jingle of a rich gold chain that hung round the Unicorn's neck and the noise of two feet and four hoofs.

They soon reached the River and turned up it where there was a grassy road: they had the water on their left and the forest on their right. Soon after that they came to the place where the ground grew rougher and thick wood came down to the water's edge. The road, what there was of it, now ran on the Southern bank and they had to ford the River to reach it. It was up to Tirian's arm-pits, but Jewel (who had four legs and was therefore steadier) kept on his right so as to break the force of the current, and Tirian put his strong arm round the Unicorn's strong neck and they both got safely over. The King was still so angry that he hardly noticed the cold of the water. But of course he dried his sword very carefully on the shoulder of his cloak, which was the only dry part of him, as soon as they came to shore.

They were now going Westward with the River on their right and Lantern Waste straight ahead of them. They had not gone more than a mile when they both stopped and both spoke at the same moment. The King said "What have we here?" and Jewel said "Look!"

"It is a raft," said King Tirian.

And so it was. Half a dozen splendid tree-trunks, all newly cut and newly lopped of their branches, had been lashed together to make a raft, and were gliding swiftly down the river. On the front of the raft there was a water rat with a pole to steer it.

"Hey! Water-Rat! What are you about?" cried the King.

"Taking logs down to sell to the Calormenes, Sire," said the Rat, touching his ear as he might have touched his cap if he had had one.

"Calormenes!" thundered Tirian. "What do you mean? Who gave order for these trees to be felled?"

The River flows so swiftly at that time of the year that the raft had already glided past the King and Jewel. But the Water-Rat looked back over its shoulder and shouted out:

"The Lion's orders, Sire. Aslan himself." He added something more but they couldn't hear it.

The King and the Unicorn stared at one another and both looked more frightened than they had ever been in any battle.

"Aslan," said the King at last, in a very low voice. "Aslan. Could it be true? *Could* he be felling the holy trees and murdering the Dryads?"

"Unless the Dryads have all done something dreadfully wrong –" murmured Jewel.

"But selling them to Calormenes!" said the King. "Is it possible?"

"I don't know," said Jewel miserably. "He's not a *tame* lion."

"Well," said the King at last, "we must go on and take the adventure that comes to us."

"It is the only thing left for us to do, Sire," said the Unicorn. He did not see at the moment how foolish it was for two of them to go on alone; nor did the King. They were too angry to think clearly. But much evil came of their rashness in the end.

Suddenly the King leaned hard on his friend's neck and bowed his head.

"Jewel," he said, "what lies before us? Horrible thoughts arise in my heart. If we had died before today we should have been happy."

"Yes," said Jewel. "We have lived too long. The worst thing in the world has come upon us." They stood like that for a minute or two and then went on.

Before long they could hear the hack-hack-hack of axes falling on timber, though they could see nothing yet because there was a rise of the ground in front of them. When they had reached the top of it they could see right into Lantern Waste itself. And the King's face turned white when he saw it.

Right through the middle of that ancient forest – that forest where the trees of gold and of silver had once grown and where a child from our world had once planted the Tree of Protection – a broad lane had already been opened. It was a hideous lane like a raw gash in the land, full of muddy ruts where felled trees had been dragged down to the river. There was a great crowd of people at work, and a cracking of whips, and horses tugging and straining as they dragged at the logs. The first thing that struck the King and the Unicorn was that about half the people in the crowd were not Talking Beasts but Men. The next thing was that these men were not the fair-haired men of Narnia: they were dark, bearded men from Calormen, that great and cruel country that lies beyond Archenland across the desert to the south. There was no reason, of course, why one should not meet a Calormene or two in Narnia — a merchant or an ambassador — for there was peace between Narnia and Calormen in those days. But Tirian could not understand why there were so many of them: nor why they were cutting down a Narnian forest. He grasped his sword tighter and rolled his cloak round his left arm. They came quickly down among the men.

Two Calormenes were driving a horse which was harnessed to a log. Just as the King reached them the log had got stuck in a bad muddy place.

"Get on, son of sloth! Pull, you lazy pig!" cried the Calormenes, cracking their whips. The horse was already straining himself as hard as he could; his eyes were red and he was covered with foam.

"Work, lazy brute," shouted one of the Calormenes: and as he spoke he struck the horse savagely with his whip. It was then that the really dreadful thing happened.

Up till now Tirian had taken it for granted that the horses which the Calormenes were driving were their own horses; dumb, witless animals like the horses of our own world. And though he hated to see even a dumb horse overdriven, he was of course thinking more about the murder of the Trees. It had never crossed his mind that anyone would dare to harness one of the free Talking Horses of Narnia, much less to use a whip on it. But as that

savage blow fell the horse reared up and said, half
screaming:

"Fool and tyrant! Do you not see I am doing all I can?"

When Tirian knew that the Horse was one of his own
Narnians, there came over him and over Jewel such a rage
that they did not know what they were doing. The King's
sword went up, the Unicorn's horn went down. They
rushed forward together. Next moment both the Calormenes lay dead, the one beheaded by Tirian's sword and
the other gored through the heart by Jewel's horn.

CHAPTER THREE

THE APE IN ITS GLORY

"MASTER Horse, Master Horse," said Tirian as he hastily cut its traces, "how came these aliens to enslave you? Is Narnia conquered? Has there been a battle?"

"No, Sire," panted the horse, "Aslan is here. It is all by his orders. He has commanded —"

"'Ware danger, King," said Jewel. Tirian looked up and saw that Calormenes (mixed with a few Talking Beasts) were beginning to run towards them from every direction. The two dead men had died without a cry and so it had taken a moment before the rest of the crowd knew what had happened. But now they did. Most of them had naked scimitars in their hands.

"Quick. On my back," said Jewel.

The King flung himself astride of his old friend who turned and galloped away. He changed direction twice or thrice as soon as they were out of sight of their enemies, crossed a stream, and shouted without slackening his pace, "Whither away, Sire? To Cair Paravel?"

"Hold hard, friend," said Tirian. "Let me off." He slid off the Unicorn's back and faced him.

"Jewel," said the King. "We have done a dreadful deed."

"We were sorely provoked," said Jewel.

"But to leap on them unawares — without defying them — while they were unarmed — faugh! We are two murderers, Jewel. I am dishonoured forever."

Jewel drooped his head. He too was ashamed.

"And then," said the King, "the Horse said it was by Aslan's orders. The Rat said the same. They all say Aslan is here. How if it were true?"

"But, Sire, how *could* Aslan be commanding such dreadful things?"

"He is not a *tame* lion," said Tirian. "How should we know what he would do? We, who are murderers. Jewel, I will go back. I will give up my sword and put myself in the hands of these Calormenes and ask that they bring me before Aslan. Let him do justice on me."

"You will go to your death, then," said Jewel.

"Do you think I care if Aslan dooms me to death?" said the King. "That would be nothing, nothing at all. Would it not be better to be dead than to have this horrible fear that Aslan has come and is not like the Aslan we have believed in and longed for? It is as if the sun rose one day and were a black sun."

"I know," said Jewel. "Or as if you drank water and it were *dry* water. You are in the right, Sire. This is the end of all things. Let us go and give ourselves up."

"There is no need for both of us to go."

"If ever we loved one another, let me go with you now," said the Unicorn. "If you are dead and if Aslan is not Aslan, what life is left for me?"

They turned and walked back together, shedding bitter tears.

As soon as they came to the place where the work was going on the Calormenes raised a cry and came towards them with their weapons in hand. But the King held out his sword with the hilt towards them and said:

"I who was King of Narnia and am now a dishonoured knight give myself up to the justice of Aslan. Bring me before him."

"And I give myself up too," said Jewel.

Then the dark men came round them in a thick crowd, smelling of garlic and onions, their white eyes flashing dreadfully in their brown faces. They put a rope halter round Jewel's neck. They took the King's sword away and tied his hands behind his back. One of the Calormenes, who had a helmet instead of a turban and seemed to be in command, snatched the gold circlet off Tirian's head and hastily put it away somewhere among his clothes. They led the two prisoners uphill to a place where there was a big clearing. And this was what the prisoners saw.

At the centre of the clearing, which was also the highest point of the hill, there was a little hut like a stable, with a thatched roof. Its door was shut. On the grass in front of the door there sat an Ape. Tirian and Jewel, who had been expecting to see Aslan and had heard nothing about an Ape yet, were very bewildered when they saw it. The Ape was of course Shift himself, but he looked ten times uglier than when he lived by Caldron Pool, for he was now dressed up. He was wearing a scarlet jacket which did not fit him very well, having been made for a dwarf. He had jewelled slippers on his hind paws which would not stay on properly because, as you know, the hind paws of an Ape are really like hands. He wore what seemed to be a paper crown on his head. There was a great pile of nuts beside him and he kept cracking nuts with his jaws and spitting out the shells. And he also kept on pulling up the scarlet jacket to scratch himself. A great number of Talking Beasts stood facing him, and nearly every face in that crowd looked miserably worried and bewildered. When they saw who the prisoners were they all groaned and whimpered.

"O Lord Shift, mouthpiece of Aslan," said the chief Calormene. "We bring you prisoners. By our skill and courage and by the permission of the great god Tash we have taken alive these two desperate murderers."

"Give me that man's sword," said the Ape. So they took

the King's sword and handed it, with the sword-belt and all, to the monkey. And he hung it round his own neck: and it made him look sillier than ever.

"We'll see about those two later," said the Ape, spitting out a shell in the direction of the two prisoners. "I got some other business first. They can wait. Now listen to me, everyone. The first thing I want to say is about nuts. Where's that Head Squirrel got to?"

"Here, Sir," said a red squirrel, coming forward and making a nervous little bow.

"Oh you are, are you?" said the Ape with a nasty look. "Now attend to me I want – I mean, Aslan wants – some more nuts. These you've brought aren't anything like enough. You must bring some more, do you hear? Twice as many. And they've got to be here by sunset tomorrow, and there mustn't be any bad ones or any small ones among them."

A murmur of dismay ran through the other squirrels, and the Head Squirrel plucked up courage to say:

"Please, would Aslan himself speak to us about it? If we might be allowed to see him –"

"Well you won't," said the Ape. "He may be very kind (though it's a lot more than most of you deserve) and come out for a few minutes tonight. Then you can all have a look at him. But he will *not* have you all crowding round him and pestering him with questions. Anything you want to say to him will be passed on through me: if I think it's worth bothering him about. In the meantime all you squirrels had better go and see about the nuts. And make sure they are here by tomorrow evening or, my word! you'll catch it."

The poor squirrels all scampered away as if a dog were after them. This new order was terrible news for them. The nuts they had carefully hoarded for the winter had nearly all been eaten by now; and of the few that were left they had already given the Ape far more than they could spare.

Then a deep voice – it belonged to a great tusked and shaggy Boar – spoke from another part of the crowd.

"But *why* can't we see Aslan properly and talk to him?" it said. "When he used to appear in Narnia in the old days everyone could talk to him face to face."

"Don't you believe it," said the Ape. "And even if it was true, times have changed. Aslan says he's been far too soft with you before, do you see? Well, he isn't going to be soft any more. He's going to lick you into shape this time. He'll teach you to think he's a tame lion!"

A low moaning and whimpering was heard among the Beasts; and, after that, a dead silence which was more miserable still.

"And now there's another thing you got to learn," said the Ape. "I hear some of you are saying I'm an Ape. Well, I'm not. I'm a Man. If I look like an Ape, that's because I'm so very old: hundreds and hundreds of years old. And it's because I'm so old that I'm so wise. And it's because I'm so wise that I'm the only one Aslan is ever going to speak to. He can't be bothered talking to a lot of stupid animals. He'll tell me what you've got to do, and I'll tell the rest of you. And take my advice, and see you do it in double quick time, for he doesn't mean to stand any nonsense."

There was a dead silence except for the noise of a very young badger crying and its mother trying to make it keep quiet.

"And now here's another thing," the Ape went on, fitting a fresh nut into its cheek, "I hear some of the horses are saying, Let's hurry up and get this job of carting timber over as quickly as we can, and then we'll be free again. Well, you can get that idea out of your heads at once. And not only the Horses either. Everybody who can work is going to be made to work in future. Aslan has it all settled with the King of Calormen — The Tisroc, as our dark faced friends the Calormenes call him. All you Horses and Bulls and Donkeys are to be sent down into Calormen to work for your living — pulling and carrying the way horses and such-like do in other countries. And all you digging animals like Moles and Rabbits and Dwarfs are going down to work in The Tisroc's mines. And —"

"No, no, no," howled the Beasts. "It can't be true. Aslan would never sell us into slavery to the King of Calormen."

"None of that! Hold your noise!" said the Ape with a snarl. "Who said anything about slavery? You won't be slaves. You'll be paid — very good wages too. That is to say, your pay will be paid into Aslan's treasury and he will use it all for everybody's good." Then he glanced, and almost winked, at the chief Calormene. The Calormene bowed and replied, in the pompous Calormene way:

"Most sapient Mouthpiece of Aslan, The Tisroc (may-he-live-forever) is wholly of one mind with your lordship in this judicious plan."

"There! You see!" said the Ape. "It's all arranged. And all for your own good. We'll be able, with the money you earn, to make Narnia a country worth living in. There'll be oranges and bananas pouring in – and roads and big cities and schools and offices and whips and muzzles and saddles and cages and kennels and prisons – Oh, everything."

"But we don't want all those things," said an old Bear. "We want to be free. And we want to hear Aslan speak himself."

"Now don't you start arguing," said the Ape, "for it's a thing I won't stand. I'm a Man: you're only a fat, stupid old Bear. What do you know about freedom? You think freedom means doing what you like. Well, you're wrong. That isn't true freedom. True freedom means doing what I tell you."

"H-n-n-h," grunted the Bear and scratched its head; it found this sort of thing hard to understand.

"Please, please," said the high voice of a woolly lamb, who was so young that everyone was surprised he dared to speak at all.

"What is it now?" said the Ape. "Be quick."

"Please," said the Lamb, "I can't understand. What have we to do with the Calormenes? We belong to Aslan. They belong to Tash. They have a god called Tash. They say he has four arms and the head of a vulture. They kill Men on his altar. I don't believe there's any such person as Tash. But if there was, how could Aslan be friends with him?"

All the animals cocked their heads sideways and all their bright eyes flashed towards the Ape. They knew it was the best question anyone had asked yet.

The Ape jumped up and spat at the Lamb.

"Baby!" he hissed. "Silly little bleater! Go home to your mother and drink milk. What do you understand of such things? But the others, listen. Tash is only another name for Aslan. All that old idea of us being right and the Calormenes wrong is silly. We know better now. The Calormenes use different words but we all mean the same thing. Tash and Aslan are only two different names for you know Who. That's why there can never be any quarrel between them. Get that into your heads, you stupid brutes. Tash is Aslan: Aslan is Tash."

You know how sad your own dog's face can look sometimes. Think of that and then think of all the faces of those Talking Beasts — all those honest, humble, bewildered Birds, Bears, Badgers, Rabbits, Moles, and Mice — all far sadder than that. Every tail was down, every whisker drooped. It would have broken your heart with very pity to see their faces. There was only one who did not look at all unhappy.

It was a ginger Cat – a great big Tom in the prime of life – who sat bolt upright with his tail curled round his toes, in the very front row of all the Beasts. He had been staring hard at the Ape and the Calormene captain all the time and had never once blinked his eyes.

"Excuse me," said the Cat very politely, "but this interests me. Does your friend from Calormen say the same?"

"Assuredly," said the Calormene. "The enlightened Ape – Man, I mean – is in the right. *Aslan* means neither less nor more than *Tash*."

"Especially, Aslan means *no more* than Tash?" suggested the Cat.

"No more at all," said the Calormene, looking the Cat straight in the face.

"Is that good enough for you, Ginger?" said the Ape.

"Oh certainly," said Ginger coolly. "Thank you very much. I only wanted to be quite clear. I think I am beginning to understand."

Up till now the King and Jewel had said nothing: they were waiting until the Ape should bid them speak, for they thought it was no use interrupting. But now, as Tirian looked round on the miserable faces of the Narnians, and saw how they would all believe that Aslan and Tash were one and the same, he could bear it no longer.

"Ape," he cried with a great voice, "you lie damnably. You lie like a Calormene. You lie like an Ape."

He meant to go on and ask how the terrible god Tash who fed on the blood of his people could possibly be the same as the good Lion by whose blood all Narnia was saved. If he had been allowed to speak, the rule of the Ape might have ended that day; the Beasts might have seen the truth and thrown the Ape down. But before he could say another word two Calormenes struck him in the mouth with all their force, and a third, from behind, kicked his feet from under him. And as he fell, the Ape squealed in rage and terror.

"Take him away. Take him away. Take him where he cannot hear us, nor we hear him. There tie him to a tree. I will – I mean, Aslan will – do justice on him later."

CHAPTER FOUR

WHAT HAPPENED THAT NIGHT

THE King was so dizzy from being knocked down that he hardly knew what was happening until the Calormenes untied his wrists and put his arms straight down by his sides and set him with his back against an ash tree. Then they bound ropes round his ankles and his knees and his waist and his chest and left him there. What worried him worst at the moment – for it is often little things that are hardest to stand – was that his lip was bleeding where they had hit him and he couldn't wipe the little trickle of blood away although it tickled him.

From where he was he could still see the little stable on the top of the hill and the Ape sitting in front of it. He could just hear the Ape's voice still going on and, every now and then, some answer from the crowd, but he could not make out the words.

"I wonder what they've done to Jewel," thought the King.

Presently the crowd of beasts broke up and began going away in different directions. Some passed close to Tirian. They looked at him as if they were both frightened and sorry to see him tied up but none of them spoke. Soon they had all gone and there was silence in the wood. Then hours and hours went past and Tirian became first very thirsty and then very hungry; and as the afternoon dragged on and turned into evening, he became cold too. His back was very sore. The sun went down and it began to be twilight.

When it was almost dark Tirian heard a light pitter-patter of feet and saw some small creatures coming towards him. The three on the left were Mice, and there

was a Rabbit in the middle: on the right were two Moles. Both these were carrying little bags on their backs which gave them a curious look in the dark so that at first he wondered what kind of beasts they were. Then, in a moment, they were all standing up on their hind legs, laying their cool paws on his knees and giving his knees snuffly animal kisses. (They could reach his knees because Narnian Talking Beasts of that sort are bigger than the dumb beasts of the same kind in England.)

"Lord King! dear Lord King," said their shrill voices, "we are so sorry for you. We daren't untie you because Aslan might be angry with us. But we've brought you your supper."

At once the first Mouse climbed nimbly up till he was

perched on the rope that bound Tirian's chest and was wrinkling his blunt nose in front of Tirian's face. Then the second Mouse climbed up and hung on just below the first Mouse. The other beasts stood on the ground and began handing things up.

"Drink, Sire, and then you'll find you are able to eat," said the topmost Mouse, and Tirian found that a little wooden cup was being held to his lips. It was only the size of an egg cup so that he had hardly tasted the wine in it before it was empty. But then the Mouse passed it down and the others re-filled it and it was passed up again and Tirian emptied it a second time. In this way they went on till he had quite a good drink, which was all the better for coming in little doses, for that is more thirst-quenching than one long draught.

"Here is cheese, Sire," said the first Mouse, "but not very much, for fear it would make you too thirsty." And after the cheese they fed him with oat-cakes and fresh butter, and then with some more wine.

"Now hand up the water," said the first Mouse, "and I'll wash the King's face. There is blood on it."

Then Tirian felt something like a tiny sponge dabbing his face, and it was most refreshing.

"Little friends," said Tirian, "how can I thank you for all this?"

"You needn't, you needn't," said the little voices. "What else could we do? *We* don't want any other King. We're your people. If it was only the Ape and the Calormenes who were against you we would have fought till we were cut into pieces before we'd let them tie you up. We would, we would indeed. But we can't go against Aslan."

"Do you think it really is Aslan?" asked the King.

"Oh yes, yes," said the Rabbit. "He came out of the stable last night. We all saw him."

"What was he like?" said the King.

"Like a terrible, great Lion, to be sure," said one of the Mice.

"And you think it is really Aslan who is killing the Wood-Nymphs and making you all slaves to the King of Calormen?"

"Ah, that's bad, isn't it?" said the second Mouse. "It would have been better if we'd died before all this began. But there's no doubt about it. Everyone says it is Aslan's orders. And we've seen him. We didn't think Aslan would be like that. Why, we – we *wanted* him to come back to Narnia."

"He seems to have come back very angry this time," said the first Mouse. "We must all have done something dreadfully wrong without knowing it. He must be punishing us for something. But I do think we might be told what it was!"

"I suppose what we're doing now may be wrong," said the Rabbit.

"I don't care if it is," said one of the Moles. "I'd do it again."

But the others said, "Oh hush," and "Do be careful," and then they all said, "We're sorry, dear King, but we must go back now. It would never do for us to be caught here."

"Leave me at once, dear Beasts," said Tirian. "I would not for all Narnia bring any of you into danger."

"Goodnight, goodnight," said the Beasts, rubbing their noses against his knees. "We will come back – if we can." Then they all pattered away and the wood seemed darker and colder and lonelier than it had been before they came.

The stars came out and time went slowly on – imagine how slowly – while that last King of Narnia stood stiff and sore and upright against the tree in his bonds. But at last something happened.

Far away there appeared a red light. Then it disappeared for a moment and came back again, bigger and stronger. Then he could see dark shapes going to and fro on this side of the light and carrying bundles and throwing them down. He knew now what he was looking at. It was a bonfire, newly lit, and people were throwing bundles of brushwood on to it. Presently it blazed up and Tirian could see that it was on the very top of the hill. He could see quite clearly the stable behind it, all lit up in the red glow, and a great crowd of Beasts and Men between the fire and himself. A small figure, hunched up beside the fire, must be the Ape. It was saying something to the crowd, but he could not hear what. Then it went and bowed three times to the ground in front of the door of the stable. Then it got up and opened the door. And something on four legs – something that walked rather stiffly – came out of the stable and stood facing the crowd.

A great wailing or howling went up, so loud that Tirian could hear some of the words.

"Aslan! Aslan! Aslan!" cried the Beasts. "Speak to us. Comfort us. Be angry with us no more."

From where Tirian was he could not make out very clearly what the thing was; but he could see that it was yellow and hairy. He had never seen the Great Lion. He had never seen a common lion. He couldn't be sure that what he saw was not the real Aslan. He had not expected Aslan to look like that stiff thing which stood and said nothing. But how could one be sure? For a moment horrible thoughts went through his mind: then he remembered

the nonsense about Tash and Aslan being the same and knew that the whole thing must be a cheat.

The Ape put his head close up to the yellow thing's head as if he were listening to something it was whispering to him. Then he turned and spoke to the crowd, and the crowd wailed again. Then the yellow thing turned clumsily round and walked – you might almost say, waddled – back into the stable and the Ape shut the door behind it. After that the fire must have been put out for the light vanished quite suddenly, and Tirian was once more alone with the cold and the darkness.

He thought of other Kings who had lived and died in Narnia in old times and it seemed to him that none of them had ever been so unlucky as himself. He thought of his great-grandfather's great-grandfather King Rilian who had been stolen away by a Witch when he was only a young prince and kept hidden for years in the dark caves beneath the land of the Northern Giants. But then it had all come right in the end, for two mysterious children had suddenly appeared from the land beyond the world's end and had rescued him so that he came home to Narnia and had a long and prosperous reign. "It's not like that with me," said Tirian to himself. Then he went further back and thought about Rilian's father, Caspian the Seafarer, whose wicked uncle King Miraz had tried to murder him and how Caspian had fled away into the woods and lived among the Dwarfs. But that story too had all come right in the end: for Caspian also had been helped by children – only there were four of them that time – who came from somewhere beyond the world and fought a great battle and set him on his father's throne. "But it was all long ago," said Tirian to himself. "That sort of thing doesn't happen now." And then he remembered (for he had always been good at history when he was a boy) how those same four children who had helped Caspian had been in Narnia over a thousand years before; and it was then that they had done the most remarkable thing of all. For then they had defeated the terrible White Witch and ended the Hundred Years of Winter, and after that they had reigned (all four of them together) at Cair Paravel, till they were no longer children but great Kings and lovely Queens, and their reign had been the golden age of Narnia. And Aslan had come into that story a lot. He had come into all the other stories too, as Tirian now remembered. "Aslan – and children from another world," thought Tirian. "They have always come in when things were at their worst. Oh, if only they could now."

And he called out "Aslan! Aslan! Aslan! Come and help us now."

But the darkness and the cold and the quietness went on just the same.

"Let *me* be killed," cried the King. "I ask nothing for myself. But come and save all Narnia."

And still there was no change in the night or the wood, but there began to be a kind of change inside Tirian. Without knowing why, he began to feel a faint hope. And he felt somehow stronger. "Oh Aslan, Aslan," he whispered. "If you will not come yourself, at least send me the helpers from beyond the world. Or let me call them. Let my voice carry beyond the world." Then, hardly knowing that he was doing it, he suddenly cried out in a great voice:

"Children! Children! Friends of Narnia! Quick. Come to me. Across the worlds I call you; I Tirian, King of Narnia, Lord of Cair Paravel, and Emperor of the Lone Islands!"

And immediately he was plunged into a dream (if it was a dream) more vivid than any he had had in his life.

He seemed to be standing in a lighted room where seven people sat round a table. It looked as if they had just finished their meal. Two of those people were very old, an old man with a white beard and an old woman with wise, merry, twinkling eyes. He who sat at the right hand of the old man was hardly full grown, certainly younger than Tirian himself, but his face had already the look of a king and a warrior. And you could almost say the same of the other youth who sat at the right hand of the old woman. Facing Tirian across the table sat a fair-haired girl younger than either of these, and on either side of her a boy and girl who were younger still. They were all dressed in what seemed to Tirian the oddest kind of clothes.

But he had no time to think about details like that, for instantly the younger boy and both the girls started to their feet, and one of them gave a little scream. The old woman started and drew in her breath sharply. The old man must have made some sudden movement too for the wine glass which stood at his right hand was swept off the table: Tirian could hear the tinkling noise as it broke on the floor.

Then Tirian realized that these people could see him; they were staring at him as if they saw a ghost. But he noticed that the king-like one who sat at the old man's right never moved (though he turned pale) except that he clenched his hand very tight. Then he said:

"Speak, if you're not a phantom or a dream. You have a Narnian look about you and we are the seven friends of Narnia."

Tirian was longing to speak, and he tried to cry out aloud that he was Tirian of Narnia, in great need of help. But he found (as I have sometimes found in dreams too) that his voice made no noise at all.

The one who had already spoken to him rose to his feet. "Shadow or spirit or whatever you are," he said, fixing his eyes full upon Tirian. "If you are from Narnia, I charge you in the name of Aslan, speak to me. I am Peter the High King."

The room began to swim before Tirian's eyes. He heard the voices of those seven people all speaking at once, and all getting fainter every second, and they were saying things like, "Look! It's fading." "It's melting away." "It's vanishing." Next moment he was wide awake, still tied to the tree, colder and stiffer than ever. The wood was full of the pale, dreary light that comes before sunrise, and he was soaking wet with dew; it was nearly morning.

That waking was about the worst moment he had ever had in his life.

CHAPTER FIVE

HOW HELP CAME TO THE KING

BUT his misery did not last long. Almost at once there came a bump, and then a second bump, and two children were standing before him. The wood in front of him had been quite empty a second before and he knew they had not come from behind his tree, for he would have heard them. They had in fact simply appeared from nowhere. He saw at a glance that they were wearing the same queer, dingy sort of clothes as the people in his dream; and he saw, at a second glance, that they were the youngest boy and girl out of that party of seven.

"Gosh!" said the boy, "that took one's breath away! I thought—"

"Hurry up and get him untied," said the girl. "We can talk, afterwards." Then she added, turning to Tirian, "I'm sorry we've been so long. We came the moment we could."

While she was speaking the Boy produced a knife from his pocket and was quickly cutting the King's bonds: too quickly, in fact, for the King was so stiff and numb that when the last cord was cut he fell forward on his hands and knees. He couldn't get up again till he had brought some life back into his legs by a good rubbing.

"I say," said the girl. "It was you, wasn't it, who appeared to us that night when we were all at supper? Nearly a week ago."

"A week, fair maid?" said Tirian. "My dream led me into your world scarce ten minutes since."

"It's the usual muddle about times, Pole," said the Boy.

"I remember now," said Tirian. "That too comes in all the old tales. The time of your strange land is different from ours. But if we speak of Time, 'tis time to be gone from here: for my enemies are close at hand. Will you come with me?"

"Of course," said the girl. "It's you we've come to help."

Tirian got to his feet and led them rapidly down hill, Southward and away from the stable. He knew where he meant to go but his first aim was to get to rocky places where they would leave no trail, and his second to cross some water so that they would leave no scent. This took them about an hour's scrambling and wading and while that was going on nobody had any breath to talk. But even so, Tirian kept on stealing glances at his companions. The wonder of walking beside the creatures from another world made him feel a little dizzy: but it also made all the old stories seem far more real than they had ever seemed before . . . anything might happen now.

"Now," said Tirian as they came to the head of a little valley which ran down before them among young birch trees, "we are out of danger of those villains for a space and may walk more easily." The sun had risen, dew-drops were twinkling on every branch, and birds were singing.

"What about some grub? – I mean for you, Sir, we two have had our breakfast," said the Boy.

Tirian wondered very much what he meant by "grub", but when the Boy opened a bulgy satchel which he was carrying and pulled out a rather greasy and squashy packet, he understood. He was ravenously hungry, though he hadn't thought about it till that moment. There were two hard-boiled egg sandwiches, and two cheese sandwiches, and two with some kind of paste in them. If he hadn't been so hungry he wouldn't have thought much of the paste, for that is a sort of food nobody eats in Narnia. By the time he had eaten all six sandwiches they had come

to the bottom of the valley and there they found a mossy cliff with a little fountain bubbling out of it. All three stopped and drank and splashed their hot faces.

"And now," said the girl as she tossed her wet hair back from her forehead, "aren't you going to tell us who you are and why you were tied up and what it's all about?"

"With a good will, damsel," said Tirian. "But we must keep on the march." So while they went on walking he told them who he was and all the things that had happened to him. "And now," he said at the end, "I am going to a certain tower, one of three that were built in my grandsire's time to guard Lantern Waste against certain perilous outlaws who dwelled there in his day. By Aslan's good will I was not robbed of my keys. In that tower we shall find stores of weapons and mail and some victuals also, though no better than dry biscuit. There also we can lie safe while we make our plans. And now, prithee, tell me who you two are and all your story."

"I'm Eustace Scrubb and this is Jill Pole," said the Boy. "And we were here once before, ages and ages ago, more than a year ago by our time, and there was a chap called Prince Rilian, and they were keeping this chap underground, and Puddleglum put his foot in –"

"Ha!" cried Tirian, "are you then that Eustace and that Jill who rescued King Rilian from his long enchantment?"

"Yes, that's us," said Jill. "So he's *King* Rilian now, is he? Oh of course he would be. I forgot –"

"Nay," said Tirian, "I am the seventh in descent from him. He has been dead over two hundred years."

Jill made a face. "Ugh!" she said. "That's the horrid part about coming back to Narnia." But Eustace went on.

"Well now you know who we are, Sire," he said. "And it was like this. The Professor and Aunt Polly had got all us friends of Narnia together –"

"I know not these names, Eustace," said Tirian.

"They're the two who came into Narnia at the very beginning, the day all the animals learned to talk."

"By the Lion's Mane," cried Tirian. "Those two! The Lord Digory and the Lady Polly! From the dawn of the world! And still in your place? The wonder and the glory of it! But tell me, tell me."

"She isn't really our aunt, you know," said Eustace. "She's Miss Plummer, but we call her Aunt Polly. Well those two got us all together partly just for fun, so that we could all have a good jaw about Narnia (for of course there's no one else we can ever talk to about things like that) but partly because the Professor had a feeling that we were somehow wanted over here. Well then you came in like a ghost or goodness-knows-what and nearly frightened the lives out of us and vanished without saying a word. After that, we knew for certain there was something up.

The next question was how to get here. You can't go just by wanting to. So we talked and talked and at last the Professor said the only way would be by the Magic Rings. It was by those Rings that he and Aunt Polly got here long, long ago when they were only kids, years before we younger ones were born. But the Rings had all been buried in the garden of a house in London (that's our big town, Sire) and the house had been sold. So then the problem was how to get at them. You'll never guess what we did in the end! Peter and Edmund – that's the High King Peter, the one who spoke to you – went up to London to get into the garden from the back, early in the morning before people were up. They were dressed like workmen so that if anyone did see them it would look as if they'd come to do something about the drains. I wish I'd been with them: it must have been glorious fun. And they must have succeeded for next day Peter sent us a wire – that's a sort of message, Sire, I'll explain about it some other time – to say he'd got the Rings. And the day after that was the day Pole and I had to go back to school – we're the only two who are still at school and we're at the same one. So Peter and Edmund were to meet us at a place on the way down to school and hand over the Rings. It had to be us two who were to go to Narnia, you see, because the older ones couldn't come again. So we got into the train – that's a kind of thing people travel in in our world: a lot of wagons chained together – and the Professor and Aunt Polly and Lucy came with us. We wanted to keep together as long as we could. Well there we were in the train. And we were just getting to the station where the others were to meet us, and I was looking out of the window to see if I could see them when suddenly there came a most frightful jerk and a noise: and there we

were in Narnia and there was your Majesty tied up to the tree."

"So you never used the Rings?" said Tirian.

"No," said Eustace. "Never even saw them. Aslan did it all for us in his own way without any Rings."

"But the High King Peter has them," said Tirian.

"Yes," said Jill. "But we don't think he can use them. When the two other Pevensies — King Edmund and Queen Lucy — were last here, Aslan said they would never come to Narnia again. And he said something of the same sort to the High King, only longer ago. You may be sure he'll come like a shot if he's allowed."

"Gosh!" said Eustace. "It's getting hot in this sun. Are we nearly there, Sire?"

"Look," said Tirian and pointed. Not many yards away grey battlements rose above the tree-tops, and after a minute's more walking they came out in an open grassy space. A stream ran across it and on the far side of the stream stood a squat, square tower with very few and narrow windows and one heavy-looking door in the wall that faced them.

Tirian looked sharply this way and that to make sure that no enemies were in sight. Then he walked up to the tower and stood still for a moment fishing up his bunch of keys which he wore inside his hunting-dress on a narrow silver chain that went round his neck. It was a nice bunch of keys that he brought out, for two were golden and many were richly ornamented: you could see at once that they were keys made for opening solemn and secret rooms in palaces, or chests and caskets of sweet-smelling wood that contained royal treasures. But the key which he now put into the lock of the door was big and plain and more rudely made. The lock was stiff and for a moment Tirian began to be afraid that he would not be able to turn it: but at last he did and the door swung open with a sullen creak.

"Welcome friends," said Tirian. "I fear this is the best palace that the King of Narnia can now offer to his guests."

Tirian was pleased to see that the two strangers had been well brought up. They both said not to mention it and that they were sure it would be very nice.

As a matter of fact it was not particularly nice. It was rather dark and smelled very damp. There was only one room in it and this room went right up to the stone roof: a wooden staircase in one corner led up to a trap door by which you could get out on the battlements. There were a few rude bunks to sleep in, and a great many lockers and bundles. There was also a hearth which looked as if nobody had lit a fire in it for a great many years.

"We'd better go out and gather some firewood first thing, hadn't we?" said Jill.

"Not yet, comrade," said Tirian. He was determined that they should not be caught unarmed, and began searching the lockers, thankfully remembering that he had always been careful to have these garrison towers inspected once a year and to make sure that they were stocked with all things needful. The bow strings were there in their coverings of oiled silk, the swords and spears were greased against rust, and the armour was kept bright in its wrappings. But there was something even better. "Look you!" said Tirian as he drew out a long mail shirt of a curious pattern and flashed it before the children's eyes.

"That's funny-looking mail, Sire," said Eustace.

"Aye, lad," said Tirian. "No Narnian Dwarf smithied that. 'Tis mail of Calormen, outlandish gear. I have ever kept a few suits of it in readiness, for I never knew when I or my friends might have reason to walk unseen in The Tisroc's land. And look on this stone bottle. In this there is a juice which, when we have rubbed it on our hands and faces, will make us brown as Calormenes."

"Oh hurrah!" said Jill. "Disguise! I love disguises."

Tirian showed them how to pour out a little of the juice into the palms of their hands and then rub it well over their faces and necks, right down to the shoulders, and then on their hands, right up to the elbows. He did the same himself.

"After this has hardened on us," he said, "we may wash in water and it will not change. Nothing but oil and ashes will make us white Narnians again. And now, sweet Jill, let us go see how this mail shirt becomes you. 'Tis something too long, yet not so much as I feared. Doubtless it belonged to a page in the train of one of their Tarkaans."

After the mail shirts they put on Calormene helmets, which are little round ones fitting tight to the head and having a spike on top. Then Tirian took long rolls of some white stuff out of the locker and wound them over the helmets till they became turbans: but the little steel spike still stuck up in the middle. He and Eustace took curved Calormene swords and little round shields. There was no sword light enough for Jill, but he gave her a long, straight hunting knife which might do for a sword at a pinch.

"Hast any skill with the bow, maiden?" said Tirian.

"Nothing worth talking of," said Jill, blushing. "Scrubb's not bad."

"Don't you believe her, Sire," said Eustace. "We've both been practising archery ever since we got back from Narnia last time, and she's about as good as me now. Not that either of us is much."

Then Tirian gave Jill a bow and a quiver full of arrows. The next business was to light a fire, for inside that tower it still felt more like a cave than like anything indoors and set one shivering. But they got warm gathering wood – the sun was now at its highest – and once the blaze was roaring up the chimney the place began to look cheerful. Dinner was, however, a dull meal, for the best they could do was to pound up some of the hard biscuit which they found in a locker and pour it into boiling water, with salt, so as to make a kind of porridge. And of course there was nothing to drink but water.

"I wish we'd brought a packet of tea," said Jill.

"Or a tin of cocoa," said Eustace.

"A firkin or so of good wine in each of these towers would not have been amiss," said Tirian.

CHAPTER SIX

A GOOD NIGHT'S WORK

ABOUT four hours later Tirian flung himself into one of the bunks to snatch a little sleep. The two children were already snoring: he had made them go to bed before he did because they would have to be up most of the night and he knew that at their age they couldn't do without sleep. Also, he had tired them out. First he had given Jill some practice in archery and found that, though not up to Narnian standards, she was really not too bad. Indeed she had succeeded in shooting a rabbit (not a *Talking* rabbit, of course: there are lots of the ordinary kind about in Western Narnia) and it was already skinned, cleaned, and hanging up. He had found that both the children knew all about this chilly and smelly job; they had learned that kind of thing on their great journey through Giant-Land in the days of Prince Rilian. Then he had tried to teach Eustace how to use his sword and shield. Eustace had learned quite a lot about sword fighting on his earlier adventures but that had been all with a straight Narnian sword. He had never handled a curved Calormene scimitar and that made it hard, for many of the strokes are quite different and some of the habits he had learned with the long sword had now to be unlearned again. But Tirian found that he had a good eye and was very quick on his feet. He was surprised at the strength of both children: in fact they both seemed to be already much stronger and bigger and more grown-up than they had been when he first met them a few hours ago. It is one of the effects which Narnian air often has on visitors from our world.

All three of them agreed that the very first thing they

must do was to go back to Stable Hill and try to rescue Jewel the Unicorn. After that, if they succeeded, they would try to get away Eastward and meet the little army which Roonwit the Centaur would be bringing from Cair Paravel.

An experienced warrior and huntsman like Tirian can always wake up at the time he wants. So he gave himself till nine o'clock that night and then put all worries out of his head and fell asleep at once. It seemed only a moment later when he woke but he knew by the light and the very feel of things that he had timed his sleep exactly. He got up, put on his helmet-and-turban (he had slept in his mail shirt), and then shook the other two till they woke up. They looked, to tell the truth, very grey and dismal as they climbed out of their bunks and there was a good deal of yawning.

"Now," said Tirian, "we go due North from here – by good fortune 'tis a starry night – and it will be much shorter than our journey this morning, for then we went round-about but now we shall go straight. If we are challenged, then do you two hold your peace and I will do my best to talk like a curst, cruel, proud lord of Calormen. If I draw my sword then thou, Eustace, must do likewise and let Jill leap behind us and stand with an arrow on the string. But if I cry 'Home', then fly for the Tower both of you. And let none try to fight on – not even one stroke – after I have given the retreat: such false valour has spoiled many notable plans in the wars. And now, friends, in the name of Aslan let us go forward."

Out they went into the cold night. All the great Northern stars were burning above the tree-tops. The North-Star of that world is called the Spear-Head: it is brighter than our Pole Star.

For a time they could go straight towards the Spear-Head but presently they came to a dense thicket so that they had to go out of their course to get round it. And after that – for they were still overshadowed by branches – it was hard to pick up their bearings. It was Jill who set them right again: she had been an excellent Guide in England. And of course she knew her Narnian stars perfectly, having travelled so much in the wild Northern Lands, and could work out the direction from other stars even when the Spear-Head was hidden. As soon as Tirian saw that she was the best pathfinder of the three of them he put her in front. And then he was astonished to find how silently and almost invisibly she glided on before them.

"By the Mane!" he whispered to Eustace. "This girl is a wondrous wood-maid. If she had Dryad's blood in her she could scarce do it better."

"She's so small, that's what helps," whispered Eustace. But Jill from in front said: "S-s-s-h, less noise."

All round them the wood was very quiet. Indeed it was far too quiet. On an ordinary Narnia night there ought to have been noises – an occasional cheery "Goodnight" from a Hedgehog, the cry of an Owl overhead, perhaps a flute in the distance to tell of Fauns dancing, or some throbbing, hammering noises from Dwarfs underground. All that was silenced: gloom and fear reigned over Narnia.

After a time they began to go steeply uphill and the trees grew further apart. Tirian could dimly make out the well-known hill-top and the stable. Jill was now going with more and more caution: she kept on making signs to the others with her hand to do the same. Then she stopped dead still and Tirian saw her gradually sink down into the grass and disappear without a sound. A moment later she rose again, put her mouth close to Tirian's ear, and said in

the lowest possible whisper, "Get down. *Thee* better." She
said *thee* for *see* not because she had a lisp but because she
knew the hissing letter S is the part of a whisper most likely
to be overheard. Tirian at once lay down, almost as silently
as Jill, but not quite, for he was heavier and older. And
once they were down, he saw how from that position you
could see the edge of the hill sharp against the star-strewn
sky. Two black shapes rose against it: one was the stable,
and the other, a few feet in front of it, was a Calormene
sentry. He was keeping very ill watch: not walking or even
standing but sitting with his spear over his shoulder and his
chin on his chest. "Well done," said Tirian to Jill. She had
shown him exactly what he needed to know.

They got up and Tirian now took the lead. Very slowly,
hardly daring to breathe, they made their way up to a little
clump of trees which was not more than forty feet away
from the sentinel.

"Wait here till I come again," he whispered to the other
two. "If I miscarry, fly." Then he sauntered out boldly in
full view of the enemy. The man started when he saw him

and was just going to jump to his feet: he was afraid Tirian might be one of his own officers and that he would get into trouble for sitting down. But before he could get up Tirian had dropped on one knee beside him, saying:

"Art thou a warrior of the Tisroc's, may he live for ever? It cheers my heart to meet thee among all these beasts and devils of Narnians. Give me thy hand, friend."

Before he well knew what was happening the Calormene sentry found his right hand seized in a mighty grip. Next instant someone was kneeling on his legs and a dagger was pressed against his neck.

"One noise and thou art dead," said Tirian in his ear. "Tell me where the Unicorn is and thou shalt live."

"B – behind the stable, O My Master," stammered the unfortunate man.

"Good. Rise up and lead me to him."

As the man got up the point of the dagger never left his neck. It only travelled round (cold and rather ticklish) as Tirian got behind him and settled it at a convenient place under his ear. Trembling he went round to the back of the stable.

Though it was dark Tirian could see the white shape of Jewel at once.

"Hush!" he said. "No, do not neigh. Yes, Jewel, it is I. How have they tied thee?"

"Hobbled by all four legs and tied with a bridle to a ring in the stable wall," came Jewel's voice.

"Stand here, sentry, with your back to the wall. So. Now, Jewel: set the point of your horn against this Calormene's breast."

"With a good will, Sire," said Jewel.

"If he moves, rive him to the heart." Then in a few seconds Tirian cut the ropes. With the remains of them he bound the sentry hand and foot. Finally he made him open his mouth, stuffed it full of grass and tied him up from scalp to chin so that he could make no noise, lowered the man into a sitting position and set him against the wall.

"I have done thee some discourtesy, soldier," said Tirian. "But such was my need. If we meet again I may happen to do thee a better turn. Now, Jewel, let us go softly."

He put his left arm round the beast's neck and bent and kissed its nose and both had great joy. They went back as quietly as possible to the place where he had left the children. It was darker in there under the trees and he nearly ran into Eustace before he saw him.

"All's well," whispered Tirian. "A good night's work. Now for home."

They turned and had gone a few paces when Eustace said, "Where are you, Pole?" There was no answer. "Is Jill on the other side of you, Sire?" he asked.

"What?" said Tirian. "Is she not on the other side of you?"

It was a terrible moment. They dared not shout but they whispered her name in the loudest whisper they could manage. There was no reply.

"Did she go from you while I was away?" asked Tirian.

"I didn't see or hear her go," said Eustace. "But she could have gone without my knowing. She can be as quiet as a cat; you've seen for yourself."

At that moment a far off drum beat was heard. Jewel moved his ears forward. "Dwarfs," he said.

"And treacherous Dwarfs, enemies, as likely as not," muttered Tirian.

"And here comes something on hoofs, much nearer," said Jewel.

The two humans and the Unicorn stood dead still. There were now so many different things to worry about that they didn't know what to do. The noise of hoofs came steadily nearer. And then, quite close to them, a voice whispered:

"Hallo! Are you all there?"

Thank heaven, it was Jill's.

"Where the *devil* have you been to?" said Eustace in a furious whisper, for he had been very frightened.

"In the stable," gasped Jill, but it was the sort of gasp you give when you're struggling with suppressed laughter.

"Oh," growled Eustace, "you think it funny, do you? Well all I can say is –"

"Have you got Jewel, Sire?" asked Jill.

"Yes. Here he is. What is that beast with you?"

"That's *him*," said Jill. "But let's be off home before anyone wakes up." And again there came little explosions of laughter.

The others obeyed at once for they had already lingered long enough in that dangerous place and the Dwarf drums seemed to have come a little nearer. It was only after they had been walking Southward for several minutes that Eustace said:

"Got *him*? What do you mean?"

"The false Aslan," said Jill.

"What?" said Tirian. "Where have you been? What have you done?"

"Well, Sire," said Jill. "As soon as I saw that you'd got the sentry out of the way I thought hadn't I better have a look inside the stable and see what really *is* there? So I crawled along. It was as easy as anything to draw the bolt.

Of course it was pitch black inside and smelled like any other stable. Then I struck a light and — would you believe it? — there was nothing at all there but this old donkey with a bundle of lion-skin tied on to his back. So I drew my knife and told him he'd have to come along with me. As a matter of fact I needn't have threatened him with the knife at all. He was very fed up with the stable and quite ready to come — weren't you, Puzzle dear?"

"Great Scott!" said Eustace. "Well I'm — jiggered. I was jolly angry with you a moment ago, and I still think it was mean of you to sneak off without the rest of us: but I must admit — well, I mean to say — well it was a perfectly gorgeous thing to do. If she was a boy she'd have to be knighted, wouldn't she, Sire?"

"If she was a boy," said Tirian, "she'd be whipped for disobeying orders." And in the dark no one could see whether he said this with a frown or a smile. Next minute there was a sound of rasping metal.

"What are you doing, Sire?" asked Jewel sharply.

"Drawing my sword to smite off the head of the accursed Ass," said Tirian in a terrible voice. "Stand clear, girl."

"Oh don't, please don't," said Jill. "Really, you mustn't. It wasn't his fault. It was all the Ape. He didn't know any better. And he's very sorry. And he's a nice Donkey. His name's Puzzle. And I've got my arms round his neck."

"Jill," said Tirian, "you are the bravest and most wood-wise of all my subjects, but also the most malapert and disobedient. Well: let the Ass live. What have you to say for yourself, Ass?"

"Me, Sire?" came the Donkey's voice. "I'm sure I'm very sorry if I've done wrong. The Ape said Aslan *wanted* me to dress up like that. And I thought he'd know. I'm not clever like him. I only did what I was told. It wasn't any fun for me living in that stable. I don't even know what's been going on outside. He never let me out except for a minute or two at night. Some days they forgot to give me any water too."

"Sire," said Jewel. "Those Dwarfs are coming nearer and nearer. Do we want to meet them?"

Tirian thought for a moment and then suddenly gave a great laugh out loud. Then he spoke, not this time in a whisper. "By the Lion," he said, "I am growing slow witted! Meet them? Certainly we will meet them. We will meet anyone now. We have this Ass to show them. Let them see the thing they have feared and bowed to. We can show them the truth of the Ape's vile plot. His secret's out. The tide's turned. Tomorrow we shall hang that Ape on the highest tree in Narnia. No more whispering and skulking and disguises. Where are these honest Dwarfs? We have good news for them."

When you have been whispering for hours the mere sound of anyone talking out loud has a wonderfully stirring effect. The whole party began talking and laughing: even Puzzle lifted up his head and gave a grand Haw-hee-haw-hee-hee; a thing the Ape hadn't allowed him

to do for days. Then they set off in the direction of the drumming. It grew steadily louder and soon they could see torchlight as well. They came out on one of those rough roads (we should hardly call them roads at all in England) which ran through Lantern Waste. And there, marching sturdily along, were about thirty Dwarfs, all with their little spades and mattocks over their shoulders. Two armed Calormenes led the column and two more brought up the rear.

"Stay!" thundered Tirian as he stepped out on the road. "Stay, soldiers. Whither do you lead these Narnian Dwarfs and by whose orders?"

CHAPTER SEVEN

MAINLY ABOUT DWARFS

THE two Calormene soldiers at the head of the column, seeing what they took for a Tarkaan or great lord with two armed pages, came to a halt and raised their spears in salute.

"O My Master," said one of them, "we lead these manikins to Calormen to work in the mines of The Tisroc, may-he-live-forever."

"By the great god Tash, they are very obedient," said Tirian. Then suddenly he turned to the Dwarfs themselves. About one in six of them carried a torch and by that flickering light he could see their bearded faces all looking at him with grim and dogged expressions. "Has The Tisroc fought a great battle, Dwarfs, and conquered your land?" he asked, "that thus you go patiently to die in the salt-pits of Pugrahan?"

The two soldiers glared at him in surprise but the Dwarfs all answered, "Aslan's orders, Aslan's orders. He's sold us. What can we do against *him*?"

"Tisroc indeed!" added one and spat. "I'd like to see him try it!"

"Silence, dogs!" said the chief soldier.

"Look!" said Tirian, pulling Puzzle forward into the light. "It has all been a lie. Aslan has not come to Narnia at all. You have been cheated by the Ape. This is the thing he brought out of the stable to show you. Look at it."

What the Dwarfs saw, now that they could see it close, was certainly enough to make them wonder how they had ever been taken in. The lion-skin had got pretty untidy already during Puzzle's imprisonment in the stable and it had been knocked crooked during his journey through the dark wood. Most of it was in a big lump on one shoulder. The head, besides being pushed sideways, had somehow got very far back so that anyone could now see his silly, gentle, donkeyish face gazing out of it. Some grass stuck out of one corner of his mouth, for he'd been doing a little

quiet nibbling as they brought him along. And he was muttering, "It wasn't my fault, I'm not clever. I never said I *was*."

For one second all the Dwarfs were staring at Puzzle with wide open mouths and then one of the soldiers said sharply, "Are you mad, My Master? What are you doing to the slaves?" and the other said, "And who are you?" Neither of their spears was at the salute now – both were down and ready for action.

"Give the password," said the chief soldier.

"This is my password," said the King as he drew his sword. "*The light is dawning, the lie broken.* Now guard thee, miscreant, for I am Tirian of Narnia."

He flew upon the chief soldier like lightning. Eustace, who had drawn his sword when he saw the King draw his, rushed at the other one: his face was deadly pale, but I wouldn't blame him for that. And he had the luck that beginners sometimes do have. He forgot all that Tirian had tried to teach him that afternoon, slashed wildly (indeed I'm not sure his eyes weren't shut) and suddenly found, to his own great surprise, that the Calormene lay dead at his feet. And though that was a great relief, it was, at the moment, rather frightening. The King's fight lasted a second or two longer: then he too had killed his man and shouted to Eustace, "'Ware the other two."

But the Dwarfs had settled the two remaining Calormenes. There was no enemy left.

"Well struck, Eustace!" cried Tirian, clapping him on the back. "Now, Dwarfs, you are free. Tomorrow I will lead you to free all Narnia. Three cheers for Aslan!"

But the result which followed was simply wretched. There was a feeble attempt from a few Dwarfs (about five) which died away all at once: from several others there were sulky growls. Many said nothing at all.

"Don't they understand?" said Jill impatiently. "What's wrong with all you Dwarfs? Don't you hear what the King says? It's all over. The Ape isn't going to rule Narnia any longer. Everyone can go back to ordinary life. You can have fun again. Aren't you glad?"

After a pause of nearly a minute a not-very-nice-looking Dwarf with hair and beard as black as soot said: "And who might you be, Missie?"

"I'm Jill," she said. "The same Jill who rescued King

Rilian from the enchantment —
and this is Eustace who did it too
— and we've come back from
another world after hundreds of
years. Aslan sent us."

The Dwarfs all looked at one
another with grins; sneering
grins, not merry ones.

"Well," said the Black Dwarf
(whose name was Griffle), "I
don't know how all you chaps
feel, but I feel I've heard as much
about Aslan as I want to for the
rest of my life."

"That's right, that's right," growled the other Dwarfs.
"It's all a plant, all a blooming plant."

"What do you mean?" said Tirian. He had not been pale
when he was fighting but he was pale now. He had thought
this was going to be a beautiful moment, but it was turning
out more like a bad dream.

"You must think we're blooming soft in the head, that
you must," said Griffle. "We've been taken in once and
now you expect us to be taken in again the next minute.
We've no more use for stories about Aslan, see! Look at
him! An old moke with long ears!"

"By heaven, you make me mad," said Tirian. "Which
of us said *that* was Aslan? That is the Ape's imitation of the real Aslan. Can't you understand?"

"And you've got a better imitation, I suppose!" said
Griffle. "No thanks. We've been fooled once and we're not
going to be fooled again."

"I have not," said Tirian angrily, "I serve the real
Aslan."

"Where's he? Who's he? Show him to us!" said several Dwarfs.

"Do you think I keep him in my wallet, fools?" said Tirian. "Who am I that I could make Aslan appear at my bidding? He's not a tame lion."

The moment those words were out of his mouth he realized that he had made a false move. The Dwarfs at once began repeating "not a tame lion, not a tame lion," in a jeering sing-song. "That's what the other lot kept on telling us," said one.

"Do you mean you don't believe in the real Aslan?" said Jill. "But I've seen him. And he has sent us two here out of a different world."

"Ah," said Griffle with a broad smile. "So *you* say. They've taught you your stuff all right. Saying your lessons, ain't you?"

"Churl," cried Tirian, "will you give a lady the lie to her very face?"

"You keep a civil tongue in your head, Mister," replied the Dwarf. "I don't think we want any more Kings – if you *are* Tirian, which you don't look like him – no more than we want any Aslans. We're going to look after ourselves from now on and touch our caps to nobody. See?"

"That's right," said the other Dwarfs. "We're on our own now. No more Aslan, no more Kings, no more silly stories about other worlds. The Dwarfs are for the Dwarfs." And they began to fall into their places and to get ready for marching back to wherever they had come from.

"Little beasts!" said Eustace. "Aren't you even going to say *thank you* for being saved from the salt-mines?"

"Oh, we know all about that," said Griffle over his shoulder. "You wanted to make use of us, that's why you rescued us. You're playing some game of your own. Come on you chaps."

And the Dwarfs struck up the queer little marching song which goes with the drum-beat, and off they tramped into the darkness.

Tirian and his friends stared after them. Then he said the single word "Come," and they continued their journey.

They were a silent party. Puzzle felt himself to be still in disgrace, and also he didn't really quite understand what had happened. Jill, besides being disgusted with the Dwarfs, was very impressed with Eustace's victory over the Calormene and felt almost shy. As for Eustace, his heart was still beating rather quickly. Tirian and Jewel walked sadly together in the rear. The King had his arm on the Unicorn's shoulder and sometimes the Unicorn nuzzled the King's cheek with his soft nose. They did not try to comfort one another with words. It wasn't very easy to think of anything to say that would be comforting. Tirian had never dreamed that one of the results of an Ape's setting up as a false Aslan would be to stop people from believing in the real one. He had felt quite sure that the Dwarfs would rally to his side the moment he showed them how they had been deceived. And then next night he would have led them to Stable Hill and shown Puzzle to all the creatures and everyone would have turned against the Ape and, perhaps after a scuffle with the Calormenes, the whole thing would have been over. But now, it seemed, he could count on nothing. How many other Narnians might turn the same way as the Dwarfs?

"Somebody's coming after us, I think," said Puzzle suddenly.

They stopped and listened. Sure enough, there was a thump-thump of small feet behind them.

"Who goes there!" shouted the King.

"Only me, Sire," came a voice. "Me, Poggin the Dwarf. I've only just managed to get away from the others. I'm on your side, Sire: and on Aslan's. If you can put a Dwarfish sword in my fist, I'd gladly strike a blow on the right side before all's done."

Everyone crowded round him and welcomed him and praised him and slapped him on the back. Of course one single Dwarf could not make a very great difference, but it was somehow very cheering to have even one. The whole party brightened up. But Jill and Eustace didn't stay bright for very long, for they were now yawning their heads off and too tired to think about anything but bed.

It was at the coldest hour of the night, just before dawn, that they got back to the Tower. If there had been a meal ready for them they would have been glad enough to eat, but the bother and delay of getting one was not to be thought of. They drank from a stream, splashed their faces with water, and tumbled into their bunks, except for Puzzle and Jewel who said they'd be more comfortable outside. This perhaps was just as well, for a Unicorn and a fat, full-grown Donkey indoors always make a room feel rather crowded.

Narnian Dwarfs, though less than four feet high, are for their size about the toughest and strongest creatures there are, so that Poggin, in spite of a heavy day and a late night, woke fully refreshed before any of the others. He at once took Jill's bow, went out and shot a couple of wood pigeons. Then he sat plucking them on the doorstep and chatting to Jewel and Puzzle. Puzzle looked and felt a good deal better this morning. Jewel, being a Unicorn and therefore one of the noblest and delicatest of beasts, had been very kind to him, talking to him about things of the sort they could both understand like grass and sugar and the care of one's hoofs. When Jill and Eustace came out of the Tower yawning and rubbing their eyes at almost half past ten, the Dwarf showed them where they could gather plenty of a Narnian weed called Wild Fresney, which looks rather like our wood-sorrel but tastes a good deal nicer when cooked. (It needs a little butter and pepper to make it perfect, but they hadn't got these.) So that what with one thing and another, they had the makings of a capital stew for their breakfast or dinner, whichever you choose to call it. Tirian went a little further off into the wood with an axe and brought back some branches for fuel. While the meal was cooking – which seemed a very long time, especially as it smelled nicer and nicer the nearer it came to being done – the King found a complete Dwarfish outfit for Poggin: mail shirt, helmet, shield, sword, belt, and dagger. Then he inspected Eustace's sword and found that Eustace had put it back in the sheath all messy from killing the Calormene. He was scolded for that and made to clean and polish it.

All this while Jill went to and fro, sometimes stirring the pot and sometimes looking out enviously at the Donkey and the Unicorn who were contentedly grazing. How many times that morning she wished she could eat grass!

But when the meal came everyone felt it had been worth waiting for, and there were second helpings all round. When everyone had eaten as much as he could, the three humans and the Dwarf came and sat on the doorstep, the four-footed ones lay down facing them, the Dwarf (with permission both from Jill and from Tirian) lit his pipe, and the King said:

"Now, friend Poggin, you have more news of the enemy, belike, than we. Tell us all you know. And first, what tale do they tell of my escape?"

"As cunning a tale, Sire, as ever was devised," said Poggin. "It was the Cat, Ginger, who told it, and most likely made it up too. This Ginger, Sire – oh, he's a sly-boots if ever a cat was – said he was walking past the tree to which those villains bound your Majesty. And he said (saving your reverence) that you were howling and swearing and cursing Aslan: 'language I wouldn't like to repeat' were the words he used, looking ever so prim and proper – you know the way a Cat can when it pleases. And then, says Ginger, Aslan himself suddenly appeared in a flash of lightning and swallowed your Majesty up at one mouthful. All the Beasts trembled at this story and some fainted right away. And of course the Ape followed it up. There, he says, see what Aslan does to those who don't respect him. Let that be a warning to you all. And the poor creatures wailed and whined and said, it will, it will. So that in the upshot your Majesty's escape has not set them thinking whether you still have loyal friends to aid you, but only made them more afraid and more obedient to the Ape."

"What devilish policy!" said Tirian. "This Ginger, then, is close in the Ape's counsels."

"It's more a question by now, Sire, if the Ape is in *his* counsels," replied the Dwarf. "The Ape has taken to drinking, you see. My belief is that the plot is now mostly carried on by Ginger or Rishda – that's the Calormene captain. And I think some words that Ginger has scattered among the Dwarfs are chiefly to blame for the scurvy return they made you. And I'll tell you why. One of those dreadful midnight meetings had just broken up the night before last and I'd gone a bit of the way home when I found I'd left my pipe behind. It was a real good 'un, an old favourite, so I went back to look for it. But before I got to the place where I'd been sitting (it was black as pitch there) I heard a cat's voice say *Mew* and a Calormene voice say 'here . . . speak softly,' so I just stood as still as if I was frozen. And these two were Ginger and Rishda Tarkaan as they call him. 'Noble Tarkaan,' said the Cat in that silky voice of his, 'I just wanted to know exactly what we both meant today about Aslan meaning *no more* than Tash.' 'Doubtless, most sagacious of cats,' says the other, 'you have perceived my meaning.' 'You mean,' says Ginger, 'that there's no such person as either.' 'All who are enlightened know that,' said the Tarkaan. 'Then we can understand one another,' purrs the Cat. 'Do you, like me, grow a little weary of the Ape?' 'A stupid, greedy brute,' says the other, 'but we must use him for the present. Thou and I must provide for all things in secret and make the Ape do our will.' 'And it would be better, wouldn't it,' said Ginger, 'to let some of the more enlightened Narnians into our counsels: one by one as we find them apt. For the Beasts who really believe in Aslan may turn at any moment: and will, if the Ape's folly betrays his secret. But those who care neither for Tash nor Aslan but have only an eye to their own profit and such reward as The Tisroc may give them when Narnia is a Calormene province, will be firm.' 'Excellent Cat,' said the Captain. 'But choose which ones carefully.'"

While the Dwarf had been speaking the day seemed to have changed. It had been sunny when they sat down. Now Puzzle shivered. Jewel shifted his head uneasily. Jill looked up.

"It's clouding over," she said.

"And it's so cold," said Puzzle.

"Cold enough, by the Lion!" said Tirian, blowing on his hands. "And faugh! What foul smell is this?"

"Phew!" gasped Eustace. "It's like something dead. Is there a dead bird somewhere about? And why didn't we notice it before?"

With a great upheaval Jewel scrambled to his feet and pointed with his horn.

"Look!" he cried. "Look at it! Look, look!"

Then all six of them saw; and over all their faces there came an expression of uttermost dismay.

CHAPTER EIGHT

WHAT NEWS THE EAGLE BROUGHT

IN the shadow of the trees on the far side of the clearing something was moving. It was gliding very slowly Northward. At a first glance you might have mistaken it for smoke, for it was grey and you could see things through it. But the deathly smell was not the smell of smoke. Also, this thing kept its shape instead of billowing and curling as smoke would have done. It was roughly the shape of a man but it had the head of a bird; some bird of prey with a cruel, curved beak. It had four arms which it held high above its head, stretching them out Northward as if it wanted to snatch all Narnia in its grip; and its fingers – all twenty of them – were curved like its beak and had long, pointed, bird-like claws instead of nails. It floated on the grass instead of walking, and the grass seemed to wither beneath it.

After one look at it Puzzle gave a screaming bray and darted into the Tower. And Jill (who was no coward, as you know) hid her face in her hands to shut out the sight of it. The others watched it for perhaps a minute, until it streamed away into the thicker trees on their right and disappeared. Then the sun came out again, and the birds once more began to sing.

Everyone started breathing properly again and moved. They had all been still as statues while it was in sight.

"What was it?" said Eustace in a whisper.

"I have seen it once before," said Tirian. "But that time it was carved in stone and overlaid with gold and had solid diamonds for eyes. It was when I was no older than thou, and had gone as a guest to The Tisroc's court in Tashbaan.

He took me into the great temple of Tash. There I saw it, carved above the altar."

"Then that – that thing – was Tash?" said Eustace.

But instead of answering him Tirian slipped his arm behind Jill's shoulders and said, "How is it with you, Lady?"

"A-all right," said Jill, taking her hands away from her pale face and trying to smile. "I'm all right. It only made me feel a little sick for a moment."

"It seems, then," said the Unicorn, "that there is a real Tash, after all."

"Yes," said the Dwarf. "And this fool of an Ape, who didn't believe in Tash, will get more than he bargained for! He called for Tash: Tash has come."

"Where has it – he – the Thing – gone to?" said Jill.

"North into the heart of Narnia," said Tirian. "It has

come to dwell among us. They have called it and it has come."

"Ho, ho, ho!" chuckled the Dwarf, rubbing his hairy hands together. "It will be a surprise for the Ape. People shouldn't call for demons unless they really mean what they say."

"Who knows if Tash will be visible to the Ape?" said Jewel.

"Where has Puzzle got to?" said Eustace.

They all shouted out Puzzle's name and Jill went round to the other side of the Tower to see if he had gone there.

They were quite tired of looking for him when at last his large grey head peered cautiously out of the doorway and he said, "Has it gone away?" And when at last they got him to come out, he was shivering the way a dog shivers before a thunderstorm.

"I see now," said Puzzle, "that I really have been a very bad donkey. I ought never to have listened to Shift. I never thought things like this would begin to happen."

"If you'd spent less time saying you weren't clever and more time trying to be as clever as you could —" began Eustace but Jill interrupted him.

"Oh leave poor old Puzzle alone," she said. "It was all a mistake; wasn't it, Puzzle dear?" And she kissed him on the nose.

Though rather shaken by what they had seen, the whole party now sat down again and went on with their talk.

Jewel had little to tell them. While he was a prisoner he had spent nearly all his time tied up at the back of the stable, and had of course heard none of the enemies' plans. He had been kicked (he'd done some kicking back too) and beaten and threatened with death unless he would say that he believed it was Aslan who was brought out and shown to them by firelight every night. In fact he was going to be executed this very morning if he had not been rescued. He didn't know what had happened to the Lamb.

The question they had to decide was whether they would go to Stable Hill again that night, show Puzzle to the Narnians and try to make them see how they had been tricked, or whether they should steal away Eastward to meet the help which Roonwit the Centaur was bringing up from Cair Paravel and return against the Ape and his Calormenes in force. Tirian would very much like to have followed the first plan: he hated the idea of leaving the Ape to bully his people one moment longer than need be. On the other hand, the way the Dwarfs had behaved last night was a warning. Apparently one couldn't be sure how people would take it even if he showed them Puzzle. And there were the Calormene soldiers to be reckoned with. Poggin thought there were about thirty of them. Tirian felt sure that if the Narnians all rallied to his side, he and Jewel and the children and Poggin (Puzzle didn't count for much) would have a good chance of beating them. But how if half the Narnians – including all the Dwarfs – just sat and looked on? or even fought against him? The risk was too great. And there was, too, the cloudy shape of Tash. What might it do?

And then, as Poggin pointed out, there was no harm in leaving the Ape to deal with his own difficulties for a day or two. He would have no Puzzle to bring out and show now. It wasn't easy to see what story he – or Ginger – could make up to explain that. If the Beasts asked night after night to see Aslan, and no Aslan was brought out, surely even the simplest of them would get suspicious.

In the end they all agreed that the best thing was to go off and try to meet Roonwit.

As soon as they had decided this, it was wonderful how much more cheerful everyone became. I don't honestly think that this was because any of them was afraid of a fight (except perhaps Jill and Eustace). But I daresay that each of them, deep down inside, was very glad not to go any nearer – or not yet – to that horrible bird-headed thing which, visible or invisible, was now probably haunting Stable Hill. Anyway, one always feels better when one has made up one's mind.

Tirian said they had better remove their disguises, as they didn't want to be mistaken for Calormenes and perhaps attacked by any loyal Narnians they might meet. The Dwarf made up a horrid-looking mess of ashes from the hearth and grease out of the jar of grease which was kept for rubbing on swords and spear-heads. Then they took off their Calormene armour and went down to the stream. The nasty mixture made a lather just like soft soap: it was a pleasant, homely sight to see Tirian and the two children kneeling beside the water and scrubbing the backs of their necks or puffing and blowing as they splashed the lather off. Then they went back to the Tower with red, shiny faces, like people who have been given an extra good wash before a party. They re-armed themselves in true Narnian style, with straight swords and three-cornered shields. "Body of me," said Tirian. "That is better. I feel a true man again."

Puzzle begged very hard to have the lion-skin taken off him. He said it was too hot and the way it was rucked up on his back was uncomfortable: also, it made him look so silly. But they told him he would have to wear it a bit longer, for they still wanted to show him in that get-up to the other Beasts, even though they were now going to meet Roonwit first.

What was left of the pigeon-meat and rabbit-meat was not worth bringing away but they took some biscuits. Then Tirian locked the door of the Tower and that was the end of their stay there.

It was a little after two in the afternoon when they set out, and it was the first really warm day of that spring. The young leaves seemed to be much further out than yesterday: the snow-drops were over, but they saw several primroses. The sunlight slanted through the trees, birds sang, and always (though usually out of sight) there was the noise of running water. It was hard to think of horrible things like Tash. The children felt, "This is really Narnia at last." Even Tirian's heart grew lighter as he walked ahead of them, humming an old Narnian marching song which had the refrain:

> Ho, rumble, rumble, rumble,
> Rumble drum belaboured.

After the King came Eustace and Poggin the Dwarf. Poggin was telling Eustace the names of all the Narnian trees, birds, and plants which he didn't know already. Sometimes Eustace would tell him about English ones.

After them came Puzzle, and after him Jill and Jewel walking very close together. Jill had, as you might say, quite fallen in love with the Unicorn. She thought – and she wasn't far wrong – that he was the shiningest, delicatest, most graceful animal she had ever met: and he was so gentle and soft of speech that, if you hadn't known, you would hardly have believed how fierce and terrible he could be in battle.

"Oh, this *is* nice!" said Jill. "Just walking along like this. I wish there could be more of *this* sort of adventure. It's a pity there's always so much happening in Narnia."

But the Unicorn explained to her that she was quite mistaken. He said that the Sons and Daughters of Adam and Eve were brought out of their own strange world into Narnia only at times when Narnia was stirred and upset, but she mustn't think it was always like that. In between their visits there were hundreds and thousands of years when peaceful King followed peaceful King till you could hardly remember their names or count their numbers, and there was really hardly anything to put into the History Books. And he went on to talk of old Queens and heroes whom she had never heard of. He spoke of Swanwhite the Queen who had lived before the days of the White Witch and the Great Winter, who was so beautiful that when she looked into any forest pool the reflection of her face shone out of the water like a star by night for a year and a day afterwards. He spoke of Moonwood the Hare who had such ears that he could sit by Caldron Pool under the thunder of the great waterfall and hear what men spoke in whispers at Cair Paravel. He told how King Gale, who was ninth in descent from Frank the first of all Kings, had sailed far away into the Eastern seas and delivered the Lone Islanders from a dragon and how, in return, they had given him the Lone Islands to be part of the royal lands of Narnia for ever. He talked of whole centuries in which all Narnia was so happy that notable dances and feasts, or at most tournaments, were the only things that could be remembered, and every day and week had been better than the last. And as he went on, the picture of all those happy years, all the thousands of them, piled up in Jill's mind till it was rather like looking down from a high hill on to a rich, lovely plain full of woods and waters and cornfields, which spread away and away till it got thin and misty from distance. And she said:

"Oh, I do hope we can soon settle the Ape and get back to those good, ordinary times. And then I hope they'll go on for ever and ever and ever. *Our* world is going to have an end some day. Perhaps this one won't. Oh Jewel — wouldn't it be lovely if Narnia just went on and on — like what you said it has been?"

"Nay, sister," answered Jewel, "all worlds draw to an end, except Aslan's own country."

"Well, at least," said Jill, "I hope the end of this one is millions of millions of millions of years away — hallo! what are we stopping for?"

The King and Eustace and the Dwarf were all staring up at the sky. Jill shuddered, remembering what horrors they had seen already. But it was nothing of that sort this time. It was small, and looked black against the blue.

"I dare swear," said the Unicorn, "from its flight, that it is a Talking bird."

"So think I," said the King. "But is it a friend, or a spy of the Ape's?"

"To me, Sire," said the Dwarf, "it has a look of Far-sight the Eagle."

"Ought we to hide under the trees?" said Eustace.

"Nay," said Tirian, "best stand still as rocks. He would see us for certain if we moved."

"Look! He wheels, he has seen us already," said Jewel. "He is coming down in wide circles."

"Arrow on string, Lady," said Tirian to Jill. "But by no means shoot till I bid you. He may be a friend."

If one had known what was going to happen next it would have been a treat to watch the grace and ease with which the huge bird glided down. He alighted on a rocky crag a few feet from Tirian, bowed his crested head, and said in his strange eagle's-voice, "Hail, King."

"Hail, Farsight," said Tirian. "And since you call me King, I may well believe you are not a follower of the Ape and his false Aslan. I am right glad of your coming."

"Sire," said the Eagle, "when you have heard my news you will be sorrier of my coming than of the greatest woe that ever befell you."

Tirian's heart seemed to stop beating at these words, but he set his teeth and said, "Tell on."

"Two sights have I seen," said Farsight. "One was Cair Paravel filled with dead Narnians and living Calormenes: The Tisroc's banner advanced upon your royal battlements: and your subjects flying from the city – this way and that, into the woods. Cair Paravel was taken from the sea. Twenty great ships of Calormen put in there in the dark of the night before last night."

No one could speak.

"And the other sight, five leagues nearer than Cair Paravel, was Roonwit the Centaur lying dead with a Calormene arrow in his side. I was with him in his last hour and he gave me this message to your Majesty: to remember that all worlds draw to an end and that noble death is a treasure which no one is too poor to buy."

"So," said the King, after a long silence, "Narnia is no more."

CHAPTER NINE

THE GREAT MEETING ON STABLE HILL

FOR a long time they could not speak nor even shed a tear. Then the Unicorn stamped the ground with his hoof, and shook his mane, and spoke.

"Sire," he said, "there is now no need of counsel. We see that the Ape's plans were laid deeper than we dreamed of. Doubtless he has been long in secret traffic with The Tisroc, and as soon as he had found the lion-skin he sent him word to make ready his navy for the taking of Cair Paravel and all Narnia. Nothing now remains for us seven but to go back to Stable Hill, proclaim the truth, and take the adventure that Aslan sends us. And if, by a great marvel, we defeat those thirty Calormenes who are with the Ape, then to turn again and die in battle with the far greater host of them that will soon march from Cair Paravel."

Tirian nodded. But he turned to the children and said: "Now, friends, it is time for you to go hence into your own world. Doubtless you have done all that you were sent to do."

"B – but we've done nothing," said Jill who was shivering, not with fear exactly but because everything was so horrible.

"Nay," said the King, "you loosed me from the tree: you glided before me like a snake last night in the wood and took Puzzle: and you, Eustace, killed your man. But you are too young to share in such a bloody end as we others must meet tonight or, it may be, three days hence. I entreat you – nay, I command you – to return to your own place. I should be put to shame if I let such young warriors fall in battle on my side."

"No, no, no," said Jill (very white when she began speaking and then suddenly very red and then white again.) "We won't, I don't care what you say. We're going to stick to you whatever happens, aren't we, Eustace?"

"Yes, but there's no need to get so worked up about it," said Eustace who had stuck his hands in his pockets (forgetting how very odd that looks when you are wearing a mail shirt). "Because, you see, we haven't any choice. What's the good of talking about our going back! How? We've got no magic for doing it!"

This was very good sense but, at the moment, Jill hated Eustace for saying it. He was fond of being dreadfully matter-of-fact when other people got excited.

When Tirian realized that the two strangers could not get home (unless Aslan suddenly whisked them away), he next wanted them to go across the Southern mountains into Archenland where they might possibly be safe. But they didn't know their way and there was no one to send with them. Also, as Poggin said, once the Calormenes had Narnia they would certainly take Archenland in the next week or so: The Tisroc had always wanted to have these Northern countries for his own. In the end Eustace and Jill begged so hard that Tirian said they could come with him and take their chance – or, as he much more sensibly called it, "the adventure that Aslan would send them".

The King's first idea was that they should not go back to Stable Hill – they were sick of the very name of it by now – till after dark. But the Dwarf told them that if they arrived there by daylight they would probably find the place deserted, except perhaps for a Calormene sentry. The Beasts were far too frightened by what the Ape (and Ginger) had told them about this new angry Aslan – or Tashlan – to go near it except when they were called together for these horrible midnight meetings. And Calormenes are never good woodsmen. Poggin thought that even by daylight they could easily get round to somewhere behind the stable without being seen. This would be much harder to do when the night had come and the Ape might be calling the Beasts together and all the Calormenes were on duty. And when the meeting did begin they could leave Puzzle at the back of the stable, completely out of sight, till the moment at which they wanted to produce him. This was obviously a good thing: for their only chance was to give the Narnians a sudden surprise.

Everyone agreed and the whole party set off on a new line — North-West — towards the hated Hill. The Eagle sometimes flew to and fro above them, sometimes he sat perched on Puzzle's back. No one — not even the King himself except in some great need — would dream of *riding* on a Unicorn.

This time Jill and Eustace walked together. They had been feeling very brave when they were begging to be allowed to come with the others, but now they didn't feel brave at all.

"Pole," said Eustace in a whisper. "I may as well tell you I've got the wind up."

"Oh *you're* all right, Scrubb," said Jill. "You can fight. But I — I'm just shaking, if you want to know the truth."

"Oh shaking's nothing," said Eustace. "I'm feeling I'm going to be sick."

"Don't talk about *that*, for goodness' sake," said Jill.

They went on in silence for a minute or two.

"Pole," said Eustace presently.

"What?" said she.

"What'll happen if we get killed here?"

"Well we'll be dead, I suppose."

"But I mean, what will happen in our own world? Shall we wake up and find ourselves back in that train? Or shall we just vanish and never be heard of any more? Or shall we be dead in England?"

"Gosh. I never thought of that."

"It'll be rum for Peter and the others if they saw me waving out of the window and then when the train comes in we're nowhere to be found! Or if they found two – I mean, if we're dead over there in England."

"Ugh!" said Jill. "What a horrid idea."

"It wouldn't be horrid for *us*," said Eustace. "We shouldn't be there."

"I almost wish – no I don't, though," said Jill.

"What were you going to say?"

"I *was* going to say I wished we'd never come. But I don't, I don't, I don't. Even if we *are* killed. I'd rather be killed fighting for Narnia than grow old and stupid at home and perhaps go about in a bath-chair and then die in the end just the same."

"Or be smashed up by British Railways!"

"Why d'you say that?"

"Well when that awful jerk came – the one that seemed to throw us into Narnia – I thought it *was* the beginning of a railway accident. So I was jolly glad to find ourselves here instead."

While Jill and Eustace were talking about this, the others were discussing their plans and becoming less miserable. That was because they were now thinking of what was to be done this very night and the thought of what had happened to Narnia – the thought that all her glories and joys were over – was pushed away into the back part of their minds. The moment they stopped talking it would come out and make them wretched again: but they kept on talking. Poggin was really quite cheerful about the night's work they had to do. He was sure that the Boar and the Bear, and probably all the Dogs would come over to their side at once. And he couldn't believe that all the other Dwarfs would stick to Griffle. And fighting by firelight and in and out among trees would be an advantage to the weaker side. And then, if they could win tonight, need they really throw their lives away by meeting the main Calormene army a few days later?

Why not hide in the woods, or even up in the Western Waste beyond the great waterfall and live like outlaws? And then they might gradually get stronger and stronger, for Talking Beasts and Archenlanders would be joining them every day. And at last they'd come out of hiding and sweep the Calormenes (who would have got careless by then) out of the country and Narnia would be revived. After all, something very like that had happened in the time of King Miraz!

And Tirian heard all this and thought "But what about Tash?" and felt in his bones that none of it was going to happen. But he didn't say so.

When they got nearer to Stable Hill of course everyone became quiet. Then the real wood-work began. From the moment at which they first saw the Hill to the moment at which they all arrived at the back of the stable, it took them over two hours. It's the sort of thing one couldn't describe properly unless one wrote pages and pages about it. The journey from each bit of cover to the next was a separate adventure, and there were very long waits in between, and several false alarms. If you are a good Scout or a good Guide you will know already what it must have been like. By about sunset they were all safe in a clump of holly trees about fifteen yards

behind the stable. They all munched some biscuit and lay down.

Then came the worst part, the waiting. Luckily for the children they slept for a couple of hours, but of course they woke up when the night grew cold, and what was worse, woke up very thirsty and with no chance of getting a drink. Puzzle just stood, shivering a little with nervousness, and said nothing. But Tirian, with his head against Jewel's flank, slept as soundly as if he were in his royal bed at Cair Paravel, till the sound of a gong beating awoke him and he sat up and saw that there was firelight on the far side of the stable and knew that the hour had come.

"Kiss me, Jewel," he said. "For certainly this is our last night on earth. And if ever I offended against you in any matter great or small, forgive me now."

"Dear King," said the Unicorn, "I could almost wish you had, so that I might forgive it. Farewell. We have known great joys together. If Aslan gave me my choice I would choose no other life than the life I have had and no other death than the one we go to."

Then they woke up Farsight, who was asleep with his head under his wing (it made him look as if he had no head at all), and crept forward to the stable. They left Puzzle (not without a kind word, for no one was angry with him now) just behind it, telling him not to move till someone came to fetch him, and took up their position at one end of the stable.

The bonfire had not been lit for long and was just beginning to blaze up. It was only a few feet away from them, and the great crowd of Narnian creatures were on the other side of it, so that Tirian could not at first see them very well, though of course he saw dozens of eyes shining with the reflection of the fire, as you've seen a rabbit's or cat's eyes in the headlights of a car. And just as Tirian took his place, the gong stopped beating and from somewhere on his left three figures appeared. One was Rishda Tarkaan the Calormene Captain. The second was the Ape. He was holding on to the Tarkaan's hand with one paw and kept whimpering and muttering, "Not so fast, don't go so fast, I'm not *at all* well. Oh my poor head! These midnight meetings are getting too much for me. Apes aren't meant to be up at night: It's not as if I was a rat or a bat – oh my poor head." On the other side of the Ape, walking very soft and stately, with his tail straight up in the air, came Ginger the Cat. They were heading for the bonfire and were so close to Tirian that they would have seen him at once if they had looked in the right direction. Fortunately they did not. But Tirian heard Rishda say to Ginger in a low voice:

"Now, Cat, to thy post. See thou play thy part well."

"Miaow, miaow. Count on me!" said Ginger. Then he stepped away beyond the bonfire and sat down in the front

row of the assembled Beasts: in the audience, as you might say.

For really, as it happened, the whole thing was rather like a theatre. The crowd of Narnians were like the people in the seats; the little grassy place just in front of the stable, where the bonfire burned and the Ape and the Captain stood to talk to the crowd, was like the stage; the stable itself was like the scenery at the back of the stage; and Tirian and his friends were like people peering round from behind the scenery. It was a splendid position. If any of them stepped forward into the full firelight, all eyes would be fixed on him at once: on the other hand, so long as they stood still in the shadow of the end-wall of the stable, it was a hundred to one against their being noticed.

Rishda Tarkaan dragged the Ape up close to the fire. The pair of them turned to face the crowd, and this of course meant that their backs were towards Tirian and his friends.

"Now, Monkey," said Rishda Tarkaan in a low voice. "Say the words that wiser heads have put into thy mouth. And hold up thy head." As he spoke he gave the Ape a little prod or kick from behind with the point of his toe.

"Do leave me alone," muttered Shift. But he sat up straighter and began, in a louder voice – "Now listen, all of you. A terrible thing has happened. A wicked thing. The wickedest thing that ever was done in Narnia. And Aslan –"

"Tashlan, fool," whispered Rishda Tarkaan.

"Tashlan I mean, of course," said the Ape, "is very angry about it."

There was a terrible silence while the Beasts waited to hear what new trouble was in store for them. The little party by the end-wall of the stable also held their breath. What on earth was coming now?

"Yes," said the Ape. "At this very moment, when the Terrible One himself is among us – there in the stable just behind me – one wicked Beast has chosen to do what you'd think no one would dare to do even if *He* were a thousand miles away. It has dressed itself up in a lion-skin and is wandering about in these very woods pretending to be Aslan."

Jill wondered for a moment if the Ape had gone mad. Was he going to tell the whole truth? A roar of horror and rage went up from the Beasts. "Grrr!" came the growls. "Who is he? Where is he? Just let me get my teeth into him!"

"It was seen last night," screamed the Ape, "but it got away. It's a Donkey! A common, miserable Ass! If any of you see that Ass –"

"Grrr!" growled the Beasts. "We will, we will. He'd better keep out of *our* way."

Jill looked at the King: his mouth was open and his face was full of horror. And then she understood the devilish cunning of the enemies' plan. By mixing a little truth with it they had made their lie far stronger. What was the good, now, of telling the Beasts that an ass had been dressed up as a lion to deceive them? The Ape would only say, "That's just what I've said." What was the good of showing them Puzzle in his lion-skin? They would only tear him in pieces. "That's taken the wind out of our sails," whispered Eustace. "The ground is taken from under our feet," said Tirian. "Cursed, cursed cleverness!" said Poggin. "I'll be sworn that this new lie is of Ginger's making."

CHAPTER TEN

WHO WILL GO INTO THE STABLE?

JILL felt something tickling her ear. It was Jewel the Unicorn, whispering to her with the wide whisper of a horse's mouth. As soon as she heard what he was saying she nodded and tip-toed back to where Puzzle was standing. Quickly and quietly she cut the last cords that bound the lion-skin to him. It wouldn't do for him to be caught with *that* on, after what the Ape had said! She would like to have hidden the skin somewhere very far away, but it was too heavy. The best she could do was to kick it in among the thickest bushes. Then she made signs to Puzzle to follow her and they both joined the others.

The Ape was speaking again.

"And after a horrid thing like that, Aslan – Tashlan – is angrier than ever. He says he's been a great deal too good to you, coming out every night to be looked at, see! Well, he's not coming out any more."

Howls and mewings and squeals and grunts were the Animals' answer to this, but suddenly a quite different voice broke in with a loud laugh.

"Hark what the monkey says," it shouted. "We know why he isn't going to bring his precious Aslan out. I'll tell you why: because he hasn't got him. He never had anything except an old donkey with a lion-skin on its back. Now he's lost *that* and he doesn't know what to do."

Tirian could not see the faces on the other side of the fire very well but he guessed this was Griffle the Chief Dwarf. And he was quite certain of it when, a second later, all the Dwarfs' voices joined in, singing: "Don't know what to do! Don't know what to do! Don't know what to do-o-o!"

"Silence!" thundered Rishda Tarkaan. "Silence, children of mud! Listen to me, you other Narnians, lest I give command to my warriors to fall upon you with the edge of the sword. The Lord Shift has already told you of that wicked Ass. Do you think, because of him that there is no *real* Tashlan in the stable! Do you? Beware, beware."

"No, no," shouted most of the crowd. But the Dwarfs said, "That's right, Darkie, you've got it. Come on, Monkey, show us what's in the stable, seeing is believing."

When next there was a moment's quiet the Ape said:

"You Dwarfs think you're very clever, don't you? But not so fast. I never said you couldn't see Tashlan. Anyone who likes can see him."

The whole assembly became silent. Then, after nearly a minute, the Bear began in a slow, puzzled voice:

"I don't quite understand all this," it grumbled, "I thought you said—"

"*You* thought!" repeated the Ape. "As if anyone could call what goes on in your head *thinking*. Listen, you others. Anyone can see Tashlan. But he's not coming out. You have to go in and see *him*."

"Oh, thank you, thank you, thank you," said dozens of voices. "That's what we wanted! We can go in and see him face to face. And now he'll be kind and it will all be as it used to be." And the Birds chattered, and the Dogs barked excitedly. Then suddenly, there was a great stirring and a noise of creatures rising to their feet, and in a second the whole lot of them would have been rushing forward and trying to crowd into the stable door all together. But the Ape shouted:

"Get back! Quiet! Not so fast."

The Beasts stopped, many of them with one paw in the air, many with tails wagging, and all of them with heads on one side.

"I thought you said," began the Bear, but Shift interrupted.

"Anyone can go in," he said. "But, one at a time. Who'll go first? He didn't *say* he was feeling very kind. He's been licking his lips a lot since he swallowed up the wicked King the other night. He's been growling a good deal this morning. I wouldn't much like to go into that stable myself tonight. But just as you please. Who'd like to go in first? Don't blame me if he swallows you whole or blasts you into a cinder with the mere terror of his eyes. That's your affair. Now then! Who's first? What about one of you Dwarfs?"

"Dilly, dilly, come and be killed!" sneered Griffle. "How do we know what you've got in there?"

"Ho-ho!" cried the Ape. "So you're beginning to think there's *something* there, eh? Well, all you Beasts were making noise enough a minute ago. What's struck you all dumb? Who's going in first?"

But the Beasts all stood looking at one another and began backing away from the stable. Very few tails were wagging now. The Ape waddled to and fro jeering at them. "Ho-ho-ho!" he chuckled. "I thought you were all so eager to see Tashlan face to face! Changed your mind, eh?"

Tirian bent his head to hear something that Jill was trying to whisper in his ear. "What do you think is really inside the stable?" she said. "Who knows?" said Tirian. "Two Calormenes with drawn swords, as likely as not, one

on each side of the door." "You don't think," said Jill, "it might be . . . you know . . . that horrid thing we saw?" "Tash himself?" whispered Tirian. "There's no knowing. But courage, child: we are all between the paws of the true Aslan."

Then a most surprising thing happened. Ginger the Cat said in a cool, clear voice, not at all as if he was excited, "I'll go in, if you like."

Every creature turned and fixed its eyes on the Cat. "Mark their subtleties, Sire," said Poggin to the King. "This cursed cat is in the plot, in the very centre of it. Whatever is in the stable will not hurt him, I'll be bound. Then Ginger will come out again and say that he has seen some wonder."

But Tirian had no time to answer him. The Ape was calling the Cat to come forward. "Ho-ho!" said the Ape. "So you, a pert Puss, would look upon him face to face. Come on, then! I'll open the door for you. Don't blame me if he scares the whiskers off your face. That's your affair."

And the Cat got up and came out of its place in the crowd, walking primly and daintily, with its tail in the air, not one hair on its sleek coat out of place. It came on till it had passed the fire and was so close that Tirian, from where he stood with his shoulder against the end-wall of the stable, could look right into its face. Its big green eyes never blinked. ("Cool as a cucumber," muttered Eustace. "*It* knows it has nothing to fear.") The Ape, chuckling and making faces, shuffled across beside the Cat: put up his paw: drew the bolt and opened the door. Tirian thought he could hear the Cat purring as it walked into the dark doorway.

"Aii-aii-aouwee! —" The most horrible caterwaul you ever heard made everyone jump. You have been wakened yourself by cats quarrelling or making love on the roof in the middle of the night: you know the sound.

This was worse. The Ape was knocked head over heels by Ginger coming back out of the stable at top speed. If you had not known he was a cat, you might have thought he was a ginger-coloured streak of lightning. He shot across the open grass, back into the crowd. No one wants to meet a cat in that state. You could see animals getting out of his way to left and right. He dashed up a tree, whisked around, and hung head downwards. His tail was bristled out till it was nearly as thick as his whole body: his eyes were like saucers of green fire: along his back every single hair stood on end.

"I'd give my beard," whispered Poggin, "to know whether that brute is only acting or whether it has really found something in there that frightened it!"

"Peace, friend," said Tirian, for the Captain and the Ape were also whispering and he wanted to hear what they said. He did not succeed, except that he heard the Ape once more whimpering "My head, my head," but he got the idea that those two were almost as puzzled by the cat's behaviour as himself.

"Now, Ginger," said the Captain. "Enough of that noise. Tell them what thou hast seen."

"Aii – Aii – Aaow – Awah," screamed the Cat.

"Art thou not called a *Talking* Beast?" said the Captain. "Then hold thy devilish noise and talk."

What followed was rather horrible. Tirian felt quite certain (and so did the others) that the Cat was trying to

say something: but nothing came out of his mouth except the ordinary, ugly cat-noises you might hear from any angry or frightened old Tom in a backyard in England. And the longer he caterwauled the less like a Talking Beast he looked. Uneasy whimperings and little sharp squeals broke out from among the other Animals.

"Look, look!" said the voice of the Bear. "It can't talk. It has forgotten how to talk! It has gone back to being a dumb beast. Look at its face." Everyone saw that it was true. And then the greatest terror of all fell upon those Narnians. For every one of them had been taught – when it was only a chick or a puppy or a cub – how Aslan at the beginning of the world had turned the beasts of Narnia into Talking Beasts and warned them that if they weren't good they might one day be turned back again and be like the poor witless animals one meets in other countries. "And now it is coming upon us," they moaned.

"Mercy! Mercy!" wailed the Beasts. "Spare us, Lord Shift, stand between us and Aslan, you must always go in and speak to him for us. We daren't, we daren't."

Ginger disappeared further up into the tree. No one ever saw him again.

Tirian stood with his hand on his sword-hilt and his head bowed. He was dazed with the horrors of that night. Sometimes he thought it would be best to draw his sword at once and rush upon the Calormenes: then next moment he thought it would be better to wait and see what new turn affairs might take. And now a new turn came.

"My Father," came a clear, ringing voice from the left of the crowd. Tirian knew at once that it was one of the Calormenes speaking, for in The Tisroc's army the common soldiers call the officers "My Master" but the officers call their senior officers "My Father". Jill and Eustace didn't know this but, after looking this way and that, they saw the speaker, for of course people at the sides of the crowd were easier to see than people in the middle where the glare of the fire made all beyond it look rather black. He was young and tall and slender, and even rather beautiful in the dark, haughty, Calormene way.

"My Father," he said to the Captain, "I also desire to go in."

"Peace, Emeth," said the Captain, "Who called thee to counsel? Does it become a boy to speak?"

"My Father," said Emeth. "Truly I am younger than thou, yet I also am of the blood of the Tarkaans even as thou art, and I also am the servant of Tash. Therefore . . ."

"Silence," said Rishda Tarkaan. "Am not I thy Captain? Thou hast nothing to do with this stable. It is for the Narnians."

"Nay, my Father," answered Emeth. "Thou hast said that their Aslan and our Tash are all one. And if that is the truth, then Tash himself is in yonder. And how then sayest thou that I have nothing to do with him? For gladly would I die a thousand deaths if I might look once on the face of Tash."

"Thou art a fool and understandest nothing," said Rishda Tarkaan. "These be high matters."

Emeth's face grew sterner. "Is it then not true that Tash and Aslan are all one?" he asked. "Has the Ape lied to us?"

"Of course they're all one," said the Ape.

"Swear it, Ape," said Emeth.

"Oh dear!" whimpered Shift, "I wish you'd all stop bothering me. My head does ache. Yes, yes, I swear it."

"Then, my Father," said Emeth, "I am utterly determined to go in."

"Fool," began Rishda Tarkaan, but at once the Dwarfs began shouting: "Come along, Darkie. Why don't you let him in? Why do you let Narnians in and keep your own people out? What have you got in there that you don't want your own men to meet?"

Tirian and his friends could only see the back of Rishda Tarkaan, so they never knew what his face looked like as he shrugged his shoulders and said, "Bear witness all that I am guiltless of this young fool's blood. Get thee in, rash boy, and make haste."

Then, just as Ginger had done, Emeth came walking forward into the open strip of grass between the bonfire and the stable. His eyes were shining, his face very solemn, his hand was on his sword-hilt, and he carried his head high.

Jill felt like crying when she looked at his face. And Jewel whispered in the King's ear, "By the Lion's Mane, I almost love this young warrior, Calormene though he be. He is worthy of a better god than Tash."

"I do wish we knew what is really inside there," said Eustace.

Emeth opened the door and went in, into the black mouth of the stable. He closed the door behind him. Only a few moments passed — but it seemed longer — before the door opened again. A figure in Calormene armour reeled out, fell on its back, and lay still: the door closed behind it. The Captain leaped towards it and bent down to stare at its face. He gave a start of surprise. Then he recovered himself and turned to the crowd, crying out:

"The rash boy has had his will. He has looked on Tash and is dead. Take warning, all of you."

"We will, we will," said the poor Beasts. But Tirian and his friends stared at the dead Calormene and then at one another. For they, being so close, could see what the crowd, being further off and beyond the fire, could not see: this dead man was not Emeth. He was quite different: an older man, thicker and not so tall, with a big beard.

"Ho-ho-ho," chuckled the Ape. "Any more? Anyone

else want to go in? Well, as you're all shy, I'll choose the next. You, you Boar! On you come. Drive him up, Calor-menes. He *shall* see Tashlan face to face."

"O-o-mph," grunted the Boar, rising heavily to his feet. "Come on, then. Try my tusks."

When Tirian saw that brave Beast getting ready to fight for its life – and Calormene soldiers beginning to close in on it with their drawn scimitars – and no one going to its help – something seemed to burst inside him. He no longer cared if this was the best moment to interfere or not.

"Swords out," he whispered to the others. "Arrow on string. Follow."

Next moment the astonished Narnians saw seven figures leap forth in front of the stable, four of them in shining mail. The King's sword flashed in the firelight as he waved it above his head and cried in a great voice:

"Here stand I, Tirian of Narnia, in Aslan's name, to prove with my body that Tash is a foul fiend, the Ape a manifold traitor, and these Calormenes worthy of death. To my side, all true Narnians. Would you wait till your new masters have killed you all one by one?"

CHAPTER ELEVEN

THE PACE QUICKENS

Quick as lightning, Rishda Tarkaan leaped back out of reach of the King's sword. He was no coward, and would have fought single-handed against Tirian and the Dwarf if need were. But he could not take on the Eagle and the Unicorn as well. He knew how Eagles can fly into your face and peck at your eyes and blind you with their wings. And he had heard from his father (who had met Narnians in battle) that no man, except with arrows, or a long spear, can match a Unicorn, for it rears on its hind legs as it falls upon you and then you have its hoofs and its horn and its teeth to deal with all at once. So he rushed into the crowd and stood calling out:

"To me, to me, warriors of The Tisroc, may-he-live-forever. To me, all loyal Narnians, lest the wrath of Tashlan fall upon you!"

While this was happening two other things happened as well. The Ape had not realized his danger as quickly as the Tarkaan. For a second or so he remained squatting beside the fire staring at the newcomers. Then Tirian rushed upon the wretched creature, picked it up by the scruff of the neck, and dashed back to the stable shouting, "Open the door!" Poggin opened it. "Go and drink your own medicine, Shift!" said Tirian and hurled the Ape through into the darkness. But as the Dwarf banged the door shut again, a blinding greenish-blue light shone out from the inside of the stable, the earth shook, and there was a strange noise – a clucking and screaming as if it was the hoarse voice of some monstrous bird. The Beasts moaned and howled and called out "Tashlan! Hide us from him!" and many fell down, and many hid their faces in their wings or paws. No one except Farsight the Eagle, who has the best eyes of all living things, noticed the face of Rishda Tarkaan at that moment. And from what Farsight saw there he knew at once that Rishda was just as surprised, and nearly frightened, as everyone else. "There goes one," thought Farsight, "who has called on gods he does not believe in. How will it be with him if they have really come?"

The third thing – which also happened at the same moment – was the only really beautiful thing that night. Every single Talking Dog in the whole meeting (there were fifteen of them) came bounding and barking joyously to the King's side. They were mostly great big dogs with thick shoulders and heavy jaws. Their coming was like the breaking of a great wave on the sea-beach: it nearly knocked you down. For though they were Talking Dogs they were just as doggy as they could be: and they all stood up and put their front paws on the shoulders of the humans and licked their faces, all saying at once: "Welcome! Welcome! We'll help, we'll help, help, help. Show us how to help, show us how, how. How-how-how?"

It was so lovely that it made you want to cry. This,

at last, was the sort of thing they had been hoping for. And when, a moment later, several little animals (mice and moles and a squirrel or so) came pattering up, squealing with joy, and saying "See, see. We're here," and when, after that, the Bear and the Boar came too, Eustace began to feel that perhaps, after all, everything might be going to come right. But Tirian gazed round and saw how very few of the animals had moved.

"To me! to me!" he called. "Have you all turned cowards since I was your King?"

"We daren't," whimpered dozens of voices. "Tashlan would be angry. Shield us from Tashlan."

"Where are all the Talking Horses?" said Tirian to the Boar.

"We've seen, we've seen," squealed the Mice. "The Ape has made them work. They're all tied — down at the bottom of the hill."

"Then all you little ones," said Tirian, "you nibblers and gnawers and nutcrackers, away with you as fast as you can scamper and see if the Horses are on our side. And if they are, get your teeth into the ropes and gnaw till the Horses are free and bring them hither."

"With a good will, Sire," came the small voices, and with a whisk of tails those sharp-eyed and sharp-toothed folk were off. Tirian smiled for mere love as he saw them go. But it was already time to be thinking of other things. Rishda Tarkaan was giving his orders.

"Forward," he said. "Take all of them alive if you can and hurl them into the stable or drive them into it. When they are all in we will put fire to it and make them an offering to the great god Tash."

"Ha!" said Farsight to himself. "So that is how he hopes to win Tash's pardon for his unbelief."

The enemy line — about half of Rishda's force — was now moving forward, and Tirian had barely time to give his orders.

"Out on the left, Jill, and try to shoot all you may before they reach us. Boar and Bear next to her. Poggin on my left, Eustace on my right. Hold the right wing, Jewel. Stand by him, Puzzle, and use your hoofs. Hover and strike, Farsight. You Dogs, just behind us. Go in among them after the sword-play has begun. Aslan to our aid!"

Eustace stood with his heart beating terribly, hoping and hoping that he would be brave. He had never seen anything (though he had seen both a dragon and a sea-serpent) that made his blood run so cold as that line of dark-faced bright-eyed men. There were fifteen Calormenes, a Talking Bull of Narnia, Slinkey the Fox, and Wraggle the Satyr. Then he heard twang-and-zipp on his left and one Calormene fell: then twang-and-zipp again and the Satyr was down. "Oh, well done, daughter!" came Tirian's voice; and then the enemy were upon them.

Eustace could never remember what happened in the next two minutes. It was all like a dream (the sort you have when your temperature is over 100) until he heard Rishda Tarkaan's voice calling out from the distance:

"Retire. Back hither and re-form."

Then Eustace came to his senses and saw the Calormenes scampering back to their friends. But not all of them. Two lay dead, pierced by Jewel's horn, one by Tirian's sword. The Fox lay dead at his own feet, and he wondered if it was he who had killed it. The Bull also was down, shot through the eye by an arrow from Jill and gashed in his side by the Boar's tusk. But our side had its losses too. Three dogs were killed and a fourth was hobbling behind the line on three legs and whimpering. The Bear lay on the ground, moving feebly. Then it mumbled in its throaty voice, bewildered to the last, "I – I don't – understand," laid its big head down on the grass as quietly as a child going to sleep, and never moved again.

In fact, the first attack had failed. Eustace didn't seem able to be glad about it: he was so terribly thirsty and his arm ached so.

As the defeated Calormenes went back to their commander, the Dwarfs began jeering at them.

"Had enough, Darkies?" they yelled. "Don't you like it? Why doesn't your great Tarkaan go and fight himself instead of sending you to be killed? Poor Darkies!"

"Dwarfs," cried Tirian. "Come here and use your swords, not your tongues. There is still time. Dwarfs of Narnia! You can fight well, I know. Come back to your allegiance."

"Yah!" sneered the Dwarfs. "Not likely. You're just as

big humbugs as the other lot. We don't want any Kings. The Dwarfs are for the Dwarfs. Boo!"

Then the Drum began: not a Dwarf drum this time, but a big bull's hide Calormene drum. The children from the very first hated the sound. *Boom – boom – ba-ba-boom* it went. But they would have hated it far worse if they had known what it meant. Tirian did. It meant that there were other Calormene troops somewhere near and that Rishda Tarkaan was calling them to his aid. Tirian and Jewel looked at one another sadly. They had just begun to hope that they might win that night: but it would be all over with them if new enemies appeared.

Tirian gazed despairingly round. Several Narnians were standing with the Calormenes, whether through treachery or in honest fear of "Tashlan". Others were sitting still, staring, not likely to join either side. But there were fewer animals now: the crowd was much smaller. Clearly, several of them had just crept quietly away during the fighting.

Boom – boom – ba-ba-boom went the horrible drum. Then another sound began to mix with it. "Listen!" said Jewel: and then "Look!" said Farsight. A moment later there was no doubt what it was. With a thunder of hoofs, with tossing heads, widened nostrils, and waving manes, over a score of Talking Horses of Narnia came charging up the hill. The gnawers and nibblers had done their work.

Poggin the Dwarf and the children opened their mouths to cheer but that cheer never came. Suddenly the air was full of the sound of twanging bow-strings and hissing arrows. It was the Dwarfs who were shooting and – for a moment Jill could hardly believe her eyes – they were shooting the Horses. Dwarfs are deadly archers. Horse

after Horse rolled over. Not one of those noble Beasts ever reached the King.

"Little *Swine*," shrieked Eustace, dancing in his rage. "Dirty, filthy, treacherous little brutes." Even Jewel said, "Shall I run after those Dwarfs, Sire, and spit ten of them on my horn at each plunge?" But Tirian with his face as stern as stone, said, "Stand fast, Jewel. If you must weep, sweetheart (this was to Jill), turn your face aside and see you wet not your bow-string. And peace, Eustace. Do not scold, like a kitchen-girl. No warrior scolds. Courteous words or else hard knocks are his only language."

But the Dwarfs jeered back at Eustace. "That was a surprise for you, little boy, eh? Thought we were on *your* side, did you? No fear. We don't want any Talking Horses. We don't want you to win any more than the other gang. You can't take *us* in. The Dwarfs are for the Dwarfs."

Rishda Tarkaan was still talking to his men, doubtless making arrangements for the next attack and probably wishing he had sent his whole force into the first. The drum boomed on. Then, to their horror, Tirian and his friends heard, far fainter as if from a long way off, an answering drum. Another body of Calormenes had heard Rishda's signal and were coming to support him. You would not have known from Tirian's face that he had now given up all hope.

"Listen," he whispered in a matter-of-fact voice, "we must attack now, before yonder miscreants are strengthened by their friends."

"Bethink you, Sire," said Poggin, "that here we have the good wooden wall of the stable at our backs. If we advance, shall we not be encircled and get sword-points between our shoulders?"

"I would say as you do, Dwarf," said Tirian. "Were it not their very plan to force us into the stable? The further we are from its deadly door, the better."

"The King is right," said Farsight. "Away from this accursed stable, and whatever goblin lives inside it, at all costs."

"Yes, do let's," said Eustace. "I'm coming to hate the very sight of it."

"Good," said Tirian. "Now look yonder to our left. You see a great rock that gleams white like marble in the firelight. First we will fall upon those Calormenes. You, maiden, shall move out on our left and shoot as fast as ever you may into their ranks: and you, Eagle, fly at their faces from the right. Meanwhile we others will be charging them. When we are so close, Jill, that you can no longer shoot at them for fear of striking us, go back to the white rock and wait. You others, keep your ears wide even in the fighting. We must put them to flight in a few minutes or else not at all, for we are fewer than they. As soon as I call *Back*, then rush to join Jill at the white rock, where we shall have protection behind us and can breathe awhile. Now, be off, Jill."

Feeling terribly alone, Jill ran out about twenty feet, put her right leg back and her left leg forward, and set an arrow to her string. She wished her hands were not shaking so. "That's a rotten shot!" she said as her first arrow sped towards the enemy and flew over their heads. But she had another on the string next moment: she knew that speed was what mattered. She saw something big and black darting into the faces of the Calormenes. That was Farsight. First one man, and then another, dropped his sword and put up both his hands to defend his eyes. Then one of her own arrows hit a man, and another hit a Narnian wolf, who had, it seemed, joined the enemy. But she had been shooting only for a few seconds when she had to stop. With a flash of swords and of the Boar's tusks and Jewel's horn, and with deep baying from the dogs, Tirian and his party were rushing on their enemies, like men in a hundred yards' race. Jill was astonished to see how unprepared the Calormenes seemed to be. She did not realize that this was the result of her work and the Eagle's. Very few troops can keep on looking steadily to the front if they are getting arrows in their faces from one side and being pecked by an eagle on the other.

"Oh well done. *Well* done!" shouted Jill. The King's party were cutting their way right into the enemy. The Unicorn was tossing men as you'd toss hay on a fork. Even Eustace seemed to Jill (who after all didn't know very much about swordsmanship) to be fighting brilliantly. The Dogs were at the Calormenes' throats. It was going to work! It was victory at last — With a horrible, cold shock Jill noticed a strange thing. Though Calormenes were falling at each Narnian sword-stroke, they never seemed to get any fewer. In fact, there were actually more of them now than when the fight began. There were more every second. They were running up from every side. They were new Calormenes. These new ones had spears. There was such a crowd of them that she could hardly see her own friends. Then she heard Tirian's voice crying:

"Back! To the rock!"

The enemy had been reinforced. The drum had done its work.

CHAPTER TWELVE

THROUGH THE STABLE DOOR

JILL ought to have been back at the white rock already but she had quite forgotten that part of her orders in the excitement of watching the fight. Now she remembered. She turned at once and ran to it, and arrived there barely a second before the others. It thus happened that all of them, for a moment, had their backs to the enemy. They all wheeled round the moment they had reached it. A terrible sight met their eyes.

A Calormene was running towards the stable door carrying something that kicked and struggled. As he came between them and the fire they could see clearly both the shape of the man and the shape of what he carried. It was Eustace.

Tirian and the Unicorn rushed out to rescue him. But the Calormene was now far nearer to the door then they. Before they had covered half the distance he had flung Eustace in and shut the door on him. Half a dozen more Calormenes had run up behind him. They formed a line on the open space before the stable. There was no getting at it now.

Even then Jill remembered to keep her face turned aside, well away from her bow. "Even if I can't stop blubbing, I *won't* get my string wet," she said.

"'Ware arrows," said Poggin suddenly.

Everyone ducked and pulled his helmet well over his nose. The Dogs crouched behind. But though a few arrows came their way it soon became clear that they were not being shot at. Griffle and his Dwarfs were at their archery again. This time they were coolly shooting at the Calormenes.

"Keep it up, boys!" came Griffle's voice. "All together. Carefully. We don't want Darkies any more than we want Monkeys – or Lions – or Kings. The Dwarfs are for the Dwarfs."

Whatever else you may say about Dwarfs, no one can say they aren't brave. They could easily have got away to some safe place. They preferred to stay and kill as many of both sides as they could, except when both sides were kind enough to save them trouble by killing one another. They wanted Narnia for their own.

What perhaps they had not taken into account was that the Calormenes were mail-clad and the Horses had had no protection. Also the Calormenes had a leader. Rishda Tarkaan's voice cried out:

"Thirty of you keep watch on those fools by the white rock. The rest, after me, that we may teach these sons of earth a lesson."

Tirian and his friends, still panting from their fight and thankful for a few minutes' rest, stood and looked on while the Tarkaan led his men against the Dwarfs. It was a strange scene by now. The fire had sunk lower: the light it gave was now less and of a darker red. As far as one could see, the whole place of assembly was now empty except for the Dwarf and the Calormenes. In that light one couldn't make out much of what was happening. It sounded as if the Dwarfs were putting up a good fight. Tirian could hear Griffle using dreadful language, and every now and then the Tarkaan calling, "Take all you can alive! Take them alive!"

Whatever that fight may have been like, it did not last long. The noise of it died away. Then Jill saw the Tarkaan coming back to the stable: eleven men followed him, dragging eleven bound Dwarfs. (Whether the others had all been killed, or whether some of them had got away, was never known.)

"Throw them into the shrine of Tash," said Rishda Tarkaan.

And when the eleven Dwarfs, one after the other, had been flung or kicked into that dark doorway and the door had been shut again, he bowed low to the stable and said:

"These also are for thy burnt offering, Lord Tash."

And all the Calormenes banged the flats of their swords on their shields and shouted, "Tash! Tash! The great god Tash! Inexorable Tash!" (There was no nonsense about "Tashlan" now.)

The little party by the white rock watched these doings and whispered to one another. They had found a trickle of water coming down the rock and all had drunk eagerly – Jill and Poggin and the King in their hands, while the four-footed ones lapped from the little pool which it had made at the foot of the stone. Such was their thirst that it seemed the most delicious drink they had ever had in their lives, and while they were drinking they were perfectly happy and could not think of anything else.

"I feel in my bones," said Poggin, "that we shall all, one by one, pass through that dark door before morning. I can think of a hundred deaths I would rather have died."

"It is indeed a grim door," said Tirian. "It is more like a mouth."

"Oh, can't we do *anything* to stop it?" said Jill in a shaken voice.

"Nay, fair friend," said Jewel, nosing her gently. "It

may be for us the door to Aslan's country and we shall sup at his table tonight."

Rishda Tarkaan turned his back on the stable and walked slowly to a place in front of the white rock.

"Hearken," he said. "If the Boar and the Dogs and the Unicorn will come over to me and put themselves in my mercy, their lives shall be spared. The Boar shall go to a cage in The Tisroc's garden, the Dogs to The Tisroc's kennels, and the Unicorn, when I have sawn his horn off, shall draw a cart. But the Eagle, the children, and he who was the King shall be offered to Tash this night."

The only answer was growls.

"Get on, warriors," said the Tarkaan. "Kill the beasts, but take the two-legged ones alive."

And then the last battle of the last King of Narnia began.

What made it hopeless, even apart from the numbers of the enemy, was the spears. The Calormenes who had been with the Ape almost from the beginning had had no spears: that was because they had come into Narnia by ones and twos, pretending to be peaceful merchants, and of course they had carried no spears for a spear is not a thing you can hide. The new ones must have come in later, after the Ape was already strong and they could march openly. The spears made all the difference. With a long spear you can kill a boar before you are in reach of his tusks and a unicorn before you are in reach of his horn; if you are very quick and keep your head. And now the levelled spears were closing in on Tirian and his last friends. Next minute they were all fighting for their lives.

In a way it wasn't quite so bad as you might think.

When you are using every muscle to the full — ducking under a spear-point here, leaping over it there, lunging forward, drawing back, wheeling round — you haven't much time to feel either frightened or sad. Tirian knew he could do nothing for the others now; they were all doomed together. He vaguely saw the Boar go down on one side of him, and Jewel fighting furiously on the other. Out of the corner of one eye he saw, but only just saw, a big Calormene pulling Jill away somewhere by her hair. But he hardly thought about any of these things. His only thought now was to sell his life as dearly as he could. The worst of it was that he couldn't keep to the position in which he had started, under the white rock. A man who is fighting a dozen enemies at once must take his chances wherever he can; must dart in wherever he sees an enemy's breast or neck unguarded. In a very few strokes this may get you quite a distance from the spot where you began. Tirian soon found that he was getting further and further to the right, nearer to the stable. He had a vague idea in his mind that there was some good reason for keeping away from it. But he couldn't now remember what the reason was. And anyway, he couldn't help it.

All at once everything came quite clear. He found he was fighting the Tarkaan himself. The bonfire (what was left of it) was straight in front. He was in fact fighting in the very doorway of the stable, for it had been opened and two Calormenes were holding the door, ready to slam it shut the moment he was inside. He remembered everything now, and he realized that the enemy had been edging him to the stable on purpose ever since the fight began. And while he was thinking this he was still fighting the Tarkaan as hard as he could.

A new idea came into Tirian's head. He dropped his sword, darted forward, in under the sweep of the Tarkaan's scimitar, seized his enemy by the belt with both hands, and jumped back into the stable, shouting:

"Come in and meet Tash yourself!"

There was a deafening noise. As when the Ape had been flung in, the earth shook and there was a blinding light.

The Calormene soldiers outside screamed. "Tash, Tash!" and banged the door. If Tash wanted their own Captain, Tash must have him. They, at any rate, did not want to meet Tash.

For a moment or two Tirian did not know where he was or even who he was. Then he steadied himself, blinked, and looked around. It was not dark inside the stable, as he had expected. He was in strong light: that was why he was blinking.

He turned to look at Rishda Tarkaan, but Rishda was not looking at him. Rishda gave a great wail and pointed; then he put his hands before his face and fell flat, face downwards, on the ground. Tirian looked in the direction where the Tarkaan had pointed. And then he understood.

A terrible figure was coming towards them. It was far smaller than the shape they had seen from the Tower, though still much bigger than a man, and it was the same. It had a vulture's head and four arms. Its beak was open and its eyes blazed. A croaking voice came from its beak.

"Thou hast called me into Narnia, Rishda Tarkaan. Here I am. What hast thou to say?"

But the Tarkaan neither lifted his face from the ground nor said a word. He was shaking like a man with a bad

hiccup. He was brave enough in battle: but half his courage had left him earlier that night when he first began to suspect that there might be a real Tash. The rest of it had left him now.

With a sudden jerk — like a hen stooping to pick up a worm — Tash pounced on the miserable Rishda and tucked him under the upper of his two right arms. Then Tash turned his head sidewise to fix Tirian with one of his terrible eyes: for of course, having a bird's head, he couldn't look at you straight.

But immediately, from behind Tash, strong and calm as the summer sea, a voice said:

"Begone, Monster, and take your lawful prey to your own place: in the name of Aslan and Aslan's great Father the Emperor-over-the-Sea."

The hideous creature vanished, with the Tarkaan still under its arm. And Tirian turned to see who had spoken.

And what he saw then set his heart beating as it had never beaten in any fight.

Seven Kings and Queens stood before him, all with crowns on their heads and all in glittering clothes, but the Kings wore fine mail as well and had their swords drawn in their hands. Tirian bowed courteously and was about to speak when the youngest of the Queens laughed. He stared hard at her face, and then gasped with amazement, for he knew her. It was Jill: but not Jill as he had last seen her, with her face all dirt and tears and an old drill dress half slipping off one shoulder. Now she looked cool and fresh, as fresh as if she had just come from bathing. And at first he thought she looked older, but then didn't, and he could never make up his mind on that point. And then he saw that the youngest of the Kings was Eustace: but he also was changed as Jill was changed.

Tirian suddenly felt awkward about coming among these people with the blood and dust and sweat of a battle still on him. Next moment he realized that he was not in that state at all. He was fresh and cool and clean, and dressed in such clothes as he would have worn for a great feast at Cair Paravel. (But in Narnia your good clothes were never your uncomfortable ones. They knew how to make things that felt beautiful as well as looking beautiful in Narnia: and there was no such thing as starch or flannel or elastic to be found from one end of the country to the other.)

"Sire," said Jill coming forward and making a beautiful curtsey, "let me make you known to Peter the High King over all Kings in Narnia."

Tirian had no need to ask which was the High King, for he remembered his face (though here it was far nobler) from his dream. He stepped forward, sank on one knee and kissed Peter's hand.

"High King," he said. "You are welcome to me."

And the High King raised him and kissed him on both cheeks as a High King should. Then he led him to the eldest of the Queens — but even she was not old, and there

were no grey hairs on her head and no wrinkles on her cheek — and said, "Sir, this is that Lady Polly who came into Narnia on the First Day, when Aslan made the trees grow and the Beasts talk." He brought him next to a man whose golden beard flowed over his breast and whose face was full of wisdom. "And this," he said, "is the Lord Digory who was with her on that day. And this is my brother, King Edmund: and this my sister, the Queen Lucy."

"Sir," said Tirian, when he had greeted all these. "If I have read the chronicle aright, there should be another. Has not your Majesty two sisters? Where is Queen Susan?"

"My sister Susan," answered Peter shortly and gravely,

"is no longer a friend of Narnia."

"Yes," said Eustace, "and whenever you've tried to get her to come and talk about Narnia or do anything about Narnia, she says, 'What wonderful memories you have! Fancy your still thinking about all those funny games we used to play when we were children.'"

"Oh Susan!" said Jill. "She's interested in nothing nowadays except nylons and lipstick and invitations. She always was a jolly sight too keen on being grown-up."

"Grown-up, indeed," said the Lady Polly. "I wish she *would* grow up. She wasted all her school time wanting to be the age she is now, and she'll waste all the rest of her life trying to stay that age. Her whole idea is to race on to the silliest time of one's life as quick as she can and then stop there as long as she can."

"Well, don't let's talk about that now," said Peter. "Look! Here are lovely fruit-trees. Let us taste them."

And then, for the first time, Tirian looked about him and realized how very queer this adventure was.

CHAPTER THIRTEEN

HOW THE DWARFS REFUSED
TO BE TAKEN IN

TIRIAN had thought – or he would have thought if he had time to think at all – that they were inside a little thatched stable, about twelve feet long and six feet wide. In reality they stood on grass, the deep blue sky was overhead, and the air which blew gently on their faces was that of a day in early summer. Not far away from them rose a grove of trees, thickly leaved, but under every leaf there peeped out the gold or faint yellow or purple or glowing red of fruits such as no one has seen in our world. The fruit made Tirian feel that it must be autumn but there was something in the feel of the air that told him it could not be later than June. They all moved towards the trees.

Everyone raised his hand to pick the fruit he best liked the look of, and then everyone paused for a second. This fruit was so beautiful that each felt "It can't be meant for me . . . surely we're not allowed to pluck it."

"It's all right," said Peter. "I know what we're all thinking. But I'm sure, quite sure, we needn't. I've a feeling we've got to the country where everything is allowed."

"Here goes, then!" said Eustace. And they all began to eat.

What was the fruit like? Unfortunately no one can describe a taste. All I can say is that, compared with those fruits, the freshest grapefruit you've ever eaten was dull, and the juiciest orange was dry, and the most melting pear was hard and woody, and the sweetest wild strawberry was sour. And there were no seeds or stones, and no wasps. If you had once eaten that fruit, all the nicest things in this world would taste like medicines after it. But I can't describe it. You can't find out what it is like unless you can get to that country and taste it for yourself.

When they had eaten enough, Eustace said to King Peter, "You haven't yet told us how you got here. You were just going to, when King Tirian turned up."

"There's not much to tell," said Peter. "Edmund and I were standing on the platform and we saw your train coming in. I remember thinking it was taking the bend far too fast. And I remember thinking how funny it was that our people were probably in the same train though Lucy didn't know about it —"

"Your people, High King?" said Tirian.

"I mean my Father and Mother — Edmund's and Lucy's and mine."

"Why were they?" asked Jill. "You don't mean to say *they* know about Narnia?"

"Oh no, it had nothing to do with Narnia. They were on their way to Bristol. I'd only heard they were going that morning. But Edmund said they'd be bound to be going by that train." (Edmund was the sort of person who knows about railways.)

"And what happened then?" said Jill.

"Well, it's not very easy to describe, is it, Edmund?" said the High King.

"Not very," said Edmund. "It wasn't at all like that other time when we were pulled out of our own world by Magic. There was a frightful roar and something hit me with a bang, but it didn't hurt. And I felt not so much scared as — well, excited. Oh — and this is one queer thing.

I'd had a rather sore knee, from a hack at rugger. I noticed it had suddenly gone. And I felt very light. And then — here we were."

"It was much the same for us in the railway carriage," said the Lord Digory, wiping the last traces of the fruit from his golden beard. "Only I think you and I, Polly, chiefly felt that we'd been unstiffened. You youngsters won't understand. But we stopped feeling old."

"Youngsters, indeed!" said Jill. "I don't believe you two really are much older than we are here."

"Well if we aren't, we have been," said the Lady Polly.

"And what has been happening since you got here?" asked Eustace.

"Well," said Peter, "for a long time (at least I suppose it was a long time) nothing happened. Then the door opened —"

"The door?" said Tirian.

"Yes," said Peter. "The door you came in — or came out — by. Have you forgotten?"

"But where is it?"

"Look," said Peter and pointed.

Tirian looked and saw the queerest and most ridiculous thing you can imagine. Only a few yards away, clear to be seen in the sunlight, there stood up a rough wooden door and, round it, the framework of the doorway: nothing else, no walls, no roof. He walked towards it, bewildered, and the others followed, watching to see what he would do. He walked round to the other side of the door. But it looked just the same from the other side: he was still in the open air, on a summer morning. The door was simply standing up by itself as if it had grown there like a tree.

"Fair Sir," said Tirian to the High King, "this is a great marvel."

"It is the door you came through with that Calormene five minutes ago," said Peter smiling.

"But did I not come in out of the wood into the stable? Whereas this seems to be a door leading from nowhere to nowhere."

"It looks like that if you walk *round* it," said Peter. "But put your eye to that place where there is a crack between two of the planks and look *through*."

Tirian put his eye to the hole. At first he could see nothing but blackness. Then, at his eyes grew used to it, he saw the dull red glow of a bonfire that was nearly going out, and above that, in a black sky, stars. Then he could see dark figures moving about or standing between him and the fire: he could hear them talking and their voices were like those of Calormenes. So he knew that he was looking out through the stable door into the darkness of Lantern Waste where he had fought his last battle. The men were discussing whether to go in and look for Rishda Tarkaan (but none of them wanted to do that) or to set fire to the stable.

He looked round again and could hardly believe his eyes. There was the blue sky overhead, and grassy country spreading as far as he could see in every direction, and his new friends all round him laughing.

"It seems, then," said Tirian, smiling himself, "that the stable seen from within and the stable seen from without are two different places."

"Yes," said the Lord Digory. "Its inside is bigger than its outside."

"Yes," said Queen Lucy. "In our world too, a stable once had something inside it that was bigger than our whole world." It was the first time she had spoken, and from the thrill in her voice, Tirian now knew why. She was drinking everything in even more deeply than the others. She had been too happy to speak. He wanted to hear her speak again, so he said:

"Of your courtesy, Madam, tell on. Tell me your whole adventure."

"After the shock and the noise," said Lucy, "we found

ourselves here. And we wondered at the door, as you did. Then the door opened for the first time (we saw darkness through the doorway when it did) and there came through a big man with a naked sword. We saw by his arms that he was a Calormene. He took his stand beside the door with his sword raised, resting on his shoulder, ready to cut down anyone who came through. We went to him and spoke to him, but we thought he could neither see nor hear us. And he never looked round on the sky and the sunlight and the grass: I think he couldn't see them either. So then we waited a long time. Then we heard the bolt being drawn on the other side of the door. But the man didn't get ready to strike with his sword till he could see who was coming in. So we supposed he had been told to strike some and spare others. But at the very moment when the door opened, all of a sudden Tash was there, on this side of the door; none of us saw where he came from. And through the door there came a big Cat. It gave one look at Tash and ran for its life: just in time, for he pounced at it and the door hit his beak as it was shut. The man could see Tash. He turned very pale and bowed down before the Monster: but it vanished away.

"Then we waited a long time again. At last the door opened for the third time and there came in a young Calormene. I liked him. The sentinel at the door started, and looked very surprised, when he saw him. I think he'd been expecting someone quite different –"

"I see it all now," said Eustace (he had the bad habit of interrupting stories). "The Cat was to go in first and the sentry had orders to do him no harm. Then the Cat was to come out and say he'd seen their beastly Tashlan and *pretend* to be frightened so as to scare the other Animals. But what Shift never guessed was that the real Tash would turn up; so Ginger came out really frightened. And after that, Shift would send in anyone he wanted to get rid of and the sentry would kill them.

And –"

"Friend," said Tirian softly, "you hinder the lady in her tale."

"Well," said Lucy, "the sentry was surprised. That gave the other man just time to get on guard. They had a fight. He killed the sentry and flung him outside the door. Then he came walking slowly forward to where we were. He could see us, and everything else. We tried to talk to him but he was rather like a man in a trance. He kept on saying Tash, Tash, where is Tash? I go to Tash. So we gave it up and he went away somewhere — over there. I liked him. And after that . . . ugh!" Lucy made a face.

"After that," said Edmund, "someone flung a monkey through the door. And Tash was there again. My sister is so tender-hearted she doesn't like to tell you that Tash made one peck and the Monkey was gone!"

"Serve him right!" said Eustace. "All the same, I hope he'll disagree with Tash too."

"And after that," said Edmund, "came about a dozen Dwarfs: and then Jill, and Eustace, and last of all yourself."

"I hope Tash ate the Dwarfs too," said Eustace. "Little swine."

"No, he didn't," said Lucy. "And don't be horrid. They're still here. In fact you can see them from here. And I've tried and tried to make friends with them but it's no use."

"*Friends* with them!" cried Eustace. "If you knew how those Dwarfs have been behaving!"

"Oh stop it, Eustace," said Lucy. "Do come and see them. King Tirian, perhaps *you* could do something with them."

"I can feel no great love for Dwarfs today," said Tirian. "Yet at your asking, Lady, I would do a greater thing than this."

Lucy led the way and soon they could all see the Dwarfs. They had a very odd look. They weren't strolling about or enjoying themselves (although the cords with which they had been tied seemed to have vanished) nor were they lying down and having a rest. They were sitting very close together in a little circle facing one another. They never looked round or took any notice of the humans till Lucy and Tirian were almost near enough to touch them. Then the Dwarfs all cocked their heads as if they couldn't see anyone but were listening hard and trying to guess by the sound what was happening.

"Look out!" said one of them in a surly voice. "Mind where you're going. Don't walk into our faces!"

"All right!" said Eustace indignantly. "We're not blind. We've got eyes in our heads."

"They must be darn good ones if you can see in here," said the same Dwarf whose name was Diggle.

"In where?" asked Edmund.

"Why you bone-head, in *here* of course," said Diggle. "In this pitch-black, poky, smelly little hole of a stable."

"Are you blind?" said Tirian.

"Ain't we all blind in the dark!" said Diggle.

"But it isn't dark, you poor stupid Dwarfs," said Lucy. "Can't you see? Look up! Look round! Can't you see the sky and the trees and the flowers? Can't you see *me*?"

"How in the name of all Humbug can I see what ain't there? And how can I see you any more than you can see me in this pitch darkness?"

"But I *can* see you," said Lucy. "I'll prove I can see you. You've got a pipe in your mouth."

"Anyone that knows the smell of baccy could tell that," said Diggle.

"Oh the poor things! This is dreadful," said Lucy. Then she had an idea. She stopped and picked some wild violets. "Listen, Dwarf," she said. "Even if your eyes are wrong, perhaps your nose is all right: can you smell *that*?" She leaned across and held the fresh, damp flowers to Diggle's ugly nose. But she had to jump back quickly in order to avoid a blow from his hard little fist.

"None of that!" he shouted. "How dare you! What do you mean by shoving a lot of filthy stable-litter in my

face? There was a thistle in it too. It's like your sauce! And who are you anyway?"

"Earth-man," said Tirian, "she is the Queen Lucy, sent hither by Aslan out of the deep past. And it is for her sake alone that I, Tirian your lawful King, do not cut all your heads from your shoulders, proved and twice-proved traitors that you are."

"Well if that doesn't beat everything!" exclaimed Diggle. "How *can* you go on talking all that rot? Your wonderful Lion didn't come and help you, did he? Thought not. And now – even now – when you've been beaten and shoved into this black hole, just the same as the rest of us, you're still at your old game. Starting a new lie! Trying to make us believe we're none of us shut up, and it ain't dark, and heaven knows what."

"There *is* no black hole, save in your own fancy, fool," cried Tirian. "Come *out* of it." And, leaning forward, he caught Diggle by the belt and the hood and swung him right out of the circle of Dwarfs. But the moment Tirian put him down, Diggle darted back to his place among the others, rubbing his nose and howling:

"Ow! Ow! What d'you do that for! Banging my face against the wall. You've nearly broken my nose."

"Oh dear!" said Lucy, "What *are* we to do for them?"

"Let 'em alone," said Eustace: but as he spoke the earth trembled. The sweet air grew suddenly sweeter. A brightness flashed behind them. All turned. Tirian turned last because he was afraid. There stood his heart's desire, huge and real, the golden Lion, Aslan himself, and already the others were kneeling in a circle round his forepaws and burying their hands and faces in his mane as he stooped his great head to touch them with his tongue. Then he fixed his eyes upon Tirian, and Tirian came near, trembling, and flung himself at the Lion's feet, and the Lion kissed him and said, "Well done, last of the Kings of Narnia who stood firm at the darkest hour."

"Aslan," said Lucy through her tears, "could you – will you – do something for these poor Dwarfs?"

"Dearest," said Aslan, "I will show you both what I can, and what I cannot, do." He came close to the Dwarfs and gave a low growl: low, but it set all the air shaking. But the Dwarfs said to one another, "Hear that? That's the gang at the other end of the stable. Trying to frighten us. They do it with a machine of some kind. Don't take any notice. They won't take *us* in again!"

Aslan raised his head and shook his mane. Instantly a glorious feast appeared on the Dwarfs' knees: pies and tongues and pigeons and trifles and ices, and each Dwarf had a goblet of good wine in his right hand. But it wasn't much use. They began eating and drinking greedily enough, but it was clear that they couldn't taste it properly. They thought they were eating and drinking only the sort of things you might find in a stable. One said he was trying to eat hay and another said he had a bit of an old turnip and a third said he'd found a raw cabbage leaf. And they raised golden goblets of rich red wine to their lips and said "Ugh! Fancy drinking dirty water out of a trough that a donkey's been at! Never thought we'd come to this." But very soon every Dwarf began suspecting that every other Dwarf had found something nicer than he had, and they started grabbing and snatching, and went on to quarrelling, till in a few minutes there was a free fight and all the good food was smeared on their faces and clothes or trodden under foot. But when at last they sat down to nurse their black eyes and their bleeding noses, they all said:

"Well, at any rate there's no Humbug here. We haven't let anyone take us in. The Dwarfs are for the Dwarfs."

"You see, " said Aslan. "They will not let us help them. They have chosen cunning instead of belief. Their prison is only in their own minds, yet they are in that prison; and so afraid of being taken in that they cannot be taken out. But come, children. I have other work to do."

He went to the Door and they all followed him. He raised his head and roared, "Now it is time!" then louder, "Time!"; then so loud that it could have shaken the stars, "TIME." The Door flew open.

CHAPTER FOURTEEN

NIGHT FALLS ON NARNIA

THEY all stood beside Aslan, on his right side, and looked through the open doorway.

The bonfire had gone out. On the earth all was blackness: in fact you could not have told that you were looking into a wood if you had not seen where the dark shapes of the trees ended and the stars began. But when Aslan had roared yet again, out on their left they saw another black shape. That is, they saw another patch where there were no stars: and the patch rose up higher and higher and became the shape of a man, the hugest of all giants. They all knew Narnia well enough to work out where he must be standing. He must be on the high moorlands that stretch away to the North beyond the River Shribble. Then Jill and Eustace remembered how once long ago, in the deep caves beneath those moors, they had seen a great giant asleep and been told that his name was Father Time, and that he would wake on the day the world ended.

"Yes," said Aslan, though they had not spoken. "While he lay dreaming his name was Time. Now that he is awake he will have a new one."

Then the great giant raised a horn to his mouth. They could see this by the change of the black shape he made against the stars. After that — quite a bit later, because sound travels so slowly — they heard the sound of the horn: high and terrible, yet of a strange, deadly beauty.

Immediately the sky became full of shooting stars. Even one shooting star is a fine thing to see; but these were dozens, and then scores, and then hundreds, till it was like silver rain: and it went on and on. And when it had gone on for some while, one or two of them began to think that there was another dark shape against the sky as well as the giant's. It was in a different place, right overhead, up in the very roof of the sky as you might call it. "Perhaps it is a cloud," thought Edmund. At any rate, there were no stars there: just blackness. But all around, the downpour of stars went on. And then the starless patch began to grow, spreading further and further out from the centre of the sky. And presently a quarter of the whole sky was black, and then a half, and at last the rain of shooting stars was going on only low down near the horizon.

With a thrill of wonder (and there was some terror in it too) they all suddenly realized what was happening. The spreading blackness was not a cloud at all: it was simply emptiness. The black part of the sky was the part in which there were no stars left. All the stars were falling: Aslan had called them home.

The last few seconds before the rain of stars had quite ended were very exciting. Stars began falling all round them. But stars in that world are not the great flaming globes they are in ours. They are people (Edmund and Lucy had once met one). So now they found showers of glittering people, all with long hair like burning silver and spears like white-hot metal, rushing down to them out of the black air, swifter than falling stones. They made a hissing noise as they landed and burnt the grass. And all these stars glided past them and stood somewhere behind, a little to the right.

This was a great advantage, because otherwise, now that there were no stars in the sky, everything would have been completely dark and you could have seen nothing. As it was, the crowd of stars behind them cast a fierce, white light over their shoulders. They could see mile upon mile of Narnian woods spread out before them, looking as if they were floodlit. Every bush and almost every blade of grass had its black shadow behind it. The edge of every leaf stood out so sharp that you'd think you could cut your finger on it.

On the grass before them lay their own shadows. But the great thing was Aslan's shadow. It streamed away to their left, enormous and very terrible. And all this was under a sky that would now be starless forever.

The light from behind them (and a little to their right) was so strong that it lit up even the slopes of the Northern Moors. Something was moving there. Enormous animals were crawling and sliding down into Narnia: great dragons and giant lizards and featherless birds with wings like bats' wings. They disappeared into the woods and for a few minutes there was silence. Then there came — at first from very far off — sounds of wailing and then, from every direction, a rustling and a pattering and a sound of wings. It came nearer and nearer. Soon one could distinguish the scamper of little feet from the padding of big paws, and the clack-clack of light little hoofs from the thunder of great ones. And then one could see thousands of pairs of eyes gleaming. And at last, out of the shadow of the trees, racing up the hill for dear life, by thousands and by millions, came all kinds of creatures — Talking Beasts, Dwarfs, Satyrs, Fauns, Giants, Calormenes, men from Archenland, Monopods, and strange unearthly things from the remote islands of the unknown Western lands. And all these ran up to the doorway where Aslan stood.

This part of the adventure was the only one which seemed rather like a dream at the time and rather hard to remember properly afterwards. Especially, one couldn't say how long it had taken. Sometimes it seemed to have lasted only a few minutes, but at others it felt as if it might have gone on for years. Obviously, unless either the Door had grown very much larger or the creatures had suddenly grown as small as gnats, a crowd like that couldn't ever have tried to get through it. But no one thought about that sort of thing at the time.

The creatures came rushing on, their eyes brighter and brighter as they drew nearer and nearer to the standing Stars. But as they came right up to Aslan one or other of two things happened to each of them. They all looked straight in his face, I don't think they had any choice about that. And when some looked, the expression of their faces changed terribly – it was fear and hatred: except that, on the faces of Talking Bears, the fear and hatred lasted only for a fraction of a second. You could see that they suddenly ceased to the *Talking* Beasts. They were just ordinary animals. And all the creatures who looked at Aslan in that way swerved to their right, his left, and disappeared into his huge black shadow, which (as you have heard) streamed away to the left of the doorway. The children never saw them again. I don't know what became of them. But the others looked in the face of Aslan and loved him, though some of them were very frightened at the same time. And all these came in at the Door, in on Aslan's right. There were some queer specimens among them. Eustace even recognized one of those very Dwarfs who had helped to shoot the Horses. But he had no time to wonder about that sort of thing (and anyway it was no business of his) for a great joy put

everything else out of his head. Among the happy creatures who now came crowding round Tirian and his friends were all those whom they had thought dead. There was Roonwit the Centaur and Jewel the Unicorn and the good Boar and the good Bear, and Farsight the Eagle, and the dear Dogs and the Horses, and Poggin the Dwarf.

"Further in and higher up!" cried Roonwit and thundered away in a gallop to the West. And though they did not understand him, the words somehow set them tingling all over. The Boar grunted at them cheerfully. The Bear was just going to mutter that he still didn't understand, when he caught sight of the fruit-trees behind them. He waddled to those trees as fast as he could and there, no doubt, found something he understood very well. But the Dogs remained, wagging their tails, and Poggin remained, shaking hands with everyone and grinning all over his honest face. And Jewel leaned his snowy white head over the King's shoulder and the King whispered in Jewel's ear. Then everyone turned his attention again to what could be seen through the Doorway.

The Dragons and Giant Lizards now had Narnia to themselves. They went to and fro tearing up the trees by the roots and crunching them up as if they were sticks of rhubarb. Minute by minute the forests disappeared. The whole country became bare and you could see all sorts of things about its shape – all the little humps and hollows – which you had never noticed before. The grass died. Soon Tirian found that he was looking at a world of bare rock and earth. You could hardly believe that anything had ever lived there. The monsters themselves grew old and lay down and died. Their flesh shrivelled up and the bones appeared: soon they were only huge skeletons that lay here and there on the dead rock, looking as if they had died thousands of years ago. For a long time everything was still.

At last something white – a long, level line of whiteness that gleamed in the light of the standing stars – came moving towards them from the Eastern end of the world.

A widespread noise broke the silence: first a murmur then a rumble, then a roar. And now they could see what it was that was coming, and how fast it came. It was a foaming wall of water. The sea was rising. In that tree-less world you could see it very well. You could see all the rivers getting wider and the lakes getting larger, and separate lakes joining into one, and valleys turning into new lakes, and hills turning into islands, and then those islands vanishing. And the high moors to their left and the higher mountains to their right crumbled and slipped down with a roar and a splash into the mounting water; and the water came swirling up to the very threshold of the Doorway (but never passed it) so that the foam splashed about Aslan's forefeet. All now was level water from where they stood to where the waters met the sky.

And out there it began to grow light. A streak of dreary and disastrous dawn spread along the horizon, and widened and grew brighter, till in the end they hardly noticed the light of the stars who stood behind them. At last the sun came up. When it did, the Lord Digory and the Lady Polly looked at one another and gave a little nod: those two, in a different world, had once seen a dying sun, and so they knew at once that this sun also was dying. It was three times – twenty times – as big as it ought to be, and very dark red. As its rays fell upon the great Time-giant, he turned red too: and in the reflection of that sun the whole waste of shoreless waters looked like blood.

Then the Moon came up, quite in her wrong position, very close to the sun, and she also looked red. And at the sight of her the sun began shooting out great flames, like whiskers or snakes of crimson fire, towards her. It is as if he were an octopus trying to draw her to himself in his tentacles. And perhaps he did draw her. At any rate she came to him, slowly at first, but then more and more quickly, till at last his long flames licked round her and the two ran together and became one huge ball like a burning coal. Great lumps of fire came dropping out of it into the sea and clouds of steam rose up.

Then Aslan said, "Now make an end."

The giant threw his horn into the sea. Then he stretched out one arm – very black it looked, and thousands of miles long – across the sky till his hand reached the Sun. He took the Sun and squeezed it in his hand as you would squeeze an orange. And instantly there was total darkness.

Everyone except Aslan jumped back from the ice-cold air which now blew through the Doorway. Its edges were already covered with icicles.

"Peter, High King of Narnia," said Aslan. "Shut the Door."

Peter, shivering with cold, leaned out into the darkness and pulled the Door to. It scraped over ice as he pulled it. Then, rather clumsily (for even in that moment his hands had gone numb and blue) he took out a golden key and locked it.

They had seen strange things enough through that Doorway. But it was stranger than any of them to look round and find themselves in warm daylight, the blue sky above them, flowers at their feet, and laughter in Aslan's eyes.

He turned swiftly round, crouched lower, lashed himself with his tail and shot away like a golden arrow.

"Come further in! Come further up!" he shouted over his shoulder. But who could keep up with him at that pace? They set out walking Westward to follow him.

"So," said Peter, "night falls on Narnia. What, Lucy! You're not *crying*? With Aslan ahead, and all of us here?"

"Don't try to stop me, Peter," said Lucy, "I am sure Aslan would not. I am sure it is not wrong to mourn for Narnia. Think of all that lies dead and frozen behind that door."

"Yes and I *did* hope," said Jill, "that it might go on for ever. I knew *our* world couldn't. I did think Narnia might."

"I saw it begin," said the Lord Digory. "I did not think I would live to see it die."

"Sirs," said Tirian. "The ladies do well to weep. See, I do so myself. I have seen my mother's death. What world but Narnia have I ever known? It were no virtue, but great discourtesy, if we did not mourn."

They walked away from the Door and away from the Dwarfs who still sat crowded together in their imaginary stable. And as they went they talked to one another about old wars and old peace and ancient Kings and all the glories of Narnia.

The Dogs were still with them. They joined in the conversation but not much because they were too busy racing on ahead and racing back and rushing off to sniff at smells in the grass till they made themselves sneeze. Suddenly they picked up a scent which seemed to excite them very much. They all started arguing about it — "Yes it is — No it isn't — That's just what I said — anyone can smell what *that* is — Take your great nose out of the way and let someone else smell."

"What is it, cousins?" said Peter.

"A Calormene, Sire," said several Dogs at once.

"Lead on to him, then," said Peter. "Whether he meets us in peace or war, he shall be welcome."

The Dogs darted on ahead and came back a moment later, running as if their lives depended on it, and barking loudly to say that it really was a Calormene. (Talking Dogs, just like the common ones, behave as if they thought whatever they are doing at the moment immensely important.)

The others followed where the Dogs led them and found a young Calormene sitting under a chestnut tree beside a clear stream of water. It was Emeth. He rose at once and bowed gravely.

"Sir," he said to Peter, "I know not whether you are my friend or my foe, but I should count it my honour to have you for either. Has not one of the poets said that a

noble friend is the best gift and a noble enemy the next best?"

"Sir," said Peter, "I do not know that there need be any war between you and us."

"Do tell us who you are and what's happened to you," said Jill.

"If there's going to be a story, let's all have a drink and sit down," barked the Dogs. "We're quite blown."

"Well of course you will be if you keep tearing about the way you have done," said Eustace.

So the humans sat down on the grass. And when the Dogs had all had a very noisy drink out of the stream they all sat down, bolt upright, panting, with their tongues hanging out of their heads a little on one side to hear the story. But Jewel remained standing, polishing his horn against his side.

CHAPTER FIFTEEN

FURTHER UP AND FURTHER IN

"Know, O Warlike Kings," said Emeth, "and you, O ladies whose beauty illuminates the universe, that I am Emeth the seventh son of Harpha Tarkaan of the city of Tehishbaan, Westward beyond the desert. I came lately into Narnia with nine and twenty others under the command of Rishda Rarkaan. Now when I first heard that we should march upon Narnia I rejoiced; for I had heard many things of your Land and desired greatly to meet you in battle. But when I found that we were to go in disguised as merchants (which is a shameful dress for a warrior and the son of a Tarkaan) and to work by lies and trickery, then my joy departed from me. And most of all when I found we must wait upon a Monkey, and when it began to be said that Tash and Aslan were one, then the world became dark in my eyes. For always since I was a boy I have served Tash and my great desire was to know more of him, if it might be, to look upon his face. But the name of Aslan was hateful to me.

"And, as you have seen, we were called together outside the straw-roofed hovel, night after night, and the fire was kindled, and the Ape brought forth out of the hovel something upon four legs that I could not well see. And the people and the Beasts bowed down and did honour to it. But I thought, the Tarkaan is deceived by the Ape: for this thing that comes out of the stable is neither Tash nor any other god. But when I watched the Tarkaan's face, and marked every word that he said to the Monkey, then I changed my mind: for I saw that the Tarkaan did not believe in it himself. And then I understood that he did not believe in Tash at all: for if he had, how could he dare to mock him?

"When I understood this, a great rage fell upon me and I wondered that the true Tash did not strike down both the Monkey and the Tarkaan with fire from heaven. Nevertheless I hid my anger and held my tongue and waited to see how it would end. But last night, as some of you know, the Monkey brought not forth the yellow thing but said that all who desired to look upon Tashlan – for so they mixed the two words to pretend that they were all one – must pass one by one into the hovel. And I said to myself, Doubtless this is some other deception. But when the Cat had followed in and had come out again in a madness of terror, then I said to myself, Surely the true Tash, whom they called on without knowledge or belief, has now come among us, and will avenge himself. And though my heart was turned into water inside me because of the greatness and terror of Tash, yet my desire was stronger than my fear, and I put force upon my knees to stay them from trembling, and on my teeth that they should not chatter, and resolved to look upon the face of Tash though he should slay me. So I offered myself to go into the hovel; and the Tarkaan, though unwillingly, let me go.

"As soon as I had gone in at the door, the first wonder was that I found myself in this great sunlight (as we all are now) though the inside of the hovel had looked dark from outside. But I had no time to marvel at this, for immediately I was forced to fight for my head against one of our own men. As soon as I saw him I understood that the Monkey and the Tarkaan had set him there to slay any who came in if he were not in their secrets: so that this man also was a liar and a mocker and no true servant of Tash. I had the better will to fight him; and having slain the villain, I cast him out behind me through the door.

"Then I looked about me and saw the sky and the wide lands, and smelled the sweetness. And I said, By the Gods, this is a pleasant place: it may be that I am come into the country of Tash. And I began to journey into the strange country and to seek him.

"So I went over much grass and many flowers and among all kinds of wholesome and delectable trees till lo! in a narrow place between two rocks there came to meet me a great Lion. The speed of him was like the ostrich, and his size was an elephant's; his hair was like pure gold and the brightness of his eyes like gold that is liquid in the furnace. He was more terrible than the Flaming Mountain of Lagour, and in beauty he surpassed all that is in the world even as the rose in bloom surpasses the dust of the desert. Then I fell at his feet and thought, Surely this is the hour of death, for the Lion (who is worthy of all honour) will know that I have served Tash all my days and not him. Nevertheless, it is better to see the Lion and die than to be Tisroc of the world and live and not to have seen him. But the Glorious One bent down his golden head and touched my forehead with his tongue and said, Son, thou art welcome. But I said, Alas, Lord, I am no son of thine but the servant of Tash. He answered, Child, all the service thou hast done to Tash, I account as service done to me. Then by reasons of my great desire for wisdom and understanding, I overcame my fear and questioned the Glorious One and said, Lord, is it then true, as the Ape said, that thou and Tash are one? The Lion growled so that the earth shook (but his wrath was not against me) and said, It is false. Not because he and I are one, but because we are opposites, I take to me the services which thou hast done to him. For I and he are of such different kinds that no service which is vile can be done to me, and none which is not vile can be done to him. Therefore if any man swear by Tash and keep his oath for the oath's sake, it is by me that he has truly sworn, though he know it not, and it is I who reward him. And if any man do a cruelty in my name, then, though he says the name Aslan, it is Tash whom he serves and by Tash his deed is accepted. Dost thou understand, Child? I said, Lord, thou knowest how much I understand. But I said also (for the truth constrained me), Yet I have been seeking Tash all my days. Beloved, said the Glorious One, unless thy desire had been for me thou wouldst not have sought so long and so truly. For all find what they truly seek.

"Then he breathed upon me and took away the trembling from my limbs and caused me to stand upon my feet. And after that, he said not much, but that we should meet again, and I must go further up and further in. Then he turned him about in a storm and flurry of gold and was gone suddenly.

"And since then, O Kings and Ladies, I have been wandering to find him and my happiness is so great that it even weakens me like a wound. And this is the marvel of marvels, that he called me Beloved, me who am but as a dog —"

"Eh? What's that?" said one of the Dogs.

"Sir," said Emeth. "It is but a fashion of speech which we have in Calormen."

"Well, I can't say it's one I like very much," said the Dog.

"He doesn't mean any harm," said an older Dog.

"After all, *we* call our puppies *Boys* when they don't behave properly."

"So we do," said the first Dog. "Or *girls*."

"S-s-sh!" said the Old Dog. "That's not a nice word to use. Remember where you are."

"Look!" said Jill suddenly. Someone was coming, rather timidly, to meet them; a graceful creature on four feet, all silvery-grey. And they stared at him for a whole ten seconds before five or six voices said all at once, "Why, it's old Puzzle!" They had never seen him by daylight with the lion-skin off, and it made an extraordinary difference. He was himself now: a beautiful donkey with such a soft, grey coat and such a gentle, honest face that if you had seen him you would have done just what Jill and Lucy did – rushed forward and put your arms round his neck and kissed his nose and stroked his ears.

When they asked him where he had been he said he had

come in at the door along with all the other creatures but he had – well, to tell the truth, he had been keeping out of their way as much as he could; and out of Aslan's way. For the sight of the real Lion had made him so ashamed of all that nonsense about dressing up in a lion-skin that he did not know how to look anyone in the face. But when he saw that all his friends were going away Westward, and after he had had a mouthful of grass ("And I've never tasted such good grass in my life," said Puzzle), he plucked up his courage and followed. "But what I'll do if I really have to meet Aslan, I'm sure I don't know," he added.

"You'll find it will be all right when you really do," said Queen Lucy.

Then they went forward together, always Westward, for that seemed to be the direction Aslan had meant when he cried out, "Further up and futher in." Many other creatures were slowly moving the same way, but that grassy country was very wide and there was no crowding.

It still seemed to be early, and the morning freshness was in the air. They kept on stopping to look round and to look behind them, partly because it was so beautiful but partly also because there was something about it which they could not understand.

"Peter," said Lucy, "where is this, do you suppose?"

"I don't know," said the High King. "It reminds me of somewhere but I can't give it a name. Could it be somewhere we once stayed for a holiday when we were very, very small?"

"It would have to have been a jolly good holiday," said Eustace. "I bet there isn't a country like this anywhere in *our* world. Look at the colours! You couldn't get a blue like the blue on those mountains in our world."

"Is it not Aslan's country?" said Tirian.

"Not like Aslan's country on top of that mountain beyond the Eastern end of the world," said Jill. "I've been there."

"If you ask me," said Edmund, "it's like somewhere in the Narnian world. Look at those mountains ahead – and the big ice-mountains beyond them. Surely they're rather like the mountains we used to see from Narnia, the ones up Westward beyond the Waterfall?"

"Yes, so they are," said Peter. "Only these are bigger."

"I don't think *those* ones are so very like anything in Narnia," said Lucy. "But look there." She pointed Southward to their left, and everyone stopped and turned to look. "Those hills," said Lucy, "the nice woody ones and the blue ones behind – aren't they very like the Southern border of Narnia?"

"Like!" cried Edmund after a moment's silence. "Why, they're exactly like. Look, there's Mount Pire with his forked head, and there's the pass into Archenland and everything!"

"And yet they're not like," said Lucy. "They're different. They have more colours on them and they look further away than I remembered and they're more . . . more . . . oh, I don't know . . ."

"More like the real thing," said the Lord Digory softly.

Suddenly Farsight the Eagle spread his wings, soared

thirty or forty feet up into the air, circled round and then alighted on the ground.

"Kings and Queens," he cried, "we have all been blind. We are only beginning to see where we are. From up there I have seen it all — Ettinsmuir, Beaversdam, the Great River, and Cair Paravel still shining on the edge of the Eastern Sea. Narnia is not dead. This is Narnia."

"But how can it be?" said Peter. "For Aslan told us older ones that we should never return to Narnia, and here we are."

"Yes," said Eustace. "And we saw it all destroyed and the sun put out."

"And it's all so different," said Lucy.

"The Eagle is right," said the Lord Digory. "Listen, Peter. When Aslan said you could never go back to Narnia, he meant the Narnia you were thinking of. But that was not the real Narnia. That had a beginning and an end. It was only a shadow or a copy of the real Narnia which has always been here and always will be here: just as our world, England and all, is only a shadow or copy of something in Aslan's real world. You need not mourn over Narnia, Lucy. All of the old Narnia that mattered, all the dear creatures, have been drawn into the real Narnia through the Door. And of course it is different;

as different as a real thing is from a shadow or as waking life is from a dream." His voice stirred everyone like a trumpet as he spoke these words: but when he added under his breath "It's all in Plato, all in Plato: bless me, what *do* they teach them at these schools!" the older ones laughed. It was so exactly like the sort of thing they had heard him say long ago in that other world where his beard was grey instead of golden. He knew why they were laughing and joined in the laugh himself. But very quickly they all became grave again: for, as you know, there is a kind of happiness and wonder that makes you serious. It is too good to waste on jokes.

It is as hard to explain how this sunlit land was different from the old Narnia as it would be to tell you how the fruits of that country taste. Perhaps you will get some idea of it if you think like this. You may have been in a room in which there was a window that looked out on a lovely bay of the sea or a green valley that wound away among mountains. And in the wall of that room opposite to the window there may have been a looking-glass. And as you turned away from the window you suddenly caught sight of that sea or that valley, all over again, in the looking glass. And the sea in the mirror, or the valley in the mirror, were in one sense just the same as the real ones: yet at the same time they were somehow different − deeper, more wonderful, more like places in a story: in a story you have never heard but very much want to know. The difference between the old Narnia and the new Narnia was like that. The new one was a deeper country: every rock and flower and blade of grass looked as if it meant more. I can't describe it any better than that: if ever you get there you will know what I mean.

It was the Unicorn who summed up what everyone was feeling. He stamped his right fore-hoof on the ground and neighed, and then cried:

"I have come home at last! This is my real country! I belong here. This is the land I have been looking for all my life, though I never knew it till now. The reason why we loved the old Narnia is that it sometimes looked a little like this. Bree-hee-hee! Come further up, come further in!"

He shook his mane and sprang forward into a great gallop – a Unicorn's gallop, which, in our world, would have carried him out of sight in a few moments. But now a most strange thing happened. Everyone else began to run, and they found, to their astonishment, that they could keep up with him: not only the Dogs and the humans but even fat little Puzzle and short-legged Poggin the Dwarf. The air flew in their faces as if they were driving fast in a car without a windscreen. The country flew past as if they were seeing it from the windows of an express train. Faster and faster they raced, but no one got hot or tired or out of breath.

CHAPTER SIXTEEN

FAREWELL TO SHADOWLANDS

IF one could run without getting tired, I don't think one would often want to do anything else. But there might be special reasons for stopping, and it was a special reason which made Eustace presently shout:

"I say! Steady! Look what we're coming to!"

And well he might. For now they saw before them Caldron Pool and beyond the Pool the high unclimbable cliffs and, pouring down the cliffs, thousands of tons of water every second, flashing like diamonds in some places and dark, glassy green in others, the Great Waterfall; and already the thunder of it was in their ears.

"Don't stop! Further up and further in," called Farsight, tilting his flight a little upwards.

"It's all very well for *him*," said Eustace, but Jewel also cried out:

"Don't stop. Further up and further in! Take it in your stride."

His voice could only just be heard above the roar of the water but next moment everyone saw that he had plunged into the Pool. And helter-skelter behind him, with splash after splash, all the others did the same. The water was not biting cold as all of them (and especially Puzzle) expected, but of a delicious foamy coolness. They all found they were swimming straight for the Waterfall itself.

"This is absolutely crazy," said Eustace to Edmund.

"I know. And yet —" said Edmund.

"Isn't it wonderful?" said Lucy. "Have you noticed one can't feel afraid, even if one wants to? Try it."

"By Jove, neither one can," said Eustace after he had tried.

Jewel reached the foot of the Waterfall first, but Tirian was only just behind him. Jill was last, so she could see the whole thing better than the others. She saw something white moving steadily up the face of the Waterfall. That white thing was the Unicorn. You couldn't tell whether he was swimming or climbing, but he moved on, higher and higher. The point of his horn divided the water just above his head, and it cascaded out in two rainbow-coloured streams all round his shoulders. Just behind him came King Tirian. He moved his legs and arms as if he were swimming but he moved straight upwards: as if one could swim up the wall of a house.

What looked funniest was the Dogs. During the gallop they had not been at all out of breath, but now, as they swarmed and wriggled upwards, there was plenty of spluttering and sneezing among them; that was because they would keep on barking, and every time they barked they got their mouths and noses full of water. But before Jill had time to notice all these things fully, she was going up the Waterfall herself. It was the sort of thing that would have been quite impossible in our world. Even if you hadn't been drowned, you would have been smashed to pieces by the terrible weight of water against the countless jags of rock. But in that world you could do it. You went on, up and up, with all kinds of reflected lights flashing at you from the water and all manner of coloured stones flashing through it, till it seemed as if you were climbing up light itself – and always higher and higher till the sense of height would have terrified you if you could be terrified, but later it was only gloriously exciting. And then at last one came to the lovely, smooth green curve in which the water poured over the top and found that one was out on the level river above the Waterfall. The current was racing away behind you, but you were such a wonderful swimmer that you could make headway against it. Soon they were all on the bank, dripping but happy.

A long valley opened ahead and great snow-mountains, now much nearer, stood up against the sky.

"Further up and further in," cried Jewel and instantly they were off again.

They were out of Narnia now and up into the Western Wild which neither Tirian nor Peter nor even the Eagle had ever seen before. But the Lord Digory and the Lady Polly had. "Do you remember? Do you remember?" they said – and said it in steady voices too, without panting, though the whole party was now running faster than an arrow flies.

"What, Lord?" said Tirian. "Is it then true, as stories tell, that you two journeyed here on the very day the world was made?"

"Yes," said Digory, "and it seems to me as if it were only yesterday."

"And on a flying horse?" asked Tirian. "Is that part true?"

"Certainly," said Digory. But the Dogs barked, "Faster, faster!"

So they ran faster and faster till it was more like flying than running, and even the Eagle overhead was going no faster than they. And they went through winding valley after winding valley and up the steep sides of hills and, faster than ever, down the other side, following the river and sometimes crossing it and skimming across mountain-lakes as if they were living speed-boats, till at last at the far end of one long lake which looked as blue as a turquoise, they saw a smooth green hill. Its sides were as steep as the sides of a pyramid and round the very top of it ran a green wall: but above the wall rose the branches of trees whose leaves looked like silver and their fruit like gold.

"Further up and further in!" roared the Unicorn, and no one held back. They charged straight at the foot of the hill and then found themselves running up it almost as water from a broken wave runs up a rock out at the point of some bay. Though the slope was nearly as steep as the roof of a house and the grass was smooth as a bowling green, no one slipped. Only when they had reached the very top did they slow up; that was because they found themselves facing great golden gates. And for a moment none of them was bold enough to try if the gates would open. They all felt just as they had felt about the fruit — "Dare we? Is it right? Can it be meant for *us*?"

But while they were standing thus a great horn, wonderfully loud and sweet, blew from somewhere inside that walled garden and the gates swung open.

Tirian stood holding his breath and wondering who would come out. And what came was the last thing he had expected: a little, sleek, bright-eyed Talking Mouse with a red feather stuck in a circlet on its head and its left paw resting on a long sword. It bowed, a most beautiful bow, and said in its shrill voice:

"Welcome, in the Lion's name. Come further up and further in."

Then Tirian saw King Peter and King Edmund and Queen Lucy rush forward to kneel down and greet the Mouse and they all cried out "Reepicheep!" And Tirian breathed fast with the sheer wonder of it, for now he

knew that he was looking at one of the great heroes of
Narnia, Reepicheep the Mouse who had fought at the
great Battle of Beruna and afterwards sailed to the
World's end with King Caspian the Seafarer. But before
he had had much time to think of this he felt two strong
arms thrown about him and felt a bearded kiss on his
cheeks and heard a well remembered voice saying:

"What, lad? Art thicker and taller since I last touched
thee!"

It was his own father, the good King Erlian: but not as
Tirian had seen him last when they brought him home
pale and wounded from his fight with the giant, nor even
as Tirian remembered him in his later years when he was
a grey-headed warrior. This was his father, young and
merry, as he could just remember him from very early
days when he himself had been a little boy playing games

with his father in the castle garden at Cair Paravel, just before bedtime on summer evenings. The very smell of the bread-and-milk he used to have for supper came back to him.

Jewel thought to himself, "I will leave them to talk for a little and then I will go and greet the good King Erlian. Many a bright apple has he given me when I was but a colt." But next moment he had something else to think of, for out of the gateway there came a horse so mighty and noble that even a Unicorn might feel shy in its presence: a great winged horse. It looked a moment at the Lord Digory and the Lady Polly and neighed out "What, cousins!" and they both shouted "Fledge! Good old Fledge!" and rushed to kiss it.

But by now the Mouse was again urging them to come in. So all of them passed in through the golden gates, into the delicious smell that blew towards them out of that garden and into the cool mixture of sunlight and shadow under the trees, walking on springy turf that was all dotted with white flowers. The very first thing which struck everyone was that the place was far larger than it had seemed from outside. But no one had time to think about that for people were coming up to meet the newcomers from every direction.

Everyone you had ever heard of (if you knew the history of these countries) seemed to be there. There was Glimfeather the Owl and Puddleglum the Marshwiggle, and King Rilian the Disenchanted, and his mother the Star's daughter and his great father Caspian himself. And close beside him were the Lord Drinian and the Lord Berne and Trumpkin the Dwarf and Truffle-hunter the good Badger with Glenstorm the Centaur and a hundred other heroes of the great War of Deliverance. And then from another side came Cor the King of Archenland with King Lune his father and his wife Queen Aravis and the brave prince Corin Thunder-Fist, his brother, and Bree the Horse and Hwin the Mare. And then – which was a wonder beyond all wonders to Tirian – there came from further away in the past, the two good Beavers and Tumnus the Faun. And there was greeting and kissing and hand-shaking and old jokes revived, (you've no idea how good an old joke sounds when you take it out again after a rest of five or six hundred years) and the whole company moved forward to the centre of the orchard where the Phoenix sat in a tree and looked down upon them all, and at the foot of that tree were two thrones and in those two thrones a King and Queen so great and beautiful that everyone bowed down before them. And well they might, for these two were King Frank and Queen Helen from whom all the most ancient Kings of Narnia and Archenland are descended. And Tirian felt as you would feel if you were brought before Adam and Eve in all their glory.

About half an hour later – or it might have been half a hundred years later, for time there is not like time here – Lucy stood with her dear friend, her oldest Narnian friend, the Faun Tumnus, looking down over the wall of that garden, and seeing all Narnia spread out below. But when you looked down you found that this hill was much higher than you had thought: it sank down with shining cliffs, thousands of feet below them and trees in that lower world looked no bigger than grains of green salt. Then she turned inward again and stood with her back to the wall and looked at the garden.

"I see," she said at last, thoughtfully. "I see now. This

garden is like the stable. It is far bigger inside than it was outside."

"Of course, Daughter of Eve," said the Faun. "The further up and the further in you go, the bigger everything gets. The inside is larger than the outside."

Lucy looked hard at the garden and saw that it was not really a garden but a whole world, with its own rivers and woods and sea and mountains. But they were not strange: she knew them all.

"I see," she said. "This is still Narnia, and more real and more beautiful then the Narnia down below, just as *it* was more real and more beautiful than the Narnia outside the stable door! I see ... world within world, Narnia within Narnia ..."

"Yes," said Mr Tumnus, "like an onion: except that as you go in and in, each circle is larger than the last."

And Lucy looked this way and that and soon found that a new and beautiful thing had happened to her. Whatever she looked at, however far away it might be, once she had fixed her eyes steadily on it, became quite clear and close as if she were looking through a telescope. She could see the whole Southern desert and beyond it the great city of Tashbaan: to Eastward she could see Cair Paravel on the edge of the sea and the very window of the room that had once been her own. And far out to sea she could discover the islands, islands after islands to the end of the world, and, beyond the end, the huge mountain which they had called Aslan's country. But now she saw that it was part of a great chain of mountains which ringed round the whole world. In front of her it seemed to come quite close. Then she looked to her left and saw what she took to be a great bank of brightly-coloured cloud, cut off from them by a gap. But she looked harder and saw that it was not a cloud at all but a real land. And when she had fixed her eyes on one particular spot of it, she at once cried out, "Peter! Edmund! Come and look! Come quickly." And they came and looked, for their eyes also had become like hers.

"Why!" exclaimed Peter. "It's England. And that's the house itself – Professor Kirk's old home in the country where all our adventures began!"

"I thought that house had been destroyed," said Edmund.

"So it was," said the Faun. "But you are now looking at the England within England, the real England just as this is the real Narnia. And in that inner England no good thing is destroyed."

Suddenly they shifted their eyes to another spot, and then Peter and Edmund and Lucy gasped with amazement and shouted out and began waving: for there they saw their own father and mother, waving back at them across the great, deep valley. It was like when you see people waving at you from the deck of a big ship when you are waiting on the quay to meet them.

"How can we get at them?" said Lucy.

"That is easy," said Mr Tumnus. "That country and this country – all the *real* countries – are only spurs jutting out from the great mountains of Aslan. We have only to walk along the ridge, upward and inward, till it joins on. And listen! There is King Frank's horn: we must all go up."

And soon they found themselves all walking together – and a great, bright procession it was – up towards mountains higher than you could see in this world even if they were there to be seen. But there was no snow on those mountains: there were forests and green slopes and sweet orchards and flashing waterfalls, one above the other, going up forever. And the land they were walking on grew narrower all the time, with a deep valley on each side: and across that valley the land which was the real England grew nearer and nearer.

The light ahead was growing stronger. Lucy saw that a great series of many-coloured cliffs led up in front of them like a giant's staircase. And then she forgot everything else, because Aslan himself was coming, leaping down from cliff to cliff like a living cataract of power and beauty.

And the very first person whom Aslan called to him was Puzzle the Donkey. You never saw a donkey look feebler and sillier than Puzzle did as he walked up to Aslan, and he looked, beside Aslan, as small as a kitten looks beside a St Bernard. The Lion bowed down his head and whispered something to Puzzle at which his long ears went down, but then he said something else at which the ears perked up again. The humans couldn't hear what he had said either time. Then Aslan turned to them and said:

"You do not yet look so happy as I mean you to be."

Lucy said, "We're so afraid of being sent away, Aslan. And you have sent us back into our own world so often."

"No fear of that," said Aslan. "Have you not guessed?"

Their hearts leaped and a wild hope rose within them.

"There *was* a real railway accident," said Aslan softly. "Your father and mother and all of you are – as you used to call it in the Shadowlands – dead. The term is over: the holidays have begun. The dream is ended: this is the morning."

And as He spoke He no longer looked to them like a lion; but the things that began to happen after that were so great and beautiful that I cannot write them. And for us this is the end of all the stories, and we can most truly say that they all lived happily ever after. But for them it was only the beginning of the real story. All their life in this world and all their adventures in Narnia had only been the cover and the title page: now at last they were beginning Chapter One of the Great Story which no one on earth has read: which goes on forever: in which every chapter is better than the one before.

that this is the sum of all the works, and we can most truly

The Chronicles of Narnia
by C. S. Lewis

C. S. Lewis's wit and wisdom, his blend of excitement and adventure with fantasy, have made this magnificent series beloved of many generations of readers. The final book, *The Last Battle*, won the Carnegie Medal for 1956.

Each of the seven titles is a complete story in itself, but all take place in the magical land of Narnia. Guided by the noble Lion Aslan, the children learn that evil and treachery can only be overcome by courage, loyalty and great sacrifice.

The titles, in suggested reading order, are as follows:

The Magician's Nephew
The Lion, the Witch and the Wardrobe
The Horse and His Boy
Prince Caspian
The Voyage of the Dawn Treader
The Silver Chair
The Last Battle